From pauperism to poverty

Karel Williams

From pauperism to poverty

Routledge & Kegan Paul
London, Boston and Henley

First published in 1981
by Routledge & Kegan Paul Ltd
39 Store Street,
London WC1E 7DD,
9 Park Street,
Boston, Mass. 02108, USA, and
Broadway House,
Newtown Road,
Henley-on-Thames,
Oxon RG9 1EN
Set in Press Roman 10 on 11 pt. by
Hope Services, Abingdon, Oxon
and printed in Great Britain by
Lowe & Brydone Ltd,
Thetford, Norfolk

British Library Cataloguing in Publication Data

From pauperism to poverty.
1. Poor – Great Britain – History – Sources
I. Williams, Karel
301.44'1   HV245   80-41577

ISBN 0 7100 0698 5

Contents

Figures and tables
(excluding those in Statistical appendix)

Tables and graphs in Statistical appendix on pauperism in England and Wales, c.1800-1939

Acknowledgments

Tony Cutler and my sister Annwyl encouraged me to read the French texts against which I defined my position.

Peter Hopkins commissioned a book and accepted an overlength and overdue typescript.

The essays would never have been finished if my wife Gwen had not helped at every stage.

Chris Branson looked after my children through the summer of 1979 while a final typescript was being prepared.

My colleague John Williams rearranged courses and took on more teaching so that I could carry on writing.

Dot Jones abstracted the relevant official statistics and organised their presentation in a statistical appendix.

Gino Bedani, Bob Bowers, John Williams, and my wife Gwen made detailed criticisms of a draft manuscript.

Rosemary Law and Susan Cadman typed and checked references. My father checked the syntax and read the proofs.

Introduction

This book collects seven hitherto unpublished essays in nineteenth-century history, three essays on the configuration of the English and Welsh poor law between 1800 and 1914, and four essays on texts of social investigation written by Mayhew, Engels, Booth, and Rowntree between the 1840s and 1940s. Each essay criticises existing historiographic work in one field and then develops an alternative analysis of text or institution. The subject matter may be esoteric but these essays are not a specialist contribution to the history of 'social thought and policy'. The treatment of the subject matter raises fundamental questions about ways of writing history. Taken together, the essays attack the *a priori* of current Anglo-American historiography and develop an alternative informally semiotic mode of analysis. This book is therefore written for any modern historian who is prepared to reflect on the procedures and presuppositions of his discourse.

Current Anglo-American historiography is not monolithic; it accommodates many different ways of writing history where the *a priori* is not always the same. The criticism in these essays fairly comprehensively surveys the existing ways of writing history because they are all represented in the existing history of the poor law and the texts of social investigation. Readers will be initially disconcerted because the essays do not take up a position within the existing field; that is to say, they do not endorse one of the current ways of writing history and ignore or condemn all others. Traditional narrative descriptive history is criticised as are the new kinds of historiography which rely on social scientific concepts and empiricist procedures.

Traditional history of ideas dominates existing writing on the texts of social investigation by Mayhew, Booth, and Rowntree. This historiography is criticised for its obsession with precursors and anticipations of modernity which are fabricated by a violent abstraction of elements from texts. The new way is to search for systems of elements, totalities called paradigms, problematics or whatever. In the essay on Engels, a critique of pre-1968 Althusserianism shows that the new way stakes its existence on a difference which is unsustainable; the finite system of elements is an object which is itself open to criticism of the sort that devastates traditional history of ideas.

Traditional, narrative, descriptive history of institutions dominates the historiography on the poor law after 1834. This is critically rejected because, as the essay on the poor law after 1834 shows, such historiography is the prisoner of confused and incoherent received ideas. The new way is to use formal social scientific concepts from economics and sociology to define new questions and obtain new answers. The historiography on the poor law before 1834 provides examples of the new economic history which is defined by its reliance on marginalist economic theory. An appendix to the chapter on the poor law after 1870 considers the concept of social control which has recently been applied to nineteenth-century social history. These new ways are rejected; first, because the social sciences cannot provide theory like the natural sciences which construct and render natural phenomena intelligible and second, because existing economic and sociological theories are particularly unsuitable for explicating cultural phenomena since these theories rely on self-constitutive subjects.

The criticism in these essays is concerned with epistemological assumptions as well as with substantive procedures in the history of ideas and institutions. These assumptions are largely unconscious in traditional historiography which, for example, assumes that the texts of social investigation are representational of a non-textual reality. They are formalised in the new historiography on the poor law before 1834 which carries out tests to establish real causal connections. Empiricism is not the source of all evil in modern historiography but, as the essay on the pre-1834 poor law demonstrates, empiricist assumptions and procedures are diversionary. There is good reason to suppose that knowledge cannot be representational in the empiricist sense. Furthermore, test procedures are futile and self-defeating in that they do not deliver the certain or probable knowledge of causal connections which they promise.

It is not possible to develop all these arguments against current historiography without criticising particular pieces of work by generalists like Thompson, Hobsbawm, and Briggs, and by specialist historians of social policy like Rose, Digby, and Brown. The essays are concerned with questions of intellectual strategy and, in this context, close attention to existing historiography has a definite rationale. In England or America, where there is almost no reflection on the *a priori* of historical knowledge, it is necessary to provide detailed critical analyses.

Furthermore, it is necessary to oppose revisionism of the new Anglo-American sort which knocks down Aunt Sallies in the form of isolated conclusions from earlier historiography. It is scandalous that, as the essays on the poor law show, so many new historians never read their predecessors and end up defining their own problems by a process of self-reference while pretending to revise an earlier orthodoxy. If I criticise others for failing to read their predecessors, I am obliged to read my contemporaries closely and critically.

If criticism is not to be completely destructive, it is necessary to develop alternatives to that which is criticised. For this reason, every essay contains a positive alternative analysis of text or institution. The alternative analyses in the various essays are not unified by one formal set or system of concepts. They are defined first by a set of specific conceptual references to work in other theoretical fields; there are important references to the 'archeology' of Michael Foucault and the literary criticism of Roland Barthes. They are defined second by general presuppositions about the nature of language which establish an *a priori* very different from that of Anglo-American historiography.

The essays on the poor law take up certain Foucauldian references. They take up Foucault's early concern with changing lines of division and exclusion which define the insane and the sick; changing exclusions are also at stake in the definition of the pauper and pauperism. They also take up Foucault's later concern, in *Discipline and Punish,* with the positive programmes and strategies which operate upon those who are excluded; strategies, albeit of a non-Foucauldian kind, figure in the analysis of the poor law after 1834. The essays on the texts of social investigation take up certain Barthesian references. They take up the concept of text as interweaving infinite chains of reference which is demonstrated in the book *S/Z* (Barthes, 1970); the texts of social investigation are reconstructed in this way. At the same time, it must be emphasised that none of the analyses is orthodoxly Foucauldian or Barthesian. An appendix to the essay on the poor law after 1870 articulates some fundamental reservations about *Discipline and Punish.*

At another and more fundamental level, the analyses in the essays are unified by certain general presuppositions about the role and nature of language in historiographic knowledge. Historiography exists in and through language; it is a form of writing that presents readings of significations in resources, whether these resources be printed texts or the traces of an institution. This point is so obvious as to be banal. But the implications are radical if the nature of language is defined in a modern post-Saussurian way so that intransitivity and polysemy are emphasised.

Anglo-American historiography accepts a common sense theory of language and the transitivity assumption that it is in the nature of language to name real pre-linguistic objects. As the essays explain, this comfortable supposition was destroyed by Saussure's conception of language as a system of differences. In this case, the possibility of representing a non-linguistic referent vanishes and we are left with signification defined by the mechanics of the differences established within language. It is not possible to discuss words as though they represented things. Thus, the essays on the poor law and on the texts of social investigation concentrate on reconstructing the differences in the resources.

Anglo-American historiography also accepts the transparency assumption and in practice supposes that it is possible for one reading to exhaust a resource so that no remainder of significance is left. This is impossible because resources are often polysemic; they contain a play of reference which obliges us to construct more than one reading of every relatively complex text or institution. For this reason, all the essays use the unfamiliar term 'resources' rather than the familiar historiographic term 'sources'. All the essays accept the necessity for reconstructing the ambiguities of words, even if this sometimes makes the argument difficult to follow. The essays on Engels and on the poor law after 1870 concretely show how polysemy in complex resources can be incorporated into an analysis which makes more than one reading.

Because of the difference of assumption at these two points, the essays on texts and institution deliver an informally semiotic analysis of language and promote a concept of knowledge as reading(s). If language is now the primary concern of progressive literary criticism, these essays mark the point of entrance of this preoccupation into historiography. Taken together, the essays are attempts at a new kind of historiography which accepts the irreducibly linguistic nature of the discourse's resources.

The primary aim is displacement of the existing historiographic *a priori,* not complete internal consistency. Indeed, there are obvious inconsistencies in the concept of language used in seven essays which were drafted at various times between 1976 and 1979. The essay on the poor law before 1834, which contains the basic critique of empiricism, uses a concept of language as a theoretical system of differences in the Saussurean sense. Later essays on the poor law after 1870 and on the texts of social investigation explicitly or implicitly use a concept of language as interweaving infinite chains of reference in the Barthesian sense. These inconsistencies are not simply a fault; they establish a displacement within the text which has certain positive advantages. The essays do not promote one narrow orthodoxy but themselves exemplify the notion of knowledge as tentative reconstruction always open to revision.

What matters is difference of *a priori* rather than difference of results. Nevertheless, when the *a priori* changes, differences of result usually follow. And in this particular case, the results of the alternative analyses in the seven essays are very different from the results in the existing commentaries on the texts of social investigation and the histories of the poor law. To begin with, the results of the seven essays are organised differently.

The results are not unified in the conventional way by the discovery that texts and institutional practices share certain conscious preoccupations of the age. On the contrary, there is often a simple disjuncture between relief practice and social investigation as in the 1840s. And where there are recurrent preoccupations, these are not necessarily of great significance; for example, from the 1860s onwards the theme of 'splitting' the deserving from the undeserving is to be found everywhere, but it is of no importance because it is only a kind of lowest common denominator in several different relief strategies and social analyses. At the same time it should be emphasised that these essays do not pursue unity and identity at a more fundamental level and, concretely, they do not presuppose that there is one stable monolithic strategy of the age. After reading these essays it is easy to see how a strategy of the age could be fabricated by, for example, taking up the reference to classification which is an important organising principle in Mayhew and Booth's texts of investigation and which is also increasingly important in relief strategy after 1870. But the essays also show how uninformative the history of such a strategy would be because classification was very differently used and articulated in different texts and institutional strategies.

The dispersion of the results is not rationalised in the conventional way as a matter of differences from a privileged modernity. The title *From Pauperism to Poverty* is intended as an ironic comment on the obsessions of other historians. Such historians evaluate the texts of social investigation as more or less successful precursors of modern discourse on poverty; hence, for example, the recent praise of Mayhew's *Morning Chronicle* articles as an investigation of poverty. Such historians also assess the operations of the poor law as more or less successful responses to a poverty problem; hence, for example, the recent reappraisal of the pre-1834 poor law as a beneficent or at least harmless response to rural poverty and the universal condemnation of the 1834 *Report* for its concern with pauperism. These judgments are possible because current historians have only half-rejected an earlier Whig historiography of the welfare state; they reject the Whig schema of steady progress towards the welfare state but they accept the Whig destination, that is, poverty as a privileged object of investigation and for remedial action. The essay on Rowntree undermines this position by showing that poverty is neither a more 'real' nor a more scientific problem than pauperism; poverty is simply a discursive invention of more recent date.

When differentiation according to distance from poverty has been rejected, the essays are free to rework existing schema of continuity and discontinuity, identity and difference between various texts of investigation, and between the operations of the poor law in different periods. Finally, this introduction will comment on some of these differences of result.

In the essays on social investigation, the results are about texts not authors; as the essay on Mayhew shows, the author does not exist except as a text effect. If these essays dispose of authorial identity and the associated notion of an *oeuvre,* they are better able to establish differences between texts. The alternative analyses set up a broad division between the Mayhew and Engels texts on the one hand and the Booth and Rowntree texts on the other.

The Booth and Rowntree texts have a reactionary academic value in that they use language to produce a world taken for granted. Booth sustained conventional late nineteenth-century identifications by retreating into an interpretative doxa about the nature of society. Rowntree promoted twentieth-century identifications by providing an opportunistic concept of primary poverty. These are contemporary texts which will mainly be of interest to those concerned with the academic dimension of the present crisis of the welfare state. The Mayhew and Engels texts have a progressive literary value in that they use language to create and question different worlds. Mayhew's texts may be only aesthetically diverting, but Engels's *Condition of the Working Class* does pose serious modern problems, whether about the nature of discourse or the definition of socialism, even if it does not provide exemplary solutions to those problems. The texts by Mayhew and Engels are modern even though they are old in calendar terms; they have not yet lost the power to subvert our conventional identifications.

The results in the essays on the poor law are not about cause and effect linkages; as the first essay shows, probable or certain knowledge about causes is unobtainable. If these essays are not preoccupied with causality, they are better able to recover differences established in and by the operations of the poor law. Recent historiography emphasises continuity in the operations of the nineteenth-century institution which was always paying out relief doles to the poor. These essays establish two major discontinuities in relief practice.

The first discontinuity concerns a change in the classes of pauper assisted after 1834. The official pauperism statistics are reprinted in the statistical appendix to this book. They show first that large numbers of able-bodied men were on relief in the decades before 1834 and second, that after 1834 a line of exclusion was drawn and unemployed men found poor relief virtually unobtainable in the second half of the nineteenth century. The 1834 to 1870 period is also defined by a repressive strategy for disciplining paupers; this strategy was materialised in the general mixed workhouses which, as the essays show, were constructed in almost every poor law union by 1870. After this date, a second discontinuity is established by the development of several new relief strategies which in practice coexisted in a complex relationship. Outdoors, in the so-called 'crusade against out-relief' in the 1870s, there was a new kind of repression which was now directed against all classes of pauper and ideally promoted a new kind of knowledge *by* the poor about relief practice. Indoors, after 1870 there was a new strategy of classification and treatment which required new and different kinds of institution. To complicate matters further, an outdoors strategy of treatment which emphasised knowledge *of* the pauper, belatedly made an appearance after the 1890s.

Part one

The poor law

followed by a work of construction in the third. This develops an alternative kind of analysis which is not preoccupied with cause and effect linkages. The third section reads the configuration of the poor law before 1834 and offers a new account of who got what from the institution. In Anglo-American terms, this alternative analysis is a recovery and rectification of earlier kinds of historiographical analysis. Furthermore, this alternative institutional analysis is not so very different from the kind of textual analysis presented in the second half of this book.

Testing in philosophy

This section analyses the immediate necessity for, and the ultimate inefficacy of, test procedures in various empiricist theories of knowledge. It does so by presenting a short and simple reading of some philosophical texts, the technical literature of empiricism. Very simple readings are possible and necessary when such technical texts are relatively far away from the pole of polysemy. At the same time, it is difficult to make the readings accessible when technical texts always presuppose familiarity with specialised procedures, equipment, and vocabulary. Those who have difficulty with the following short account of empiricism, could refer to my earlier, more extended, account of 'Popperism' (Williams, 1975).

In empiricist philosophy, from Hume to Popper, test procedures were discussed and promoted as part of a solution to problems in the theory of knowledge. Most discussion of empirical testing was concerned with the question of justifying the rationality of such procedures in terms of their results. However, it is equally, or more, important to consider the problem situation which established the necessity for test procedures as part of the pursuit of empiricist knowledge. This problem situation goes all the way back to the eighteenth century and Hume.

For Hume, whether in the *Treatise* (Hume, 1911) or the *Enquiry* (Hume, 1902), the knowledge process was a matter of mind passively sampling reality. In its general form, the problem of knowledge concerned the difficulty of identifying and inductively generalising about the causal connections between empirical observables and events on the basis of limited experience (Hume, 1902, pp. 25-39). In its singular form, the problem concerned the difficulty of identifying the causal antecedents of one object or event out of a multiplicity of temporal antecedents. All subsequent empiricists have either accepted or made limited restatements of this Humean problem of knowledge. They have then tried to solve this problem. Before going on to consider these solutions, it is worth making two points concerning Hume's presuppositions about the form and ends of knowledge.

The Humean definition of the problem of knowledge introduced a presupposition about the form of knowledge. With a few exceptions such as formal mathematical proofs, almost all knowledge was typed by Hume as knowledge about 'matters of fact' which took the form of cause and effect sequences between empirical objects and events. In prescriptive mood, subsequent empiricists have often supposed that the one legitimate and proper form of knowledge concerned causal relations between observables. Less obviously, Hume smuggled in a prescriptive definition of the ends of the knowledge process. If knowledge was about cause and effect sequences, then the only knowledge worth having was probable or certain knowledge. In this way, Hume committed empiricism to the pursuit of probability.

The dilemma of inductive empiricism was that such knowledge is unattainable for reasons which were already clear in Hume's texts. Hume realised that analogy was the necessary basis of inductive generalisation.

> All our reasonings concerning matter of fact are founded on
> a species of analogy, which leads us to expect from any
> cause, the same events which we have observed to result
> from similar causes (Hume, 1902, p. 104).

Hume defined a 'cause' very simply as an observable object or event prior in space and time to the effect (Hume, 1902, p. 76), so he set up a mechanical universe consisting of sequences of empirical objects and events. The problem was that this concept of a mechanical universe of observables put insurmountable difficulties in the way of any induction based on analogy. Discrete empirical objects and events might resemble each other, but they were never identical. Relatively complex objects and events would be similar and different in a large number of observable characteristics. Without the benefit of a theoretical specification of the situation, there would be no reason to single out one small set of observable characteristics as necessarily relevant to a causal sequence. In this case, analogy or similarity of objects in some few respects would not provide a secure basis for the identification of causal relations. Such relations might well be determined by some of the unconsidered similarities and differences, while the number of such points would be so large that all the similarities and differences could not be considered.

The problem, as Hume left it, was that any inductivist discussion of a restricted number of natural cases was caught up in problems about a need for similarity which could not be satisfied. Thus, modifications of the Humean problem situation were attractive. The term systematic empiricism can be used to denote the modifications proposed in the mid-nineteenth century by J. S. Mill in his *System of Logic* and subsequently refined by the British statisticians, Pearson and Galton.

The systematic empiricists questioned none of Hume's presuppositions about the form and ends of knowledge. Their aim was the restricted one of reducing the radical uncertainty about the identity of causes within this framework. Their chosen means were new statistical techniques which promised to identify the causal relations present in a set of associations between empirical variables. And, at this point, explicit test procedures made their appearance. For it was generally supposed that the new statistical techniques should be used in conjunction with experimental tests and the manipulation of observables to control their variation. It is also worth noting that systematic empiricists increasingly accepted that the results of their tests would not be certain, universal causal statements but would be probabilistic generalisations derived from, and restricted to, a finite number of past cases.

However, as the Willers (1973) have recently argued, even these modest results were unattainable by systematic empiricist tests. If the tests were to be rigorous, there would have to be controls for almost every observable characteristic of the members of the population being studied. Control, like housework, was never done. So systematic empiricism required standards which could not, in practice, be attained in empirical work. The old problem about the infinite similarities and differences of discrete empirical objects and events was simply re-inscribed within the systematic empiricist test. In any case, experimental manipulation could succeed only in producing artificial cases which were a poor basis for induction because they were unlike natural cases.

Inductive empiricism was therefore caught in a double bind. Case study of the sort that Hume envisaged was so natural as to founder directly on the myriad similarities and differences between empirical variables. Experimental tests of the sort recommended by systematic empiricists were artificial and practically useless when control was an endless task. With or without tests, the inductive empiricists did not have a method that plausibly secured the knowledge they wanted about causal relations between empirical variables.

This conclusion has long since been accepted by twentieth-century empiricists like Carnap, Hempel, or Popper who were impelled to make further modifications to the Humean problem situation. This group of philosophers could be called the theoretical empiricists because so many of their modifications were made with the aim of accommodating natural scientific theory and rationalising its success in empiricist terms. Popperian falsificationism will now be considered as an example of this genre of empiricism. This example was chosen for two reasons. First, Popperism is the best known of these empiricisms since alternatives such as Carnap's have never been popularised in the same way. Second, Popperism represents a kind of limit position in theoretical empiricism. With his subsequent proposals for evaluating research programmes, Lakatos (1970) has shown that it is possible to refine the Popperian rules only at the expense of turning empiricism into a radical conventionalism.

Theoretical empiricists like Popper never really questioned the empiricist definition of the form and ends of knowledge, but they did go beyond a simple redefinition of the theoretical means of knowledge. Characteristically, they reconceptualised the stuff of knowledge so as to concede its linguistic, theoretical nature. Observable reality did not directly enter into knowledge for Popper; it was impossible to get beyond an intervening linguistic level where the factual evidence of empiricism consisted of test or observation statements which spoke of the effects of physical reality (Popper, 1974, p. 1120). Furthermore, although knowledge retained its causal form, the causal connections which concerned Popper were withdrawn into a discursive universe of theory which was supposed to consist of universal causal statements or laws. When knowledge was so clearly defined as a matter of discursive explanation rather than real connection, the problem of changes in explanation became very much more important; Popper was especially concerned with this problem and the defence of such changes as rational in empiricist terms.

Popper's methodology then became a do-it-yourself guide concerned with how to work in and on theoretical languages so as to obtain problems and theories which were rationally and objectively preferable to their predecessors because they uncovered 'real aspects or real layers of the world' (Popper, 1969, p. 115). Popper latterly represented the growth of knowledge by the following schema

$$P_1 \rightarrow TT \rightarrow EE \rightarrow P_2$$

By this, Popper (1972, pp. 106-52, 206-53) denoted the movement of knowledge from problem to problem via an intervening tentative theory and process of error elimination. The promise of the method was that, if at the stage of error elimination, the rules for working in and on language were obeyed, then the growth of knowledge would be rational. The Popperian rules prescribed two necessary operations of critical discussion and empirical test. So Popperism maintained test procedures in a key position and their role can now be considered in greater detail.

Given the retreat into language, Popper's tests could not involve a comparison with reality. Instead they involved bringing together test statements and universal laws so as to establish a rational relation between them. This relation could not be one of induction because a limited series of test statements could never justify an explanatory universal theory, nor for technical reasons could inductive testing result in a rigorous probability (Popper, 1968, p. 278; 1972, p. 265). The only possible rational relation between test and universal statement was one of deductive falsificationism because there was an asymmetry between verification and falsification such that the falsity of universal theories could be deduced when they clashed with basic statements. More exactly, Popper's falsificationism was of a sophisticated variety and a theory was not to be rejected because of one contrary test statement (Popper, 1974, p. 1035). Popper admitted that there were usually degrees of dissonance between theory and evidence. In this situation, the injunction was to seek and choose greater truth content or verisimilitude after testing (Popper, 1969, pp. 231-6, 391-7; 1972, pp. 47-53).

Popper's recognition of the existence of language was a huge advance over Hume and the systematic empiricists who had simply assumed that language was a perfect instrument, transparent to the order of things. Popper's particular conceptualisation of the role of language also got round the difficulties of inductivism which have already been considered. On the inductivist account, experience of empirical objects and events brought back so many similarities and differences as to undermine the determination of cause and effect linkages. On Popper's account, linguistic theory entered into the formulation of the hypothesis to be tested, the pertinent cause and effect variables, and in some cases the direction of the causal linkages. The only similarities or differences that could be relevant were those expressed within theoretical language. For Popper, language was so fundamentally constraining and directing as to remove the problem of the infinite similarities and differences between empirical objects.

When the problems of inductive empiricism were resolved in this way, the danger was that knowledge would end up in a prison house of language. Where language constrained, then successive theories could not be engaged with each other in a crucial test if they were formulated in radically different languages. At this point, incommensurability always threatened to undermine the rationality of Popperian tests. This was especially so because Popper clearly denied the existence of any kind of universal linguistic basis for knowledge. Test statements were concerned with the behaviour of physical bodies in space and time as in the assertion 'at the time x, the planet y was in position z' (Popper, 1968, p. 43). But although these statements were sometimes called basic statements, they were not so simple and unproblematic as to be universally acceptable test evidence. A particular theory defined the categories and measurement procedures in a series of test statements so that each theory defined the test evidence used in its own evaluation (Popper, 1968, p. 246).

In this case, Popper had to make certain assumptions about the organisation and nature of theoretical languages if his tests were to allow a choice between theoretical explanations which was rational in empiricist terms. To begin with, a certain organisation of knowledge was necessary and the alternative theories under consideration had to be competing. Formally, the theories had to contain intersecting sets of test statements or, less formally, the theories had to have common problems or results in approximation (Popper, 1969, p. 315; 1972, pp. 15-16; 1974, pp. 104-7). If this condition was not satisfied, then the common empirical basis disintegrated and theories would become incommensurable because it would be impossible to arrange a crucial test or to make the comparative measurement of truth content which was crucial to this sophisticated falsificationism (Popper, 1968, p. 277; 1969, p. 177; 1972, p. 52).

If the intersection assumption was necessary for rational tests, the transitivity assumption was necessary if Popper was to stay in the empiricist game about reality. Popper's instructions for working within language were in many ways instructions for behaving as though there was nothing but language upon language. It was altogether appropriate that Popper was an enthusiast for the Tarskian definition of truth as a purely linguistic affair between languages (Popper, 1972, pp. 319-40). But Popper was enough of the traditional empiricist to maintain a residual supposition of transitivity, that is, to assume that it was in the nature of language to name real pre-linguistic objects. This surfaced in the Popperian concept of the test statement as that which spoke of physical reality and in Popper's development of Buhler's theory of language which insisted it was in the nature of language to provide descriptive statements which described facts.

The key critical question about Popper is whether he can be allowed his transitivity and intersection assumptions or, more exactly, in what terms is he to be denied them?

Most recent discussion of Popper has been concerned with whether he was empirically correct to suppose that theories in the natural sciences have intersecting classes of basic statements. For example, was there such a relation of intersection between successive theories in physics from Kepler and Galileo to Newton, and from Newton and Maxwell to Einstein (Popper, 1968, p. 276; 1969, pp. 173, 199, 220; 1972, pp, 202, 262, 289)? The spectre of incommensurability was raised by Kuhn (1962) who argued that knowledge was organised into large incommensurable unities called paradigms, not umpteen competing theories. If paradigms existed, then Popper had all along been specifying controls for a subsidiary and unimportant choice situation, intra-paradigm choice, and empirical test cannot be determinant of inter-paradigm choice.

There is a high price attached to such criticism because, if it is accepted, then the next step is the kind of empty nihilism now represented by Feyerabend. *Against Method* (Feyerabend, 1975) is simply empiricism, minus the orthodox presuppositions about the means and end of knowledge, and with nothing in the empty places. Because of incommensurability, it is impossible to have progress in the Popperian sense of hypotheses with greater content. So Feyerabend cheerfully recommends the motto 'anything goes' as most likely to secure progress 'in any of the senses we choose' (Feyerabend, 1975, p. 27). The end result is a kind of carousel theory of knowledge where everything from folk tale to abstract scientific explanation goes up and down and round and round, periodically reappearing to make a contribution 'to the enrichment of our culture' (Feyerabend, 1975, p. 30). Because critics like Feyerabend never step outside the circle of empiricism's presuppositions, they can do no better than celebrate empiricism's failure as serendipity. This is the nihilistic consequence of the objection that Popper is wrong about theories intersecting.

The real problem, however, is that the whole post-Kuhnian debate about intersection is insufficiently radical. Such criticism accepts that theories have one objective structure and such criticism also accepts that this theory structure is a language in the Popperian sense. It is these claims, especially the transitivity assumption, which should be scrutinised. But such scrutiny is impossible when both Popper and his critics never challenge a common-sense representational concept of language as a serial naming of things whereby each word corresponds to a thing or class of things: by a process of conventional decision, object one is called a tree, object two is called grass, and so on to infinity. Once the objects are named, there is a one-to-one link between words and things, substantial identities on either side of a linguistic bar. By introducing the notion of theory-relative basic statements, Popper only added the possibility of successive different namings of things.

But the possibility of such transitivity was completely destroyed by Saussure in his *Course in General Linguistics,* first published in 1916. Saussure argued that there is no natural reason why, for example, the sound image 'tree' should be associated with the concept 'tree' in a linguistic sign. The association is not determined by a natural, or any other, kind of link between sound image and concept but by a difference which is sustained phonically and conceptually: the sound image 'tree' is defined by its difference from other sound images (treat, trot, etc.) and the concept 'tree' by its difference from other concepts (bush, forest, etc.). The implication is that 'the idea or phonic substance that a sign contains is of less importance than the signs that surround it' (Saussure, 1960, p. 120). The point seems rather unexciting in this form but it does have radical implications for transitivity.

Linguistic entities cannot have substantial identity and a connection to the real if they are constituted by a system of linguistic differences,

> language has neither ideas nor sources that existed before
> the linguistic system, but only conceptual and phonic
> differences that have issued from the system (Saussure,
> 1960, p. 120).

Furthermore, within one linguistic system, changes in the surrounding system of differences must affect the value of signs which literally remain the same. Consider, for example, an artificial language like Morse code which has a very simple task of representing alphabetical letters. Change some of the dot and dash denotations and the value of the other denotations is changed even if they still use the same dots and dashes to represent a letter. In complicated linguistic systems, the empiricist's real referent must vanish completely to the profit of signification determined by the changing mechanics of difference within linguistic systems.

This conceptualisation also and incidentally sees off the intersection assumption. For Saussure, each individual language is a self-contained system of differences and it is definitionally impossible that languages could overlap or intersect. For example, it is a nonsense to suppose that Morse code could intersect or overlap with a system of signalling at sea by means of flags. The two systems of differences have to be completely separate if each is to work, and there is therefore no area where statements common to both languages can be found. It is of course possible to move between systems and translate statements from one language to another; but such translation is never perfect even in natural languages because it involves a movement between systems. It is possible to say something according to one set of differences and then say something else according to another set of differences, but it is never possible to say the same thing in different languages.

In conclusion, modern empiricist philosophy has retreated into the area of the theory of language and here the development of the science of linguistics has pulled the rug out from under empiricism. Language cannot play the role that it must if test procedures are to be a rational device for theoretical empiricists. Popper's key assumptions are not so much empirically wrong as conceptually unacceptable because they rest on an anachronistic pre-Saussurean concept of language and they deny the constitutive systematicity of language. In the end, the problem with empiricism is not simply that it does not work in its own terms but that its whole problem situation is unacceptable. The procedures, like testing, that empiricism recommends are hardly therefore something to be slavishly imitated in social science or historiography.

Testing in historiography

Almost all the history written in the twentieth century has subscribed to the transitivity assumptions of empiricism; historiography still seeks to offer representations of reality even if it no longer hopes for an ultimate representation of how it really was. However, test procedures of the sort recommended by systematic and theoretical empiricism were hardly used in the history written before about 1960. In the 1940s theoretical empiricists like Hempel (1965) identified historiography as an anomalous form of knowledge which did not rely on empiricist procedures. At this stage, the philosopher's project was to explain away the anomaly and to reconcile historiography as it was with the empiricist image of scientificity.

By the 1960s the historian's project was to change historiography and to reconstruct the discourse in the image of empiricist scientificity. With or without the aid of social scientific theory, explicit hypotheses and formal procedures for testing causal statements made their appearance. The results were dramatic because other and more traditional types of analysis were usually excluded from texts which used the new techniques. In some areas of historiography, especially in economic history, texts in the new empiricist mode came to dominate the field. The old poor law was one such area and this section will consider articles by Baugh (1975), Blaug (1963, 1964), Huzel (1969) and McCloskey (1974) as examples of the new kind of empiricist historiography. Just as there are systematic and theoretical empiricists in philosophy, so there are two corresponding kinds of testers in historiography. Both kinds are represented in the articles on the poor law; testers like Huzel imitate systematic empiricism whereas testers like Blaug and McCloskey rely on theory to sort out causal variables and relations prior to test.

If the rest of this section is to be concerned with criticising these new kinds of historiography, the first point which should be made is that the presence of empiricist terminology and procedures does not justify the summary condemnation of any substantive discourse, historiography or otherwise. To issue such condemnations would be to invert the presumptuous legislative claims of empiricist philosophy of science. Popper searched for testability and test procedures and, where these were absent as in Marx and Freud, Popper confidently condemned whole discourses as metaphysics rather than science. It would be equally unsatisfactory to condemn whole discourses because test procedures were present. An anti-empiricist demarcation of discourses must be rejected because, like an empiricist demarcation, it presupposes that discourses are unitary homogeneous things wherein the epistemological is dominant so that the presence or absence of epistemologically approved procedures determines everything that happens in a discourse. This is unacceptable for two reasons: first, the relation between the epistemological and the other levels of discourse is not necessarily one of coherence and determination; second, the discursive existence and effect of epistemologically prescribed procedures is in each case an object for specification and investigation.

Test procedures, therefore, cannot be blamed for everything that has gone wrong in recent work on the old poor law. By way of illustration, we can consider the role of a stereotyped 'literature survey' in recent articles. Such literature surveys exist in the shadow of empiricism in that their function is to provide hypotheses for test. This partly explains how and why the testers decompose the texts surveyed into atomic statements about cause and effect. On the other hand, empiricism cannot be blamed for the carelessness of some recent literature surveys.

In the literature survey, the testers read and report on earlier historiography. Blaug's work inaugurates the current discussion of the old poor law and in his first article Blaug introduces the notion of the 'standard analysis' or the 'traditional indictment' of the old poor law (Blaug, 1963, p. 152). In a series of texts from the 1834 *Report* onwards this analysis was simply a set of 'conclusions' about the effects of the institution; 'the old poor law demoralized the working class, promoted population growth, lowered wages, reduced rents, destroyed yeomanry and compounded the burden on ratepayers' (Blaug, 1963, p. 151). The supposed cause of these effects was the 'allowance system' of adding to the labourers' wages from the rates (Blaug, 1963, p. 152). McCloskey (1974) has exactly the same approach as Blaug to the construction of a post-1834 orthodoxy about effects (McCloskey, 1974, pp. 420-1). Baugh (1975, p. 70) and Huzel (1969, pp. 431-2) again offer similar lists of effects.

But allegations about ill-effects are absent, or heavily qualified, or not important in earlier analyses of the old poor law. Consider, for example, the accounts of the Webbs (1927-9) and the Hammonds (1927). The Webbs used the same adjective 'calamitous' again and again in their description of the allowance system (e.g. Webbs, 1927-9, pp. 154, 212, 423). But nowhere did this text specify and detail the effects produced by the allowance system and the mechanisms through which these effects were realised. From a few scattered indicators in the text (e.g. Webbs, 1927-9, p. 154), it is not at all clear that the Webbs supposed allowances had dramatic effects on the cost of relief or population increase. The Hammonds were rather different because their text did list every ill-effect mentioned in the literature surveys (Hammonds, 1911, pp. 225-31). It is, however, doubtful whether statements about ill-effects occupied a privileged place in the Hammonds' text.

In different ways both the Hammonds and the Webbs identified allowances in aid of agricultural wages as an undesirable type of social and economic policy, and allowances were undesirable not because of their ill-effects but because alternative policies would have had beneficial effects. The Hammonds identified allowances as a token economic redistribution which was politically necessary if landlords and tithe owners were to continue to enjoy the 'surplus profits' of agriculture (Hammonds, 1911, p. 169). As good Hobsonian liberals, the Hammonds favoured a more radical redistribution to benefit the labourer. The Webbs identified allowances as a form of industrial subsidy by means of payments to an underemployed workforce (Webbs, 1927-9, p. 423). Their preferred alternative was the policy of 'the national minimum' which they had expounded in their *Minority Report* of 1909.

By emphasising the catalogue of ill-effects, the testers fail to engage the texts of the Webbs and the Hammonds. They do not identify the precariousness of these earlier analyses which can avoid anachronism only by presenting some of the policy proposals of the 1790s as basically Edwardian. Furthermore, the testers never identify the obsolescence of the analyses of the Webbs and the Hammonds. These analyses are not obsolete because they misrepresent the effects of allowances; they are obsolete because it would now be quixotic to analyse the old poor law's operations as a deviation from redistributive radicalism or the policy of the minimum.

If the testers do not engage their precursors, they cannot establish significant differences of analysis. The literature surveys that we have considered are devices for generating a wayward disengagement from earlier historiography. The necessary result in Blaug and his successors is a revisionism that defines its own problems by a process of self-reference, while all the time professing to revise an orthodoxy which it has fabricated in a literature it does not understand. But this discovery finally brings us back to the procedures of testing which are crucial to the process of self-reference. For, in all the recent articles, a superstructure of tests is erected on the basis of the literature survey and the imitation of empiricist techniques in this superstructure generates massive problems. To consider first the case of those who imitate systematic empiricist procedures, the problem is that they succeed too well in their imitation. The work of Huzel (1969) on the poor law and population increase provides a perfect illustration of such procedures carried out by a historian who subscribes completely to the inductivist creed about the form, ends, and means of knowledge.

In such work, tests expand to fill the textual space available because other kinds of general argument are palpably unrigorous in empiricist terms. Consider, for example, the fall in fertility which supposedly occurred in the 1820s *before* the reform of the poor law (Huzel, 1969, pp. 442-3). This does not establish anything about the effect of relief practice, and more especially of allowances in aid of wages, upon fertility. Common sense can proliferate a multiplicity of 'factors' that may have influenced fertility in different directions: variability in economic opportunity, institutional arrangements like living-in, employability of children, availability of consumer goods, and so forth. The inductivist cannot by inspection rigorously identify one or more of these factors as the cause of the fertility fall and the causal role of the poor law must remain obscure. To emphasise the role of relief practice would be to replicate the errors of previous historians of the old poor law whom Huzel condemns for failure to 'isolate the allowance system as a variable' (Huzel, 1969, p. 439).

The good inductivist in historiography needs a more rigorous procedure which will secure probable knowledge of causal relations.

Unfortunately, there are strict limits on the possibility of deploying systematic empiricist techniques in historiography. As a form of knowledge about the past, historiography has a limited capacity to generate and manipulate the evidence it requires. Sometimes only a restricted number of 'natural' cases can be investigated and usually there are severe limits on the possibility of experimental manipulation and control. In inductivist terms, history is like survey-type social science with the added disadvantage that there are absolute limits in historiography on the possibility of experimental manipulation as an adjunct or alternative procedure. Case study and especially the matching of 'natural' cases is almost necessarily the dominant technique in this kind of historiography.

This is certainly so in Huzel's article whose centrepiece is a case study of two Kent villages situated some 15 miles apart. The two parishes were different in respect of poor relief policy; Barham was a strict relief parish which gave no allowance in aid of wages, while Lenham operated a generous system of allowances (Huzel, 1969, pp. 415-16). In a number of other respects, the two parishes were similar; for example, both parishes had a similar economic basis in agriculture. Having matched cases in this way, Huzel is explicit about the hypothesis that if,

the allowance system was a prime factor in promoting
population increase, one would expect that parishes in
which the allowance system was in force would reveal
markedly higher birth and especially marriage rates than
parishes which gave no allowances, given roughly similar
social and economic structures and geographical conditions
(Huzel, 1969, p. 445).

Empirical measurements then show that population growth was faster in Barham and the implication is that the allowance system was not 'a prime factor'.

Huzel has instituted a procedure of case study like that recommended by inductivist epistemology and his conclusions can therefore be confounded by concrete variants on the sceptical arguments which have already been used against such epistemology. As the epistemology requires a similarity of empirical objects so Huzel requires 'roughly similar social and economic structures and geographic conditions'. This similarity cannot be established because, however carefully the villages may have been matched, they were different in a number of respects pertinent to the rate of population increase and its possible causes. To illustrate this point, the issues of emigration and occupational structure will be briefly considered.

Between 1801 and 1821 the generous relief parish of Lenham lost one in twenty of its population through emigration while Barham had virtually no net loss (Huzel, 1969, p. 448). Directly, had the emigrants stayed in Lenham then that parish would have had a faster rate of population increase than Barham (Huzel, 1969, p. 448). Indirectly, the effects could well have been dramatic if the emigrants were single persons of marriageable age. Huzel tries to dispose of this possibility by citing one piece of literary evidence (Huzel, 1969, p. 449), but this is hardly conclusive. It is therefore all the more unfortunate that Huzel's demographic information is presented almost entirely in the form of crude birth and marriage rates per 1,000 of population. Such measurements are directly biased by differences in age structure of population, rather than controlled for such differences - as is the case with age specific fertility and mortality. So poor law allowances may have been promoting faster population increase in Lenham, but, because of emigration, this may not have been reflected in population totals and crude demographic measures.

On the other hand, if population was growing faster in Lenham, this may have been because of differences in occupational structure rather than because of differences in poor law practice. From 1811 to 1831, Lenham had one in eight families engaged in 'other activities' outside agriculture, manufacture and trade, while Barham had nearly one in four families so engaged (Huzel, 1969, p. 445). Lenham also typically had a smaller household size. Both differences suggest that there were fewer domestic servants in Lenham. Other things being equal, a smaller proportion of Lenham's population was therefore engaged in a kind of employment where freedom to marry was often substantially curtailed.

Empiricist historiography would of course prefer to introduce differences one at a time and thus maintain the appearance of an orderly and constructive debate on the poor law and population increase. Such contributions are well regarded and help fill the pages of many historical journals. But it must now be clear that one step at a time movement arbitrarily calls a halt at the edge of a precipice. There is no reason why differences between empirical cases could not and should not be multiplied until the argument reaches total agnosticism about the causes of population increase and the effects of allowances. The differences already established illustrate that the matching of empirical cases can never be perfect and these imperfections undermine any certainty about cause and effect. The procedures of inductivist case study in historiography are futile in their own terms because they cannot arrive at probable knowledge about causal relations.

The theoretical testers are an altogether difference case. They use social scientific theory to specify a list of possible causes and effects and thus avoid the difficulties of naïve inductive empiricism. Furthermore, the theoretical testers in historiography are immune to criticism of the kind used against theoretical empiricism, because these historians do not carry out theoretical empiricist procedures – even when they claim to do so – and use the empiricist jargon about hypothesis, test, proof, and disproof.

In the theoretical 'tests' of this historiography, while empirical hypotheses are continually 'proved' or 'disproved', major theoretical structures are never put at risk nor is there any question of choice between such structures. This is transparently so in general terms in the area of the new economic history where the theoretical testers are dominant. The new economic history does not doubt and test marginalism but presumes that the world is as marginalist theory constructs it. What new economic historian has ever found one major proposition of marginalism to be invalid, or preferred an alternative explanation rigorously specified in neo-Ricardian or Marxist terms? If such results are inconceivable, it is clear that theoretical testing is not going on.

It is then necessary to examine specific texts so as to establish what is being done. Here Blaug (1963) and McCloskey (1974), the two marginalist historians of the old poor law, provide excellent examples of the kind of work undertaken by historians who depend on social scientific theory. As is usually the case, their articles are given over to this kind of work; the manipulation of theory is a technical business which takes up a lot of space if the appearance of rigour is to be maintained.

Blaug theoretically constructs the effects of poor law allowances in aid of wages using marginalism and development economics. His point of departure is the empirical circumstance that, in the early nineteenth century, allowances in aid of wages correlated very strongly with low wages (Blaug, 1963, p. 158). The question is how is a causal relation to be established. Blaug wants to refute arguments that suppose allowances cause low wages. Theoretical ingenuity is required to obtain a relationship whereby low wages cause allowances while remaining loyal to a marginal productivity theory of wage determination which prima facie points the other way. Blaug solves this difficulty by supposing that the usual relation between productivity and wages is reversed in the one special case of an underdeveloped economy in whose backward agricultural sector wages are below a 'biological minimum' and the food intake of workers is too low to allow maximum effort per unit of time (Blaug, 1963, p. 154).

In this special case, allowances in aid of wages could repair nutritional deficiencies and raise productivity and wages among the underemployed surplus labour in the agricultural sector (Blaug, 1963, p. 176). The remaining work now involves fitting the empirical case into the theoretical box that Blaug has constructed. To this end, Blaug presents evidence about conditions in the backward agricultural sector of the early nineteenth-century English economy. Wages were always very low in the large agricultural sector and significantly lower than in other sectors (Blaug, 1963, pp. 160-1). Beyond this, there is evidence of underemployment for labourers in wintertime in wheat-growing agricultural areas (Blaug, 1963, pp. 170-1).

McCloskey (1974) theoretically constructs the effects of allowances on real wages and hours worked in strictly marginalist terms. The elementary implications of supply and demand curve analysis allow him to refute the possibility that allowances simultaneously depressed wages and hours. Allowances in aid of wages will normally move the supply curve of labour in or out (e.g. Figure 1, S_2 versus S_3).

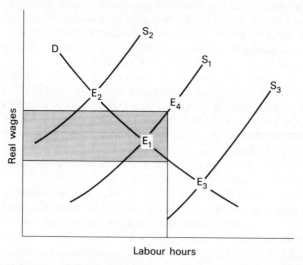

Labour hours

Figure 1   Wage subsidy
S_1/E_1 = pre-allowance supply of labour with E_1 equilibrium.
S_2/E_2 = post-allowance, lesser supply of labour with E_2 equilibrium.
S_3/E_3 = post-allowance, greater supply of labour with E_3 equilibrium.
S_1/E_4 = post-allowance, a labour supply curve with movement upwards to E_4,
with shaded area underneath equalling the portion of the wage bill
paid out of allowances.

As long as the demand curve is constant, after allowances have been introduced, either real wages will fall or hours worked will fall (e.g. Figure 1, E_3, versus E_1), but both wages and hours cannot fall at the same time. The way in which allowances are administered will determine which of the two effects is realised. If allowances are administered as a wage subsidy proportionate to hours worked and to earnings, the result will be more labour hours worked and lower real wages. In this case the labour supply curve will shift outwards (e.g. Figure 1, S_1 to S_3) or, alternatively, there will be a movement up a given supply curve (e.g. Figure 1, S_1) above the unsubsidised equilibrium point (McCloskey,

1974, p. 428). If allowances are administered as an income subsidy, wages will be made up with a lump-sum payment independent of hours worked and earnings, and the result will be fewer labour hours worked and higher real wages. In this case the labour supply curve will shift inwards (e.g. Figure 1, S_1 to S_2).

The remaining work for McCloskey now involves fitting the empirical circumstances into the appropriate box. Having set up the theoretical possibility of two distinct effects, McCloskey's empirical question is which effect was dominant in the England of the early nineteenth century. A brief survey of administrative details suggests that the poor law was administered as an income subsidy rather than a wages subsidy (McCloskey, 1974, p. 435). If the subsidy was not related to hours worked and earnings, then the effect in marginalist terms must necessarily have been to diminish the supply of labour and to increase wages for the effort that was supplied. The allowance system in early nineteenth-century England was a case which fitted the theoretical box of inwards shift of supply curve (e.g. Figure 1, S_1 to S_2).

Historians like Blaug and McCloskey undertake two distinct kinds of work. The first kind of work is theoretical (re)specification of terms and linkages. In all this they are using marginalism (which they never question) to redefine the nature and direction of the causal linkages posited in the atomic statements that they abstract from earlier historiography. When such historians have finished turning round the causal arrows, they begin a second kind of work which involves fitting the empirical case into an appropriate theoretical box. Here it is a question of working up empirical data using marginalist categories which are never in question. These two kinds of work are complementary parts of a procedure which could be called operationalisation so as to distinguish it from theoretical testing which is probably a chimerical representation necessary to certain kinds of empiricist philosophy. Operationalisation is what is left when this epistemological wrapping has been discarded.

If operationalisation is now going on in historiography, this establishes a link with the natural sciences rather than philosophy. Operationalisation is the routine kind of work undertaken by natural scientists in the modern period. In most kinds of natural scientific theory, there is scope for filling the empty boxes. And much of the time, in laboratory experiments and 'applied' calculations using theory, natural scientists are simply engaged in filling the boxes. In such inquiries, given a particular theoretical specification of the terms and relations, empirical values can be specified and relations or values not initially known can be calculated. The whole philosophical problem of knowledge is more or less irrelevant here. As most natural scientists claim, it is enough to know that the procedures of operationalisation usually work since they rationalise and explain empirical behaviour. For example, we live in a world where, thanks to Newtonian theory and computerised calculation, it is possible to build bridges that do not fall down and cars that crumple safely under impact in accidents. There seems no reason to make a great epistemological fuss about why and how. But at the same time it is of course true that this procedure of operationalisation has to be carried out with technical competence and the procedure does require appropriate theoretical resources.

In historiography, the problems concern the competence of the operationalisers *and* the absence of appropriate theoretical resources. These two points will now be considered in turn, beginning with the point about competence. This point is worth developing because it is not generally realised that much work in areas like the new economic history is technically questionable. This can only be demonstrated by taking specific examples and the work of Blaug and McCloskey can again be used for this purpose.

In so far as operationalisation is a technical procedure, the criteria of competence are straightforward. The work of theoretical specification involves taking bits from a construction kit, manipulating them, and fitting them together to construct a theoretical box. At this point, incompetent operationalisation involves a failure of rigorous theoretical specification and poor construction of the box. After this first stage, there is then the operation of fitting circumstances to boxes. Most empirical circumstances can be reconciled with the theory as so many different cases, but, of course, particular empirical circumstances will not fit every box. If the case is claimed to, but does not, fit the box then that again is incompetent operationalisation. Blaug and McCloskey's work can be criticised on both counts.

To begin with Blaug and his construction of a theoretical case, the marginalism and the development economics hardly fit together smoothly. Blaug's special case presupposes a convenient lapse from marginalist rationality whereby the employers never identified their interest in well-fed workers before allowances were introduced. More seriously, all of Blaug's ingenuity is a flight of speculation when he never actually specifies the point of the natural biological minimum. He speaks of 'minimum caloric requirements' (Blaug, 1964, p. 242) but never specified what these might be or the period of time over which they are to be measured. Without this specification, Blaug can label anything he likes as a special case and therefore does not really have a theoretical box at all.

Blaug's fitting of the English case into the box raises even more serious problems. It is not at all clear that the resources will sustain an identification of agriculture in early nineteenth-century England as the backward sector of a dual economy where wages were below the minimum. To begin with, the existence of open unemployment and under-employment in English agriculture is a disturbing anomaly. As Blaug himself argues, if wages are below a biological minimum, there should be 'disguised unemployment', that is, the semi-starved work-force should be so inefficient that the situation should give the appearance of a 'labour deficit' (Blaug, 1963, p. 171). Of course it could be argued that the appearance of labour deficit would only be found before allowances were paid. But that does not help Blaug because in a subsequent article he presents evidence that shows disguised unemployment after allowances; more than half the parishes in areas supposedly paying allowances reported disguised unemployment in 1832 (Blaug, 1964, p. 236). Furthermore, the payment of such allowances apparently did not necessarily increase labour productivity. As often as not, on Blaug's own evidence, the effect of allowances on productivity was perverse; nearly half the parishes in areas supposedly paying allowances reported declining productivity of labour (Blaug, 1964, p. 236).

McCloskey's work shows similar lapses and lacunae. To begin with, McCloskey's information on the English case is quite inadequate. It is not enough to know that allowances were usually administered as an income subsidy. Without some empirical information about the slope of, and shifts in, the supply and demand curves, it is by no means certain that modest allowances would have had significant effects upon hours worked. There is also the complication that, as the next section will show, the system of allowances in aid of wages had a strong discretionary element. This discretion may well have been exercised in the direction of controlling rational marginalist responses; those who responded to an income subsidy by reducing the number of hours worked may well have been simply struck off the relief rolls.

There are even more serious problems about McCloskey's neglect of the theoretical and empirical possibility of a downward shift in the demand curve for labour. *Both* real wages and hours worked can decline in the case of a downward shift in the demand curve for labour (e.g. Figure 2, D_1 to D_2). Depending on the slopes of the curves, a fall in both wages and hours is still possible even if, after a downward shift of the demand curve, allowances administered as an income subsidy are introduced and the supply curve for labour shifts inwards (e.g. Figure 2, S_1 to S_2). There is therefore no theoretical logic in marginalism which prevents both wages and hours falling. McCloskey simply neglects the theoretical box which is crucial to the argument he is trying to demolish. He then does not seriously consider whether early nineteenth-century England fits the case of a downward shift in the demand curve for agricultural labour. In marginalist terms, this demand curve is the marginal revenue product curve of the factor, and in any industry the demand curve will shift downwards if, per unit of labour input, there is a 'shrinkage' of output in terms of physical quantity and/or price. This seems to be at least a possibility in England after 1815 when agricultural prices were depressed and the efficiency of labour was often alleged,

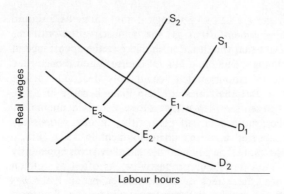

Figure 2   Wage subsidy with downward shift of demand curve

D_1/E_1 = original demand for labour with E_1 equilibrium.
D_2/E_2 = lower level of demand for labour with E_2 equilibrium.
$S_1/E_1, E_2$ = pre-allowance supply of labour with equilibria E_1 and E_2.
S_2 = post-allowance supply of labour with allowances administered as an income subsidy and E_3 equilibrium.

and sometimes reported, to be declining. McCloskey ignores these potentially embarrassing empirical circumstances.

Even if Blaug and McCloskey's manipulation of theory was faultless, that would not save them because they do not have access to the basic theoretical resources for operationalisation.

The operationalisers in historiography do not have such resources because they have relied on social scientific theory which is not up to the work of operationalisation. Sociology can only provide a few conceptual odds and ends about social control, class and so forth for the writing of modern social history. Here, there is simply not enough formal interconnected theory to allow a process of operationalisation. There is a corpus of theory in economics, and the new economic history has drawn heavily on marginalism in its rewriting of modern economic history. But there are severe limitations on the usability of this body of marginalist theory in a process of operationalisation. A long time ago Clapham joked about the empty theoretical boxes in economics. However, he never properly identified the basic problem which is that the boxes are necessarily empty because of difficulties about the scale of the theory and what it can handle operationally.

Marginalist theory can define determinative results and connections for small-scale problems; theorists like Alfred Marshall were masters of elegant trivialities like the effects of the abolition of postage charges on consumer surplus. But marginalist theory cannot define determinative results and connections for large-scale problems involving complicated change across a whole economy. In such cases the results are defined by *ad hoc* supplementary assumptions. This point was given away by Fogel (1964) right at the beginning of the new economic history when he envisaged an alternative non-railroad future with the American Mid-West criss-crossed by canals. The whole debate about counterfactuals in the new economic history is a confused recognition that marginalist economic theory cannot do the job which it has to do if operationalisation is going to work. It is true that operationalisation of marginalist theory can give determinative solutions in non-trivial cases for middle-scale problems; but that is not very much help because it provides us with the economic analogue of a physics which can calculate stress within structures and decide whether bridges will fall down but can only do so for footbridges under 10 metres span.

Even for middle-scale problems, marginalism is of no use to historical analysis because it proposes a universal calculus of economic rationality. Much of marginalist theory is taken up with elaborating such a calculus; the apparatus of consumer indifference and utility is erected around *Homo economicus* and the theory of the firm is added to provide another level of the same rationality. This rationality is universally applied in the reconstruction of the economics of the Stone Age, the Industiral Revolution, or Monopoly Capitalism. Any other calculus is judged as a deviation from the universal rational norm. The result is patently anti-historical. A serious historiography must be dedicated to recovering the different definitions of economic sanity and insanity which in modern times must surely have changed at least as often as the definitions of clinical sanity and insanity. Marginalist economics is a device for suppressing the different cultural calculi of economic rationality and for erecting a spuriously natural rationality. This economics must therefore be rejected by every economic historian.

The new kind of historiogaphy that tries to carry out operationalisation is thus in a hopeless position because it does not have the requisite theoretical resources. Meanwhile, it is not worth hanging around waiting for something to turn up in orthodox social science, or imagining that the requisite resources do exist to the left of social science. When negative criticism has liberated us from the incubus of an empiricist scientificity which cannot and will not work in philosophy or history, the positive alternative is to begin other styles of work.

The poor law's configuration before 1834

How is an alternative mode of analysing the poor law to be defined and obtained? The starting point here must be rejection of the currently favoured procedures of testing. If these procedures are rejected, that leaves, as a residual, the testers' presuppositions about the virtuous form and ends of knowledge; historiographical knowledge is, or should be, a representational knowledge which recovers probable causal sequences between real objects and events.

These presuppositions have naturalised themselves in Anglo-American historiography over the last twenty years so that it is easy to forget that many other kinds of historiography have managed to dispense with some of these presuppositions. Consider, for example, the question of causal analysis. It is impossible to abjure all forms of causal and quasi-causal inference in historical argument; but historiography does not have to dedicate itself to an understanding of the past through analysis of causal sequences, and many existing kinds of historiography find little room for such analysis. This is true, for example, of the Webbs whose histories of trade unionism and local government are the model of an older English institutional history. As we have already seen, the Webbs discussed the pre-1834 poor law at length, without analysing the effects of the institution in detail. Much the same kind of point could be made about the analyses of Michel Foucault which are now the model of an *avant-garde* anti-history. There have been many shifts of position in Foucault's texts from *Madness and Civilisation* to *Discipline and Punish,* but all these texts display the same indifference to causal analysis.

In many ways, therefore, this chapter proposes a recovery, rectification and reinstatement of other modes of analysis which have been consigned to the periphery of current Anglo-American economic and social history. But, at the same time, there is something new in this chapter because there is no existing historiography that rejects all the presuppositions of the testers. There are two ways of approaching and specifying a new alternative based on complete rejection: first, it is possible to elaborate the formal difference of an alternative historiography in a series of dogmatic theses; second, it is possible to establish specific differences from existing historiography on the poor law. This section now turns to the definition of an alternative in these terms, and it begins with a series of dogmatic general assertions.

First, an alternative analysis is concerned with significations rather than with the status of the signifying as something which is empirically observable or related to the empirically observable. The significations are so many names of things which have taken on an intransitive linguistic life of their own, enmeshed in complex networks of differences. Analysis will be concerned with the relation between significations which can be reconstructed as chains of reference. But analysis will not try to resolve such relations into causal relations.

This differentiation defines an alternative historiographical inquiry as a kind of reading. That is to say, the primary concern of historiography should be with questions of legibility and intelligibility. It should be emphasised that the readable does not have to be restrictively and logocentrically defined as that which is to be found on the pages of books; the traces of an institution or state apparatus are just another text and these traces include, for example, surviving buildings as well as printed records. Thus, in principle, the kind of institutional analyses offered in the first half of this book need not be so very different from the textual analyses offered in the second half.

Second, with regard to the ends of knowledge, it is not necessary to presuppose that these ends should be probability or certainty. An alternative reading of signification can aim not at certainty but at difference from previous identifications. Perhaps this point is best illustrated with a concrete example from the second half of this book. Later chapters present alternative readings of Mayhew or Engels which do not have to aspire to certainty in order to attain significance. They achieve significance because, in a reasoned way, they handle reference differently. In much the same way, readings of institutional configuration do not have to be promoted or preferred on grounds of their probable or certain truth; an argued difference of reading is enough.

This differentiation defines an alternative kind of historiographic knowledge which sidesteps the relativism and scepticism shadowing the empiricist pursuit of probability or certainty. A knowledge staked on certainty must always fear a relativistic failure; if its favoured procedures like testing are not followed, or, worse, if these procedures are ineffectual, then the result will be a complete and total relativism where one thing is as good as another. An alternative knowledge staked on difference cannot fail in the same way. Such an alternative can accept that in the long run we are all wrong just as surely as we are all dead, and that most of our errors cannot be justified as necessary steps on an upward path to enlightenment. But this does not mean that at any moment of time in the development of a knowledge, one thing is as good as another, or more specifically, that anything will do as the next step. In an alternative kind of historiographic knowledge, there will always be scope and need for reasoned argument about the differences which are to be established as the next step.

At this point, it becomes necessary to examine the specific historiographic field within which an alternative analysis is to be established. Programmatic assertions about signification and difference do not directly define a substantive series of questions; concretely, it is always necessary to redefine and reformulate the questions which construct particular problems in a specific field of historiography. Moreover, in any historiographic investigation, there are problems and differences relating to the particularity of the resources which are or can be used; concretely it is never possible to answer any and every question. Even when a question is clearly answerable, different answers can be obtained depending on the procedures and presuppositions of the analysis. Thus, it is necessary to examine critically, first, the existing questions and answers of poor law history and, second, the resources available for rewriting poor law history.

Subsequent historiography has revised but not replaced the Webbs' massive history of the poor law; so we can begin by considering this text. The prime objective in the Webbs' institutional history was to define one institutional configuration in each period. Hence their poor law history put much effort into developing constructs like 'Speenhamland' for the pre-1834 poor law and the 'retreat from principles of 1834' for the post-1834 period. In their history of trade unionism it was the same story, only with different constructs like 'new unionism' or 'new model unionism'. If the Webbs can be congratulated for asking questions about institutional configuration, they can be criticised for their answers and their treatment of resources. Basically, the problem here concerns their presupposition of unitary meaning and the way in which they constructed such meanings by cutting off and rearranging reference into convergent patterns. For the Webbs, defining an institutional configuration was a matter of stringing references along one or two chains to define a regional mechanism of the age. Configurations like 'Speenhamland' were non-transcendental, non-idealist regional substitutes for the spirit of the age. Within each separate age, the dominance of one configuration was a matter of methodological assumption rather than practical demonstration. Partly for this reason, the Webbs neglected the official statistics which are a key resource for the writing of poor law history because questions about the national parameters of relief practice can be answered most economically from these official statistics. The Webbs dutifully acknowledged the existence of these resources and then effectively neglected them, except for the statistics on cost of relief which they dismissed as unreliable.

As we have already seen, the recent historiography of the testers is diverted into asking unprofitable questions about cause and effect relations. Apart from this, it must now be insisted that the testers' incidental treatment of institutional configuration and their relation to resources is markedly inferior to that of the Webbs.

Far from advancing beyond the Webbs' presupposition of unitary meaning, in their treatment of institutional configuration, recent historians of the old poor law have actually moved backwards because they have tried to reduce such a meaning to its natural economic secret. Blaug tried to naturalise and explain away the relief practice of the institution through economic reductionism. He identified the supplementation of labourers' wages as a response to underemployment in the backward agricultural sector of the economy; the real problem was that 'wages were too low to provide a minimum standard of living' (Blaug, 1963, p. 169). This reductionism was only a prelude to a later comprehensive attempt by Baugh to explain relief expenditure in economic terms. Pre-1814 expenditure was referred to the variability of the harvest (Baugh, 1975, pp. 55-9); post-1814 relief expenditure was explained in terms of chronic post-war unemployment (Baugh, 1975, p.

64). In both periods, 'what mattered was the shape of the poverty problem and that shape changed' (Baugh, 1975, p. 67). With Baugh, we reach a historiography that is not interested in recovering the cultural configuration of the institution but which is obsessed with passing off the institutional configuration as a natural response to economic conditions. Against this, it must be insisted that economic conditions may, for example, make relief expenditure fluctuations more intelligible, but they can never determine, nor render intelligible, relief practice with regard to who was relieved and how.

As for the relation to resources, the problem is that recent historiography has a completely opportunistic relation to resources. Consider, for example, the treatment of official statistics. Recent historians raid individual resources so as to abstract the elements that are immediately useful to their tests about the effects of relief practice. Only the statistics of annual expenditure on poor relief are regularly considered in this recent historiography. But the expenditure statistics yield little information when they are disconnected from the other available statistics about numbers on relief and types of relief practice. Discussions of these other statistics usually consider one official return at a time, concentrate on one small section of the return, and never effectively cross-refer between the different returns. For example, Blaug (1963), in his first article, relied on replies to one question in the Select Committee *Abstract of Returns* for 1824 (BPP, 1825, XIX). In his second article Blaug (1964) discussed two questions in the Royal Commission *Answers to Rural and Town Queries* of 1832 (BPP, 1834, XXX–XXXVI) but this second article did not properly cross-refer back to 1824, nor discuss the *Abstract of Returns* for 1802–3 (BPP, 1803–4, XIII), although these returns contain the most detailed information on the composition of the pauper host and cover almost every parish in England and Wales. Amazingly, in the post-1963 historiography, there is only one brief discussion of this *Abstract of Returns* for 1802–3 (Marshall, 1968, pp. 31–5). Given their treatment of the pre-1834 statistics, it is hardly surprising that none of the revisionist historians cross-refers to the post-1834 statistics.

Matters are further complicated by premature local studies of the operation of the old poor law in Neumann's (1972) article and several unpublished theses. The local study can only be worth while and effective as an adjunct to national study which defines the configuration of the institution; local and regional differences can only be rendered intelligible in a national context. But the necessary national studies are non-existent or inadequate for the reasons we have analysed. Recent local studies must, therefore, make a virtue out of necessary illegibility and celebrate diversity, improvisation and local autonomy as primary themes. Thus, Neumann (1972, p. 109) finds that in pre-1834 Berkshire there was not a Speenhamland system in the sense of a universally applied bread scale used in the assistance of the able-bodied. So what was the institution doing in Berkshire? All Neumann will say is that there were many ephemeral schemes to assist the able-bodied before and after 1795; 'the parishes gave this relief (to the able-bodied) precisely as often, widely and generously as they chose' (Neumann, 1972, p. 108). The Webbs' bogus order of 'Speenhamland' is dissolved into chaotic disorder. This is a pseudo-resolution that avoids all the difficult problems which concern the necessity for reconceptualising the configuration of the institution.

It is to this task of reconceptualisation that we now turn. In principle, it is not difficult to produce a concrete analysis of the nineteenth-century poor law which is consonant with this section's programmatic generalities about chains of reference and significations enmeshed in networks of differences. The poor law before or after 1834 can be defined and delimited as a network of differences. It is easy to see that penality differentiates crimes and punishments just as medicine differentiates illnesses and treatments. In a similar way, the nineteenth-century poor law differentiated various kinds of indigence which were to be rewarded and punished in different ways. Practically, several classes of pauper subject (able-bodied men, widows, the old, etc.) were differentiated as objects for relief strategies of assistance, repression, or treatment. Ancillary roles for a bureaucracy and different types of institution were organised around these strategies of relief practice. Above all, an alternative analysis must describe how these differentiations shifted and changed as relief practice defined new objects and new strategies.

This description is obtained by reading the available resources as a kind of text. The crucial resources in the pre-1834 period are the official statistics and these make a short text with many lacunae. Although the pre-1834 period was not a pre-statistical era, it was a period dominated by the *ad hoc* special return. The only regular continuously available information concerns expenditure after 1812 when an annual series begins. Apart from this, statistics were collected occasionally and any analysis must adapt itself to the particularity of the information which is available in the three major *ad hoc* returns on paupers and how they were assisted: the *Abstract of Returns* for 1802-3 (BPP, 1803-4, XIII), the Select Committee *Abstract of Returns* for 1824 (BPP, 1825, XIX), and the Royal Commission *Answers to Rural and Town Queries* for 1832 (BPP, 1834, XXX-XXXVI). The categories used in any one of these special returns do not necessarily recur in the others and the information on class of pauper, numbers, mode of assistance, and cost is always extremely skeletal.

It is unprofitable to lament an infinite richness which is lost behind these poor resources; one of the founding presuppositions of our analysis is that there is no referent behind these textual significations.

The term 'resources' has been deliberately used to suggest that there is always the possibility of, and necessity for, reconstructing these statistics; they are not conceptualised as a source in the orthodox historiographic sense of a primary and original source of signification. But the meagre statistical resources do establish limits on the kinds of analysis that are possible; it is impossible to read an unwritten text and difficult to read a fragmentary text. For these reasons, the configuration of the poor law before 1834 can be constructed only very simply as a few cuts or lines of division on a social surface. The specifiable differences here concern what kind of relief allowance the poor law was offering to whom. It is difficult to establish even a few elementary lines of this sort when there are many gaps in the available statistical resources which can only be filled by assumptions.

The reliance on assumptions at several key points in the ensuing argument must raise the issue of whether this chapter adopts a double standard on speculation. Does it condemn empiricist speculation about cause only to prefer its own anti-empiricist speculation about configuration? This objection misunderstands the nature of an alternative analysis which aims at difference of identification. Any alternative analysis is improbable in the sense that it offers a provisional reconstruction of meaning. Thus, the immediately relevant question about the pre-1834 poor law is not whether the alternative gets it right, but whether the alternative establishes that Blaug and others have got it wrong? Although the following reconstruction is defensible in these terms, because of the resource constraint, it is hardly a model alternative analysis. After 1834, official statistics and other resources are abundant, so that it is possible in the next chapters to offer a more complex analysis of the new poor law. And, in the second half of this book, the analysis of the texts of the empirical investigators is even less constrained by resource limitations. In these fields an alternative analysis can be fully developed and vindicated.

To turn now to the analysis of the pre-1834 poor law, the obvious starting point is the *Abstract of Returns* for 1802-3 which asked eight questions about expenditure and eight about numbers on relief through the year Easter 1802 to Easter 1803. The replies are especially valuable because question thirteen asked 'what was the total number of persons relieved who were above sixty years or disabled from labour by permanent illness or other infirmity?' Never again before 1834 is it possible to define the relative importance of the group of aged and infirm paupers. The other positive advantage of the *Abstract* for 1802-3 is that there was a very high response rate to its questions; only some 1,000 of the 15,500 parishes in England and Wales failed to return answers. By way of contrast, the information for 1824 and 1832 covers only a small sample of these parishes.

Nevertheless there are problems about the answers returned for

1802-3. These difficulties arise because the questions about total numbers relieved did not clearly specify whether parishes were to return an average load figure or a total of all paupers relieved in the year Easter 1802 to Easter 1803. If parishes returned the latter kind of total, they may either have double-counted or made allowance for repeated relief applications by the same individual. However, the importance of these difficulties should not be exaggerated. The uncertainty about what kind of total was returned must primarily affect those returned as 'occasionally relieved' in replies to question twelve. It is only here that the discrepancy between the different kinds of total would be very large. But the group of those 'occasionally relieved' only accounted for one-third of all paupers. It is also significant that this percentage of 'occasionally relieved' is remarkably constant if the replies are considered on a county by county basis; thirteen of the fifteen agricultural counties were within six percentage points of the group average (see Statistical appendix, Table 4.2). This consistency suggests that those who filled in the returns understood the questions in one sense. The replies to the *Abstract* for 1802-3 (see Statistical appendix, Table 4.2) therefore allow us to answer questions about how paupers were relieved and about what classes of pauper obtained relief. When answers have been obtained for 1802-3, it will be possible to bring in the other available resources and answer questions about what changed in the period between 1802 and 1834. The issue of how paupers were assisted will be considered first.

The poor law in 1802-3 was not paying allowances universally to all the individuals who were aged or had young dependants. This is clear from a comparison of the total number on relief in 1802-3 and the age structure of population data which first became available twenty years later after the census of 1821. In 1802-3, the 1,040,000 paupers made up 9 per cent of population in England and Wales. In 1821, men and women aged sixty years and over alone made up 7.5 per cent of population and adult men in the age group twenty to fifty years made up 17.4 per cent of population. If the age structure of 1802-3 was anything like this, then the poor law must have been selectively assisting some of the old and some of the men with dependent children. Furthermore, the poor law was not operating a system of permanent pensions for the fortunate few who were assisted. Individuals who were assisted often received discontinuous relief; in 1802-3, 305,000 paupers, or almost one-third of the total number in England and Wales, were directly returned as 'occasionally relieved'.

Those who received relief typically continued to live in their own homes. Out of the 1,040,000 men, women, and children, only 83,000 were returned as 'in workhouses or houses of industry' in replies to question ten. The vast majority of the paupers who were not institutionalised received small doles. Excluding legal and other expenses, total expenditure on out-relief was £3,061,000. If it is assumed that the pauper totals are average load figures, then the weekly dole per pauper works out as just under one and a quarter (1.23) shillings a week in an era when even an underpaid agricultural labourer could expect to earn the better part of ten shillings a week. Such a weekly dole figure is a crude 'guestimate' which rests on a large assumption. It is nevertheless significant because on any plausible assumption the results would be much the same. The allowances must have been supplementary to other sources of income because they were typically too small to support an individual fully.

In conclusion, in its mode of assistance in 1802-3, poor relief was thus selective, discontinuous, and supplementary. This does not establish that the poor law was an unimportant institution with a marginal role. Such a verdict can be sustained only if anachronistic standards of judgment are applied. It would be futile to condemn the poor law in the 1800s for not paying universal full subsistence allowances when these were only put on the agenda in the 1940s by the *Beveridge Report*. The point is rather that the emphasis on selectivity, discontinuity, and supplementarity in a preliminary way establishes a difference in the kind of assistance offered by the early nineteenth-century poor law and late twentieth-century social security.

The available resources suggest there was no great change in the kind of relief offered before 1834. On selectivity and supplementarity, the main consideration has to be the level of expenditure on relief in real terms. This is best assessed by means of the index of real relief expenditure which Blaug (1963, p. 180) calculated by using wheat prices to adjust the official statistics of total expenditure on relief. It is a crude real index because wheat was only the invariable consumption staple of the poor in the southern and eastern wheat-growing counties; but this index does give a rough guide to major changes in expenditure levels. The year 1802-3 was an average one in terms of harvest and wheat prices and 1802-3 expenditure is taken as a base of 100. Blaug's calculations then show that expenditure was consistently higher after 1812. But in the twenty-two years from 1812 to 1833 inclusive, expenditure was only running at twice the 1802 level for one year (1822) and through the whole period real expenditure was running at an average index level of 165. Given that population was also increasing, the increase in real expenditure is sufficiently moderate to suggest continuity in mode of relief. Before 1834, the poor law never spent the huge sums of money which would have been necessary if the system was to move towards universality and away from the selective system of 1802-3. Moreover, in this case there was necessarily a straight trade off between selectivity and supplementarity. When real expenditure levels increased relatively moderately, the institutions could only have supported a very much larger number of paupers by offering them even more meagre supplementary doles.

As for the importance of occasional and irregular relief, there is direct evidence for the years 1813 to 1815 that occasional relief was still important. The *Abstract of Returns* for 1813-15 (BPP, 1818, XIX) included replies to a question about the 'numbers of parishioners occasionally relieved'. In the three years 1813, 1814, and 1815, annual totals of between 400,000 and 440,000 paupers were returned as occasionally relieved and in all three years this group made up almost exactly 45 per cent of all paupers (BPP, 1818, XIX). It should be emphasised that this percentage is not directly comparable with the 30 per cent returned as 'occasionally relieved' in 1802-3. The later totals do not include relief to non-parishioners which was included in the earlier totals. It can nevertheless be reasonably claimed that from 1813-15, just as in 1802-3, there was an important place for occasional relief.

The kind of assistance offered to paupers did not change much before 1834. And, as chapter 2 will show, the mode of assisting paupers survived the 1834 reform, although there were dramatic changes in the classes assisted. To understand these post-1834 changes, it is first necessary to understand what classes of pauper obtained relief before 1834.

The discussion now turns to the question of who was assisted in the 1800s. If poor relief in 1802-3 was selective, discontinuous and supplementary, then the mode of assistance did not establish a firm line of division between pauper and non-pauper; selective, discontinuous out-relief doles would ensure constant movement of individuals across a line which was necessarily ill-defined if the institution's role was to give supplementary doles. Nevertheless, some kind of line of division between pauper and non-pauper could still have been established by relief decisions on what classes of pauper were assisted and not assisted.

Before 1834 relief practice did not establish a line that excluded definite classes of pauper. The statistics for 1802-3 directly show relief being given not only to the chronic sick and elderly but also to very large numbers of able-bodied men and their families. A relatively small proportion of those on relief was returned as aged and sick; only 16 per cent of the total number of paupers were returned as 'persons above sixty years of age, or disabled from labour by permanent illness or other infirmity'. But this 16 per cent amounted to 167,000 individuals, so the line with regard to who was assisted had hardly been set to exclude the old and sick. On the contrary, the proportion of old and sick was low simply because the line of division had been set so it included very large numbers of young, healthy, employable adults and their dependent children. Such men, women, and children totalled 874,000 and accounted for 84 per cent of all paupers.

In conclusion, the classes assisted in 1802-3 included not only the unemployed, the temporarily sick, and young widows, but also the old and chronically sick. In nineteenth-century terms, the classes assisted included the able-bodied as well as the non-able-bodied. In terms of classes assisted, the poor law of 1802–3 is both similar to and different from modern social security. Within a framework of assistance for all classes of the poor, the late twentieth-century system works by differentiating the assistance given to various groups; for example, some of the short-term unemployed receive earnings-related insurance benefits while the long-term unemployed receive non-contributory social security at a reduced rate. In these terms, the early nineteenth-century poor law can be identified as social security minus a detailed differentiation of beneficiaries. But modern social security is in no way a direct descendant of the early nineteenth-century poor law. In an intervening stage in the later nineteenth century, the poor law operated in quite a different way because a line of exclusion was then drawn against able-bodied men, or, more specifically, the unemployed, so that relief was concentrated on the old and chronically sick. This elementary point will now be established by a comparison of the classes obtaining relief in 1802–3 and 1901.

It has already been shown that through the year 1802–3, 16 per cent of paupers were aged and infirm adults. But, on a day count basis, in January 1901 48 per cent of paupers were aged and chronically infirm adults (see Statistical appendix, Table 4.39). Furthermore, a distinct new group of the chronic sick was defined and increased steadily in relative importance in the second half of the nineteenth century; on a day count basis, the insane accounted for 12 per cent of all paupers by 1901 (see Statistical appendix, Table 4.39). On a broad definition that includes mental and physical infirmity, the group of aged and infirm accounted for 60 per cent of all paupers by 1901. This spectacular rise in the relative importance of the group was not accounted for by a generous extension of relief to the aged and physically infirm adult. Such adult paupers accounted for roughly similar percentages of total population at the beginning of each century; 1.4 per cent of population in 1802–3 on a year count basis is not so very different from 1.2 per cent of population in 1901 on a day count basis. After 1821 when age structure of population figures are available, the census shows that the over-seventy age group was a roughly constant 2.5 to 3.0 per cent of total population through the nineteenth century. So it is reasonable to suppose that the poor law assisted not dissimilar proportions of the population of elderly and infirm adults in 1802 and 1901.

The explanation for the rise in relative importance of relief to aged and infirm adults is to be found in the absolute and relative decline of relief to able-bodied men. A January 1901 day count showed only some 7,000 unemployed men receiving relief (see Statistical appendix, Table 4.39). As chapter 2 will show, this day count total is not a freak or aberration but is typical of the totals of the 1890s and 1900s; by this time, the poor law had effectively stopped assisting the unemployed.

The number of unemployed men assisted through the year 1802-3 was very much larger and it is perhaps worth making a 'guestimate' of the total number. The *Abstract* for 1802-3 gives a total of 874,000 able-bodied adults and dependants. First, it can be assumed that approximately one-third of this group were young widows or temporarily sick men with dependants; this sub-group could only be very much larger if there was a very generous system of medical relief and widows' pensions. On the basis of this first assumption, there were approximately 600,000 able-bodied men and their dependants on relief through the year 1802-3. Second, it can be assumed that the typical able-bodied family consisted of man, wife, and four children; this assumption is consonant with the later evidence of the 1824 *Returns* which shows much relief assistance was then being channelled to men with two or more children. On the basis of the second assumption, through the year 1802-3 100,000 adult men obtained relief because they were unemployed, underemployed, or in full-time employment at low wages.

This total is a guestimate, but it does establish a remarkable contrast. The total population of England and Wales in 1901 was almost exactly three times larger than that of 1802. But on a day count basis, the poor law in 1901 assisted a number of unemployed men which was more than ten times smaller than the number assisted through the year 1802-3. However, the assumptions underlying the guestimate are varied, and it is difficult to avoid the conclusion that the line on classes assisted was set to include unemployed men in 1802-3 and to exclude unemployed men in the 1890s or 1900s. This elementary point has never been established in the recent literature on the old poor law because this literature fails to make any long-run comparison of the classes assisted and because this literature accepts J. D. Marshall's misleading analysis of the 1802-3 *Abstract*.

In the one modern account of the *Abstract* for 1802-3, Marshall (1968, pp. 30-6) argues that up to 70 per cent of paupers were not able-bodied adults and shows that, if the remainder divided equally by sex, then the able-bodied males accounted for 'considerably less than 20 per cent of the pauper "host", and not much more than 2 per cent of the entire population' (Marshall, 1968, p. 35). The obvious but unstated implication is that relief to the able-bodied male was relatively unimportant. Marshall's assumptions are reasonable, his arithmetic is impeccable, but his logic is dubious. To begin with, his demonstration of the unimportance of able-bodied pauperism rests on the separation of labouring men from their dependants. This is absurd when it has always been accepted that such men drew relief because of large families. If the typical client family consisted, for example, of labourer, wife and three dependent children, then it would be absolutely impossible for the percentage of labouring men to rise above 20 per cent of those on relief. As for the 2 per cent of total population figure, it has already been emphasised that relief to the able-bodied does not have to be universal to be significant. And, for obvious reasons, the incidence of selective relief to able-bodied labouring men is best measured against the total male population in the age group from say, twenty to fifty years, rather than against total population of both sexes. If, for example, the age structure of the 1802-3 population was similar to that disclosed by the 1821 census, then all males twenty to fifty years made up 17 per cent, or approximately 1,556,000, out of the total England and Wales population. It has already been guestimated that 100,000 unemployed men drew relief through the year 1802-3, and the poor law was thus assisting around one in fifteen of the male population in the age group twenty to fifty years.

If the line of division with regard to who was relieved shifted so fundamentally in the nineteenth century, then the next question is: when did the line shift? In a subsequently much cited and universally accepted article Blaug (1964) argued that the 1834 reform was a non-event because already by this date relief to the male labourer had diminished in quantity and changed form so that only a system of child allowances survived. Did a withdrawal of assistance to the able-bodied take place before 1834? Or, if there were not great changes before 1834, how soon afterwards was the line of division redrawn to exclude the able-bodied male? These questions will be considered in the rest of this chapter and in chapter 2.

Blaug discussed changes in relief practice between 1824 and 1832, but the line of division may have been redrawn several times before 1834. Hence it is necessary as a preliminary to consider the period between 1802 and 1824. In this period, the main object of analysis must be the relation between county relief expenditure and the age structure of population in these counties as disclosed by the 1821 census; this relation is an obvious indicator of the bias of the institution towards relieving the old. Of course, the Webbs hinted that the relief expenditure figures were unreliable measures of what was being spent on relief. The published figures of county expenditure in the parliamentary papers were derived from parochial accounts kept by amateurs who, no doubt, incorrectly entered some debits and credits and also imperfectly separated expenditure on relief from other types of rate-aided expenditure. The key question, however, is whether these errors were usually significant and all in one direction? The answer to this question is probably no, because over county-sized or larger areas a multiplicity of small errors of different kinds probably cancelled each other out.

What, then, was the relation between relief expenditure and age structure of population? The counties with more elderly populations did not consistently spend more on poor relief; Tucker (1975, p. 229) has calculated that there is only a weak negative relation (-0.07) between county relief expenditure in the years 1817 to 1821 and the proportion of the population aged sixty and over in 1821. As a tester, Tucker is surprised and puzzled by this relation which can only appear 'perverse' (Tucker, 1975, p. 245) to a historiography that raids individual resources. But if the relation between relief expenditure and age structure of population is referred back to the configuration of the institution in 1802–3, then it is not at all perverse. The obvious explanation is that the institution of 1817 to 1821 still had as its major role, assistance to the able-bodied male labourer; a weak negative relation between high expenditure and a high proportion of the elderly in county population is what one would anticipate if the vast majority of relief payments were to the able-bodied and their dependants.

In any analysis of what changed after 1821, the two key resources must be the Select Committee *Abstract of Returns* for 1824 and the Royal Commisssion *Rural and Town Queries* of 1832. Both resources record the replies of parishes to questions about whether they gave various kinds of relief to able-bodied men. By tabulating the replies to these questions, it is possible to calculate not only the extent of different kinds of relief to the able-bodied, but also the aggregate amount of relief to the able-bodied which is the sum of the different kinds of relief given. It is on such a tabulation of the replies that Blaug bases his argument about a pre-1834 reform of the poor law which dramatically reduced assistance to the able-bodied. The rest of this section presents the results of a retabulation and comes to different conclusions about the persistence of relief to the able-bodied right up to 1832. Two tables in the Statistical appendix (Tables 4.3 and 4.4) present the results of this retabulation and the footnotes to those tables fully explain the procedures adopted in arriving at these figures. The following account outlines the major results and how they were produced.

The retabulation is concerned with those questions of 1824 and 1832 which inquired about three general kinds of relief paid to different classes of the able-bodied: child allowances given to the low paid, payment of wages out of the rates for the underemployed, and work or doles for the unemployed.

The three separate sets of questions all took up the issue of child allowances (see Statistical appendix, Section A, Footnote 11). In this form of relief, allowances were given on account of the number of children in a family, with payments typically beginning at the third child. Such payments were made to one general class of the able-bodied, that is, those who were low paid. For example, question two in the *Returns* for 1824 inquired 'is it usual in your district for married labourers having children, to receive assistance from the parish rate?' Two of the three sets of questions, namely the 1824 *Abstract* and the 1832 *Rural Queries*, asked in different ways about another form of relief.

The second sub-section of question 24 in the first issue inquired abruptly 'whether any wages [are] paid out of the poor's rate' and, in the third issue, inquired more specifically and clearly 'is any work done for individuals and partly paid for by the parish?' These were questions asked about direct wage subvention and payments to those who would otherwise be unemployed.

It must be emphasised that these questions about child allowances and payment of wages out of the rates will necessarily leave important gaps in knowledge about relief to the able-bodied.

To begin with, the questions of 1824 and 1832 will only yield national information about the extent of child allowances. The questions about payment of wages out of the rates will only disclose the extent of this practice in the rural areas. In 1824 the relevant question asked only about payment of wages out of the rates to those labourers 'employed by the farmers'. In 1832, the *Town Queries* omitted a specific question about payment of wages out of the rates; only those places that answered the *Rural Queries* in the first and third issues directly answered a question about this practice. But, even if every parish had answered general questions about child allowances and payment of wages out of the rates, the replies would not disclose the total extent of assistance to the able-bodied. Questions about these modes of relief would produce answers about the extent of assistance to the low paid and underemployed. They would not produce answers about the extent of assistance to the unemployed or the manner in which such assistance was given. For this reason, the 1832 *Town Queries* is especially valuable. This set did include questions that allow us to judge the extent and nature of assistance to the unemployed in the urban areas. Question thirty included a very general query which should pick up *any* outdoor relief to the able-bodied, and questions thirty-four and thirty-five inquired more specifically about the offer of parish work or doles to the able-bodied.

If the questions of 1824 and 1832 limit the possibility of an exhaustive national analysis, the answers of 1824 and 1832 may set even narrower limits on the kinds of analysis that is possible. In both 1824 and 1832, the questions were answered by a relatively small proportion of the 15,000 parishes in England and Wales. In the *Returns* for 1824, parishes that answered the questions were grouped into 'districts' or 'hundreds' and the total number of districts replying was 382. As 'districts' were groups of parishes, in 1824 answers were returned by perhaps 10 per cent of English and Welsh parishes. In 1832 parishes that answered the questions were grouped into 'places' and the total number of places replying to *Rural and Town Queries* was 1,444. As places usually included more than one parish, in 1832 answers were returned by more than 10 per cent of parishes.

Is this 'sample' absolutely or relatively too small to sustain our analysis? For the anti-empiricist, a sample does not have to consist of

look-alikes that are similar in an infinite number of respects. It is however essential that the sample be representative in one respect, namely,
the relief policies in the samples of 1824 and 1832 should be representative of the whole range of different relief policies. Representativeness
is not guaranteed by the absolute or relative size of the sample; for the
anti-empiricist there are no general statistical criteria about the size of
the sample necessary for valid inference. Our critical questions must
concern the nature of the sample and whether the answers of 1824 and
1832 record only a restricted range of differences in relief policy.

It is necessary to consider the two possibilities of self-selection by
the parishes or pre-selection of the parishes. To begin by considering
self-selection, if there was widespread criticism of relief to the able-
bodied, did parishes with generous policies to the able-bodied not
reply or misrepresent their practices? In the answers, this would show
up in the form of consistently low percentages admitting relief to the
able-bodied in any form. But the answers of 1824 and 1832 do not fit
this pattern; the percentage admitting relief in different forms varies
dramatically from over 90 to under 10 per cent. This leaves the second
possibility of pre-selection. Were the parishes in the sample pre-selected
so as to justify the indictment of the institution, and more especially
of certain practices of assisting the able-bodied, along pre-determined
lines? This would show up in complete consonance between the
answers of 1824 and 1832 and the analysis and indictment of the
institution made in the relevant reports, the 1824 *Select Committee on
Labourers' Wages* and the 1834 *Report from the Commissioners for
Inquiry into the Poor Laws.* But there is not a pattern of complete consonance. Most notably, the answers to the 1832 *Town Queries* disclosed
extensive urban assistance to the unemployed which barely figured in
the 1834 *Report.*

Even if the answers were not self-selected or pre-selected, there is
always the possibility that the parishes replying to the questions did not
understand the distinctions between different modes of relief which we
have reconstructed. The main problems here centre on the apparent
ambiguity of the distinction between 'child allowances' and 'payment
of wages out of the rates', when child allowances could be construed
either as a separate form of relief or as one way of paying wages out of
the rates. This chapter treats child allowances as a separate form of relief
as did the parishes, at least in 1824. In no other way is it possible to
explain the pattern of answers in 1824, when almost all the respondents
went on to admit child allowances immediately after more than half
had denied any payment of wages out of the rates.

The parishes not only understood the questions, they also returned
answers that are reasonably clear and unambiguous. Many parishes
did not answer questions about relief practice with a direct 'yes' or 'no';
instead, they preferred to describe their policy in a sentence or a few

words. But it is usually possible, on the basis of the policy description, to classify the answer as 'effectively yes' or 'effectively no'. The re-tabulation in this chapter measures the extent of a particular relief practice by counting the number of places in each sample which answered 'yes' or 'effectively yes' to questions about that practice. Of course, in any parish a particular form of relief could be given universally, usually, or occasionally to the relevant group of the able-bodied. The classification of a parish reply as 'effectively yes' must depend on a decision about what level of relative frequency qualifies as 'yes'. Such a decision is necessary not because of ambiguity in the original replies, but because we wish to avoid ambiguity in our analysis. In this chapter's retabulation, one simple relative frequency criterion was applied to all the answers; an answer was classified as 'yes' if any relief in the relevant form was admitted. This criterion was applied for two reasons. First, this criterion directly follows the adverbial qualification in the original questions; with the exception of the 1824 question about child allowances, all the questions about relief practice inquired whether 'any' relief in particular form was given. Second, this criterion provides the best measure of the extent of a system of relief to the able-bodied which we know from earlier official statistics to have been selective in its operation.

In conclusion, the sample of different relief policies is not impossible, the questions are tolerably unambiguous, and the answers can be tabulated with some precision. But the arguments about these issues are such that it would be unwise to make too much of small differences in percentages of the sample giving relief in various forms. This is especially so with regard to comparisons between 1824 and 1832 when the samples and the questions were different. To be ultra-cautious, if the results of the tabulation are calculated in percentage terms, an error allowance of plus or minus 25 per cent could be entered after each figure. This very generous allowance for errors of one sort or another does not completely undermine the results of the retabulation which remain valid in what might be called all or nothing terms. That is to say, the margin of error may be considerable, but cannot under-mine the results of the retabulation where these show that almost all or virtually none of the parishes gave relief.

To begin with, it is possible to calculate the extent of child allowances to the low paid in 1824 and 1832. On the basis of replies in 1824, relief in this form was given in nearly every district; in the sample, 344 districts, or 90 per cent of those replying, admitted child allowances (see Statistical appendix, Table 4.3, col. III). In 1832, relief in this form was given by more than half the places; in the sample, 726 places or 55 per cent of all those replying to the town and rural questions admitted paying child allowances (see Statistical appendix, Table 4.3, col. VI). The most cautious conclusion, assuming a large measure of overstatement in these results, would be that child allowances were given in most parishes in 1824 and at least in a large minority of parishes in 1832.

We only have information on the extent of payment of wages out of the rates to the underemployed in the countryside in 1824 and 1832. But from this, it would appear that paying wages out of the rates was a relief practice which was less commonplace than child allowances. On the basis of replies in 1824, relief in this form was given by less than half the districts; in the sample, 157 districts, or 41 per cent of all those replying, admitted paying wages out of the rates to 'labourers employed by farmers' (see Statistical appendix, Table 4.3, col. III). It is possible that in 1824 some of those parishes who denied paying wages to agricultural labourers were assisting other kinds of labourers in this way. In 1832 we have no information on the urban areas, but we do know that relief in this form was then given by less than one in ten rural places; in the sample, only eighty places, or 7 per cent of all those replying to the *Rural Queries*, admitted paying wages out of the rates (see Statistical appendix, Section A, footnote 15). From these results, the only cautious conclusion possible is that, even assuming significant understatement, payment of wages out of the rates was probably not an important practice in 1832.

The picture is not much changed if we analyse how these two practices of relief – child allowances and payment of wages out of the rates – fitted together. In 1824, when almost all rural and urban districts paid child allowances, payment of wages out of the rates was an extra offered by a rural sub-set of these districts; 344 districts offered child allowances and 158 of these also paid wages out of the rates to 'labourers employed by farmers' (see Statistical appendix, Table 4.3, col. III). Only five districts admitted paying wages out of the rates and then denied giving child allowances. In 1832, it is directly possible to compare the relation between child allowances and payment of wages in the 1,070 places replying to the rural questions; 629 places gave child allowances and seventy also paid wages out of the rates. Only ten places admitted paying wages out of the rates and then denied paying child allowances (see Statistical appendix, Section A, footnote 15). At least in the rural areas, the figures for child allowances therefore mark the effective limits of the system's payment of child allowances and wages out of the rates. Put another way, these figures mark the limits of the system's assistance to the able-bodied, underemployed, and low paid.

However, the argument so far does not imply that relief to the able-bodied was effectively diminished and transformed into a system of child allowances by 1832. The *Town Queries* provides information on the extent of relief to the unemployed in the urban areas. And on the basis of replies in 1832, in the urban areas relief to the unemployed in one form or another was widespread. Around two-thirds of all places replying to the *Town Queries* admitted giving money to the unemployed; in the sample, 179 places, or 68 per cent of all those replying, admitted paying relief in money to the unemployed and 157 places, or 60 per cent of all those replying, admitted giving relief in the form of work (see Statistical appendix, Table 4.4.). The most cautious conclusion, assuming a large measure of overstatement in these results, would be that in one form or another, the unemployed were assisted in a substantial minority of urban places in 1832.

The results are even more striking if we analyse how these two relief practices - work and doles - fitted together. Here it was not the case that virtually all the places giving relief in one form also gave relief in the other form; when 179 places admitted giving money to the unemployed and 157 places admitted giving work, only ninety-six places admitted giving both forms of relief (see Statistical appendix, Table 4.4). In the urban areas, the proportion of districts giving relief in some form to the unemployed can be measured by adding together the places admitting relief in employment only, the places admitting relief in doles only, and the places admitting relief in both forms. When the three groups of places have been added together, the result is that some relief to the unemployed was given in 240, or 92 per cent, of the 262 urban places in the sample of 1832. It is this last figure that marks the limits of the system's assistance to the unemployed in the urban areas. Even if one cautiously assumes overstatement in these tabulation results, it must be conceded that most urban places assisted the unemployed in 1832.

When the town questions have been properly tabulated, the general conclusion must be that the poor law was massively involved in relief to the able-bodied in 1832, just as it had been in 1824 and earlier years. This point has not been properly appreciated by recent historians who have never revised the one modern account of the 1824 *Returns* and the 1832 *Queries* in Blaug's (1963, 1964) articles. It can now be shown that Blaug spreads confusion at every stage in his analysis of the questions and answers of 1824 and 1832.

Blaug's tabulation of the 1824 and 1832 material is marked by a general imprecision and lack of clarity. He omits all the fine detail and qualifications that are relevant to his tabulation decisions and to the interpretation of his results. He does not emphasise that the information on the extent of payment of wages out of the rates is confined to country areas by the nature of the questions in 1824 and the sample in 1832. He overlooks the relative frequency issue and even his actual tabulations appear to be inconsistent about what level of relative frequency qualifies as 'yes'. Nor does Blaug investigate or make any assumption about the relation between different relief practices. Again this issue is simply ignored. It is almost inevitable, therefore, that Blaug emphasises the importance of child allowances; this is the practice that is unlikely to be missed on the roughest tabulation of the available resources for 1824 and 1832.

If the Blaug tabulation gets child allowances right, it gets everything else wrong through errors of commission and omission. The main error of commission is a mis-specification of the conceptual distinction between child allowances and payment of wages out of the rates. Blaug never establishes the nature of this distinction, partly because he mistakes the key question (rural question 24) that parishes answered in 1832. Blaug's rural question 24 is: 'Have you any, and how many, able-bodied labourers in the employment of individuals, receiving allowance or regular relief from your parish on their own account, or on that of their families . . .?' (Blaug, 1964, p. 231). But none of the parishes answered Blaug's question 24 which was printed on a fold-out sheet as an aid to the reader of the relevant volume of parliamentary papers. Blaug's question 24 was a composite of the differently worded questions asked in three separate issues of the rural questions. And 1,070, or 90 per cent of places answering the rural questions, answered issues one and three which, as the Statistical appendix (Section A, footnotes 11 and 12) shows, made a perfectly clear distinction between child allowances and payment of wages out of the rates. Blaug argues that (composite) question 24 is the means whereby the Royal Commission confused the distinction between child allowances and another mode of relief (Blaug, 1964, p. 231). It would be fairer to say that failure to read (the separate issues of) question 24 is the pre-condition for Blaug's mis-specification of this other mode of relief as something which he calls 'Speenhamland'. Subsequent local studies (Neumann, 1972; Baugh, 1975) have criticised Blaug's concept of 'Speenhamland' but without reinstating payment of wages out of the rates as the complement of child allowances and without retabulating the answers of 1824 and 1832.

In any case, Blaug's errors of commission about relief to the low paid and underemployed are compounded by a massive error of omission about urban assistance to the unemployed. Blaug never appreciates the importance of those questions in the *Town Queries* which produced answers about the work given or doles paid to the urban unemployed; he never tabulates the extent of assistance in these forms to the unemployed. This is the crucial deficiency in his tabulation. The essential difference of this chapter's retabulation is that it shows urban assistance to the unemployed was widespread in 1832. This result undermines the Blaug argument that the poor law was effectively reformed before 1834, because able-bodied relief was reduced to a rump of child allowances by 1832. This thesis, which is not challenged in the subsequent literature, must be completely rejected.

The present retabulation of the answers for 1824 and 1832 does show changes in the extent and form of assistance to the able-bodied. A comparison of any two years between 1802 and 1834 would probably disclose changes in the extent and form of assistance to the able-bodied. This supposition is coherent with the earlier conclusion about a mode of assistance which was characteristically selective, discontinuous, and supplementary. If there were constant changes in the extent and form of assistance offered, the key question is: how radically did these changes affect relief to able-bodied men? As this chapter has shown, the available resources disclose something about assistance to the able-bodied in four years between 1802 and 1832; there is direct evidence on numbers in 1802-3, indirect evidence on age structure versus expenditure level around 1821, and direct evidence on relief practices in 1824 and 1832. These resources independently show extensive assistance to the able-bodied in all four years. On this evidence, in the last thirty years of the old poor law before 1834, able-bodied men were consistently included among the classes obtaining relief. Chapter 2 will argue that under the new poor law after 1834, a line of exclusion was drawn so that from the 1840s onwards able-bodied men did not receive relief in significant numbers. In these terms, the definition of institutional configuration was stable under the old poor law and then changed quickly and fundamentally after 1834.

October, 1978

Appendix   The 1834 *Report*

This appendix examines the 1834 *Report from the Commissioners for Inquiry into the Poor Laws* (Checkland (ed.), 1974) which has been much criticised in recent historiography. Blaug's (1964, p. 243) verdict on the 1834 *Report* has been generally accepted:

> The evidence they collected in the town and rural queries should have taught the commissioners that they had mis-interpreted the consequences of the old poor law. But their minds were made up, and where they did not ignore the findings, they twisted them to suit their preconceived opinions. The *Report* of 1834 is not only a 'wildly un-historical document' as Tawney once said, but also a wildly unstatistical one.

This verdict is already indirectly challenged by the previous chapter which shows that Blaug's own tabulation of the 1832 answers is 'wildly unstatistical'. More directly, the first section of this appendix takes up the question of the relation between the problem definition in the 1834 *Report* and the evidence of the 1832 answers. Was there a contradiction between problem definition and evidence? Or, more specifically, did the 1834 *Report* make unsustained and unsustainable allegations about the effects of relief practice? When these questions have been answered, it will be clear that, although the 1834 *Report* can be criticised, the recent historiographic criticisms are misdirected and unjustified. This reappraisal of the 1834 *Report* is a necessary postscript to the analysis of the pre-1834 poor law in chapter 1.

The second section of this appendix examines the policy recommendations of the 1834 *Report*. What was the strategy of 1834? Or, more specifically, what classes of pauper were differentiated in the *Report* and how were they to be treated? In answering these questions, we are rectifying an error of omission in recent historiography; because it has been so distracted by condemnation of the 1834 *Report*, recent historiography has failed to characterise the differentiations proposed in the *Report*. A brief account of these differentiations is a necessary preliminary to chapter 2's analysis of official strategy after 1834.

Problem definition

The 1834 *Report* claimed that 'the great source of abuse is the outdoor relief afforded to the able-bodied on their own account or on that of their families' (Checkland (ed.), 1974, p. 82). More specifically, the objection was to outdoor relief in money (rather than in kind), paid to able-bodied *male* labourers. The *Report* did not condemn the payment of 'pensions' to young able-bodied widows with dependants (Checkland (ed.), 1974, p. 114); and the *Report* was not much concerned about relief to the non-able-bodied, the aged, and infirm – this subject was perfunctorily treated in a couple of pages after some thirty had been devoted to describing the objectionable practices of outdoor relief to the able-bodied.

The rationalistic general arguments about the effects of relief (Checkland (ed.), 1974, pp. 140 *et seq.*) finally directed attention towards relief practices in the countryside because the *Report* argued that outdoor relief to the able-bodied labourer had more serious effects in the countryside. But, up to this point, the text of 1834 indirectly suggested that the objectionable relief practices were to be found throughout England and Wales. This impression was obtained by the careful choice of illustrating examples, as when the section describing the practice of paying allowances to able-bodied men included rural and urban, and southern and northern examples (Checkland (ed.), 1974, pp. 90-120).

More generally, the *Report* did develop an exhaustive classification of five different forms in which money relief to the able-bodied was given; relief without labour, the allowance system, the roundsman system, parish employment, and the labour rate system (Checkland (ed.), 1974, p. 88). But the *Report* never tried to measure the extent of the different systems; it contains no tabulation of the proportion of places giving relief in various forms. Instead, individual answers to the *Town* and *Rural Queries* of 1832 provided illustrations which were fitted into the classificatory schema and the general arguments about effect. In the same way, the *Report* only cited short extracts from the regional reports of the peripatetic assistant commissioners. The *Report* made an illustrative, anecdotal use of the evidence which it obtained.

This conclusion does not justify an immediate condemnation of the *Report*. There is not much point in criticising the 1834 *Report* for failing to measure accurately what it never tried to measure, that is, the extent of different forms of relief to able-bodied men. As we have shown, the *Report*'s problem definition implied or assumed that, in the aggregate, there was large-scale, nation-wide assistance to able-bodied men. But this assumption is quite reasonable, on the basis of chapter 1's retabulation of the answers of 1832. It is also consonant with all the other evidence of widespread assistance to the able-bodied going back to 1802. The presentation of evidence may be anecdotal, but there is no gross contradiction between the problem definition of 1834 and the resources of 1832 or earlier.

The preoccupation of the 1834 *Report* with relief to the able-bodied may be justifiable. But does not the 1834 *Report* provide a prototype of the list of the ill-effects of such relief and have not these ill-effects now been disproved? It has already been shown in chapter 1 that recent historians are unable to vindicate their alternative accounts of cause and effect linkages. It must now be shown that the 1834 *Report* does include arguments about the effects of relief practice, but such arguments are constructed in such a way that they are immune to empirical refutation in simple non-theoretical tests. This point will be established by considering two major arguments in the *Report* about the cost of relief and the effects of relief upon the labourer.

The argument about cost is apparently very simple; in 1831-2 expenditure on poor relief was over £7,000,000 and only just below the level of expenditure in the crisis year of 1818 (Checkland (ed.), 1974, p. 128). But the *Report*'s cost argument is not simply about the trend of expenditure out of the rates. It is also about the trend of a kind of shadow expenditure which is supposed to cost as much as direct expenditure on poor relief; 'a great part of the expense is incurred, not by direct payment out of the rates, but by purchase of unprofitable labour' (Checkland (ed.), 1974, p. 128). The introduction of the notion of shadow expenditure must rule out the possibility of simply testing cost effects by reference to the official expenditure statistics.

The argument about the effects upon the labourer is much more complicated. It is part of a developed analysis of the effects of relief upon the three Ricardian classes - proprietors, employers, and labourers. With regard to the labourer, the *Report* discriminated separate effects according to whether labourers did, or did not, receive relief, and labourers receiving relief were differently affected according to whether or not they were employed in agriculture. It will now be shown that all these arguments about effects upon the labourer were set up so that it is difficult or impossible to test the crucial linkages.

If relief was made available to the married pauper with no savings, the report argued that those labourers who did not receive relief were effectively being punished for acts of prudence and self-denial such as saving money and deferring marriage. The necessary consequences would be a decline in such acts of self-denial. But at this point the *Report* added an important qualification:

> Self-respect however, is not yet so utterly destroyed among
> the English peasantry as to make this [effect] universal.
> Men are still to be found who would rather derive a smaller
> income from their own funds, or their own exertions, than
> beg a larger one from the parish (Checkland (ed.), 1974, pp.
> 156-7).

When this qualification is inserted, this argument becomes very difficult to test: how does one test the proposition that the end of the world has not yet happened, but might happen in the near future?

As for the effect upon labourers receiving relief, the *Report* argued that such payments had the effect of diminishing or even destroying the qualities of skill, diligence, and honesty which were necessary in the agricultural labourer (Checkland (ed.), 1974, pp. 144-5). Allowances made 'worse workmen' and the *Report* was categorical on this point; 'the replies [to the *Rural Queries*] vary according to the poor law administration of the district' (Checkland (ed.), 1974, p. 46). At this point, there is perhaps the possibility of a test, but such a test would hardly be crucial when the *Report* clearly identified other non-economic effects upon the labourer as more important. The *Report* emphasised that the 'worst results' of allowances were domestic (Checkland (ed.), 1974, p. 177). Domestic economy suffered so that the homes of paupers were dirty and unsavoury. Worse still, the conventional pattern of 'domestic affections' was destroyed because parish allowances undermined the mutual dependence between working adults, their young children, and their aged parents (Checkland (ed.), 1974, p. 177). Such arguments would obviously be very difficult to test.

If the 1834 *Report*'s key arguments about effect are immune to test, or can only be tested with difficulty, so are the arguments about effect in other early nineteenth-century analyses of the old poor law by Malthus (1826) or Ricardo (1817). Early nineteenth-century analysts of the poor law were not such fools as late twentieth-century testers make them out to be; they were all careful to set up their theoretical arguments so that they could not easily be contradicted on empirical grounds. And the deficiencies of the effect arguments in the 1834 *Report*, or in Malthus and Ricardo, have nothing at all to do with the relation or non-relation of these arguments to the evidence. The problem is rather that all these treatments of the operation of the poor law depend on the presupposition of rational hedonism; society is presented as the sphere of operation of self-interest where rationally hedonistic individuals calculate their interest in particular relief arrangements and adjust their behaviour accordingly so as to produce the tendencies and effects described in the analysis.

This pervasive rationalism can be illustrated by considering the 1834 *Report*'s condemnation of out-relief. The *Report* presumed that three conditions obtained in the grant of out-relief: first, there was diminishing reluctance to claim relief; second, especially in the towns, there was the difficulty of assessing the circumstances of applicants; third, individuals such as tradesmen and farmers had private motives to provide unnecessary relief. These rationalistic general arguments sustained a dire conclusion and prediction that out-relief 'appears to contain in itself the elements of an almost indefinite extension; of an extension in short, which may ultimately absorb the whole fund out of which it arises' (Checkland (ed.), 1974, p. 115). Malthus and Ricardo arrived at equally dire conclusions by a similar route.

All such arguments about effect can be condemned as dogmatic *a priorism*; they presuppose that a whole social process is determined by the existence of a unitary subject capable of identifying his interests and making rational calculations on that basis. It is neither profitable nor necessary to construct things in this way. Recent historians like Blaug and McCloskey fail to make this critical point about the 1834 *Report,* which is not surprising when their own marginalism is just another dogmatic rationalism which depends on the existence of a subject – economic man. The criticisms Blaug does make can now be seen to be completely beside the point; the *Report*'s arguments were proof against simple contrary evidence and it is in any case hardly profitable to indict a dogmatic rationalism for failing to stand in a relation of virtue to the evidence.

The strategy of 1834

The 1834 *Report* proposed a radical reorganisation of the existing administrative structure of the poor law. The 15,000 parishes were to be grouped into 'incorporations' at least for the purposes of work-house management (Checkland (ed.), 1974, p. 434). These new local authorities were to be divested of all 'discretionary power' in the administration of relief; they would work within a framework of uniform national 'regulations'. A new 'central board' would promulgate the regulations and more generally control the administration of the poor law (Checkland (ed.), 1974, p. 418).

Within this new administrative structure, the strategy was to differentiate the kind of relief given to one class of pauper. Thus, the section on 'remedial measures' began by establishing an order of priorities,

> The most pressing of the evils which we have described are
> those connected with the relief of the able-bodied. They are
> the evils, therefore, for which we shall first propose
> remedies (Checkland (ed.), 1974, p. 334).

Nowhere did the *Report* make recommendations for radical reform of the relief given to groups such as young widows, the sick, or the old. The recommendations of 1834 were concerned with one class of paupers, able-bodied men.

The *Report* announced that all relief to this class should satisfy the principle of 'less eligibility',

The first and most essential of all conditions . . . is that his
[the pauper's] situation on the whole shall not be made
really or apparently so eligible as the situation of the independent labourer of the lowest class (Checkland (ed.),
1974, p. 335).

According to the *Report,* the end of less eligibility could be most
effectively secured in a 'well regulated workhouse'. The *Report* recommended that, after a transition period of two years, the central authority
should prohibit all outdoor relief to the able-bodied (Checkland (ed.),
1974, pp. 375 and 419).

All this is to be found in the textbooks on social policy which,
nevertheless, are unsatisfactory in two respects: first, they blur the
distinction between able-bodied persons and able-bodied men; second,
they fail to characterise the 'well regulated workhouse' which was the
crucial instrument in the 1834 strategy. The rest of this section will be
concerned with the *Report's* definition of the 'well regulated workhouse'

The *Report* recommended no change in the balance between workhouse and outdoor relief for the non-able-bodied. It simply presumed
that the workhouses of a reformed poor law would contain some old
and sick persons. The *Report* hedged on the question of how this group
was to be treated inside the workhouse. At one point, it did suggest
that the bracing regime intended for the able-bodied might also be
appropriate for the non-able-bodied (Checkland (ed.), 1974, p. 336).
More generally, however, the *Report* was committed to 'the principle
of separate and appropriate management'. Workhouse inmates should
be divided into at least four classes: the aged and impotent, the
children, and the able-bodied females, and the able-bodied males. The
Report envisaged that, in a union of parishes, different classes of
pauper would often, or usually, be assigned to different workhouses.
By means of classification within one institution, or by means of the
establishment of specialised institutions:

Each class might thus receive an appropriate treatment;
the old might enjoy their indulgences without torment
from the boisterous; the children be educated, and the able-
bodied subjected to such courses of labour and discipline as
will repel the indolent and vicious (Checkland (ed.), 1974,
p. 430).

As this quotation indicates, the institutional regime for the able-
bodied would have two main features – work and discipline. Like the
old 'houses of industry', the new workhouses were to be institutions
where the able-bodied were obliged to work diligently. The novelty in

the 1834 proposals was the insistence that 'discipline' could be used in a supplementary way to make workhouses thoroughly unattractive to the able-bodied poor:

> But it is not by means of labour alone that the principle
> [of less eligibility] is applicable, nor does it imply that the
> food or comforts of the pauper should approach the lowest
> point at which existence may be maintained. Although the
> workhouse food may be more ample in quantity and better
> in quality than that of which the labourer's family partakes
> and the house in other respects superior to the cottage, yet
> the strict discipline of well regulated workhouses, and in
> particular the restrictions to which the inmates are subject
> in respect to the use of acknowledged luxuries such as
> fermented liquors and tobacco are intolerable to the
> indolent and disorderly (Checkland (ed.), 1974, p. 336).

To secure less eligibility, it was not necessary to over-work or freeze or starve paupers to death; 'strict discipline' would do the job silently and economically.

If the new strategy promoted discipline to a central place, it must also be insisted that the *Report* favoured a particular kind of blind, repressive discipline without knowledge. Investigation of pauper cases was rejected on the grounds that it only set up clumsy and partial barriers against fraud and misrepresentation (Checkland (ed.), 1974, p. 386). The correct procedure was not to investigate but simply to offer all applicants relief in a disciplinary workhouse. Such an offer was,

> a self-acting test of the claim of the individual. . . . If the
> claimant does not comply with the terms on which relief is
> given to the destitute, he gets nothing; and if he does com-
> ply, the compliance proves the truth of the claim – namely
> his destitution (Checkland (ed.), 1974, p. 378).

A reformed poor law should not seek or acquire any knowledge about the merits of applicants for relief; destitution was to be the sole criterion for receipt of relief and this was automatically tested by the 'offer of the house' (Checkland (ed.), 1974, p. 392).

In conclusion, therefore, the strategy of the 1834 *Report* was to use a blind, repressive discipline so as to reduce able-bodied male pauperism.

The poor law after 1834 2

The recent historiography on the pre-1834 poor law represents the new style of Anglo-American history; it is dominated by the procedures of testing and the concepts of social science. But the recent historiography on the post-1834 poor law represents an older style of academic historiography; it includes only one or two articles (e.g. Holderness, 1972) in the new style. Generally, the post-1834 historiography manages without formal methodological or theoretical means of support; this is history such as used to fill the academic journals twenty years ago.

The first section of this chapter considers this kind of history without theory, explains how it works and arrives at its conclusions; the historiography on the poor law after 1834 here provides the material for a case study. It will be argued that this kind of historiography depends on received ideas and that, in this particular case, the received ideas are thoroughly confused and misrepresent the official strategy in the poor law after 1834. The next section of this chapter will show that, partly in consequence of these confusions and misrepresentations, recent historiography has misconstructed relief practice after 1834. These errors will be redressed by presenting an alternative account that emphasises some differences in relief practice established after 1834 and before 1870. First, it will be argued that a line of exclusion was drawn against able-bodied men after 1850; in accordance with official strategy, unemployment-related relief was virtually abolished by the middle of the century. Second, it will be argued that the instruments of a strategy of repression were fabricated and distributed before 1870; in the thirty years after 1834, new workhouses were constructed in almost every union.

Received ideas

Since the early 1960s, there has been a flood of doctoral theses, articles, and books on the post-1834 poor law. This academic literature has three general characteristics: first, it is history without a historiographic past; second, it is history of the locality; and third, it is history without overt theoretical or methodological commitments.

The historiographic past of the poor law is dominated by the Webbs and their massive general history (Webbs, 1927-9) which was preceded by an analysis of central policy (Webbs, 1910). Recent work includes unavoidable references to the Webbs on matters of details; but in the whole of the recent literature there is not one account, not even a couple of paragraphs, on how the Webbs went about the business of history writing. Because they do not have any kind of developed intellectual position on the Webbs, the recent historians of the post-1834 poor law are condemned to announcing and elaborating a 'change of focus' (Digby, 1978, p. ix): the national history of the poor law has been written by the Webbs; the remaining task is to fill in the gaps and revise the outline of that historiography by means of local studies.

In line with this analysis, recent writing on the poor law after 1834 has taken the form of local studies. The bibliography in a recent collection of essays on the new poor law gives a list of thirty-six recent theses; from their titles no fewer than thirty-three of them take the form of local studies of the operation of the poor law in a city, county, or region (Fraser, 1976, pp. 203-4). It is also true that most of the studies that appear to take a different object, turn out to be local studies in disguise. Thus Brundage's (1978) book on *The Making of the New Poor Law* promises a study of the poor law as a political institution, but the centrepiece is a regional study of the implementation of the poor law in the rural Midlands and East Anglia.

All the recent historians reject a 'purely administrative approach' to poor law history in favour of one that emphasises 'the economic, social and political context' (Digby, 1978, p. ix). Indeed, some historians make large claims about 'restoring the Poor Law to its proper place within Victorian society' (Fraser, 1976, p. 21). But this historiography does not rely on formal, social scientific concepts which are being so widely used elsewhere to rewrite nineteenth-century economic and social history. How can the programmatic aims be realised in a historiography which has turned its back on formal conceptual resources? To put the question more concretely, how can a reasonably assiduous postgraduate student set to work without concepts and in three years produce a regional study of poor law administration in its social and economic context?

Such regional studies are possible because the recent history of the poor law after 1834 relies on a small stock of notions or received ideas.

These terms are used deliberately to suggest something vaguer and less well-defined than the social scientific concepts being deployed in history of the poor law before 1834. These received ideas are not so much a systematic framework as a set of themes or references which make intelligible the operations and activities of the poor law. This section will first describe and then criticise three of the more important sets of received ideas: the first set concerns the objectives of the central authority; the second set concerns the real problems confronting the local authorities; and the third set concerns the obstructive resistance put up by those local authorities.

Detailed local studies of the implementation of the new poor law are written around these references. In marked contrast to the pre-1834 historiography which uses different bits of social science in different ways, the post-1834 historiography is a stereotyped formula history where the same received ideas are used in an identical way in one local study after another. The notions were first formulated in doctoral theses of the 1960s by historians like Rose, Midwinter, and Boyson. They subsequently acquired the status of received ideas and can be traced in any of the local studies. They were also incorporated into survey articles that generalised about the poor law after 1834 and synthesised the results of the local studies. In order to consider fairly broad generalisations, the illustrative examples in the rest of this section are taken from three survey articles: Rose (1966) on the allowance system, Ashforth (1976) on the urban poor law, and Digby (1976) on the rural poor law. These three articles are representative in their formulation and usage of the received ideas.

The 1834 Poor Law Amendment Act set up a central authority responsible for the supervision and direction of relief administration by local authorities. A first set of received ideas concerns the objectives of the central authority. Many recent historians claim or assume that the recommendations of the 1834 *Report* included the abolition of out-door relief to all classes of the able-bodied poor; the appendix to chapter 1 shows this assumption is untrue because the strategy of 1834 was preoccupied with able-bodied males. But Rose (1966, p. 607), Digby (1976, p. 149) and Ashforth (1976, p. 129) do not dissent from the conventional analysis of the 1834 recommendations and make similar claims about the objectives of the central authority after 1834. Their thesis is that the central authority after 1834 sought and failed to achieve the abolition of outdoor relief to able-bodied paupers, or even sought and failed to achieve the complete abolition of outdoor relief.

Only extended quotation can show the apparent lucidity and plausibility of these accounts. Rose, for example, summarises seventy years of poor law administration as follows:

It is, of course, well known that this [1834 *Report*]

recommendation [against outdoor relief to able-bodied
persons] was never fully carried out. In many of the new
poor law unions, especially those in the northern manufacturing districts, no 'workhouse test' was ever applied.
In the 1870s, the 'crusade against out-relief' conducted by
the Local Government Board and its inspectors succeeded
in reducing the numbers of outdoor paupers, but never
completely abolished this method of relieving the able-
bodied poor. Not only did the central authority for poor
law administration fail to end the system of outdoor relief,
it also failed to stamp out the allowance system, which
had been regarded in 1834 as the very worst feature of outdoor relief (Rose, 1966, p. 607).

Digby makes almost exactly the same points. This is her summary of
sixty years of rural poor law administration:

That outdoor allowances were normal rather than
exceptional [in the countryside] indicated that the central
board established in the 1834 Act was impotent to enforce
its relief policies on local boards of guardians in the countryside. . . . In spite of sixty years of nominal operation, the
principles of the new poor law had not been firmly established in rural areas (Digby, 1976, p. 170; see also p. 158).

Having established a presumption of failure, the historian's next
question becomes: why did the central authority fail? The stereotyped
answer then invokes two more sets of received ideas: the notion that
the real situation was thoroughly unfavourable to the achievement of
central authority objectives, and the notion that local authorities were
unsympathetic and frustrated the central authority.

The economic situation is usually invoked as the underlying cause
of the central authority's failure. All historians agree that the local
authorities faced a real problem of 'economic conditions' (Digby,
1976, p. 165) or, more exactly, cyclical unemployment in the
industrial areas and seasonal underemployment in the agricultural
areas. Ashforth and Digby provide perfect examples of these notions
in their surveys of urban and rural poor law. Ashforth emphasises 'the
massive temporary unemployment encountered in the textile manufacturing districts' (Ashforth, 1976, p. 129). This was the urban reality
which rendered the workhouse irrelevant because, when unemployment
was high 'the workhouse system was simply not capable of coping'
(Ashforth, 1976, p. 129). Digby emphasises that rural underemployment persisted after 1834 when 'the real difficulty in many rural areas'
of southern England continued to be that of surplus labour (Digby,

1976, p. 152). This reality was 'a key factor' in determining the relief policy of rural boards of guardians and predisposed the boards to offer doles which would tide the underemployed labourer over the slack winter season (Digby, 1976, p. 115).

Recent historians stress that relief was not simply adjusted to economic conditions, since the process of adjustment also involved an articulation and accommodation of political interest because the poor law was a political institution. It could hardly be anything else when the Poor Law Amendment Act amalgamated parishes into poor law unions where elected boards of guardians administered relief. Brundage (1978) has emphasised that at the implementation stage, landed aristocrats and gentry were conciliated over such matters as the boundaries of the new unions. However, the emphasis is more conventionally placed on the attitudes and interests of the farmers and shopkeepers who dominated the new boards when they began to function.

For recent historiography, these elected guardians exerted a force acting in an opposite direction to the force exerted by the central authority; the guardians pushed for outdoor relief while the central authority pushed for indoor relief. The guardians are identified as the more powerful force and therefore the outcome is the continuation of the out-relief system. Rose claims that 'the chief reason for the survival of the outdoor system lay in the desire of the boards of guardians to continue it' (Rose, 1966, p. 612). Historiography explains the guardians' motivations and the pre-conditions of their success in stereotyped terms.

Rose accounts for the guardians' attachment to outdoor relief by using the explanatory terms 'humanity' and 'economy' (Rose, 1966, pp. 612-13), which are simply repeated by Ashforth (1976, pp. 135-9). Guardians believed first, that a policy of outdoor doles was more humane than offering the workhouse and second, that this policy was also more economical. In an institution whose operations were locally financed from the rates, Rose sees economy as 'the crux of the problem' (Rose, 1966, p. 613). Guardians calculated that their interests as rate-payers were best served by small out-relief allowances which supplemented other sources of income. Under the alternative policy of indoor relief, the guardians would have to bear the full cost of maintenance in a workhouse. Both Rose and Ashforth are primarily discussing the northern and urban areas, while Digby refines and restates the economy argument for rural poor law unions, especially those in the arable south and east. Here farmer guardians calculated that their economic interests were best served by outdoor allowances which not only made for cheap relief but also retained a pool of cheap labour in the area to meet the peaks of summer demand for labour (Digby, 1976, p. 157).

The weakness of the central authority is identified as the pre-condition for the maintenance of out-relief policies. The central authority established by the 1834 Act had very limited formal powers of compulsion; Ashforth, for example, observes that the central authority could not require the construction of a workhouse essential for the operation of an indoor policy (Ashforth, 1976, p. 132). Furthermore, the 1844 and 1852 General Orders restricting outdoor relief contained 'loopholes'. As Rose claims: 'one reason for the con-tinuance of the allowance system after 1834 was the total failure of the central authority to draft and enforce an effective order prohibiting outdoor relief' (Rose, 1966, p. 609). This point is endorsed by Ashforth who quotes Rose's metaphor about loopholes large enough to drive a coach and four through (Ashforth, 1976, p. 136). Again Digby develops a special case argument applicable to the rural unions where underemployed labourers received relief 'on the ostensible grounds of sickness in the family' (Digby, 1976, pp. 157 and 166).

It is now necessary to turn to detailed criticism of the three sets of received ideas which have been outlined. The ostensible function of the received ideas is to render the operations of the institution intelligible, but the received ideas cannot discharge this function because they are confused and incoherent. The criticism will begin by considering the account of the objectives of the central authority. It will be argued that the central authority had a strategy about who was to obtain relief and on what terms, but this strategy is misrepresented in the recent historiographical account of objectives.

The analysis that follows will concentrate on the terms of the central authority orders which were issued in final form as the *Outdoor Relief Prohibitory Order* of 1844 and the *Outdoor Relief Regulation Order* of 1852. In every poor law union, one of these two *Orders* provided a legally binding set of regulations about what classes could obtain out-relief and on what conditions. Strategy, of course, cannot always be identified with such formal frameworks. By a variety of informal means, unions could be encouraged or persuaded to do more than, or other than, the *Orders* prescribed. After 1870, as we shall see in chapter 3, a new strategy was defined by coherent informal recommendations and concerted informal suasion. But there is no evidence that pre-1870 strategy had a predominant, or even an important, informal dimension. Thus the formal regulations of 1844 and 1852 are the crucial resource for any reconstruction of pre-1870 strategy.

To begin with, neither the 1844 nor the 1852 *Orders* tried to restrict outdoor relief given to the able-bodied. The 1852 *Regulation Order* restricted relief given to 'able-bodied *male* persons' (my emphasis); this was made explicit in articles one and six which specified the restrictive conditions under which out-relief could be granted (Glen, 1898, pp. 512 and 516). The 1844 *Prohibitory Order* did formally prohibit relief to able-bodied persons; but under clause five of that *Order*'s first article, able-bodied widows with dependent children were specifically exempted from the general prohibition on relief. The central authority acquiesced in unconditional out-relief to widows with young children. Thus the strategy of the 1850s and the 1860s was concerned not with able-bodied persons but able-bodied males.

More precisely, the strategy of the 1850s and 1860s was concerned with those able-bodied men who were 'in health' rather than 'temporarily sick'. Under clause two of the 1844 *Order*'s first article, sick persons were specifically exempted from the general prohibition on out-relief (Glen, 1898, p. 491). Similarly, under clause two of the 1852 *Order*'s seventh article, the restrictions on out-relief were suspended for sick men (Glen, 1898, p. 517). The central authority acquiesced in unconditional out-relief for sick men, and the prohibitions and restrictions were reserved for those men who tried to draw relief for unemployment-related reasons. The strategy of the 1850s and the 1860s was concerned with those able-bodied men who were unemployed, underemployed, or low paid.

Furthermore, although the strategy was concerned to restrict outdoor relief given to such able-bodied men, there was no attempt to abolish out-relief completely to this group. Prohibition was formally required only in those unions subject to the *Prohibitory Order*; these numbered 396 in 1847 and 307 in 1871 (Webbs, 1910, p. 38). In both years, there were more than 200 other unions subject to the 1852 *Regulation Order* or the 1844 *Order* supplemented by a *Labour Test Order*. In either case, able-bodied men could receive outdoor relief provided they performed task work for the guardians. Thus the strategy of the 1850s and 1860s admitted out-relief conditional upon a labour test as well as, or instead of, indoor relief and the workhouse test for able-bodied men.

Such provisions are sometimes represented as a retreat from the recommendations of 1834, but this interpretation is incorrect. The strategy's preoccupation with unemployment-related relief to able-bodied men was coherent with the problem definition in the 1834 *Report*. A large role for the labour test in the strategy did represent a significant shift from the 1834 *Report* which adumbrated, rather than positively recommended, the use of a labour test. Nevertheless, this was hardly a major retreat. Translated into 1834 terms, the labour test was simply another means of pursuing the end of less eligibility, which the *Report* had argued should be secured by the workhouse test; if a labour test were rigorously applied this would make relief less eligible just as surely as a well-regulated workhouse. The strategy of the 1850s simply reflected the discovery that there is more than one way to skin a (tom) cat.

All this is lost in misrepresentation in so far as historiography credits the central authority in the pre-1870 period with a generalised hostility to outdoor relief to the able-bodied. The error here can be defined in another way by saying that recent historiography conflates the pre-1870 strategy with the post-1870 strategy which did involve a generalised hostility to out-relief. This post-1870 out-relief strategy will be analysed in detail in chapter 3; at this point it is only necessary to make a provisional and tentative characterisation of the difference of the later strategy.

In every sense the post-1870 out-relief strategy went beyond the pre-1870 one. At the level of technical means, the new strategy went beyond the legal obligations in the *Orders* governing relief; the post-1870 strategy relied on supplementary suasion applied by the central bureaucracy's travelling inspectorate. At the level of ends, the strategy went beyond restriction of out-relief given to one class; the post-1870 strategy concerned restriction of relief given to all classes, not only able-bodied men but also able-bodied women such as widows with young children, and also the non-able-bodied such as the aged and chronically infirm. This, of course, implies that recent historiography is also confused about the post-1870 strategy; this later out-relief strategy was not particularly about restricting relief to the able-bodied poor as historiography might lead us to believe.

In summary, therefore, historiography conflates and misrepresents the distinct strategies of the pre- and post-1870 periods. If historiography's account of central authority objectives is simply wrong, the account of local authority objectives is unprofitably speculative.

The terms 'humanity' and 'economy' were not invented by Rose, but were borrowed from official discussions of the late 1860s and early 1870s (e.g. Wodehouse, (1871-2), pp. 96-7, in LGB, *First Annual Report,* 1871-2). Not surprisingly, they fix historiography into a sterile debate about the relative merits of indoor and outdoor policies. Rose (1966, p. 620), Ashforth (1976, p. 135), and Digby (e.g. 1978, pp. 112-13) are eager to take up positions in a debate about whether out-relief was humane. They do not recognise that this is a cosmic question which can only be speculatively answered by someone who makes an assumption about the essence of man in relation to which the humanity of different policies can be judged. The question about the economy of indoor policies is equally unanswerable. At least, there is no general answer, because the 'economy effect' obviously depends on the variable cost of, and deterrence produced by, workhouses which, as we shall see in chapter 3, were very different institutions in 1850 and 1900. As for the guardians' own calculations, this is surely another unprofitable question. The universe of the poor law can hardly be represented as one filled with calculations of private interest; in so far as they do represent the poor law in this way, historians are merely replicating the worst features of the 1834 *Report.*

The mis-specification of objectives allows historiography to set up an adversary relation between central and local authority, although the existence of any such relation is doubtful. One must be even more sceptical about the presuppositions that the relation of conflict was resolved in favour of the local authorities, because real economic problems were pressing and because the central authority was effectively powerless.

Unemployment and underemployment are not real problems; they are discursive problems that fit into a broader definition of the social problem that dates from the 1880s. These problems are not more real than the 1834 problem of pauperism, they are simply cultural inventions of more recent date. Those historians who see their own cultural categories as reality are committing the sin of naturalising culture. Given that the mutation in the definition of the social problem dates from the 1880s, they are also guilty of anachronism. It is impossible to suppose that pre-1870 policy responses could be determined by, or practical calculations based upon, a problem of unemployment or underemployment.

It should also be noted that recent historians have grossly exaggerated the impracticability of dispauperisation by means of the workhouse. This became part of official strategy in the 1870s and it was then found to be perfectly practicable in urban and industrial areas. Indeed, the unions that severely restricted out-relief in the 1870s were concentrated in the major conurbations; as we shall see in chapter 3, by 1893 four million lived in poor law unions in the big cities where less than one in three paupers was outdoors. Furthermore, some big city unions maintained indoors policies under conditions of severe economic stress; the classic examples would be unions like Whitechapel and Saint George in the East of London from the mid-1870s onwards. At other times and places, local poor law authorities may have preferred to offer out-relief doles, but they were not compelled to do so by economic circumstances.

It should not be assumed that relief practice before or after 1870 was smoothly adjusted to conform with official strategy. The *General Orders* of 1844 and 1852 did represent a major accession of formal power to the central authority, but their restrictive provisions were much less fierce than they might appear.

To begin with, the term 'able-bodied' was not clearly defined in either general order. The prohibitions and restrictions in the 1844 and 1852 *Orders* were qualified, in article one and article seven respectively, by exceptions 'in case of sudden and urgent necessity' or 'in case of sickness, accident or mental infirmity' (Glen, 1898, p. 41). In any case, effective prohibition of relief to certain classes of able-bodied men probably required a workhouse, and the central authority could not order the construction of a workhouse without the consent of a majority of the guardians in a union. As for the labour test, the 1852 *Order* required such a test but did not specify the nature of the task work; guardians had only to report their arrangements to the central authority (Glen, 1898, pp. 516-17). Finally, guardians could legally dispense relief to paupers in contravention of either the 1844 prohibition or the 1852 restriction, provided that they reported such cases to the central authority for approval (Glen, 1898, pp. 504 and 518).

There can be no dispute therefore that the formal power of the central authority was effectively restricted. But only in Utopia is there absolute power, transmitted with 100 per cent efficiency through a complex institutional structure. The 1834 *Report* had dreamt of such a Utopia governed by one rule against outdoor relief, a rule clear beyond the possibility of misconstruction, and a rule about which local authorities would have no discretion. Is it surprising that the new poor law deviated from this ideal of the exercise of power? And is it so important to recover every detail of the institution's deviation from this ideal? Surely the more important question is, given the weakness of the prime mover/central authority and the inefficiency of the transmission system, to what extent was relief practice modified and changed? This question can only be settled by an examination of relief practice.

Relief practice

In chapter 1, it was argued that any analysis of relief practice must take as its object, differences in the classes obtaining relief and the kind of relief obtained. This is correct but obviously too formal because the question is: which differences should be reconstructed? Common-sense discriminations about what kind of relief was offered to whom can provide a starting point, as they do in chapter 1 on the pre-1834 poor law. But this is less than ideal because the resulting analysis is fairly obviously diffuse and ill-focused. Fortunately, the reform of the poor law in 1834 provides us with a new point of departure. After 1834, the relevant difference in relief practice and thus the object under analysis can be defined by the official strategy of the newly created central authority. In this case, there are two key issues: the first issue concerns the nature and extent of relief to able-bodied men which the central authority always sought to repress; the second one concerns the nature and extent of workhouse construction which was essential if deterrent institutional relief was to have any place in relief practice.

If these differences defined by official strategy are to be the object of analysis, then the official statistics on poor relief after 1834 are the privileged resource for answering questions about practice. There is a profusion of post-1834 statistics, often available in continuous series over many years and usually organised into categories relevant to our questions. This is no accident; after all, the official categories were designed to provide operational measures of the success of the official strategy. Of course, particular measures are often less than conceptually ideal because the categories are ambiguous and ill-defined. The time series raise problems of a sort familiar to most users of official statistics; problems about gaps in individual series, discontinuities between successive series, changes in categories and the time base of the calcula-tion, and so forth. But these particular conceptual problems are seldom insuperable; they will be explained, assessed, and dealt with on an *ad hoc* basis in this section.

More generally, the statistics are, for our purposes, a reliable enough guide to relief practice. The analysis of this section does not presume or require completely accurate statistical measures. The two key con-clusions concern the small number of able-bodied men on relief after 1850 and the large number of new workhouses built by 1870. These conclusions can only be undermined if it is proved that the relevant statistics are completely bogus; in the case of able-bodied men, it would be necessary to prove that the official statistics understate by a margin of several hundred per cent. The detailed discussions later in this section will show that there is reason to suppose that the margins of error in the relevant official statistics are very much smaller than this.

If relief to able-bodied men is considered first, what questions should be asked about relief to this group? The key question is defined by our knowledge of the difference between post-1834 strategy and pre-1834 relief practice. After 1834, the official strategy was to grant able-bodied men relief subject to the deterrent conditions of work-house and labour test with the aim of ensuring small numbers of able-bodied men on relief. Before 1834, as chapter 1 showed, it was routine practice to grant relief in one form or another to unemployed and underemployed able-bodied men, and large numbers of men regularly drew relief. The key question therefore is: how many men continued to draw relief and for how long after 1834? Or, in the terminology of chapter 1, when was the line of exclusion against able-bodied men drawn?

This question can be directly answered from the available statistical resources; the answer can be obtained simply by looking at the relevant columns in tables published as appendices to the annual reports of the poor law central authority. The central authority produced these tables by collating, tabulating, and arranging the regular statistical returns which local authorities were obliged to produce. Three different series on unemployment-related outdoor relief to able-bodied men were produced by successive central authorities: the Poor Law Commission series from 1839 to 1846 (see Statistical appendix, Table 4.9), the Poor Law Board series from 1849 to 1861 (see Statistical appendix, Table 4.10), and the Local Government Board series from 1884 to 1912 (see

Statistical appendix, Table 4.11). These series were separated not only by time but also by differences in categories and bases of calculation; these differences have to be explained before it is possible to answer any questions with precision.

In the first period, from 1839 to 1846, the annual series comprehensively covered outdoor relief to unemployed, underemployed, and underpaid men (see Statistical appendix, Table 4.9). The total number of men relieved outdoors for unemployment-related reasons can be obtained by adding together two sub-totals of numbers relieved 'on account of insufficiency of earnings' and 'on account of want of work' (see Statistical appendix, Table 4.9, cols i and ii). To guard against understatement, it would be wise to add the sub-totals in a third residual category of men relieved for 'other causes not being sickness, accident or infirmity' (see Statistical appendix, Table 4.9, col. iii). All three categories gave total numbers of men relieved in the January to March quarter of each year, that is, 'the quarter ended Lady Day'. There must be an element of overstatement in these sub-totals because of the double-counting of individual men who made more than one successful application for relief during the quarter. Even with the benefit of this overstatement, when the three 1840s categories are added together, the result is a modest total number of able-bodied men on relief for unemployment related reasons; from 1839 to 1846, the total was never above 43,000 men in England and Wales and in four of these eight years, the total was near 20,000 (see Statistical appendix, Table 4.9, col. iv).

After a break of two years, when no statistics were published, the series resumed in a slightly different form in 1849 (see Statistical appendix, Table 4.10). The difference was such that there must be doubt about the comprehensiveness of all post-1849 statistics. The two later series simply listed men relieved outdoors because of 'want of work' and dropped the earlier category of men relieved due to 'insufficiency of wages'. Thus we lose specific information on the group of underemployed and underpaid men and can only conjecture that such men must have been returned and included in the one remaining category. But this problem is less serious than it might appear. Already in the 1840s, the total number of underemployed men returned as relieved 'on account of insufficiency of earnings' was tiny; even with double-counting in a quarterly total, the number of underemployed men was always under 13,000 and averaged 9,500 (see Statistical appendix, Table 4.9, col. ii). If the numbers of underemployed and underpaid remained small, it is hardly crucial to know whether and how they were returned in the 1850s and after. In any case, the loss of specific information about this group was more than counterbalanced by a useful gain in precision. From 1849 onwards, the totals of those in want of work were 1 January day counts and thus the problem of double-counting was completely eliminated in the later series.

The two later series show quite insignificant numbers of unemployed able-bodied men drawing outdoor poor relief. Over the whole period of the first series, from 1849 to 1861, the day count totals averaged 5,700 in England and Wales (see Statistical appendix, Table 4.10, col. i). The totals in this category did rise and fall over the trade cycle, but even in seriously depressed years the totals were remarkably low. In 1858, when trade union unemployment was running at nearly 12 per cent, there were only 12,000 able-bodied men in England and Wales receiving outdoor relief on account of want of work (*ibid.*). After a twenty-year break, the annual series resumed in 1884. The totals for the 1880s and after are exactly comparable with those of the 1850s because the basis of enumeration and the categories were the same. Over the whole period of the second series, from 1884 to 1912, the day count totals averaged 2,250 in England and Wales (see Statistical appendix, Table 4.10, col. 1; Table 4.11, col. i). And in this second period, the trade cycle had quite negligible effects: from 1889 to 1904 the total was consistently at or below 3,000 and this level was maintained even in 1893 with 10.2 per cent trade union unemployment (*ibid.*).

It is unfortunate that there was a twenty-year gap between 1861 and 1884 when no regular annual totals were published by the Poor Law Board or Local Government Board. But unemployed able-bodied men would hardly have found it easy to obtain out-relief in the latter part of this period; in the crusade against out-relief in the 1870s, paupers of all classes were being struck off the relief rolls. Furthermore, we do have a special return for 1872 which gave a day count total for one year in the middle of the twenty-year break. This return showed a total of 2,100 able-bodied men receiving outdoor relief on account of want of work (see Statistical appendix, Table 4.10 col. i). This result is completely in line with the regular annual totals in the series on either side of the break. Except during the period of the cotton famine, it is reasonable to assume that the number of unemployed on outdoor relief was always very low.

The statistics on outdoor relief to unemployed and underemployed men show the drawing in of a line of exclusion. In the 1840s, the number of unemployed men assisted outdoors by the poor law was already moderate, and from the early 1850s, the number of such men was negligible; from 1852 to 1912 inclusive, the day counts show 5,000 or fewer men 'in want of work' relieved outdoors in thirty-eight of the forty-one years for which statistics are available. This pattern is strikingly different from that prevailing before 1834 when the poor law was massively involved in the outdoor relief of the unemployed and underemployed; in chapter 1 it was estimated that 100,000 able-bodied men drew relief through the year 1802-3 when the population was very much smaller than in the second half of the nineteenth century.

Nevertheless, it is necessary to be cautious because the statistics so far cited cannot and do not prove that unemployed men failed altogether to obtain relief after 1834. Such men were not necessarily returned in the official statistics in the category 'relieved outdoors on account of want of work'. There are two other ways in which unemployed men could have been relieved and returned in the official, statistics. First, significant numbers of unemployed men may have been relieved indoors, inside a workhouse. Second, significant numbers of unemployed men may have been relieved but misrepresented and returned in another category where unemployment was not the ostensible cause of relief. There is a third possibility that unemployed men were relieved but not returned at all in the official statistics of numbers on relief. But this can be discounted because such local practice would have produced financial discrepancies which could hardly have been concealed from the auditor. Therefore, the working hypothesis must be that if unemployed men were obtaining relief in large numbers then they must be returned somewhere in the official statistics and the historian's job is to check out the likely places.

It is difficult to be decisive about indoor relief to unemployed men because, before 1891, there are no available statistics on relief to this group. Contemporaries assumed and historians have always accepted that there were few employable men in the workhouses of the new poor law. But the question must be: how few? The most significant piece of evidence here is undoubtedly the absence of official statistics on this group in an era when, especially after 1870, the central bureaucracy took infinite pains to acquire statistical information on every aspect of pauperism; if there were more than a few thousand unemployed indoors then it is likely that the central authority would have started a series to establish the dimensions of the problem.

The statistical evidence after 1891 lends some confirmation to the supposition that there were very few unemployed men in the workhouse. A series on able-bodied men 'in health' shows an average of 10,100 men relieved indoors in winter day counts for the twenty years from 1891 to 1912 (see statistical appendix, Table 4.11, col. iii). It is important to realise that this bureaucratic definition of health is different from the commonsense definition. In the official statistics, 'in health' was a residual category where workhouse masters returned those men who were not elsewhere recorded as temporarily sick or aged and (chronically) infirm; in practice, the line of division between the categories was set so that 'in health' meant under sixty years of age and not on a special workhouse diet such as was granted to the sick. The poor law inspectorate alleged that only a small number of those able-bodied men 'in health' was employable in the sense that they could have left the workhouse to take up any kind of regular employment at standard wages. For this reason, the average figure of 10,100 must substantially overstate the number of men in English and Welsh work-houses who could reasonably be termed unemployed (see Statistical appendix, Section D, footnote 9).

The only remaining possibility, therefore, is that unemployed men were relieved in significant numbers but misrepresented and returned in another category by local authorities. The question in this case is: in which category would the men have been hidden? The answer is straightforward on the assumption that the most attractive misrepresentation was one that was hardest to detect and most difficult to prove where detected. On either count, the first choice would be to relieve outdoors, and return paupers as relieved under the various exception clauses and more especially the sickness exception clauses in the 1844 and 1852 *Orders*; in this case, the unemployed man would have been represented as relieved on account of his own sickness or sickness in the family.

What official statistics are available on the numbers of men relieved outdoors under the various exception clauses? There is nothing available for the Poor Law Commission period in the 1840s when the numbers of men relieved under the exception clauses is irrecoverably lost in larger totals. In this period, for example, men relieved under the sickness exception clause could have been entered in the unemployment-related categories as relieved 'on account of insufficiency of earnings' or, could have been entered among the aged and infirm as non-able-bodied. But matters were rather different under the Poor Law Board. For each year from 1849 to 1861, the Board published a January and July day count of the total number of men in England and Wales relieved under each of the three exception clauses: first, 'adult males relieved in cases of sudden and urgent necessity'; second, 'adult males (married or single) relieved on account of own sickness, accident or infirmity'; third, 'adult males relieved on account of sickness, accident or infirmity of any of the family or of a funeral' (see Statistical appendix, Table 4.17).

The statistical evidence on the exception clauses may be incomplete, but it does provide everything we need to assess the importance of misrepresentation. First, the statistics cover the decade of the 1850s which, according to Digby, is the key period when 'local administrators discovered that in practice they had substantial autonomy over relief policies in the rural areas' (Digby, 1976, p. 149). Second, the statistics give totals of the number of men relieved under all the exception clauses; if these 'loopholes' were being used to a significant extent, then the numbers relieved under some or all the headings should be large. More importantly, an annual series, which gives summer and winter day counts, allows an assessment of how many of those returned in these categories were cyclically unemployed industrial workers or seasonally underemployed agricultural labourers being rested here by devious local poor law authorities.

The first issue, therefore, is the total number of men relieved under the various exception clauses. Seasonal and cyclical variations can be ironed out by considering an average for the decade of the 1850s or, more exactly, an average of twenty day counts made summer and winter in each of the ten years from 1849 to 1858 inclusive. On this basis, an insignificant average of 193 men were relieved 'on account of sudden and urgent necessity' (see Statistical appendix, Table 4.17, col. i). But an average 18,092 men were relieved 'on account of their own sickness' and 7,166 'on account of sickness in their family' (see Statistical appendix, Table 4.17, cols ii and iii). That is to say, the two sickness loopholes together accounted for an average of 25,000 men on a day count basis. This average total is fairly modest when the poor law was, for example, supporting twice as many able-bodied widows through the 1850s. It must also be obvious that the total is only significant if most of these 25,000 men were unemployed and underemployed masquerading as sick.

But the pattern of trade cycle and seasonal variation suggests that most of the 25,000 men were genuinely sick and thus perfectly legitimately receiving relief under the exceptions terms of the various orders. To consider trade cycle variations first of all, the number of sick men was never fewer than 20,000 in any day count in the 1850s, and numbers did not greatly increase in the years of high unemployment like 1852 or 1858; with an annual mean trade union unemployment rate of 11.9 per cent in 1858, the January day count showed 27,000 men on relief because of their own or their families' sickness and the July day count showed only 21,000 such men (see Statistical appendix, Table 4.17, cols ii and iii). Large numbers of unemployed industrial labourers cannot have been obtaining relief in this way.

As for seasonal variation, in every year of the 1850s there was a reduction between January and July in the number of men receiving relief on account of their own or their families' sickness. But every class of nineteenth-century pauper, with the exception of lunatics, was more numerous in winter than in summer. And, in proportional terms, the seasonal reduction in the 'sickness' category was fairly modest; only once (in 1850) was the July figure more than 20 per cent below the January figure (see Statistical appendix, Table 4.17, cols ii and iii). More decisively, the difference in absolute numbers between summer and winter day counts was very small indeed; in the ten years 1849 to 1858 inclusive, the seasonal reduction was always under 6,500 and averaged just over 3,500 (see Statistical appendix, Table 4.17, cols ii and iii). If the seasonal variation was so small, virtually no agricultural labourers could have been misrepresented as sick and supported as such by the poor law through the winter months.

In summary, therefore, the poor law relieved negligible numbers of unemployed men outdoors, indoors, or under the exception clauses.

In the twenty years after 1834, a line of exclusion was drawn against able-bodied men. Relief to unemployed and underemployed men was effectively abolished and this abolition was not a temporary or local phenomenon; it was national practice for sixty years from 1852 to 1912. This was the brilliant triumph of an official strategy for the repression of able-bodied male pauperism. Up to 70 per cent of the national population were wage labourers, or the dependants of wage labourers, living in an economic world of cyclical fluctuations and structural disorders; but when they were unemployed or under-employed these wage labourers obtained no assistance from the poor law. Having established this point about relief to unemployed men, this section now turns to the second issue of workhouse construction.

The key questions about workhouse construction are defined by our knowledge of the difference between post-1834 strategy and pre-1834 relief practice. After 1834, the official strategy conceded a large role for out-relief, but the strategy did prescribe indoor relief for certain classes in certain places; as we have seen, between 1844 and 1870, over half the unions were subject to an *Order* formally prohibiting outdoor relief to able-bodied men. Before 1834, most parishes did not maintain paupers in workhouses; a return of 1802–3 showed only 3,765 parishes, or 26 per cent of those making returns, admitted maintaining poor in workhouses (BPP, 1803–4, XIII). The crucial question therefore is: how many new workhouses were built? When this question has been answered, it is possible to ask supplementary questions about where and when the new workhouses were built and how they differed from the old pre-1834 workhouses. There is also the related question about cost: how much money was spent in the pre-1870 period on construct-ing new workhouses?

None of these questions can be immediately answered from the available statistical resources. Statistical information was collected on this strategic question of workhouse construction, but the kind of information obtained and published was biased by the central authority's exercise of administrative control. Thus, the relevant continuous series records the capital expenditure authorisations made by the central authority. From 1835 onwards, the central authority annual reports record every individual authorisation and give separate annual totals of all expenditure authorised for two purposes, namely, 'new workhouses ordered to be built' and 'existing workhouses altered and enlarged'. Because of the administrative bias, these statistics are not immediately useful to the historian. Expenditure authorised is not capital cost actually incurred, because some of the 'workhouses ordered to be built' may not have been built within a few years or even at all.

However, answers to all these questions can be pieced together from this expenditure series and other statistical resources if the references to construction are exploited diligently. The primary aim of any historical work on these statistics must be to obtain the key missing resource, namely, a list of all workhouses built between 1834 and 1870. Such a list would immediately provide answers to the questions about how many workhouses were built, where, and when. From such a list, it would also be possible to calculate what proportion of 'workhouses ordered to be built' were actually constructed and, with this information, total expenditure authorised could be deflated as necessary to obtain a measure of cost incurred.

A good substitute for a list of workhouses built can be obtained by a roundabout route. To begin with, some of the workhouses built between 1835 and 1854 are included in two *ad hoc* lists. A list of unions returning new workhouses 'completed and in operation' appeared in the appendix to the Fifth Annual Report of the Poor Law Commission (BPP, 1839, XX).

This list can be updated to 1854 by using information from a special return on 'the cost of building workhouses in England and Wales' (BPP, 1857-8, XLIX, pt 1). The return recorded capital cost and current expenditure on food and clothing for the paupers in each workhouse; it is reasonable, therefore, to presume that all the workhouses on this list were also constructed and in operation. However, the 1858 list is known to be incomplete, because approximately one in three unions failed to make any return to the central authority. Thus, even after exploiting this second list, it is necessary to cross-check on the two available lists and to construct a third list for the years 1854 to 1870.

The available resources will not directly fill in these gaps. But it is possible to construct a further list of new workhouses by processing the references to construction in the expenditure authorisation series from 1835 onwards. The series identified and separately listed every initial authorisation for workhouse construction and every supplementary authorisation for this purpose; supplementary authorisations were routine because unions commonly underestimated costs of construction and then obtained a supplementary authorisation when they had spent the sum initially authorised. If every union is allocated an individual file card and if every authorisation for that union is serially recorded on that card, then it is possible to estimate workhouse construction. In cases when unions obtained an initial authorisation and then returned for a supplementary authorisation within five years, we have references to highly probable construction. In cases where only one authorisation is recorded, we have a reference to possible construction; workhouses may well have been built out of an initial authorisation but this cannot be demonstrated satisfactorily from a single reference. In this way, it is possible to read through the one text on expenditure authorisation, not so as to arrive at 'reality', but so as to produce another text on workhouse construction. By processing reference in this way, a third list of probably and possibly constructed workhouses has been produced. It should also be noted that this third list is of first workhouses built after 1834. This qualification is necessary to avoid double-counting in the case of the very small number of unions that obtained authorisations to build new workhouses more than once before 1870.

Having explained how the available resources can be exploited, it is now possible to answer the questions, beginning with: how many new workhouses were built between 1834 and 1870? By 1870 a total of 492 unions in England and Wales had certainly, or very probably, built new workhouses; 396 unions appear on one of the two *ad hoc* lists and ninety-six unions appear in the expenditure series as requiring more than one authorisation within five years (see Statistical appendix, Table 4.33(a), cols i and ii). The total of new union workhouses rises to 548 if one adds a further fifty-six workhouses which only appeared once in the expenditure series (see Statistical appendix, Table 4.33 (a), col. iii). There were 647 poor law unions in England and Wales so, in percentage terms, 76 per cent of poor law unions certainly or very probably built a new union workhouse before 1870 and, if all the possibles are then added, the percentage increases to 85 per cent.

The conclusion must be that a very large proportion of poor law unions built completely new workhouses before 1870; three out of four certainly or very probably did so and, if it is assumed that half the 'possible' workhouses were built, then four out of every five unions did build before 1870. It is not worth worrying over this last assumption when the margin of uncertainty about possible construction is so small; only 9 per cent of all unions fall into the group where workhouses were possibly built. Including all possible as well as certain or probable new workhouse construction would not therefore introduce a large element of overstatement. Nevertheless, to be ultra-cautious, all subsequent calculations in this section are based on totals of 'workhouses built' which exclude *all* possibles and include *only* probable and certain workhouses.

A remarkable proportion of the new union workhouses were built in a first phase of construction in the very early years of the new poor law. The lists show that 492 unions certainly or very probably built new workhouses before 1870. Only five years after 1834, 331 unions, or just over two-thirds of those which ever built, had new workhouses in operation or under construction (see Statistical appendix, Table 4.33(a), col. iv). Afterwards, for the next twenty years, there was a steady filling in of the remaining, mainly urban, gaps in the national system of union workhouses. Twenty-five years after 1834, 456 unions, or 93 per cent of the whole group, had built their new workhouses (see Statistical appendix, Table 4.33(a), col. iv). Construction of new union workhouses slowed down in the 1860s simply because there were relatively few remaining unions without a recently built general mixed workhouse.

The argument up to this point ignores a residual group of nearly one in five unions which do not figure on any list of new workhouses built. It would be significant if these unions had no workhouses, especially if they were concentrated in one area like the industrial north. But we know that from 1850 onwards, the number of unions without any workhouse was insignificant; by 1854, only thirteen unions did not have a workhouse in operation or under construction and by 1870, there were only four such unions (see Statistical appendix, Table 4.33(b)). By implication, therefore, almost all the unions that did not build a new workhouse before 1870 were operating a converted pre-1834 workhouse. Furthermore, the unions without workhouses were marginal to the system because they were concentrated in Wales and especially in rural mid-Wales: Wales accounted for over half the unions without workhouses in 1854, and by 1870, three of the remaining four unions without workhouses formed a bloc in rural mid-Wales (see Statistical appendix, Table 4.33(b)). After 1850, therefore, virtually every union had a workhouse in operation and most of these workhouses were newly built.

This conclusion does, however, still leave the possibility that new and old workhouses were differentially distributed around the regions of England and Wales. The question here is whether the new workhouses were concentrated in rural and agricultural, or in urban and industrial areas. This question can only be answered on the basis of some classification of unions. Unfortunately there is no suitable classification of unions available for the mid-century period. However, there is Booth's 1894 (pp. 58-67, 86-95) classification of every individual union according to degree of rurality. Alternatively, and less satisfactorily, the unions can be grouped by county into fifteen agricultural counties and ten industrial counties using the early nineteenth-century classification of individual counties already used in the analysis of pre-1834 statistics.

But, the two available classifications do give roughly similar results and it must be doubtful whether the results would be materially different if a mid-century classification were used. On the Booth classification, 73 per cent of the 170 most rural unions had built new workhouses by 1870, while 76 per cent of the 147 most urban (but non-metropolitan) had built workhouses by 1870 (see Statistical appendix, Table 4.34, cols iii and iv). On a county basis, 76 per cent of all unions in Wales and the fifteen English agricultural counties had built new workhouses by 1870; 75 per cent of all unions in the ten English industrial counties had built workhouses. There are thus only very small differences between urban industrial unions and rural agricultural unions. The conclusion must be that an almost uniformly high proportion of unions in all areas built completely new workhouses.

The phasing of the construction over the 1834 to 1870 period was different in the rural and urban areas. This point can be most easily demonstrated by considering dates of construction in Booth's two groups of the 170 most rural and the 147 most urban unions. Up to 1839, rural unions building new workhouses outnumbered their urban counterparts by two to one; by this date, 62 per cent of rural unions had acquired new workhouses while only 31 per cent of urban unions had acquired them (see Statistical appendix, Table 4.34, cols iii and iv). If rural unions typically built their workhouses before 1840, many urban unions did not build until the 1840s and 1850s; 36 per cent of urban unions built their new workhouses in these two decades (see Statistical appendix, Table 4.34, col. iv). The urban unions thus caught up on rural building rates so that by 1870, as we have seen, both groups had a uniformly high building rate.

In plan and internal layout, the workhouses built between 1834 and 1870 were very different from earlier and later workhouses; these differences will be considered in chapter 3. All that need now to be said is that 1834 to 1870 construction took the form of a programme for replacing many small parish workhouses with fewer large union workhouses. This was also a programme for redistributing workhouse accommodation because parish workhouses were eccentrically dotted around the country while union workhouses were planned so that there was one per union. In these respects, high building rates significantly changed the character of the stock, and network of workhouses. It is difficult to measure these changes when there are only fragmentary statistics about the pre-1834 system, and when measures of available workhouse accommodation depended on variable cultural norms about the facilities and space required per pauper.

A return of 1776 showed 1,970 workhouses, that is, there was approximately one workhouse for every seven parishes or places making a return (see Statistical appendix, Table 4.37, col. i). Individual workhouses were often used by more than one parish; a return of 1802-3 showed 3,765 parishes or places, approximately one in four of those making a return, maintained some of their poor in a workhouse (BPP, 1803-4, XIII). It is difficult to say very much more about pre-1834 workhouses because the institutional stock included some large-scale 'houses of industry' as well as many poor houses built on a domestic scale. Smaller institutions probably predominated right up to 1834. The 1776 return showed that 1,970 workhouses could accommodate a modest average of forty-six paupers per institution (see Statistical appendix, Table 4.37, col. iv).

After 1834, more than 600 poor law unions each grouped an average of twenty-five parishes for purposes of poor law administration. Use of the new workhouses by different parishes in the same union may have been impeded by the mid-Victorian arrangements for apportioning institutional costs among those parishes. But the construction programme was such that after twenty years the workhouse system approximated closely to the post-1834 administrative ideal of one workhouse per union; by 1854, there were 647 poor law unions and 725 poor law institutions, most of which were general mixed workhouses (see Statistical appendix, Table 4.37, col. i). The new union workhouses were typically very much larger than earlier institutions; in 1854 the 725 institutions could accommodate an average of 190 paupers (see Statistical appendix, Table 4.37, col. iv). Nominally, the institutions of 1854 were nearly four times as large as those of 1776.

The character of the institutional stock and network changed as union workhouses replaced parish workhouses. But, throughout these changes, the ratio of available accommodation to population remained much the same, because population increased as fast as did available accommodation under the rebuilding programme after 1834. In 1776, available accommodation was returned as 90,000, or 1.2 per cent of estimated population in England and Wales (see Statistical appendix, Table 4.37, col. iii). In 1854, available accommodation was returned as 212,000 or again, 1.2 per cent of estimated English and Welsh population (see Statistical appendix, Table 4.37, col. iii). The exact coincidence of the percentages in 1776 and 1854 is just that, but it does underline the point that the 1834 to 1870 programme was about building different accommodation, not about building more accommodation.

Even so, the construction of new union workhouses must have been expensive. We shall never know exactly how expensive, because the expenditure authorisation series provides only an approximate guide to the cost incurred. The authorisation series does not overstate cost because it lists large numbers of unbuilt workhouses; it has already been shown that nearly four out of five unions certainly or very probably built new workhouses. On the contrary, the authorisation series probably understates cost in the early years, when some expenditure on workhouse construction was not being properly authorised; for the years 1838 to 1840 inclusive, a special return of cost incurred showed higher levels of expenditure than those recorded in the authorisation series (BPP, 1841, XXI). An altogether more serious problem is the obscurity of central authority accounting conventions. Before the early 1860s, it is not clear whether the expenditure authorisations consistently include or exclude expenditure on land purchase and on fitting out the shells of new union workhouses, nor is it clear how the central authority treated offsetting income from the sale of parish workhouses and land; receipts from this source were certainly significant in the early days of the new poor law.

Authorisation figures may be uncertain guides to cost incurred, but they do show a pattern of expenditure consonant with the data on new workhouse construction. To begin with, the cost of constructing completely new workhouses greatly exceeded that of renovating old workhouses; by 1868, £6,008,000 had been authorised for new workhouses compared with £1,071,000 for alteration of existing workhouses (see Statistical appendix, Table 4.32, cols iii and iv). This pattern is what would be expected when so many unions built completely new workhouses. The total amount authorised for new workhouse construction moved erratically up and down and year by year, depending on how major building projects were bunched. But, if this variation is averaged out by taking ten-year periods, then the authorisations show steady expenditure right through the period. Over £2,000,000 had been authorised by 1840, over £3,000,000 by 1850, and nearly £4,500,000 by 1860. This pattern is again what would be expected when the rural, agricultural unions built early and the urban, industrial unions built late.

The total of approximately £6,000,000 spent on new workhouses by 1868 is so large as to be meaningless. It is more significant if it is expressed in the form of an average: if 600 unions spent £6,000,000, then each spent an average of £10,000 on building a new workhouse. Such an average is still uninformative since it does not indicate how much accommodation was bought by this commitment of resources. In the middle of the 1834 to 1870 period, the authorisation figures show that it cost between £25 and £30 to create one pauper place in a completely new workhouse; in eighty-four workhouses built between 1840 and 1854, the average cost per pauper place created was £28.53 (BPP, 1857–8, XLIX, pt 1). At this rate, the sum of £6,000,000 would have bought institutional accommodation in completely new workhouses for over 200,000 paupers. To express the same result in another way, an average expenditure of £10,000 per union was sufficient to build a completely new workhouse for about 330 paupers.

The average workhouse is an imaginary building, but as we have already seen, it would not be much of an exaggeration to say that every poor law union acquired a union workhouse by 1870. In the thirty years after 1834, four out of every five unions built new union workhouses that were typically large institutions accommodating several hundred paupers. These buildings were an enormous monument to the strategy of the central authority. The monument still exists because many of these buildings survive as the geriatric homes of the welfare state.

Misrepresenting relief practice

It is quite startling to find that recent historiography recognises neither the abolition of relief to unemployed men nor the national programme of union workhouse construction. Misleading claims about relief practice by Rose, Digby, and Ashforth will be considered to illustrate this point.

These historians claim directly that relief to able-bodied men continued after the middle of the nineteenth century. Rose, for example, claims that,

> despite the fierce condemnation in 1834 of relief to make
> up the earnings of able-bodied men, this type of relief con-
> tinued into the 1860s especially in the northern manu-
> facturing towns and may well have survived into the
> twentieth century, or been revived particularly in the more
> rural areas (Rose, 1966, p. 616).

Ashforth comes to very similar conclusions (Ashforth, 1976, p. 314); and so does Digby, who argues that there were few men on relief for unemployment-related reasons in the countryside because they were being misrepresented as sickness cases and obtained out-relief via this 'loophole'. Rose claims more generally that,

> there is little doubt that boards of guardians took full
> advantage of these escape clauses in order to give outdoor
> relief unhindered by workhouse or work test (Rose, 1966,
> p. 611).

The historians' claims and assumptions are equally misleading about workhouse construction. Rose (1966, p. 613) chooses to ignore com-pletely the issue of workhouse construction and concentrate on the guardians' supposed reluctance to use workhouses. But other historians make confident and misleading claims about urban resistance to work-house construction. Consider, for example, Digby, who is unusual in that she does emphasise the extent of rural construction:

> country workhouses usually had smaller, newer buildings
> with a better standard of accommodation than those in
> large towns or cities which often had to utilise old, sub-
> standard workhouses built under the old poor law (Digby,
> 1976, p. 162).

Ashforth argues that, in the industrial north, many of these old build-ings were closed before replacement union workhouses were built; in the 1840s 'northern unions were far busier closing old workhouses than opening new ones' (Ashforth, 1976, p. 133). He does later concede that workhouse construction was 'under way' from the early 1850s, but that concession does not amount to much when he presents no statistics on the number and proportion of unions building new workhouses.

On our alternative account, the exclusion of unemployed men from the classes obtaining relief and the wholesale construction of new union workhouses were the two most conspicuous discontinuities in the poor law of the mid-nineteenth century. But here are specialist historians of the institution who neglect, overlook, or even deny these developments. How are such massive oversights possible? The general answer must be that the current received ideas have distracted recent historians in two ways. First, the received ideas promote the pursuit of anecdotes that corroborate rather than challenge the received ideas. Second, the received ideas promote confusions about which categories in the official statistics are relevant. Both these points can now be developed with illustrations again taken from the articles by Rose, Digby, and Ashforth.

Anecdotes are all-pervasive in the recent history of the new poor law. If we consider the syntheses of Rose, Digby, and Ashforth, then in all three cases the anecdote is the characteristic item of information recovered from the recent local studies. Here synthesis becomes a scissors and paste job whereby anecdotes are cut out from local studies and then stuck in at a suitable point in the story of the new poor law. The anecdotes usually take one of two classic forms; either they retail the occasional opinions of authority figures or they present vignettes of relief practice.

One paragraph from Rose will show how the opinions of authority figures in the central bureaucracy can be invoked to justify received ideas:

> After 1852 no statistics of the amount of outdoor relief
> afforded in aid of wages, seem to have been published,
> although officials at the Poor Law Board and their
> successors at the Local Government Board after 1871 were
> aware of the continued existence of the system. The Poor
> Law Board's annual report for 1870 remarked that 'relief
> is freely given in aid of wages in several parts of London'.
> Three years later an inspector in the north-east told the
> Local Government Board that in his area, 'cases of relief
> given in aid of small earnings are of course frequent
> enough'; and, in 1881, the Local Government Board stated,
> on examining the statistics of outdoor relief in England and
> Wales, that 'practically the old abuse of relief in aid of
> wages must largely prevail in some form or another' (Rose,
> 1966, pp. 608-9).

It is unusual for such a sequence of opinions to be offered one after the other, but other historians often do retail such opinions. Digby tries to buttress her arguments about the sickness loophole in exactly the same way (Digby, 1976, pp. 157-8).

It is appropriate that Ashforth should provide some examples of the vignette, since his article is dominated by such anecdotes. Consider, for example, how he introduces some regional non-events of the 1840s to prove the point about the guardians' reluctance to build new work-houses:

> No workhouses were built in the West Riding during the
> 1840s (though Leeds built an industrial school); in
> Lancashire (though Manchester authorised the building of
> a new workhouse and Liverpool spent £22,500 on the en-
> largement of its existing buildings) the general response was
> equally poor (Ashforth, 1976, p. 133).

Ashforth then goes on to introduce more anecdotes in support of the supplementary point that existing parish workhouses were being closed in this period:

> Blackburn closed four of its five poorhouses, Bradford
> four out of its six. In Todmorden the guardians sold all the
> workhouses and managed without (Ashforth, 1976, p.
> 133).

For anyone who has cause to doubt the received ideas, these opinions and vignettes are thoroughly ambiguous and indecisive. The significance of a practice like wage subvention must depend on the relative fre-quency of the practice. But the official opinions cited by Rose do not clearly imply any particular frequency; these opinions use undefined adjectival and adverbial qualifications like 'many', 'several', 'frequent enough', and 'largely' in a variety of contexts at different times and places between 1851 and 1871. As for Ashforth's vignettes of relief practice, their significance is not clear when incidents and events of a quite different sort can be obtained by a slightly different zigzag through space and time. Indeed, Ashforth himself is sufficiently un-dogmatic to include counter-instances of workhouse construction and use (Ashforth, 1976, pp. 133 and 136).

Recent historians do not, however, doubt the received ideas. It never occurs to them that practice might be different from the way it is repre-sented in their received ideas. Hence the ambiguities in the anecdotes do not exist for recent historiography, or, more exactly, the ambiguities are always resolvable in one way, thanks to the contiguity of received ideas. The anecdotes can therefore function as illustrative and corrob-orative material; they are the empirical stuff that fills in the spaces between the sub-conceptual clichés. Things have gone desperately wrong for a historiography which is constructed like this. The discourse has turned away from asking questions where the answers are open, and turned towards repeating received ideas and corroborating anecdotes that mark out a closed circle.

At the same time, it is important not to condemn this anecdotalism for the wrong reasons. It is easy to make a systematic empiricist critique of unsystematic empiricism, and to argue that anecdotes do not have a proof value that can be obtained through the procedures and methods of systematic empiricism. At a more common-sense level, there is Clapham's argument that anecdotes should be eschewed and the investigator should simply count relative frequency – how many and how often. Both these arguments must be rejected because they set up an alternative which will not work. As chapter 1 demonstrated, systematic empiricism does not deliver on the certainty or probability that it promises; nor will simple questions about how many and how often uncover significant differences if the discourse is burdened with confused received ideas, as is recent historiography on the post-1834 poor law. It is worth developing this important point.

Recent historians do sometimes ask how many and how often questions about post-1834 relief practice. The answers do not disclose much about relief practice because there are confusions built into the questions. Most importantly, the received ideas generate confusions about what categories in the official statistics are relevant, and the historians end up counting how many and how often in categories that are irrelevant. Two major confusions will be considered in turn: the first confusion substitutes the category able-bodied persons for able-bodied men; the second confusion substitutes misleading measures of workhouse use for statistics on workhouse construction.

All the recent historians prominently cite statistics about relief to able-bodied persons. The first statistics Rose cites are about wage supplementation of able-bodied persons in 1839 and 1846 (Rose, 1966, p. 608). At this point and later, Rose also brings in a special return of the number of persons receiving relief in aid of wages in one week in 1852. Digby and Ashforth also presume this category is relevant; they cite figures for the proportion of able-bodied paupers relieved outdoors (Ashforth, 1976, p. 134; Digby, 1976, p. 162). These same historians in these and other articles also cite occasional national or regional totals of able-bodied men on relief for unemployment-related reasons (e.g. Rose, 1966, pp. 608 and 614; Digby, 1975, pp. 72-3; Digby, 1978, p. 111). These latter totals are usually displayed less prominently.

The issue is which of the two categories – able-bodied persons or able-bodied men – provides the appropriate measure. Recent historiography emphasises the category of able-bodied persons because of the received idea that the central authority was concerned with relief to able-bodied persons. It follows that, as Digby claims in her recent book, 'the most significant statistics concerning relief policies are those for the adult able-bodied poor' (Digby, 1978, p. 110). But, as we have seen, the pre-1870 official strategy was concerned with relief to able-bodied men. Given this strategy, only statistics on able-bodied men are relevant. There is, after all, little point in investigating whether the central authority did succeed in abolishing the outdoor relief to able-bodied widows which it never tried to abolish in the pre-1870 period.

The introduction of the irrelevant category is of some practical importance since there is a large discrepancy between the totals in the categories able-bodied persons and able-bodied men. As we have already seen, the number of able-bodied men was small; but the number of able-bodied persons on relief was large, because the latter group included many able-bodied widows with dependent children. By the 1850s, the day counts showed over 50,000 able-bodied widows on relief (see Statistical appendix, Table 4.20), and these widows with their dependent children accounted for one in five paupers. By emphasising the large number of able-bodied persons on outdoor relief, it is possible to produce a completely misleading impression of central authority 'failure'. The small number of able-bodied men is the relevant measure of the success of official strategy.

The historiography confusion about able-bodied persons is complemented by an allied confusion about the object under investigation. In 1966, Rose conceived this object to be the so-called 'allowance system', that is, the grant of poor relief in aid of wages, as discussed by Blaug and others in articles on the pre-1834 poor law. This supposition completely distorts Rose's discussion of the official statistics of able-bodied male pauperism. In discussing the 1840s statistics, he ignores the 'on account of want of work' category and only gives totals for those on relief 'on account of insufficiency of earnings' (Rose, 1966, p. 614). Because this last category is dropped in 1846, Rose loses interest in the later statistics and does not cite the later Poor Law Board and Local Government Board series; instead he offers opinions and anecdotes about the continuation of allowances to able-bodied men in the north of England. It is worth exposing these confusions because the notion of the 'allowance system' is still alive and well in the most recent work of Digby (1978, pp. 105–14).

After 1834, the 'allowance system' can only be a legitimate object for investigation if official strategy was preoccupied with this 'system' of wage subvention. This condition is not satisfied. As we have seen, the central authority was hostile to all unemployed-related relief to able-bodied men. Consequently, the object for investigation should be the dimensions of such relief in all its forms. At a practical level, too, it is unreasonable for historiography to be preoccupied with that portion of the unemployment-related relief which was officially returned as given 'in aid of wages'. However it may have been returned, most unemployment-related relief, like most other outdoor relief, was in one way or another given in aid of wages. This was inevitable when, through-out the nineteenth century, all classes of outdoor pauper typically received small doles which were in aid of another source of income, whether from work, charity, or family. Full maintenance allowances paid in all the vicissitudes of wage labouring life may now appear to be natural, but they were only put on to the agenda by the *Beveridge Report* of 1942.

The misrepresentations so far considered involve errors of commission. The neglect of workhouse construction is a rather different case, because it involves one major error of omission: recent historiography has failed to produce a national list of workhouses built before 1870. But it is also true that the historiographic promotion of workhouse use as an alternative issue depends on quite subtle and plausible confusions.

To begin with, if we ignore any confusion about central authority strategy, the issue of workhouse use would appear to have priority over the issue of workhouse construction. Surely, it is more important to know how the new union workhouses were used rather than how many were built. The rejoinder to this argument must be that construction cannot be separated from use in the long run. The construction programme equipped the poor law with new technical instruments for a policy of repression. This new technical resource shifted the bounds of what was possible in the institution and permitted new kinds of strategy. These abstract points can be illustrated by considering the crusade against out-relief in the 1870s. The crusade was what happened when the union workhouses had been built. Around 1870, strategy shifted, the central authority's inspectorate began discouraging out-relief to all classes, and in the five years from 1871 to 1876, 276,000 paupers, or almost exactly one in three of those on outdoor relief, were cleared off the relief rolls (see Statistical appendix, Table 4.5, col. iii). The crusade did not happen because the workhouses were built, but it would have been technically impossible without the workhouses.

At the same time, it must be emphasised that recent historians provide a confused and misleading treatment of their chosen issue – workhouse use. The main problems arise from their choice of two technical measures of workhouse use: possible use is measured by the ratio of available accommodation to population and actual use by the percentage of paupers remaining outdoors. It will now be shown that Digby and Ashforth promote these statistical measures of workhouse use, and then it will be argued that both measures are unsatisfactory.

Recent historians emphasise that the possible role of the work-house inside the new poor law was circumscribed, because poor law unions generally had workhouse accommodation for only a small percentage of the local population. Ashforth, for example, notes that 'as late as 1854', only a minority of West Riding unions had accommodation for 1 per cent of their inhabitants (Ashforth, 1976, p. 133).

The implication is that the poor law unions did not have the institutional accommodation to implement a policy of 'offering the house'. The immediate rejoinder to this is that pre-1870 official strategy did not insist on indoor relief for all classes of paupers; even the prohibition on outdoor relief to able-bodied male paupers was never universal. But there is also a more fundamental critical point about the nature of the measure that is being used.

The issue here is whether the ratio of available accommodation to population is a good measure of the possible role of the union workhouse. This ratio is a reasonable measure of the possible roles of institutions of treatment such as nineteenth-century prisons and hospitals; the institution is designed to administer curative treatment and the possibility of such treatment depends on the availability of a cell or bed. But the new union workhouses of the mid-century were institutions of deterrence, not treatment; if they were constructed and managed properly, few paupers who were offered the workhouse should accept and those who did accept should not become permanent residents. Here it is the deterrent quality of the accommodation that is decisive, rather than the quantity of accommodation available. It is therefore not accidental that, as we have seen, the construction programme of 1835 to 1860 universally provided different institutions, but did not increase the amount of available accommodation much beyond the 1 per cent of population mark. This amount of accommodation was adequate in the 1840s when the unemployed men were being cleared off relief and it was again adequate in the 'crusade' of the 1870s when the out-relief lists were being cleared. The 'crusade' itself raises the question of workhouse use which can now be considered.

Recent historians prominently cite statistics about the importance of outdoor relief. Ashforth estimates that in most urban unions, in most years, the percentage indoors was only 6 to 15 per cent of all those receiving relief (Ashforth, 1976, p. 135). He claims that the small percentage of paupers indoors was 'the system's most striking feature' (Ashforth, 1976, p. 134). Digby is greatly impressed by the persistence of outdoor relief from the 1840s to the 1890s for able-bodied adults in Norfolk (Digby, 1976, p. 162). More generally, across the whole country, she considers 'the high ratio of outdoor to indoor relief' among all classes of paupers right up to 1909 to be the decisive measure of the central authority's failure in the countryside (Digby, 1976, p. 170).

But the percentage of paupers outdoors is a poor measure of workhouse use in an institution dedicated to dispauperisation by means of deterrent institutions. We can consider, first, the case where the workhouse is to be offered to only one group of paupers. Abstractly considered, the percentage of paupers outdoors is a poor guide to the implementation of any such strategy. A high percentage of paupers out-doors could indicate either that the strategy is not being implemented, because paupers in the relevant group are not sent to the workhouse, or that the strategy is being implemented, with deterrent workhouses ensuring that few paupers in the relevant group take up the offer of relief in an unattractive form. Practically, the pre-1870 poor law strategy approaches the one group case; the central authority acquiesced in unconditional out-relief for all classes except for able-bodied men who were to be offered the workhouse or out-relief subject to labour test. As the total number of men in this group who obtained relief in any form was small, one would expect a high percentage of paupers to be outdoors under all circumstances.

Even where the strategy is to 'offer the house' to all groups of paupers, as in the 'crusade' after 1870, the percentage of paupers out-doors is a poor guide to the role of the workhouse. Abstractly con-sidered, the percentage of paupers outdoors is an inadequate measure of changes in the availability of out-relief where a strategy of 'offering the house' to all or most groups of paupers is being implemented. Over a period of time, dynamic changes in this percentage depend on the trade-off relation between reductions in outdoor relief and increases in indoor relief, which are not an inevitable corollary if workhouses are sufficiently deterrent. The percentage of paupers outdoors will change dramatically if many of the paupers denied outdoor relief obtain indoor relief instead, but the percentage will not change dramatically if the paupers denied outdoor relief cease to draw relief in any form. These abstract arithmetical considerations are perfectly illustrated by the experience of the 1870s when, in the period of the 'crusade', out-relief generally became very much more difficult to obtain. The crucial point is that in the years 1871 to 1876, the paupers struck off the out-relief rolls ceased to draw relief in any form; a reduction of 30 per cent in outdoor relief numbers was actually accompanied by a small decrease in numbers indoors in the workhouses. The percentage of paupers outdoors hardly fell at all in these years; 86.5 per cent of all paupers were outdoors in 1871 and 83.3 per cent in 1876 (see Statistical appendix, Table 4.5, cols i and vi). If the first major discontinuity in relief practice under the new poor law was the abolition of relief to un-employed men, the second was the purge of the out-relief rolls in the 1870s. This discontinuity has simply vanished from recent general accounts of the new poor law, because these accounts use a poor measure of the relative importance and availability of outdoor relief.

In summary, at every point where they cite official statistics, Rose, Digby, and Ashforth are so committed to received ideas that they end up misrepresenting relief practice. More generally, the received ideas dominate, so that almost all of the available local studies depend on the same bogus measures and misrepresentations that we have considered in the three national accounts. Most tragically, the received ideas are so powerful that they can assimilate and suppress the obvious anomalies turned up by the two most serious of the existing local studies – Boyson (1960) on north-east Lancashire and Dunkley (1974) on Durham.

Boyson's article on the Lancashire poor law was written in 1960 before the ossification of the currently received ideas. He shows early local resistance to the implementation of the new poor law; but he then goes on to show that, in several significant respects – for example workhouse construction – this resistance was overcome by the 1860s. Thus, Boyson emphasises that 'the central authority was prepared to wait' (Boyson, 1960, p. 35). This point should have made historians of the new poor law reflect whether their local studies arrive at predetermined conclusions because they concentrate on the early years of the implementation of the new poor law. But the subsequent local studies and general accounts do not take up this issue. Here Boyson figures only as a chronicler of resistance and a source of adversary local opinions (e.g. Ashforth, 1976, p. 135).

Dunkley's article appeared more than ten years later. He shows that the new poor law was smoothly implemented in the North-East, then goes on to show that local practice about unemployment-related relief was exceedingly stringent. This class of pauper found any kind of in-door or outdoor relief virtually unobtainable in a severe local depression in the early 1840s (Dunkley, 1974, pp. 335 and 337). This point should have made historians of the new poor law reflect; were the numbers of unemployed men on relief elsewhere and after the 1840s as trivial as in County Durham? This issue was never taken up, partly because Dunkley devalued his discovery by suggesting that what happened in Durham was a question of short-run response to economic circumstance (Dunkley, 1974, p. 329). Thus, in her recent book, Digby is able to incorporate Dunkley's results; what happened in Durham simply illustrates the extent of local discretion (Digby, 1978, p. 11).

The discoveries of Boyson and Dunkley have been hidden just like the purloined letter which could not be found under the mattress, beneath the floor boards, or behind the skirting. Any unexpected and anomalous results from the local studies are interleaved with taken for granted results and enveloped in received ideas, just like the purloined letter which had been hidden among other papers in the letter rack. By these means, the historians of the new poor law have produced a discourse where anomalies and threating discoveries are lost as though they had never been made.

May, 1979

The poor law 1870-1914

3

The poor law after 1870 illustrates the possible complexity and ambiguity of institutional configurations. This chapter will reconstruct the complexity of the poor law by differentiating three distinct relief strategies that coexisted in a complex relationship by the early twentieth century. First, there is the strategy of the 'crusade against out-relief' after 1870; this was an inordinately ambitious attempt to educate the poor which degenerated into more repression of pauperism. Second, there is an indoors strategy of classification and treatment; this required new kinds of specialised institutions which were very different from the pre-1870 general mixed workhouse. Third, by 1900 the repression of outdoor pauperism was qualified by an outdoor strategy of treatment which was belatedly making an appearance.

Before we can begin differentiating the strategies, it is necessary to clear away the obstacles created by existing historiographical accounts of the poor law after 1870. The Webbs' (1927-9) *English Poor Law History* has recently been supplemented, revised, and challenged by specialist articles concerned with aspects of poor law practice and strategy after 1870 (Crowther, 1978; Duke, 1976; Flinn, 1976; Rose, 1979; Ryan, 1978; Vorspan, 1977). The first section of this chapter will argue that this recent literature, first, fails to identity the deficiencies of Webbian analysis and, second, introduces new confusion into historiographic discussion.

An appendix explains why this chapter's alternative analysis of the poor law does not use the concepts of social control theory or of recent Foucauldian analysis. Both these conceptual frameworks will be critically examined and finally rejected, because they conjure away the kinds of complexity which our alternative analysis tries to recover.

Misrepresenting relief practice after 1870

This section will criticise historiographic accounts that are specifically focused on the operations of the poor law from 1870 to 1914. For more than forty years, this historiography has been completely dominated by the Webbs' *Poor Law History* (1927-9), which was preceded by their earlier analysis of *Poor Law Policy*. The recent specialist articles have discussed the Webbs in sharp, one-sentence asides (e.g. Crowther, 1978, p. 40; Ryan, 1978, p. 56), so it is worth devoting a few paragraphs to the Webbs' analysis of the poor law after 1870.

According to the Webbs, in the second half of the nineteenth century there was a movement away from the 'principles of 1834' and the relief of destitution under deterrent conditions in the interest of repressing pauperism (Webbs, 1910, p. 58). At the same time, there was a movement towards relief based on the idea of treatment: 'the mere relief of destitution has been progressively replaced by a policy of preventive and curative treatment' (Webbs, 1927-9), vol. 2, p. 1015). The new kind of relief existed in a broader framework for the prevention of destitution embodied in the factory code, the education and public health Acts, and national insurance (Webbs, 1927-9, vol. 1, p. vi). This progress culminated in the Webbs' own 1909 *Minority Royal Commission Report* which made comprehensive proposals for the treatment of different social problem groups in order to prevent the occurrence of destitution.

This schema of transition rationalised the Webbs' own position as progressive social reformers and served as a discursive reassurance that history was going their way. But it is doubtful whether this schema of transition can now be profitably used as a framework for constructing the development of poor law strategy and practice after 1870.

The development of indoor relief was overemphasised because it could easily be constructed in terms of the Webb transition. The *Poor Law History*'s long chapter on the poor law from 1848 to 1908 separately analysed the relief obtained by different classes of pauper – children, the sick, the aged, etc. In each case, the story was of 'the breakdown of the principles of 1834' which took the form of,

> attempts to take out of the general mixed workhouse and
> to transfer to specialised institutions or other forms of
> treatment, one class of paupers after another; the children,
> the vagrants, the persons of unsound mind, those suffering
> from infectious disease, other sick persons, the blind, the
> deaf and dumb, the crippled, the sane epileptics, the
> chronically infirm or even feeble-minded, the aged and even
> the able-bodied unemployed (Webbs, 1927-9, vol. 1, p. 140).

The development of outdoor relief was underemphasised, because it could not easily be reconciled with the Webb schema of transition. The Webbs presented the continued existence of outdoor relief as a massive oversight on the part of the central authority:

> It was, in fact, the Poor Law Commissioners who started the practice, which continued under the Poor Law Board and the Local Government Board, of taking no cognisance of the paupers on outdoor relief (Webbs, 1927–9, vol. 1, p. 151).

The main discontinuity in outdoor relief strategy and practice was the so-called 'crusade against out-relief' in the 1870s, which the Webbs defined as 'a persistent crusade against outdoor relief, as such, to any class or section of the pauper host' (Webbs, 1927–9, vol. 1, p. 436). This apparent renewal of the repression of pauperism forty years after 1834 could not be fitted into any schema of a progressive transition to treatment. It was symptomatic of this difficulty that, in the *Poor Law History*, the crusade was dealt with in an appendix to the long chapter on the poor law from 1848 to 1908.

The history of the poor law after 1870 cannot be written around the Webbs' two references to 'treatment' and the 'principles of 1834'. Treatment can perhaps be represented as a kind of 'supplementary policy' (Webbs, 1910, p. 58). But, in this case, the question must be: how was treatment supplementary and to what other kinds of 'policy' was it supplementary? It certainly should not be presumed that reference to the 'principles of 1834' identifies another, or the other, 'policy'. In the later nineteenth century, the 1834 *Report* was a scriptural text whose 'principles' were reconstructed by exegesis and then used to justify a variety of strategies. It is therefore necessary to inquire, for example, whether the crusade represented a new kind of strategy rather than a reassertion of the 'principles of 1834'.

Furthermore, the formal essence of the Webb schema of transition must be regarded with some suspicion. If the institution was moving from one unitary configuration to another, then contradictoriness and complexity had to be identified as transitional phenomena that emerged and existed only so long as the institution was in transition from the repressive principles of 1834 to the treatment principles of 1929. But, it is by no means clear that the principle of treatment was ultimately triumphant and all-conquering; so any new historical inquiry must ask how different strategies and practices fitted together at different times, and ask, specifically, whether everything did increasingly 'hang together in theory and practice' (Webbs, 1927–9, vol. 2, p. 1020) in the early years of the twentieth century?

The Webb analysis raises questions rather than provides answers.

These questions are not, however, recognised in the recent articles on the poor law after 1870. The articles by Rose (1966), Digby (1976) and Ashforth (1976) that were criticised in chapter 2 contain general analyses of the operation of the poor law after 1834; the articles that will now be considered concentrate on specialised aspects of relief strategy and practice after 1870. Three of them examine the relief offered to one class or group of paupers: Flinn (1976) considers medical services and the sick, Duke (1976) considers education and pauper children, and Vorspan (1977) considers casual wards and vagrants. Crowther (1978), rather differently, takes an institutional point of reference and writes about the general mixed workhouse after the turn of the century; Ryan (1978) makes a case study of the one dissident union of Poplar.

In this specialised literature, poor law strategy and practice after 1870 is broken into pieces. Very different conclusions can obviously be obtained by examining different bits of strategy and practice. Any discoveries about practice and strategy are meaningless until the bits are fitted together in some configuration or, more exactly, established in some kind of dispersion of differences. But all these articles on the poor law after 1870 are so specialised that they cannot pose the problem of the existence of different strategies and practices in a complex combination. Indeed, the authors of these articles do not appear to accept the necessity for posing this problem.

By default, therefore, the recent articles favour a more analytic approach than that of the Webbs. The Webbs used an explicit general interpretation to make sense of similarities and differences in the treatment of particular classes. For the same purpose, the recent articles characteristically rely on two inexplicit presuppositions: first, they presuppose that the discursive framework around strategy remains the same for long periods of time; or second, they presuppose that the changes may be understood as a matter of approximations to modernity. The next few paragraphs will show how these presuppositions are used and why they are objectionable.

Some of the recent articles presuppose that choice of strategy occurs within an intellectual framework which stays the same for thirty or even seventy years. For example, Crowther supposes that, from 1832 to 1929, there was always a choice between specialised and general institutions. Thus the Webbs in 1929 advocated 'the same solution as the 1832 commissioners: separate institutions for the different categories of inmates' (Crowther, 1978, p. 40). Vorspan argues that the discrimination of two groups of deserving and undeserving vagrants was 'a consistent phenomenon' for thirty years from the 1870s onwards (Vorspan, 1977, p. 80).

In her emphasis on the importance and persistence of this division, Vorspan represents a broader tendency in the recent historiography of 'social policy'. Splitting the deserving and undeserving was emphasised by Stedman Jones (1971) in his study of London's crisis in the 1880s, and 'splitting' is now increasingly being emphasised in studies of the 1860s and the 1870s. In a forthcoming article on the crusade against out-relief, Rose will emphasise that the social problem of the 1860s was, in part, about the existence of an undeserving 'residuum', and the social policy response was splitting, that is, an 'attempt to remodel the poor law/philanthropic system so that it could distinguish between, and adequately treat, both the "deserving poor" and the "residuum" ' (Rose, 1979, p. 5).

But, whatever historians may suppose, the value of distinctions and differences does not usually stay the same for long periods of time. Crowther misrepresents the choice between institutional forms when both the general and the specialised institutions of the 1900s were very different from those of the 1830s or the 1860s. The proper historiographic task is to reconstruct the different kinds of institutions built at different times and to establish how their various regimes and internal layouts fitted into different strategies. For much the same general reasons, Vorspan and all the other historians who emphasise the persistence of the distinction between the deserving and undeserving simply miss the point. The deserving versus undeserving distinction was a recurrent theme that was endlessly repeated and elaborated on all sides from 1860 to 1914. But that was exactly because the aim of splitting did not require any one specific kind of strategy, but could be articulated in various ways in strategies which differed radically about what kinds of relief should be offered to paupers and for what ends. The primary task of poor law historiography should be to differentiate the various post-1870 strategies and not to identify the recurrent theme of splitting.

Some of the recent articles represent the changes in strategy and practice as a matter of approximations to modernity. For example, Flinn presents the development of medical services as the story of the gradual overcoming of financial and ideological obstacles to 'efficiency' (Flinn, 1976, p. 53). In similar vein, Ryan presents 'Poplarism' as a defensive campaign in the modern class war. The practice of this dissident union,

> represented a deliberate attempt to use the existing institu-
> tions of local government to protect and maintain working
> class living standards in the periods of crisis 1903–6 and
> 1908–9 and in the continuous depression of the 1920s
> (Ryan, 1978, p. 56).

But, the emphasis on approximate similarity undermines the possibility of establishing the differences which separate past and present. The task of historiography is to reconstruct those differences and, concretely in this area, to specify how the ends and means of the pre-1914 poor law were not modern. Thus, it is doubtful whether the Poplar guardians pursued the end of 'defending the working class' in 1903–4, because they used such distinctly unmodern means; around 1903, their leading ideologue, Lansbury, was an enthusiast for sending the unemployed to farm colonies. As for 'efficiency' and medical services, efficiency is not an end in itself, but a measure of the attainment of certain ends. And the ends of poor law medical services were often different from modern ones; for example, considerations of efficient treatment were obviously irrelevant in the crusade, in so far as those on outdoor medical relief were not exempted from the general purge.

Our consideration of the Webbs and of recent historians has produced many new questions to be answered and assertions to be justified. The rest of this chapter will seek to identify and differentiate the various relief strategies of the poor law in the late nineteenth century.

The crusade against out-relief

This section will examine the crusade against out-relief and its impact on relief practice. It will begin by asking whether there was a distinct strategy of the crusade and, if so, what was its nature? This question will be answered initially by analysing Inspector Henry Longley's (1874) report on *Outdoor Relief in the Metropolis* which appeared in the Local Government Board's *Third Annual Report* for 1873–4 (pp. 136–209). It is appropriate to consider a poor law inspector's report, because the crusade was a campaign whose strategy was formulated and pressed upon boards of guardians by these peripatetic civil servants, each of whom was responsible for poor law administration in one region. This particular report is chosen for two further reasons: first, the Longley report was widely recommended and circulated in the 1870s as an authoritative statement of sound principles of administration; second, the report contains a more extended, clearer, and more subtle statement of a new out-relief strategy than any other official or quasi-official pronouncement of the 1870s.

It is best to begin by conceding that Longley proposed 'splitting' the deserving from the undeserving and offering them different kinds of relief. Within the poor law, the offer of out-relief was to be restricted to 'deserving cases' (Longley, 1874, p. 207). Co-operation between the poor law and organised private charity would ultimately allow charity to assume responsibility for such deserving cases; but this discovery does not tell us very much, and crucially it provides no basis for differentiating Longley from so many of his contemporaries and successors, who also proposed to split the deserving and the undeserving. It is altogether more interesting to examine Longley's detailed proposals for the relief of pauperism; what were the ends of relief practice and by what means were they to be secured? If these questions are answered, some differences can be established and a distinct crusade strategy can be defined.

Longley's report specified the ends of relief practice negatively and positively. The text denied that the object of relief practice was 'a mere diminution of pauperism, irrespective of the general condition and welfare of the poor' (Longley, 1874, p. 197). In this case, the institution would play a repressive role where 'its highest function is to do as little harm as possible' (Longley, 1974, p. 207). The text claimed, positively, that the object of relief practice was to 'administer relief so as to offer the minimum of discouragement to the formation by the poor of provident and independent habits' (Longley, 1874, p. 198; see also pp. 139, 143, 207). The institution could play a more positive educative role if relief was administered according to some 'definite principle' so as 'to encourage providence' (Longley, 1874, p. 195). This emphasis on a positive, educative role already establishes one important difference between Longley and the strategy of 1834.

The Longley report carefully specified the means by which an educative end could be attained. Poor law relief practice should rely on two instruments: first, a greatly extended use of the already traditional instrument of workhouse test; and, second, a new instrument in the form of published codes of rules specifying the terms on which relief could be obtained.

To begin with the familiar, the Longley report insisted that the proper end of relief practice 'can be fully reached only by that system of administration which is commonly known as the "workhouse system"' (Longley, 1874, p. 139). Thus Longley could pose as a traditionalist who advocated the master remedy of 1834 which had subsequently been vindicated by 'the practical experience of nearly forty years' (Longley, 1874, p. 139). The workhouse was simply to have a very much larger role under the Longley strategy; the workhouse test after 1834 was for able-bodied men, while the workhouse test after 1874 was for all classes of paupers. Therefore Longley proposed 'an attack upon out-relief which shall have for its object to throw upon the applicant the burden of showing cause why he should be excepted from the rule on indoor relief' (Longley, 1874, p. 207). The Longley report accepted that this required 'the existence of sufficient workhouse accommodation and the maintenance in workhouses of a deterrent discipline' (Longley, 1874, p. 200). But, as the text recognised, this was hardly a problem in 1874 after the wholesale construction of general mixed workhouses.

It was also necessary to remove any uncertainty about the outcome of a relief application and to convince the working class that an application for out-relief would not be granted:

> That which an applicant does not know certainly that he
> will not get, he readily persuades himself, if he wishes for it,
> that he will get; and the poor to whom any inducement is
> held out to regard an application for relief as a sort of
> gambling speculation, in which, tho' many fail, some will
> succeed, will, like any other gamblers, reckon upon their
> own success (Longley, 1874, p. 143).

There was thus an important role for a new and unfamiliar policy instrument, the published code of rules specifying the terms on which relief could be obtained. In each union, relief should be administered according to 'rules of practice which convey to the poor, with clearness, with precision and, above all, with certainty, the measure of their relations with the poor law' (Longley, 1874, p. 143). In the Longley strategy, these rules would prevent applications by establishing a 'knowledge possessed by the poor of the course of practice adopted by the guardians' (Longley, 1874, p. 201).

Rules governing relief practice were not new. In effect, the 1834 *Report* had proposed one master rule against out-relief. But the Longley report's specimen rules were different because they did not formally prohibit out-relief but laid down complex sets of conditions which positively specified the criteria that applicants of a particular class would have to meet if they were to obtain out-relief. For example, these were the specimen rules for 'the disabled class', that is, the aged and infirm:

> No out-relief should be given to applicants of the disabled
> class (being capable of removal to the workhouse):-
> (a) where their home is such that they cannot properly be
> cared for there
> (b) where they are of bad character
> (c) where it appears that they have relatives able or liable to
> contribute to their maintenance, who refrain from doing so
> (d) where they have made no provision for their future
> wants, having been previously in receipt of such wages as to
> allow them to do so (Longley, 1874, p. 205).

In one way there was not much difference between these conditional rules and direct prohibition. Particularly in the case of the rules regarding relief to widows (Longley, 1974, pp. 204-5), the rules were so strict that very few working-class applicants would satisfy the specified conditions and obtain out-relief. But the conditions were very different from direct prohibition since they gave the working class an educative opportunity to reflect on the reasons why an application for out-relief would not be successful. Ideally, the conditions would make the working classes reflect on their own shortcomings: their failure to practise thrift, their deficient sense of family obligation, their dirty and unsavoury homes. At the same time, the conditions were an assurance that virtue would not go unrewarded; after a lifetime of thrift, caring for elderly relatives, and house cleaning, the virtuous would be rewarded with an out-relief dole.

The education of the poor, like all education, would proceed slowly, one lesson at a time. The strategy of 1834 was to compel guardians to change their practice within a few years by issuing orders that were legally binding. But Longley explicitly refused to recommend the issuing of new orders prohibiting out-relief. The strategy of 1874 was to persuade guardians to accept codes of rules after 'ample and timely notice to the poor of definite changes ... in the administration of relief' (Longley, 1874, p. 200). The Longley strategy was necessarily a gradualist strategy because 'abrupt changes of practice bear hardly upon a body of poor who have been educated by a former laxity of administration, to an undue reliance upon poor law relief' (Longley, 1874, p. 201).

The 'principles of 1834' may have been invoked to justify the crusade, but the strategy of 1874 was different from that of 1834. The 1834 *Report* had proposed negatively to deter able-bodied males via the workhouse, while the 1874 Longley report proposed positively to educate the poor via the rules. Furthermore, the Longley outdoor strategy was different from the indoor strategy of classification and treatment which was already being developed in the 1870s. The main difference here is that the 1874 strategy emphasised knowledge *by* the poor, while strategies of classification and treatment emphasised knowledge *of* the poor, and the role of expert auxiliary judgment which was crucial to any attempt at treatment.

The Longley report relegated knowledge of the poor to a subsidiary place. Longley did make proposals that were designed to increase knowledge of the applicant for relief; most notable here were the recommendations for reform of the relieving officer's application and report book which was the primary source of information for relief decisions. But the Longley report maintained that investigation of the pauper could not play a primary role:

> it can scarcely be that any system of inquiry, however minute and elaborate, can cope effectively with the fraud and concealment which are so strongly prompted by the supposed interests of the applicant (Longley, 1874, p. 167).

Moreover, Longley insisted that expert technical judgment should have a very limited place in the relief decision. There was to be no system of 'doctors' papers' entitling individuals to certain benefits; the poor law medical officer might decide, for example, the medicines necessary in a particular case but 'it is for the guardians, and for them alone, to determine whether or not the patient shall receive these necessaries from their hands' (Longley, 1874, p. 190).

If one considers absences as well as presences in the Longley report, there is one other significant indicator of the difference between the 1874 strategy and a treatment strategy. The Longley report was not at all concerned with those who did not apply for relief, those who were refused relief, and those who were struck off the out-relief rolls; the existence of such individuals was a sign of the institution's success because they were all in a condition of independence and it was unnecessary to know more. But in the strategy of treatment, there was always a concern with the problem of 'take up': those who did not apply for relief, or who were denied relief, were a problem for the institution and a sign of its failure. It is significant, for example, that in the 1909 Royal Commission, the Webbs, who were enthusiasts for treatment, initiated a special inquiry into what happened to those who were refused out-relief.

The Longley report therefore defined a crusade strategy for out-relief which differed from the strategy of repressing able-bodied male pauperism proposed in 1834 and, with modifications, implemented by the middle of the century. The out-relief strategy of the Longley report also differed from the strategy of classification and treatment which, as we shall see in the next section, was already being developed as an indoor strategy in this period. When these points have been made, the next question is: how did out-relief practice change from the early 1870s onwards?

The crusade went according to plan in that the emphasis was on voluntarily adopted local rules rather than on legally binding orders. The legal framework of the 1844 and 1852 *Orders* was never modified; it remained perfectly legal to give unconditional out-relief to all classes of paupers except able-bodied men. Instead, the poor law inspectorate persuaded guardians to adopt codes of rules that attached conditions to out-relief. Such codes of rules were, however, never universally adopted; according to the Webbs, rather more than one-third of all unions adopted codes of formal rules (Webbs, 1927-9, vol. 1, p. 444). It must also be presumed that many of these codes of rules were not in the form of sets of conditions. Even the famous Manchester regulations, which were sometimes recommended as a model, did not specify a set of conditions which had to be met before out-relief would be granted to widows or the aged; here, out-relief was to be denied only where 'intemperance' or 'improvidence' was the immediate cause of the relief application (Manchester rules, in Jennur-Fust, 1912, pp. 43–5). The institution, as a whole, never functioned educatively by means of published rules.

Nevertheless, the institution may have educated the poor in a second-best way by means of concrete relief decisions. Even those unions that did not follow explicit published codes of rules often followed implicit rules in their relief decisions. On this issue, the only available resource is Booth's (1894) classification of practice with regard to the aged in 285 unions right at the end of the crusade period.

The Booth tabulation showed that there was a wide variation in practice and therefore the education which the poor received varied according to the union in which they lived. But, in most unions, the poor were gently educated by relief decisions. The common practice was to attach moderate conditions to out-relief, that is, out-relief was given subject to good character, actual destitution, and contributions from legally liable relatives. Of the 263 provincial unions that replied to Booth, a group of 193 unions, or nearly 75 per cent, favoured such policies of moderate restriction (Booth, 1894, p. 19). And ninety unions, almost half the group of 193, did not insist on these conditions in all cases (Booth, 1894, p. 19). Even by the end of the crusade, the institution as a whole was not educating strictly by means of concrete relief decisions.

The Booth tabulation also showed that the unions with 'strict' out-relief practice were not necessarily the unions with the smallest numbers on relief. The virtual complete refusal of out-relief appeared to work in that it was associated with small numbers on relief; only 11 per cent of old persons drew relief in the five provincial unions which effectively prohibited out-relief. But the practice of attaching strict conditions to out-relief appeared not to work in that it was associated with larger numbers on relief than any other policy; 33 per cent of old persons drew relief in the provincial unions which offered out-relief subject to strict conditions (Booth, 1894, p. 19). In the 'strict' unions, there was a trade-off relation between reduction in outdoor numbers and increase in indoor numbers; the group of fifteen 'strict' unions had relatively small numbers of old people outdoors, but relatively large numbers of old people indoors (Booth, 1894, p. 19). Thus 'strictness' of the Longley type apparently did not prevent relief applications; it appeared to have only altered the form in which applicants obtained relief.

The Longley strategy was never implemented. The educative ends of the crusade were never approached by exemplary 'strict' rules or relief decisions, and the apparent results of 'strictness' in a few unions were disappointing. It should not, therefore, be concluded that, because of this 'failure', the crusade was a non-event or a debâcle; the crusade simply turned into a rather different kind of event. The perpetual failure to achieve educative ends allowed a displacement of goals whereby crudely repressive ends were promoted and became predominant. Because the Longley strategy never worked, the outdoor strategy of the crusade was in practice redefined as dispauperisation by any and every means.

The change of goal was reflected in the annual reports in which each poor law inspector surveyed poor law administration in his area. The Longley report had implied that statistical measures of pauperism would not necessarily measure the progress of the education of the poor. But, in the 1870s and afterwards, inspectors routinely assessed poor law administration in their regions by means of simple statistical measures of pauperism – the ratio of all paupers to population and, more especially, the ratio of outdoor paupers to population. Success was identified with small numbers on relief and failure with large numbers on relief. This was the crude logic of practical dispauperisation.

It is possible to analyse the success and failure of the crusade in these terms. Some key figures have been abstracted from the Statistical appendix (Table 4.5, cols I–IV) and are presented in Table 3.1. All the totals in this table give the mean of two (summer and winter) day counts and exclude lunatics and vagrants whose numbers were not affected by the administration of out-relief.

Table 3.1   The crusade

Year	Outdoor paupers		Indoor paupers	
	number ('000s)	per 1,000 total population	number ('000s)	per 1,000 total population
1871	843	37.5	140	6.2
1876	567	23.6	125	5.2
1893	505	17.2	169	5.7

In dispauperisation terms, the crusade was a brilliant short-run success. In five years from 1871 to 1876, the total number of outdoor paupers fell by 276,000 – or some 33 per cent. This reduced the percentage of total population drawing out-relief from 3.8 to 2.4 per cent. Two supplementary points should be made here. First, reductions in outdoor numbers were not achieved at the expense of increases in indoor numbers. From 1871 to 1876, indoor numbers did not increase, but actually declined by 15,000, or some 11 per cent. Those who were struck off the out-relief rolls typically ceased to draw relief in any form. Second, numbers of paupers had fluctuated before 1871, but there was no precedent for a reduction such as was achieved by 1876, when there were only 567,000 outdoor paupers. In the ten years before 1871, outdoor pauper numbers never dropped below 700,000 and in the five years before 1871 numbers were never significantly below 750,000. Average outdoor numbers in the decade before 1871 were even higher; by coincidence, in both the five- and ten-year periods before 1871 an average of 791,000 outdoor paupers drew relief.

After 1876, the central authority's almost unqualified enthusiasm for the restiction of out-relief continued for at least another fifteen years. The first formal sign of a change in central policy came with the circular of 1896 which accepted outdoor relief for the deserving (*Circular*, 11 July 1896, in Local Government Board, Twenty-sixth Annual Report for 1896-7). Two years earlier the Local Government Act of 1894 had changed the poor law electoral franchise and the guardians' property qualification. Thus, the end of the crusade is conventionally fixed in 1893, which was the last year of operation of the old-style institution dedicated to dispauperisation. What success in dispauperisation terms had been achieved by 1893?

Dramatic reductions in the total number of outdoor paupers did not continue after 1876. The number of outdoor paupers in 1893 was actually 16,000, or some 3 per cent, higher than in 1876. But in the years between 1876 and 1893, absolute numbers of outdoor paupers were stabilised at the lower levels reached by 1876. The number of outdoor paupers was never much above 550,000 or much below 500,000 and averaged 542,000 over the sixteen years 1877 to 1892 inclusive. Population increased steadily over this period, so that in relative terms the number of outdoor paupers decreased significantly from 2.4 to 1.7 per cent of population between 1876 and 1893. On the other hand, after 1876, indoor numbers increased significantly, albeit from a small numerical base; by 1893, indoor numbers had increased by 44,000, or 35 per cent since 1876. Therefore, after 1876, the crusade could only be presented as a qualified success in dispauperisation terms.

The aggregate national statistics show a dramatic reduction in absolute numbers on out-relief in the five years after 1871, and a sustained reduction in relative numbers on relief in the next twenty years. This aggregate conclusion raises two questions about the breadth of the changes. First, were the reductions in total numbers achieved by reductions in all pauper classes or by disproportionately large reductions concentrated in one or two pauper classes? Second, were the reductions in total numbers achieved by changes in practice in a large number of unions or by really dramatic changes of practice in a small number?

Throughout the period of the crusade, the two largest classes on relief were the aged and infirm adults who accounted for 44 per cent of all paupers in 1872, and the widows with dependent children who accounted for 25 per cent of all paupers in the same year (see Statistical appendix, Table 4.39). A comparison of percentage rates of reduction of outdoor pauperism shows that neither of these classes was singled out for especially harsh treatment during the period of the crusade. Over all, there was a reduction of 40 per cent in outdoor pauperism between 1871 and 1893. By way of comparison, there was a 39 per cent reduction in the number of widows and children on outdoor relief between 1872 and 1893 (see Statistical appendix, Table 4.20) and there was a 33 per cent reduction in the number of adult non-able-bodied paupers on outdoor relief between 1871 and 1893 (see Statistical appendix, Table 4.23). By implication, therefore, the crusade worked by means of a broad-front reduction in the numbers of all the more important classes of pauper drawing outdoor relief.

If we are going to answer questions about whether, and how, a large or small number of unions was implicated in the crusade, it is first necessary to define the extent of *de facto* severe restrictions of out-relief, that is, restriction of out-relief irrespective of the means by which this was attained. Using the criterion of less than 30 per cent of all paupers on outdoor relief on 1 January 1893, it is possible to define a group of forty-one unions that restricted out-relief. The 30 per cent cut-off point is arbitrary, but it does define a group of unions where out-relief was unusually restricted; on the same basis, nationally, 74 per cent of all paupers were on outdoor relief on 1 January 1893. It must also be emphasised that the 1893 list of 'restricters' includes more or less the same unions as would an 1883, or even an 1873, list of restricters. Few unions lapsed from restriction over these twenty years; for example, the group of forty-one in 1893 includes all but one of thirteen model unions which, according to Chance (1895, p. 82), led the way in restriction. The main changes in the composition of the group of restricters were caused by the addition of latecomers to restrictions; a couple of urban unions such as Birmingham and Reading only seriously embarked on restriction in the 1880s.

To begin with, it must be emphasised that a significant proportion of total population lived in the forty-one unions where out-relief was unusually restricted. Of the 452 unions classified by Booth in 1894 as rural or half rural, only seven unions had less than 30 per cent out-relief. These seven rural unions had a total population of only 154,000 (see Table 3.2). But, of the 170 unions classified by Booth in 1894 as mostly or wholly urban, thirty-four unions had less than 30 per cent out-relief. These thirty-four urban unions had a total population of 4,362,000; around 15 per cent of the total population of England and Wales lived in these urban unions where the availability of out-relief was severely restricted. The proportion of the big city population affected by out-relief restriction was even higher; 3,242,000 lived in London unions and 752,000 in Liverpool, Birmingham, and Manchester unions, where out-relief was severely restricted.

If severe restriction of out-relief was not a marginal phenomenon, what was the role of the group of restricters in the national reduction in

Table 3.2   Unions restricting out-relief

Seven rural or semi-rural unions with less than 30 per cent of
all paupers outdoors in 1893

Union	Population
Brixworth (N'ants)	12,186
Bradfield (Berks)	18,017
Tenterden (Kent)	9,966
Wallingford (Berks)	14,706
Milton (Kent)	24,968
Faversham (Kent)	25,770
Atcham (Salop)	48,346
Total	153,959

Thirty-four urban or semi-urban unions with less than 30 per cent of
all paupers outdoors in 1893

Union	Population
Semi-urban	
Madeley (Salop)	23,114
Preston (Lancs)	143,541
Richmond (Surrey)	41,548
Provincial urban	
Liverpool (Lancs)	156,981
Manchester (Lancs)	145,100
Birmingham (Warwick)	245,503
Gravesend & Milton (Kent)	23,876
Salford (Lancs)	204,522
Reading (Berks)	60,054
Oxford (Berks)	75,308
London	
Bethnal Green	129,312
St George's in the East	45,795
St Saviour's	203,275
Holborn	141,920
Shoreditch	124,009
Stepney	57,376
Whitechapel	74,462
Westminster	37,312
Poplar	166,748
Strand	28,440
St Giles & St George	39,782
Chelsea	96,253
Mile End Old Town	107,592
Camberwell	234,762
St George, Hanover Sq	134,138
Greenwich	165,413
St Pancras	234,739
Hackney	229,542
St Marylebone	142,404
Kensington	166,308
Fulham	188,878
Wandsworth & Clapham	307,500
Paddington	117,846
Hampstead	68,416
Total	4,361,769

Source: Booth, 1894, pp. 58–98.

numbers on relief after 1871? The group of forty-one restricters achieved a proportional reduction in numbers on outdoor relief which was greater than that achieved in England and Wales as a whole. In the period 1871–6, the group of forty-one achieved a 57 per cent reduction in outdoor numbers against a national 35 per cent reduction and, in the period 1871–93, the group of forty-one achieved a 68 per cent reduction in outdoor numbers against a national 37 per cent reduction (Table 3.3). But the dispauperisation record of the restricters was not

Table 3.3   Restriction and reduction in pauper numbers

Forty-one unions with less than 30 per cent of all paupers outdoors (1st Jan. 1893)

Pauper numbers (thousands)

1st Jan.	Outdoors	Indoors	Total population
1871	140	46	} 3,670
1876	61	46	
1893	65	68	4,460

Reduction in outdoor numbers (thousands)

Period	Reduction (thousands)	% reduction
1871–6	80	57
1871–93	94	68

All unions in England and Wales

Pauper numbers (thousands)

1st Jan.	Outdoors	Indoors	England and Wales population
1871	918	168	} 22,706
1876	601	152	
1893	577	207	29,403

Reduction in outdoor numbers (thousands)

Period	Reduction (thousands)	% reduction
1871–6	316	35
1871–93	341	37

Sources: Poor Relief Annual Returns (1st Jan.) BPP. Booth, 1894, pp. 59–99.

such that this group of forty-one unions accounted for a large proportion of the total national reduction in numbers on out-relief during the crusade. The group of forty-one restricters, which included about 16 per cent of national population, accounted for only 25 per cent of the national reduction in outdoor numbers in the period 1871–6 and 28 per cent of the national reduction in outdoor numbers in the period 1871–93. By implication, therefore, the national reduction in outdoor numbers was achieved by broad-front changes in practice in many unions.

If education of the poor did not work, repression of pauperism did work since, in a large number of unions after 1871, most classes of pauper found it increasingly difficult to obtain out-relief; in 1871, 3.8 per cent of population drew out-relief and by 1893, only 1.7 per cent of population drew out-relief (see Statistical appendix, Table 4.5). There were significant changes in outdoor relief practice after 1870, but these changes were of a cruder and coarser kind than those envisaged in the Longley report; the crusade turned into a purge of the out-relief rolls. So, in relief practice, there was a large measure of continuity and development between the outdoor strategies before and after 1870. By the 1860s, outdoor relief to able-bodied men had been virtually abolished; in the 1870s, outdoor relief to all other classes was substantially diminished. Under the new poor law, before 1870, the poor were repressed into assuming responsibility for unemployment and after 1870, the poor were increasingly repressed into assuming responsibility for the other vicissitudes of a working-class life. In practice, the education of the poor, before or after 1870, was a matter of brutal dispauperisation.

Classification and treatment indoors

So far the crusade, or the repression of outdoor pauperism, has been considered as if it were the one and only strategy of the poor law in the 1870s. But the configuration of the institution after 1870 was never so simple, and the trend of poor law expenditure during the period of the crusade from 1871 to 1893 provides a first indication that the repression of outdoor relief was articulated with a new kind of indoor strategy. Some key figures of poor law expenditure have been abstracted from the Statistical appendix and are presented in Table 3.4.

As the crusade progressed, fewer outdoor paupers required doles, so substantial savings were made in the cost of outdoor relief. In five years from 1871 to 1876, the cost of out-relief fell by some 25 per cent, or £903,000; and in the next seventeen years to 1893, during a period of falling prices, the cost of out-relief was easily reduced by a further £390,000. But, between 1871 and 1876, the total cost of all poor relief fell by only 7 per cent, or some £551,000; and from 1876 onwards, despite a falling general price level, total cost rose fairly steadily year by year, except for a short period in the late 1880s.

Table 3.4   Relief expenditure, 1871-93

Year ending March	In- maintenance	Out- relief	Maintenance of lunatics	Loan charges	Salaries	Other	Total
	£	£	£	£	£	£	£
1871	1,525	3,664	746	291	838	822	7,886
1876	1,534	2,761	883	275	943	940	7,336
1893	2,106	2,371	1,393	640	1,567	1,141	9,218

Source: Statistical appendix, Table 4.6.

By 1893, total cost was 17 per cent, or £1,331,000, above the 1871 level.

Total expenditure increased as the cost of building and running poor law institutions rose during these years. The direct cost of 'in-maintenance' was substantially the same in 1871 and 1876; but the indirect costs of indoor relief were already showing an upward trend, even if one excludes the 'salaries' which were in many cases being paid to institutional staff. The cost of maintaining pauper lunatics rose over the five years to 1876, and loan charges would also have risen had it not been for a fortuitous fall in the rate of interest. By 1893, despite a fall in the general price level, the direct and indirect costs of building and running institutions had increased substantially since 1871; 'in-maintenance', maintenance of lunatics, and loan charges had together increased by 62 per cent, or £1,577,000.

Increasing institutional costs after 1870 are an index of the development of a new strategy of classification and treatment for indoor paupers. To understand the nature of this strategy, it is necessary to analyse the architecture of, and the regimes in, the poor law institutions which were built before and after 1870. We can begin by considering the general mixed workhouses which, as we have shown, were built in most unions before 1870. Our examination of the general mixed workhouse will first consider the institutional regime prescribed in those sections of the 1847 poor law *Order* on 'Government of the Workhouse' (1847 *Order*, in Glen, 1898, pp. 264-332); it will then consider the specimen workhouse plans published by the Poor Law Commissioners in 1835 (First Annual Report, Appendix (A), no. 10).

The 1847 *Order* required that indoor paupers be divided into seven classes: aged or infirm men, able-bodied males over thirteen years, boys between seven and thirteen years, aged or infirm women, able-bodied women and girls over sixteen years, all children under seven years (1847 *Order*, article 98, in Glen, 1898, p. 277). Within the workhouse, these classes were to be segregated into different wards, day rooms, and exercise yards. These divisions were neither subtle nor complex; they prescribed the minimum age and sex segregation necessary for the maintenance of 'decency'. No doubt the segregation had the incidental benefit of rendering the workhouse thoroughly uncongenial to those accustomed to family life.

The 1847 *Order* came close to requiring one uniform institutional regime for all seven classes. There was one fixed timetable that laid down the times at which all paupers got up, ate, and went to bed (1847 *Order*, article 102, in Glen, 1898, p. 304). All classes of paupers were to be employed in the workhouse every day of the year except Sunday, Good Friday, and Christmas Day (1847 *Order*, article 112, in Glen, 1898, p. 309). There was to be one standard diet for all classes of paupers, except those exempted by order of the medical officer (1847 *Order*, article 107, in Glen, 1898, p. 316). All classes of paupers were subject to the same restrictions with regard to alcohol or tobacco (1847 *Order*, articles 107 and 121, in Glen, 1898, pp. 306 and 318). There was one formula with regard to temporary leave of absence which applied to all classes of paupers (1847 *Order*, article 116, in Glen, 1898, pp. 313-14).

Thus the 1847 *Order* required a workhouse that would deter all classes of paupers by means of one uniform disciplinary regime whose key instrument was the stereotyped timetable and the divisions marked by 'the ringing of a bell' (Glen, 1898, p. 304) which summoned all paupers to rise, to eat, and to work – always under supervision. Paupers could have been frozen or starved in almost any kind of structure, but, if the strategy was to deter through discipline, it was necessary to have appropriate institutional architecture. It is therefore important to examine the four model plans published by the Poor Law Commission (First Annual Report, Appendix (A), no. 10); these plans are key resources because the Poor Law Commission never issued any other detailed instructions for the construction of union workhouses.

The first of the model plans, designed by Head, was for a freakishly large 'rural workhouse'. Here 500 persons were accommodated in more than fifty single room 'cottages' (15 X 10 feet) arranged in a rectangular court. Less eligibility was secured by applying domestic architectural standards; as the legend explained, 'in the construction of a rural work-house, the height of the rooms, the thickness of the walls, etc. etc., shall not exceed the dimensions of the cottage of the honest, hard-working, independent labourer'. The other three model plans, designed by Sampson Kempthorne, are altogether more interesting. Here two or three hundred paupers were to be accommodated in what might be called 'hub and spokes' structures, because the paupers were accommodated in three or four wings radiating like spokes from a central hub. Here, as we shall see in the next few paragraphs, less eligibility was secured by internal partitioning and division of space.

The 'hexagon plan' for 300 paupers illustrated in Figures 1a-d is representative of the hub and spokes workhouses designed by

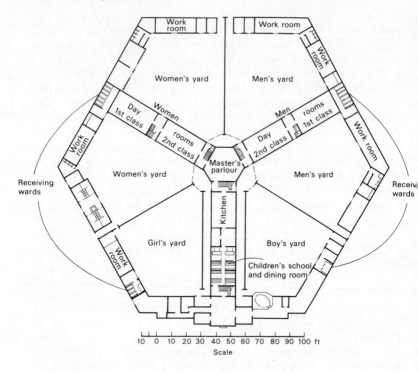

Figure 3   Hub and spokes model: An 1835 model workhouse
(a) Ground plan
Source: Poor Law Commission, First Annual Report, Appendix (A), no. 10

Kempthorne. At the hub of the structure were the workhouse master's quarters which formed a central block directly connected to the pauper accommodation which consisted of two- or three-storey wings with day rooms on the ground floor and dormitories above. The wings radiated out like spokes and were separated by exercise yards. Common facilities like kitchen and dining hall-cum-chapel were grouped together in one of the wings, while work-rooms for the different classes were arranged around the perimeter wall of the institution. The question about this plan must be whether it was appropriate for the segregation of classes and a uniform disciplinary regime as prescribed by the 1847 *Order*.

The hub and spokes structure directly established simpler age and sex divisions than those prescribed in the 1847 *Order*; it was simply designed to break up families into men, women, and children. But, with a few extra partitions, the structure could be easily adapted so that it was suitable for a seven-class division; it would, for example, be easy to separate able-bodied and aged men when the plan already

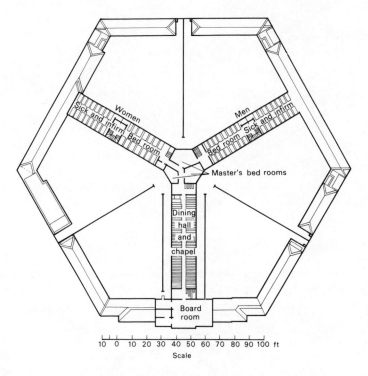

Figure 3   Hub and spokes model: An 1835 model workhouse
(b) First-floor plan
Source: Poor Law Commission, First Annual Report, Appendix (A), no. 10

provided two separate day rooms for 'first' and 'second class' men, and when the plan also provided segregated sleeping areas for 'sick and infirm' and 'other' men. The structure was thus not unsuitable for a seven-class division and much the same point could be made about the possibility of instituting a disciplinary regime.

The hub and spokes structure was biased towards the provision of one regime for all classes; this was the corollary of the physical proximity and interconnection of accommodation for different classes of pauper, all of whom, in any case, used common facilities like dining hall and chapel. The institution of a disciplinary regime might be hindered by the relatively small space allowed for work-rooms around the perimeter of the institutions. But this deficiency would not matter if there were relatively few able-bodied men in the workhouse; other classes of paupers would have been employed mainly on domestic service and not on tasks like stone-breaking which required purpose-built sheds.

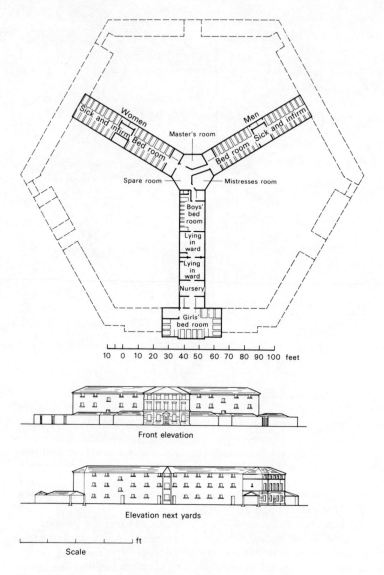

10 0 10 20 30 40 50 60 70 80 90 100 feet

Front elevation

Elevation next yards

├─────┴─────┴─────┤ ft
      Scale

Figure 3   Hub and spokes model: An 1835 model workhouse
(c) Second-floor plan
(d) Architect's view
Source: Poor Law Commission, First Annual Report, Appendix (A), no. 10

In conclusion, the institutional regime prescribed in 1847 and the model plans of 1835 were complementary; together they made possible a particular kind of repressive disciplinary regime. This was discipline without knowledge *of* paupers. The model plans of 1835 and the *Order* of 1847 both limited possible knowledge. The hub and spokes structures were not true panopticons where the paupers were always visible; the paupers were only clearly visible from the master's quarters when they were in the exercise yards. Moreover, the 1847 *Order* did not require the development of a knowledge about paupers. Such knowledge would require documentary support in the form of dossiers on paupers. But the general mixed workhouse only kept a stock-taking record of paupers in the form of an admission and discharge register that serially recorded name, age, and address of those who entered and left the workhouse. The workhouse before 1870 was dedicated to a blind, repressive discipline.

When all this has been said, it is necessary to add some careful qualifications. So far, in discussing the 1847 *Order*, we have considered the one workhouse regime that guardians were legally *required* to establish. But, even without breaking the law, guardians could have instituted differences of treatment under certain terms of the 1847 *Order* which permitted such differences. Guardians were allowed to make concessions about bedtimes and employment for the aged and infirm or for children (1847 *Order,* in Glen, 1898, pp. 304 and 306). The segregation of sexes was qualified when guardians were allowed not to separate aged married couples (1847 *Order*, in Glen, 1898, p. 291). Guardians were also permitted to sub-divide the seven classes according to 'moral character or behaviour or ... previous habits' (1847 *Order*, in Glen, 1898, p. 280).

The extent of deviation from disciplinary uniformity depended on the architecture of the new union workhouses. If the workhouses constructed before 1870 were on the hub and spokes plan, their architecture impeded the provision of different regimes and subdivision of the seven classes. It is significant here, that a special return of 1854 (BPP, 1854, LV) inquiring, among other things, about the subdivision of able-bodied women according to character, produced many replies to the effect that 'the workhouse does not permit this subdivision'.

The specialist literature on poor law architecture claimed that many early workhouses were build on the hub and spokes model:

A large majority of these new workhouses were arranged in accordance with the plans issued by the Commissioners – indeed Mr Kempthorne was employed in connection with a great number of the new workhouses, and they, for the most part, were carried out upon the model plans (Knight, 1889, p. 4).

But, no sources were cited in support of this claim and, of course, many workhouses were built after the early 1840s.

We do not know how many of the pre-1870 workhouses conformed to the model plans and in what ways others may have deviated from the model. These questions cannot easily be answered from central resources, because the available workhouse plans in the Public Record Office are chaotically organised and often undated. No doubt much could be done by painstaking local research. Meanwhile, the only readily available and useful resources are a handful of mid-century workhouse plans and descriptions published in the building trade press: the City of London workhouse (*Builder*, 25 August 1849), Carlisle workhouse (*Builder*, 30 January 1864), West London workhouse (*Builder*, 23 December 1864), Oxford workhouse (*Builder*, 4 February 1865).

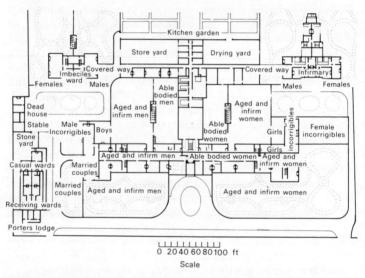

Figure 4   Main block and annexe: a West London workhouse
(a) Ground plan
Source: Builder, 3 December 1864

The fragmentary trade press evidence is interesting even though it covers so few workhouses. Fifteen to thirty years after the model plans and the first wave of workhouse construction, the four descriptions suggest that urban unions were building workhouses of one stereotyped kind. The West London workhouse plan illustrated (see Figures 4a and b) is representative of these mid-century urban workhouses. Two general features are prominent in these plans; first, a large rectangular main block and, second, a number of smaller blocks disposed around the main block.

INTENDED NEW WORKHOUSE, WEST LONDON UNION, IN UPPER HOLLOWAY.—Messrs. Searle, Son, & Yelf, Architects.

Figure 4   Main block and annexe: a West London workhouse
(b) Architect's view
Source: Builder, 3 December 1864

These workhouses were usually dominated by a large main block which was absent only in the City of London plan. The rectangular main block was, in effect, a hub and two spokes, because administration and reception facilities were arranged around a central entrance to the block, and male and female accommodation was provided in two wings on either side of the entrance. The wings were usually 50 feet wide, and day rooms and dormitories were arranged on both sides of a central access corridor which ran the whole length of the building. Different classes of pauper were separated by iron gates set at appropriate intervals across the central corridor. Up to the late 1860s, the wings were simply built as long as was necessary to accommodate the intended number of pauper inmates; thus in West London, the whole main block was 300-feet long, in Oxford 200-feet long, and in Carlisle 250-feet long. The apotheosis of this style of architecture was the Sheffield union proposal to build a main block which was 900-feet long (*Builder*, 2 October 1875).

These workhouse plans always show a number of smaller separate blocks. In this respect they show the breakdown of the physical articulation and connection which was a striking feature of the hub and spokes plan. As early as 1849, the City of London workhouse plan shows a cruciform structure with breaks and open spaces between the main wings. The later plans all show a proliferation of smaller blocks which are separate from, but sometimes connected to, the main block by covered walkways; the infirmary is always separate and the casual ward is often so. The smaller blocks were used to accommodate specific classes of paupers and thus the new form provides the architecture for a greater sub-division of paupers. The West London workhouse, for example, had accommodation for more than seven classes of paupers; the plan provided additional accommodation for casuals, married couples, 'incorrigibles', and the infirm.

In conclusion, these workhouse plans suggest that, by the 1850s and 1860s, urban workhouses were not being built strictly according to the hub and spokes plan of 1835. After thirty years, this model workhouse was beginning to break up; paupers were classified more finely into classes which were increasingly segregated in separate blocks on the one workhouse site. The 1868 official *Memorandum* 'Points to be Attended to in the Construction of Workhouses' (in Smith, 1901, pp. 41–97) brought order and principle into the dispersion of workhouse buildings which was already developing. The recommendations of this memorandum will now be considered.

The 1868 *Memorandum* insisted that it was no longer acceptable to separate the seven classes of the 1847 *Order* within one building. It recommended a finer classification which was to be materially supported by the provision of separate buildings for different classes. In new workhouses, at least eight separate buildings should be provided: entrance building, main building (for able-bodied, aged, and infirm), imbecile wards, school building, sick wards, and isolation wards (1868 *Memorandum*, in Smith, 1901, pp. 42–3). A larger number of separate buildings might well be necessary because 'when the numbers are large, provision should be made, as far as is practicable, for the sub-division of classes' (1868 *Memorandum*, in Smith, 1901, p. 59). Complicated internal partitioning would certainly be necessary within some of the buildings when the *Memorandum* recommended, for example, the classification of infirmary cases into no fewer than fifteen separate groups (1868 *Memorandum*, in Smith, 1901).

If the 1868 *Memorandum* recommended separate buildings on one site, by the end of the century official pronouncements recommended separate buildings on separate sites. As Smith, the Local Government Board architect, observed, by 1900 official permission would not have been given for the construction of an imbecile ward, or a sick ward, as an addition to an existing workhouse, or as part of a new workhouse. By the turn of the century, the official strategy was to remove groups like imbeciles and children to completely separate specialised institutions (e.g. *Circular*, 4 August, 1900; in Jenner-Fust, 1907, p. 564). This strategy implied that the general mixed workhouse would gradually wither away and be replaced by separate specialised institutions which were not recommended in 1868.

However, the 1868 *Memorandum* did not simply rationalise existing construction practice represented, for example, in the West London workhouse already considered. The *Memorandum* of 1868 reflected and recommended a radical change in the ideal size and disposition of the blocks on any site. The *Memorandum* still recommended a 'main building', but it firmly rejected existing construction practice based on one large main block; 'in arranging the buildings of a workhouse, care must be taken to avoid aggregating large numbers of inmates in a single block' (1868 *Memorandum,* in Smith, 1901, p. 44). In plan form, both general purpose and specialised institutions were not to look very different, because they would be built on one of two new architectural models – the 'pavilion system' or the 'domestic system'.

Under the pavilion system, the buildings were divided into separate blocks or pavilions which would each hold a maximum of 200 healthy or 100 sick persons (see Figure 5a). The separate pavilions would be

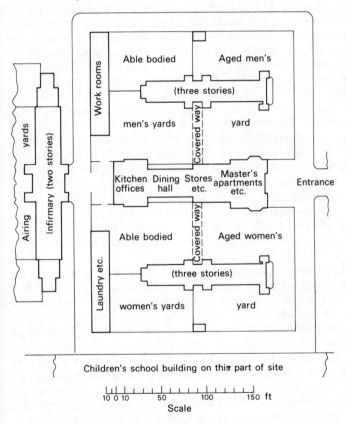

Figure 5   The Pavilion system (a) Ground plan of 1889 model workhouse
Source: Knight's Guide (1889), Diagram II

spaced out in parallel rows up to 100-feet apart; pavilions were never arranged radially at right or acute angles as in hub and spokes structures, and were never as close together as the blocks in mid-century workhouses. The pavilions were completely separate and connected only by walkways which were either open, or covered but cross-ventilated. This form of construction was first used for hospitals; the Herbert military hospital built at Woolwich between 1860 and 1864 was the first English institution built on the pavilion system (Knight, 1889, p. 8; Mouat and Snell, 1883, p. 3). This system was subsequently recommended for other types of institution – such as prisons, barracks, and lunatic asylums. The 1868 *Memorandum* explicitly recommended the use of the pavilion system in workhouse construction; 'it will usually be necessary to sub-divide the several buildings into separate blocks or pavilions' (1868 *Memorandum, in* Smith, 1901, p. 44).

From the early 1870s, there was an approved alternative form of construction, which was sometimes known as the 'villa system' when it was used in institutions for lunatics. Here it will be called the domestic system, because its basic units were buildings 'more in the form of houses than in the form of large ward blocks' (Smith, 1901, p. 34). Inside the poor law, the domestic system was recommended especially, but not exclusively, for the construction of children's homes. The houses were very much smaller than pavilions; the 1904 *Memorandum* 'On the Provision of Grouped Cottage Homes for Children' (in Jenner-Fust, 1907, p. 582) recommended a maximum number of fifteen children in one cottage/house. As Smith, the Local Government Board architect, wrote, 'the prime object is to assimilate the cottage home, as far as possible, to the general working-class dwelling' (Smith, 1901, p. 16). Thus, the 1904 *Memorandum* did not require the provision of plumbed-in washbasins and lavatories upstairs, and the architect Smith opposed such provision on the grounds that the average working-class home did not have such facilities (Smith, 1901, pp. 17-18).

So far, mainly by analysing the 1868 *Memorandum,* we have discovered a new indoor strategy which prescribed a finer classification of paupers in general purpose and specialised institutions which were all now to be built on new architectural models. These changes made it easier to institute different regimes of treatment for different classes of paupers. But, if we have discovered a major displacement in the techniques and objectives of indoor relief after 1870, it must also be emphasised that this displacement does not seem to be reflected in new policy pronouncements by the central authority. There was no modification of the 1847 *Order* which legally governed the indoor relief regime. Even circulars containing general recommendations for changes in regime were only issued late in our period; the first such set of general recommendations came in 1895, with the *Circular* on 'Workhouse

Administration' (*Circular,* 29 January 1895; in Jenner-Fust, 1907, pp. 547–53).

This was partly a matter of practicality when the indoor strategy required new kinds of buildings. It would be pointless to issue new circular recommendations or legally binding orders, if the institutional stock was such that most unions could not carry out the recommendations and would have to be exempted from the terms of the orders. In any case, many changes of regime and deviations from uniformity were possible under the permissive terms of the 1847 *Order* which have already been discussed. It is significant here that the 1895 *Circular* on 'Workhouse Administration' aimed, in part, to 'call attention to' 'frequently overlooked' permissive clauses in the 1847 *Order* and other legislation which allowed sub-division of classes, non-separation of married couples, and variation of the timetable for the aged and the young (*Circular,* 29 January 1895, in Jenner-Fust, 1907, pp. 549–51). The 1896 *Circular* on 'Classification in Workhouses' also began by 'drawing attention to' the provisions of the 1847 *Order* which allowed sub-division of classes (*Circular,* 31 July 1896, in Jenner-Fust, 1907, p. 557).

When circular recommendations were finally formulated in the 1890s, they did unmistakably recommend a departure from disciplinary uniformity. The emphasis on treatment was reflected in recommendations for the employment of specialised technicians who were necessary in any regime of treatment. Thus, an 1892 *Memorandum* on 'Nursing in Workhouse Sick Wards' recommended the employment of paid, trained nurses, rather than the use of pauper inmates to care for the sick (*Memorandum,* April 1892, in Jenner-Fust, 1907, pp. 553–6). The break-up of one uniform regime is reflected in the recommendations for different regimes for different classes and sub-division of classes. Consider, for example, the recommendations for the treatment of the 'respectable' or deserving aged which were made after 1892 and were finally codified in the 1900 *Circular* on 'The Aged Deserving Poor' (*Circular,* 4 August 1900; in Jenner-Fust, 1907, pp. 563–6). The privilege of the 'deserving aged' was to be physical segregation from the 'disreputable', and treatment appropriate to their merits. Thus the aged deserving paupers, as a group, were to have their own day rooms, dining arrangements, and sleeping accommodation in separate cubicles with personal lockers. And the appropriate treatment for this group was a relaxation of discipline; the 'deserving aged' were to have 'privileges' about hours of going to bed and rising, 'liberty' about leave of absence from, and visitors to, the workhouse and an inalienable right to smoke and brew up a cup of tea.

There was a strategy of classification and treatment for indoor paupers, but the tardy policy pronouncements suggest that practice may have changed slowly. How did indoor relief practice change after

1870? The available resources do not allow us to define the chronology, nature, and extent of changes of regime inside the poor law institutions of England and Wales. However, they do allow us to analyse the programme of construction and reconstruction after 1870 and to trace the development of new kinds of institution. We can therefore at least determine whether the architectural pre-conditions for a transformation of indoor relief practice were established by 1914. In this investigation, the first question must be whether unions built institutions on the new architectural models after 1870.

From the mid-1860s, poor law infirmaries, whether attached to workhouses or on separate sites, were usually built on the pavilion system. In the early 1870s, workhouses with large main blocks were still being built. However, the Prestwich union workhouse, near Manchester, shows the pavilion principle already infiltrating the main block; here there was a light airy corridor on one side of the main block (*Builder*, 17 August 1872). And from the early 1880s, the *Builder* provides many descriptions of new workhouses which were virtually all built on the pavilion principle. Subsequent development took the form of a refinement of the pavilion system, with first, a proliferation of special blocks such as 'test' blocks for the able-bodied 'loafer', and second, more partitioning inside the pavilions to create, for example, several separate day rooms within one pavilion. The Greenwich union workhouse at Grove Park is a classic example of the pavilion system in its final developed form (*Builder*, 19 April 1902; see also Freeman, 1904).

To illustrate the difference of the new pavilion-type institutions of the 1880s, a plan of the Holborn union workhouse at Mitcham is given (Figures 5b and 5c). This was not the first workhouse to be built completely on the pavilion principle (*Builder*, 3 March 1883; 30 October 1886), but it is a model since it shows what a specialist poor law architect, like Saxon Snell, was designing on green field sites in the 1880s and 1890s. It is a textbook pavilion structure with its parallel blocks connected by covered walkways.

It is interesting to compare this pavilion structure with the original hub and spokes structure and the intermediate main block structures. A comparison will show show Mitcham represents radical new principles of division applied to the construction of institutions for paupers. The hub and spokes structure relied on division by means of the solid walls which were everywhere – around the perimeter of the workhouse, between the exercise yards, and between the separate classes in the wings. Mitcham workhouse relied on division by means of airy, open space; the high, blank perimeter wall had been replaced by railings and

Figure 5   The Pavilion system (b) Ground plan of Holborn union workhouse
Source: Builder, 23 October 1886

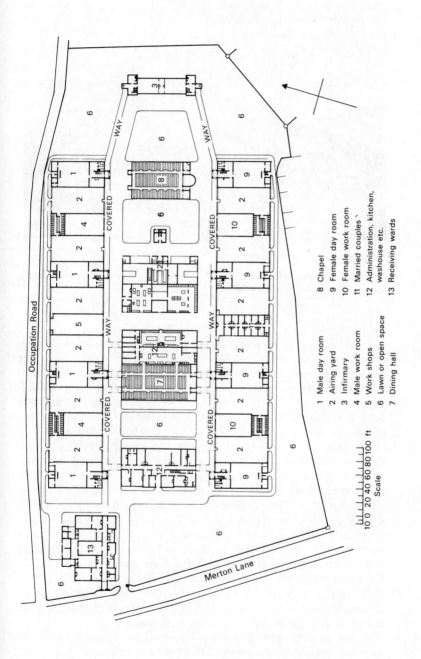

1 Male day room
2 Airing yard
3 Infirmary
4 Male work room
5 Work shops
6 Lawn or open space
7 Dining hall
8 Chapel
9 Female day room
10 Female work room
11 Married couples
12 Administration, kitchen, washhouse etc.
13 Receiving wards

Scale
10 0 20 40 60 80 100 ft

Occupation Road

Merton Lane

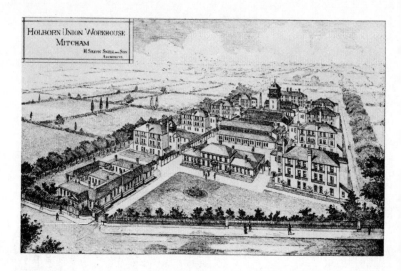

Figure 5   The Pavilion system (c) Architect's view of Holborn union workhouse
Source: Builder, 23 October 1886

the blocks were separated by the open space of lawns and walkways. The old means of division have been replaced by new means of division. Comparison with main block and annexe structures opens up another contrast which concerns the actual divisions established on the Mitcham plan. The pavilions at Mitcham were designed to allow a fine classification of male and female paupers; there were four blocks for males and four for females with one more for married couples. This is all the more striking because many of the groups who had been accommodated in main block and annexe structures were not provided for at Mitcham; there was no accommodation for epileptics, lunatics or children, and only a very small infirmary, clearly intended as a sick bay for inmates of the institution who fell ill. The absence of accommodation for these classes was an index of the degree to which, in London by the 1880s, these classes had already been removed from the general mixed workhouse; although the Mitcham institution was officially described as a workhouse, it could be more fairly described as a home for the aged and infirm. It should also be noted that there was no accommodation for a workhouse master at Mitcham. In this home for the aged, the staff were no longer disciplinary supervisors who must always be present; the staff were now the technicians of treatment who lived out and came in as and when their services were required.

If the Mitcham plan is testimony to the rise of specialised institutions on separate sites, in the poor law, the domestic system was used in the construction of one kind of specialist institution, the children's home. By 1901, fifty-five unions had built cottage homes for children (Smith, 1901, pp. 22-3); most of these grouped up to twenty 'cottages' on one site. The illustration of one such cottage at Bridgend children's home (Figure 6) shows the overgrown domestic scale of such structures. Overgrown is the appropriate adjective when this 'cottage' had two main bedrooms, in size 18 by 15 feet and 18 by 11 feet. But, although the size of the structure was scaled-up, the layout was domestic; the foster-parent slept upstairs in a separate bedroom, sat downstairs in a parlour, and prepared at least some of the 'family' meals in a kitchen.

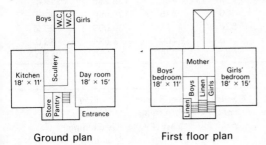

Ground plan   First floor plan

Figure 6   The domestic system: Plan of cottage home for children at Bridgend and Cowbridge Union
Source: Smith (1901), facing p. 18

If the unions did build institutions on the new models, the remaining questions concern first, how much money was spent on constructing new model institutions and reconstructing old ones after 1870, and second, how many new model institutions were built and how was the institutional stock transformed by the early 1900s? Before these questions are answered, it must be shown that constructing and reconstructing institutions according to the norms of classification and treatment was a very much more expensive business than building old-style general mixed workhouses.

It is possible to demonstrate how expensive new specialised institutions were. Smith's book on poor law architecture contains lists of 'generally typical' workhouses and infirmaries built between 1876 and 1900 (Smith, 1901, pp. 39-40). Seven workhouses and eight infirmaries were chosen at random from these lists and the cost of constructing each institution was calculated from the expenditure authorisation series in the Local Government Board annual reports. The results are given in Table 3.5. Cost of land purchase was not usually a major item as the table shows, but, to remove any suspicion that late nineteenth-century institutions were more expensive because land values rose over the nineteenth century, the cost of land purchase has been excluded in the calculation of cost per pauper place.

Table 3.5   Cost of constructing seven workhouses and eight infirmaries, c. 1884–1900

Workhouses

Date	Union	Number of paupers	Land purchase cost (£)	Erection and furnishing cost (£)	Cost per pauper (excluding land) (£)
1894	Mildenhall	115	460	11,000	95.7
1887	Gateshead	916	12,000	55,000	60.0
1899	Wolverhampton	1,230	1,400	138,280	112.4
1897	St Olakes	800	578	195,000	243.8
1898	Steyning	520	75	50,000	96.2
1898	Hastings	730	2,400	49,634	68.0
1899	Hursley	50	1,040	10,850	217.0

Infirmaries

Date	Union	Number of sick	Erection and furnishing cost (£)	Cost per pauper (excluding land) (£)
1894	King's Norton	250	24,000	96.0
1897	Wallingford	60	6,500	108.3
1884	St Saviour's	700	113,163	161.7
1893	Brentford	250	37,800	151.2
1900	Southampton	300	74,340	247.8
1892	Burnley	160	35,500*	221.9*
1898	Hendon	300	95,510	318.4
1882	Leigh	122	10,000	82.0

*Includes land.

By the turn of the century, constructing and fitting out an economy workhouse cost around £70 per pauper place, and a best practice classified workhouse could cost more than £200 per pauper place. Infirmaries were even more expensive, partly because of their more extravagant use of many smaller pavilions and partly because of the expense of medical fixtures and fittings. By the turn of the century, an economy infirmary cost £100 per pauper place, and it was commonplace for constructing and fitting out infirmaries to cost between £200 and £300 per pauper place. The institutions of the 1880s unquestionably cost less to build, but the average cost per pauper place was always very much higher than it had been before 1870. Excluding cost of land purchase, our sample of seven workhouses built between 1887 and 1900 cost an average of £128 per pauper place, and our sample of eight infirmaries built between 1882 and 1900 cost an average of £174 per

per pauper place. Per pauper place, these institutions of the late nineteenth century cost from four to six times as much as the general mixed workhouses of the mid-nineteenth century; eighty-four workhouses built between 1840 and 1854 cost an average of £29 per pauper place and this figure may well have included the cost of land purchase in some or all cases (BPP, 1857–8, XLIX).

In retrospect, pre-1870 workhouses were bargains, but, as chapter 2 showed, large sums of money had been spent before 1870 on building workhouses. In the thirty-five years up to and including 1869, the central authority authorised expenditure of £7,497,000 by guardians for constructing new workhouses and altering existing ones (see Statistical appendix, Table 4.32). Up to 1869, a further £806,000 was authorised for the construction of specialised institutions, mainly by the Metropolitan Asylums Board and Schools Districts (Poor Law Board, 22nd Annual Report, 1869–70). Thus, in the first thirty-five years of the new poor law, construction expenditure averaged £237,000 per annum. As we have seen, this expenditure ensured that most unions acquired a general mixed workhouse that was perfectly adequate by pre-1870 standards.

Nevertheless, in the next generation, after 1870, a very much larger sum of money was spent on constructing and reconstructing institutions to meet the new norms of classification and treatment. In the thirty-five years from 1870 to 1904 inclusive, the central authority authorised expenditure of £23,420,000 by guardians for constructing new institutions and altering existing ones (see Statistical appendix, Table 4.32). Between 1870 and 1904, a further £6,558,000 was authorised for the construction of specialised institutions, mainly by the Metropolitan Asylums Board and the Metropolitan Sick Asylum Districts (Local Government Board, 34th Annual Report, 1904–5). Thus, in the second thirty-five year period of institutional construction and reconstruction, expenditure for these purposes averaged £857,000 per annum. After 1870, guardians spent nearly four times as much per annum on institutional construction and reconstruction as they did before 1870.

Even though new construction was expensive, an expenditure of more than £30,000,000 bought many new buildings. The remainder of this section will be concerned with defining the nature of the great rebuilding after 1870. The immediate question must be: how many new institutions of different types were built and how were existing institutions reconstructed? This question can be answered in a preliminary way by working through the expenditure authorisation series in the annual reports, counting the number of new workhouses and specialised facilities which were authorised. Authorisation is not construction, but the authorisation totals can be taken as a rough guide to numbers of workhouses and specialised facilities built after 1870.

New workhouses are clearly identifiable in the expenditure authorisation series which lists seventy new workhouses between 1870 and
1914 (see Statistical appendix, Table 4.32). This is a relatively small
total which implies that there was no wholesale replacement of
existing workhouses with new ones in the 600 unions after 1870. Put
another way, the conclusion must be that the post-1870 construction
programme was heavily biased towards building new specialised
accommodation. The scale of specialised construction can be defined
in a preliminary way by adding together *all* the authorisations for
specialised accommodation whether in the form of additional blocks
at existing workhouse sites, or in the form of completely new institutions on separate sites. There are no fewer than 902 such authorisations between 1870 and 1914; this total includes 384 infirmary blocks
or separate site infirmaries, 175 children's blocks or separate children's
homes, and 255 casual blocks which would all have been constructed
on existing workhouse sites.

If the authorisation series shows that there was much activity in
building specialised accommodation, it is not possible to define the
nature of the activity from this one resource. The description of each
project in the authorisation series is so brief that it is impossible to
discriminate between the two different kinds of new specialised construction - specialised institutions on separate sites and specialised
blocks on existing workhouse sites. For this reason, a 1908 list of the
number of, and available accommodation in, specialised institutions
separate from existing workhouses is particularly valuable (see Statistical
appendix, Table 4.36). By using this list, and by cross-referring to the
authorisation totals, we can answer questions about the nature of
specialised construction and accommodation.

The 1908 list shows that, nationally, specialised institutions on
separate sites had not replaced the general workhouse; there were only
201 separate specialised institutions in 1908, when there were 682
workhouses (see Statistical appendix, Table 4.36). It must be emphasised,
however, that the 1908 table excludes county or county borough
asylums, which were separate-site specialised institutions, managed
by non-poor law authorities, but used by the guardians who paid for
the maintenance of pauper lunatics in such institutions. As use, rather
than managerial responsibility, is the relevant consideration for our
purposes, the best measure of the development of specialised institutions is obtained by adding together the available accommodation in
the poor law's own specialised institutions, and available accommodation in county asylums. On this basis, in 1908, there was available
accommodation for 59,000 paupers in the poor law's specialised institutions, and available accommodation for approximately 90,000 pauper
lunatics in county and county borough asylums (see Statistical
appendix, Table 4.31, col. III); on the same date, there was available

accommodation for 241,000 paupers in workhouses (see Statistical appendix, Table 4.36). Thus by 1908, 38 per cent of the institutional accommodation available for paupers was in non-workhouse, separate-site specialised institutions. Such institutions were well developed by 1908 but, with over half the indoor paupers still in workhouses, the poor law, nationally, was still nowhere near the first-best solution of accommodating most paupers in specialised institutions on separate sites.

Institutions called 'workhouses' dominated the institutional stock in 1908, as in 1870, but a comparison between the 1908 list and our tabulation of the authorisation series shows that the 'workhouse' was much modified between 1870 and 1914. As we have seen, the authorisation series up to 1914 shows 384 authorisations for specialised infirmary accommodation, 175 authorisations for specialised children's accommodation, and 255 authorisations for specialised vagrants' accommodation. But the 1908 list of separate-site specialised institutions shows only forty-three separate infirmaries, forty-nine grouped cottage homes, and no specialised institutions for casuals. It is impossible to obtain a precise result by subtracting the second set of totals from the first; the total number of authorisations includes the construction of 1909 to 1914 and a few authorised but unbuilt facilities, while some unions may have built more than once for a particular class. However, ignoring these complications, subtraction suggests that approximately half the 600 unions built additional infirmary blocks at the workhouse, rather less than half built additional casual blocks at the workhouse, and around one quarter built additional children's blocks at the workhouse. In this way, the institutional stock of workhouses was modified but hardly transformed to satisfy completely the requirements of classification and treatment. It is probable that the addition of extra pavilions only brought many of the oldest workhouses up to the best practice standards of the 1850s and 1860s when, as we have seen, new workhouses typically featured blocks for the infirm, children, and casuals that were disposed around the main structure.

The final point that should be emphasised is that the development of the poor law's own specialised institutions on separate sites was geographically very uneven. Before 1870, general mixed workhouses had been built in almost every urban and rural union. After 1870, the poor law's own specialised institutions on separate sites were built in the big cities – and especially in London. By 1908, in London, there were ninety-three non-workhouse institutions and fifty-one workhouses, while, in the whole of the rest of England and Wales, there were 108 non-workhouse institutions and 631 workhouses (see Statistical appendix, Table 4.36). Again it must be remembered that the non-poor law managed county or county borough asylums played an important role in the provinces. But, even when this accommodation for approximately 90,000 pauper lunatics is taken into account, in the provinces there was available accommodation for only 112,000 paupers in separate-site specialised institutions (see Statistical appendix, Table 4.36). London alone had accommodation for 59,000 paupers in its broad range of poor law-managed specialised institutions (see Statistical appendix, Table 4.36). Thus, 53 per cent of all available accommodation in specialised institutions was in London.

In conclusion, therefore, the first-best solution of specialised institutions on separate sites was only approached in London which had its own peculiar arrangement for financing poor law institutions from the pooled funds of the London unions. London had almost half its indoor paupers lodged in a comprehensive range of non-workhouse institutions (see Statistical appendix, Table 4.36), and this undoubtedly meant that London was approaching the point where its 'workhouses' were functioning as specialised institutions for the aged and infirm. Elsewhere, by adding pavilion blocks at existing workhouse sites, a second-best solution was gradually approached. By this very expensive policy of make do and mend, provincial unions, especially those provincial unions outside the big conurbations, simultaneously met the requirements of population increase which pushed them towards workhouse extension, and the requirements of classification and treatment which pushed them towards the reconstruction of workhouses. In this context, perhaps the fatal weakness of the pavilion system was that it lent itself so well to the piecemeal modification of existing institutions with the addition of extra pavilions.

Our conclusions may be qualified by local study of changes in regime inside poor law institutions, but it is unlikely that they will be undermined by any such local study. After all, our basic conclusion is that the architectural prerequisites for a transformation of regime were not satisfied. Thus, a study of construction patterns shows that the strategy of classification and treatment was not triumphant indoors. Relief practice indoors was not transformed but modified by a patchwork series of concessions to classification and treatment.

Treatment outdoors

After 1870, the configuration of the poor law becomes complicated because the institution operates two distinct strategies. Outdoors after 1870, there is the strategy of the crusade which aims to educate the poor and degenerates into a repressive purge of all classes on out-relief. Indoors after 1870, there is the strategy of classification and treatment which works gradually – mainly through a piecemeal modification of existing institutions. Matters are further complicated by the belated appearance of treatment as an outdoor strategy after the mid-1890s.

In the 1890s and 1900s, the central authority very slowly formulated an outdoor strategy of treatment. The aged and infirm and widows with children were the most important groups on out-relief; taking indoor and outdoor relief together, these groups accounted for nearly two out of every three paupers in the 1900s (see Statistical appendix, Table 4.39). New recommendations about out-relief to the aged were made in circulars of 1896 and 1900 (*Circular*, 11 July 1896, in Local Government Board, Annual Report, 1896-7; *Circular*, 4 August 1900, in Jenner-Fust, 1907, pp. 563-6). But new recommendations about out-relief to widows were not formulated until 1910 (*Circular*, 18 March 1910, in Jenner-Fust, 1912, pp. 46-59). This 1910 circular on 'The Administration of Out-Relief' contained the first generalised formulation of a new outdoor strategy.

By examining these policy pronouncements of 1896 to 1910, we can define the nature of the new strategy. The next few paragraphs will show the new strategy recommended, first, that out-relief should be used as a treatment in some cases and second, that a new kind of 'adequate' out-relief should be given where out-relief was appropriate.

In the case of the aged, out-relief should be granted in recognition of past, 'decent' and 'deserving' lives. The 1900 *Circular* (in Jenner-Fust, 1907, p. 564) therefore proclaimed:

> The Board consider that aged deserving persons shall not
> be urged to enter the workhouse at all unless there is some
> cause which renders such a course necessary, such as
> infirmity of mind or body, the absence of house accom-
> modation or of a suitable person to care for them, or some
> similar cause, but that they should be relieved by having
> adequate outdoor relief granted to them.

In the case of young widows with children, out-relief should be granted where it was in the interest of future lives. The 1910 *Circular* insisted that 'the interests of the children must always be kept in view' (in Jenner-Fust, 1907, p. 55). It followed that 'outdoor relief should not be given to widows with children unless they and their children are living under proper conditions' (in Jenner-Fust, 1912, p. 55).

In the cases so far considered, the strategy recommended that the guardians should passively adjust the kind of relief offered according to the past or present behaviour of the claimant. In some other cases, the strategy also recommended that the guardians should actively compel an adjustment of behaviour. The key provisions here were those of the 1905 *Relief Order* (26 April 1905, in Jenner-Fust, 1912, pp. 65-71) which was applicable to schoolchildren 'in a state of destitution for want of sufficient nourishment'. This *Order* contained provisions for compelling parents to discharge their 'natural' obligations to their children; when a child was undernourished because of parental neglect, the child should be offered relief on loan and the cost of such relief was then to be recovered from the delinquent parent.

As for the kind of out-relief which should be offered to outdoor paupers, the most obvious novelty was the recommendation of 'adequate' out-relief in both the 1900 and 1910 circulars. It was made clear in the 1910 *Circular* that the requirements of adequacy could not be met simply by paying larger out-relief doles; 'the guardians will, of course, realise that a mere increase of the amount of money granted as relief does not necessarily ensure that these requirements will be met' (in Jenner-Fust, 1912, p. 49). Adequate out-relief was relief that was adequate to the circumstances of the case. A new kind of knowledge of paupers was prerequisite for such relief. Thus, in discussing 'general principles governing outdoor relief' the 1910 *Circular* (in Jenner-Fust, 1912, p. 47) began by insisting,

> It is clear that the first point to be observed in a proper and
> businesslike administration of relief is that the guardians
> should endeavour to acquire a complete knowledge of the
> circumstances and needs of the applicants and should
> inform themselves, by every means in their power, of the
> resources of the applicant, so that they may be in a position
> to form a considered judgment as to the necessities of the
> case and the right mode of dealing with it.

This new strategy was distinct and different from the earlier crusade strategy; the strategy of the 1900s was neither a reversal nor a continuation and development of that earlier strategy. Reversal is quite implausible. The crusade may have in practice represented out-relief restriction, but, as we have seen, the new strategy did not directly reverse this by unreservedly recommending the universal grant of out-relief. Development is superficially more plausible because there are elements of continuity between the strategy of the 1900s and the strategy of the crusade; for example, both strategies emphasised that out-relief was to be a privilege dependent upon deserving behaviour. But such recurrent elements are articulated in strategies that differ fundamentally about the proper ends and means of relief practice. These differences are related to the very different roles that knowledge plays in the two strategies. In the subtle Longley version, the crusade strategy was an educative strategy that sought to promote a knowledge *by* the poor of relief practice; this knowledge might deter applications and modify behaviour. In this strategy of the 1900s, the poor law guardians were to develop a knowledge *of* paupers; this knowledge was necessary to the administration of proper treatment.

It is in this context that the otherwise puzzling 1911 *Relief Regulation*

Order (in Jenner-Fust, 1912, pp. 7–30) makes sense. This *Order* was issued to all unions as a replacement for the 1844 and 1852 *Orders* which up to 1911 continued, in unmodified form, to provide the legal framework governing the grant of outdoor relief. This 1911 *Order* has been completely ignored by recent historians and was neglected by the Webbs who regarded all measures of internal reform in the poor law after 1910 as a poor substitute for the 'break-up of the poor law' which they had advocated in their Royal Commission *Minority Report*.

It must be admitted that, on a first reading, the 1911 *Order* appears to be an unimportant piece of administrative rationalisation, which amalgamated and tidied up the different provisions of the 1844 and 1852 *Orders*. A covering circular sent to the guardians claimed that, in the new order, 'no far reaching changes are proposed and . . . no alteration is made in the broad principles governing the administration of outdoor relief by the guardians' (*Circular,* 29 December 1911; in Jenner-Fust, 1912, p. 31). This claim was justified in so far as the 1911 *Order* made no radical changes in the classes allowed out-relief, or in the terms upon which different classes might obtain relief. On these matters, there were only changes in emphasis and form of words about out-relief to the aged and to the unemployed persons who earlier orders had referred to as able-bodied men.

Under article two of the 1911 *Order* (in Jenner-Fust, 1912, p. 10), those who were infirm through old age were explicitly and specifically excluded from any general prohibition on out-relief. But, by ignoring the question of relief to the non-able-bodied, both the 1844 and 1852 *Orders* had implicitly taken up exactly the same position. More significantly, under article eleven of the 1911 *Order* (in Jenner-Fust, 1912, p. 26), *all* unions could now offer out-relief with a labour test to the unemployed man and his family. But before 1911, such out-relief was perfectly legal in a clear majority of the poor law unions under the 1852 *Order*; such relief was simply, in practice, unobtainable in almost every union, as chapter 2 showed. The departmental committee, which drafted the 1911 *Order*, did not envisage that practice would change significantly (see Jenner-Fust, 1912, pp. 5 and 29). Moreover, the central authority, under the 1911 *Order*, obtained the formal power to control any board of guardians which got out of line; under article nine of the 1911 *Order* (in Jenner-Fust, 1912, p. 24), the central authority could order any board of guardians to close its labour yard and stop out-relief to the unemployed 'at any time'.

If access to out-relief was hardly changed by the 1911 *Order*, the kind of out-relief offered was dramatically changed by the new *Order*. This *Order* established a new legally binding framework which would oblige guardians to acquire that knowledge of outdoor paupers which was essential to the operation of an outdoor strategy of treatment. The new framework was established by three key provisions in the

1911 *Order*: first, and most importantly, the provision for the obligatory, universal use of 'case papers'; second, the rules about the regular review of out-relief cases; and, third, the provisions that redefined the role of the poor law medical officer. These provisions will now be outlined and their significance explained.

Under article five of the 1911 *Order* (in Jenner-Fust, 1912, pp. 18-24), guardians were obliged to keep 'case papers' on all paupers. The case paper was a form which was filled in by the relieving officer who investigated the case and was then presented to the guardians in up-to-date form 'on each occasion on which the case is considered by them' (1911 *Order,* in Jenner-Fust, 1912, p. 18). The case paper recorded information about claimants under stereotyped headings – name, age, family, condition of home, length of residence, occupation, earnings, etc. (1911 *Order,* in Jenner-Fust, 1912, p. 19). Similar kinds of information had hitherto been recorded in the relieving officer's application and report book. But it was not easy to cross-refer between different applications by the same individual, when the application and report book was a ledger that serially recorded all applications. The successive entries on one case paper allowed the history of the case to be seen at a glance. It was recommended that the case papers on the members of one family should be kept together in one file (*Circular,* 18 March, 1910, in Jenner-Fust, 1912, p. 53), and thus the guardians would acquire a dossier of information on each client family.

By means of case papers filed in family dossiers, the poor law would, for the first time, acquire a systematic knowledge of those on outdoor relief. Those on relief would cease to be 'paupers' or objects for repression and become so many 'cases' or objects for treatment. Each case would be defined by and exist in a type of systematic documentation whose paradigm has always been the medical record. The *Circular* (29 December 1911, in Jenner-Fust, 1912, pp. 32-3) accompanying the 1911 *Order* was explicit about the rationale for such documentation:

> the information acquired will enable the guardians to pro-
> vide such treatment as may be appropriate to the particular
> case.

A quasi-clinical knowledge of outdoor paupers was necessary to a new strategy of treatment.

The 1911 *Order* also introduced rules requiring that all out-relief cases be reviewed by the guardians at regular intervals. Hitherto, most unions had tended to have a category of 'permanent' outdoor paupers, mainly young widows and old people whose relief entitlement was more or less automatically renewed so that they drew relief continuously for long periods. Now, such cases would have to be regularly reviewed.

Under article six of the 1911 *Order* (in Jenner-Fust, 1912, pp. 20-1), ordinary out-relief cases were to be first reviewed after six weeks on relief and subsequently reviewed every fourteen weeks if they remained on relief. Under article eleven of the 1911 *Order* (in Jenner-Fust, 1912, p. 26), the cases of unemployed men in the labour yard were to be reviewed every fortnight. At every review, the relevant case papers had to be laid before the guardians (1911 *Order*, in Jenner-Fust, 1912, p. 18).

The provision in the 1911 *Order* for regular review of outdoor cases is interesting, because this practice had also been recommended in the crusade of the 1870s. Then, it was a negative part of a strategy of dispauperisation: regular review would allow unions to stop paying out-relief where it was no longer necessary. In the 1900s, regular review was a positive part of a strategy of treatment: the 1910 *Circular* (18 March 1910, in Jenner-Fust, 1912, p. 48) explained that regular reviews allowed alteration of treatment according to changes in the circumstances of the applicant. There was no presumption that this 'alteration of treatment' would necessarily take the form of a refusal of out-relief. Thus provision for a regular review of cases was incorporated as an integral part of a flexible policy of treatment.

Finally, the role of the poor law medical officer was significantly changed by the 1911 *Order*. Under article four (1911 *Order*, in Jenner-Fust, 1912, p. 16), the poor law medical officer was required to examine applicants and provide a 'medical certificate' in all cases where applicants obtained out-relief on grounds of infirmity. Thus, in adjudicating on such cases, the guardians would have before them a case paper and 'a written statement of a medical officer showing the nature of the disability in a particular case' (1911 *Order*, in Jenner-Fust, 1912, p. 10). This provision was to be applied to all the infirm, including the aged who obtained out-relief on grounds of infirmity. Local authorities protested that, in this case, one in three paupers would have to obtain doctors' papers, and the central authority relented and finally exempted the infirm and aged from the conditions of article four (*Circular*, 29 December 1911, in Jenner-Fust, 1912, p. 32).

Provision for medical certificates is significant because it represents the incorporation of an expert auxiliary judgment in the relief decision. The medical officer's expert technical knowledge was to be brought in, as and when necessary, to judge the appropriateness of the poor law's classification of the case and the success of the treatment. The 1911 *Order* went as far towards accommodating expert auxiliary judgment as was possible in an institution dedicated to the relief of only that group of the infirm who were destitute in the technical sense that they were unable to pay for appropriate medical treatment. It established a kind of joint decision and division of responsibility which the drafting committee (in Jenner-Fust, 1912, p. 17) described as follows:

the function of the medical officer is to declare the
existence of a particular disability and its degree; it is for
the relieving officer to furnish the guardians with the
information necessary to enable them to determine whether
the case is one that should receive relief from the poor
rates.

If a strategy of classification and treatment for outdoor paupers was formulated after 1896, how did out-relief practice change before 1914? The official statistics on pauper numbers and cost provide a preliminary overview of out-relief practice in this period.

In a number of respects, the official statistics show that out-relief was of diminishing relative importance after 1897. First, outdoor numbers did not increase steadily but population did, so there was a small decline in the proportion of population obtaining outdoor relief; in 1897 the proportion was 17.1 per 1,000 of population and in 1910 the proportion was 15.2 per 1,000 (see Statistical appendix, Table 4.5). Second, outdoor numbers did not increase steadily but, even if casuals and lunatics are excluded, indoor numbers did. Thus, the balance between outdoor and indoor relief shifted against outdoor relief; in 1897, there were 2.9 outdoor paupers for every one indoor pauper and in 1910, there were only 2.0 outdoor paupers for every one indoor pauper (see Statistical appendix, Table 4.5).

It is probably more important to emphasise that, in terms of total numbers and cost, out-relief practice does not change significantly before 1910. The number of outdoor paupers fluctuated in a range between 490,000 and 540,000 (see Statistical appendix, Table 4.5), while the average weekly dole per pauper increased slightly from 1‥11¼d in 1897 to 2‥4½d in 1910 (see Statistical appendix, Table 4.6). There were significant changes in practice after 1910, but these were the corollary of social reform measures outside the poor law. A dramatic reduction in the number of outdoor paupers after 1910 is associated with the introduction of old-age pensions in 1909 and, more especially, the removal of the pauper disqualification attached to such pensions before January 1911. A total of 122,415 persons in receipt of poor relief on 31 December 1910 subsequently received old-age pensions and ceased to be chargeable to the poor law during the four weeks ended 29 January 1911 (see Statistical appendix, Section F, footnote 8).

If the poor law statistics do not show any transformation of out-relief practice in terms of numbers and cost before 1910, this is not decisive because it is not clear that the new strategy required changes of this sort. The central authority pronouncements, as we have seen, did not directly recommend a shift towards outdoor relief and an expansion in the numbers on such relief. The 1900 *Circular* (4 August

1900, in Jenner-Fust, 1907) acquiesced in the *status quo* in so far as it was already 'commonly the practice' to give out-relief to the deserving aged. Nor did the central authority pronouncements simply recommend larger doles. As we have seen, 'adequate' relief was not identified with larger doles. It was not so much the quantity of out-relief but the quality of out-relief as a treatment which was the prime concern in the new strategy.

In any qualitative changes, the key technical instrument was the case paper. The extent of case paper use is undoubtedly the best single measure of the development of the new strategy; without case papers, the new strategy was simply not viable in relief practice. The 1911 *Order* requiring guardians to keep case papers only came into force in 1912 and thus compulsion came too late to have a significant effect on pre-1914 relief practice. Before they were made compulsory, case papers were used by only a very small number of unions. They were first introduced in Paddington union in 1890, and subsequently voluntarily adopted in Eastbourne, Eccleshall Bierlow, Kensington, Bethnal Green, Bristol, and 'some few other unions' (see Webbs, 1927-9, vol. 11, p. 725). Clearly, therefore, treatment never amounted to much in outdoor practice before 1914 and there was much slower development of treatment outdoors than of classification and treatment indoors.

The general conclusion must be that things did not, as the Webbs supposed, increasingly hang together in the poor law of the early twentieth century. Early in the crusade, from 1871 to 1876, the repression of outdoor pauperism had its moment of triumph which was marred because the developments of this period represented the failure of more ambitious educative aims. By the 1900s, treatment was beginning to qualify, but did not replace, the repression of pauperism in outdoor relief practice; even in policy pronouncements, selective repression was still alive and well when, for example, there was virtually no dissent from the repressive assumption that the poor law should assist the smallest possible number of able-bodied men. Although there was no necessary connection between outdoor repression and indoor classification, the two were in practice intertwined. The repression of outdoor pauperism was carried furthest in the big cities and especially in London; no fewer than thirty of the group of forty-one 'restricters' were London unions. Elsewhere, the indoor strategy of classification and treatment developed slowly; by the mid-1900s, indoor classification had made great advances but still did not clearly dominate indoor relief practice. Therefore, in the early twentieth century, there was not one dominant strategy; the three strategies differentiated in this chapter were intertwined in an increasingly complex relation which defined the poor law.

September 1979

Appendix   (Re)writing social history

This appendix explains why the previous chapter's alternative analysis of the poor law does not use the new conceptual frameworks which have recently been proposed – and which could be used – for (re)writing the history of an institution like the poor law. The question will be answered by critically considering the two currently available models for such a (re)writing: first, the English new model which uses sociology and especially the concept of social control; and, second, the French new model which uses the conceptualisation of a technology of power developed in Michel Foucault's recent texts, especially in the text *Discipline and Punish* (Foucault, 1977). This appendix will argue that both models are an unsatisfactory basis for any rewriting of social history, and, more especially, of poor law history.

Social control

Recent English social historians have tried to establish a social history to sociology relationship of the sort that the new economic historians have established between economic history and economics. Since sociology is not a unified theoretical field containing large slabs of formally interconnected theory, social historians have eclectically borrowed individual concepts. Social control has recently been promoted by Donajgrodzki as a strategic concept that promises 'a broadened perspective on the question of order in society' (Donajgrodzki, 1977, p. 9). Generally, the concept encapsulates the sociological supposition that 'social order is maintained not only, or even mainly by, legal systems, police forces and prisons, but is expressed through a wide range of social institutions, from religion to family life, and including, for example, leisure and recreation, education, charity and philanthropy' (Donajgrodzki, 1977, p. 9).

According to Donajgrodzki's (1977, pp. 9-15) own brief history of the concept, it has been used in a bewildering variety of ways in different sociologies. The concept has been used at a 'micro' level in the analysis of individual institutions and small-scale social systems, although it is also used in the interpretation of 'macro' social processes. At a macro level, the concept has been used in conservative sociologies that presuppose social consensus and in radical sociologies that presuppose social conflict. Generally, it has been argued that deviancy necessitates social control, but some radical sociologists have recently argued that social control creates deviancy. The control mechanism itself has been

variously identified as an internal ideal restraint within the individual
agent (Ross, Landis, Durkheim) and as an external, material, institutional restraint (Parsons).

To complicate matters, social historians have not borrowed one of
these theoretical definitions and consistently used it at one level of
application; they have used very different concepts of social control in
their analyses and definitions of substantive problems. Two recent
articles, by Hay and Brown, illustrate this point. Hay's (1978) article
considers 'employers' attitudes' to social policy between 1900 and
1920, while Brown's article considers the restrictions and obligations
attached to the welfare benefits introduced in the 'modernisation of
social policy', 1890 to 1929.

For Hay (1978, pp. 108-9), social control equals the conscious con-
spiracy of the ruling classes to retain power:

> Here the term 'social control' is used solely to encompass
> the activities, actions and influence of the ruling class in
> Britain by which they attempted to retain the existing
> social basis of social relationships. It is used throughout to
> apply to conscious action.

The emphasis on conscious action is reinforced, for example, by a
quotation from a 1911 cabinet paper on industrial unrest: 'some effort
should be made to maintain control' (Hay, 1978, p. 109). This leads on
to a study of employers and welfare which comes as something of an
anti-climax because Hay cannot find much evidence of conscious con-
spiracy among the fraction of the ruling class which he terms 'employers'.

Brown takes a very different Durkheimian definition of social control as 'the exercise of authority backed by sanctions to conform to
rules'. Here social control is an unconscious meaning that is immanent
in the legislation and bureaucratic rules of a welfare state. As Brown
says explicitly, 'in places any study of social control moves into the
area of largely unacknowledged motives and unspoken assumptions'
(Brown, 1977, p. 129). This definition leads on to a neat study of the
nature of the legal requirements and disqualifications built into Edwardian old-age pensions and social insurance legislation. The concept of
social control is used to draw attention to the restrictions which are in-
separable from the expanded social rights granted by such measures,

> The rights or entitlements in legislation cannot be separated
> from the restrictions, obligations and disqualifications.
> Both form part of a code of authoritative rules (Brown,
> 1977, p. 126).

The problem with the concept of social control is not that it has many meanings in sociology or social history. The different definitions and usages represent coherent choices between various options available in the sociological field. The problem is that the general sociological field is such that none of the possible options is viable.

To begin with, social control enters as a possible explanation after one kind of general problem has been posed in conservative and radical sociology or in orthodox Marxism. All these theories pose a problem about the general conditions necessary for the persistence, or revolutionary transformation, of some kind of social totality called society or capitalism. But it is difficult to solve such a problem without making a theory to reality slide. Orthodox Marxism can be used to illustrate this point. At a conceptual level, the Marxist social totality is blown apart by the principle of the contradiction between the forces and relations of production. Few Marxist social theorists can then resist the apparently obvious corollary that contradictions must tend to blow apart real capitalist social formations. But why should theoretical necessity establish real necessity? And why should real connections and sequences mimic theoretical sequences? Such mimicry can only be established by sleight of hand in a theory which sets itself up ambiguously between theoretical and real poles.

The discovery of this sleight of hand discredits the whole functionalist and empiricist problem situation which requires social control as a solution. Furthermore, social control is not an exemplary solution for a bad problem. This will become obvious if we consider the options about who controls whom.

Donajgrodzki or Hay define the controlling social group variously and vaguely as the 'rich', the 'ruling classes' and the 'employers' as a fraction of the ruling class. The basic problem here is that all these controlling groups have an essential identity in the form of a set of attributes, interests, and capacities that pre-date their entry into any substantive power relation. In this respect, the 'ruling class' is just like economic man, that is to say, it is another self-constitutive subject. Such a theoretical point of departure sets up familiar problems. The discourse easily becomes preoccupied with working out the implications of the existence of a subject and with discovering what is there in the beginning. This development is most painfully obvious in the Hay schema of a 'dialectical relationship' of challenge and response between the ruled and the ruling classes.

The emphasis on conscious control in Donajgrodzki and Hay creates further specific problems. As Donajgrodzki admits, nineteenth-century contemporaries thought in social control terms; 'magistrates, policemen, employers, philanthropists, clergymen, educators, and civil servants often expressed views and attitudes rather like those of [the sociologists] Ross or Landis' (Donajgrodzki, 1977, p. 16). This is to admit that social control analysis is merely a reinscription of nineteenth-century analyses. The only practical difference seems to be that recent champions of the concept usually have radical doubts about who profits from social control. In historiography, we are all destined to write commentaries, texts about texts, and discourses upon discourses, but it is obviously pretty hopeless if all we can do is reinscribe earlier discourses.

The problem, however, is not simply the particular identity of Hay and Donajgrodzki's naïvely material conscious subject, the ruling classes. Brown goes to the other extreme and introduces an ideal subject in the form of an unconscious meaning immanent in legislative-cum-bureaucratic rules. This solves nothing, and really changes nothing, since it simply redefines the attributes of the subject and relocates them in an ideal structure rather than in material agents. The problem is the constitutive subject in social control theory, not the definition of the identity of that subject in particular social control theories.

At the end of this rather abstract argument, it is important to insist that the introduction of a subject practically limits the analyses of these social historians which are impoverished in a number of significant respects. By way of example, consider Hay and Donajgrodzki's treatment, or, more exactly, their non-treatment, of the training of social agents and the forms in which social control is exercised.

Analysts of social control presuppose that individuals and institutions can be expressive of social control. Donajgrodzki recognises the implication is that 'controllers and the controlled are, as it were, trained to their roles' (Donajgrodzki, 1977, p. 15). But, in this literature, there is no detailed discussion of how this amazing feat of training is achieved; in Hay and Donajgrodzki's class war, the soldiers apparently never have to go through rifle drill. Perfectly trained individuals are miraculously produced when the attributes of a general theoretical subject are speculatively projected on to, and realised in, concrete historical subjects. Thus social control theory does not require any specification of training procedures.

Even more notably, social control analyses neglect the question of the forms in which social control is and can be exercised. Hay only commits himself to the unspecific generality that 'certain forms of control seem specific to certain social formations or stages of society' (Hay, 1978, p. 110). Donajgrodzki suggests there was a general transition in the nineteenth century away from control through personal relations and towards control through formal institutions (Donajgrodzki, 1977, pp. 21-2). However, this only gives the game away. Donajgrodzki is simply relocating the attributes of the subject in the social structure rather than in the individual agent. As these attributes always exist in a relation of expression, the question of the form in which social control is exercised, is not and cannot be a problem.

Techniques of punishment

Michel Foucault's (1977) text *Discipline and Punish* is immediately interesting because it is immune to criticism of the sort that damages social control theory. First, Foucault's problem is not the functionalist sociological one about the conditions of persistence, or transformation, of a social order. This text's problem is to conceptualise the different ways in which power can be exercised. Second, Foucault's analysis does not set up constitutive subjects that exist prior to their entry into power relations. In this text, subjectivity is defined by the power relations themselves because the occupant of a particular place in an apparatus necessarily acquires a certain identity; this is true, for example, of the prisoner in his cell and the warder in his watch tower. Third, Foucauldian analysis does not neglect the question of the material apparatus and the forms of control. On the contrary, this text is preoccupied with analysing the significance of timetables, cell systems, examinations, Black Marias, and so forth. If power is about 'who does what to whom', Foucault is the first analyst of power to put 'does what', and the question of the technology of power, in a privileged and primary place.

According to *Discipline and Punish*, we live in a 'disciplinary society' which is the result of a 'historical transformation' that took the form of 'the gradual extension of the mechanisms of discipline through the seventeenth and eighteenth centuries, their spread throughout the whole social body' (Foucault, 1977, p. 216). A whole series of institutions form a 'carceral archipelago' spread out across our society. All the institutional islands of the archipelago are alike in that they use some of the 'carceral methods', if not the compact prison model; thus 'the prison is like a rather disciplined barracks, a strict school, a dark workshop, but not qualitatively different' (Foucault, 1977, p. 233). In this way, Foucault at least comes close to proposing that the modern age has one simple unitary meaning; there is a universal disciplinary mechanism of the modern age which is a kind of late twentieth-century, technical, non-transcendental substitute for the spirit of the age. This is nicely ironic when Foucault has always been so hostile to any history of ideas concerned with the mentality or the spirit of the age.

If *Discipline and Punish* avoids the elementary traps that ensnare social control theory, the Foucauldian alternative is incredible in so far as it ends up making wild claims about a mechanism of the age. The obvious question is: why does the analysis miscarry in this way? The answer to this is that *Discipline and Punish* makes a schematic analysis of stages of punishment and the over-simplifications of this schema are not contained and held in check because the text's account of modern disciplinary techniques is radically flawed. These points will now be developed.

In France, and more generally in Europe, since early modern times, Foucauldian analysis discovers 'three ways of organising the power to punish' (Foucault, 1977, p. 130). These stages are differentiated, first, in terms of how the body figures as point of application or object of punishment and, second, in representational terms, according to what, how, and for whom punishment signifies. Stage one was torture and hanging which survived into the late eighteenth century (Foucault, 1977, pp. 32-69). Such punishments directly marked the body with public torture of the condemned finally manifesting the sovereign power harmed by the crime. Stage two was late eighteenth-century penal reform (Foucault, 1977, pp. 73-120) which sought in a novel way to insert punishment completely into the element of representation so as to construct a 'theatre of punishment'. The aim of this theatre was to prevent offences against society by putting representational obstacles before the idea of crime. Stage three was inaugurated in the nineteenth century by the proliferation of modern disciplinary institutions which did not employ either marks upon the body or signs; instead, such institutions operated 'methods of training the body' (Foucault, 1977, p. 131) with the aim of correcting behaviour. The representation necessary to the operation of these new methods is a private knowledge whereby the disciplinary authority observes and judges those who are disciplined.

Discipline and Punish develops an interesting concept of the power to punish; this power does not simply punish those who have broken the rules, but also makes an example of somebody. However, Foucault's concept of the variation of such punishment is very schematic. Stage two is clearly labelled as an eighteenth-century penal reformers' 'Utopia' which never practically functioned as a transitional period between stages one and three. Effectively, Foucault sets up a qualified binary opposition with stage one (torture) and stage three (modern punishment) as the key terms which are antithesised. In consequence, *Discipline and Punish* locates one massive transformation from nonmodern to modern punishment around the decade of the 1830s. In this respect, Foucault's history of punishment is similar to his earlier histories of madness (Foucault, 1967) and of clinical medicine (Foucault, 1973) which also presuppose an early nineteenth-century inauguration of modernity after which not very much happens.

What is wrong with such a hypothesis about punishment? To begin with, the schema of the stages is not a hypothesis in the empiricist sense; the schema is a basic analytical device for constructing what happened and, as such, it is immune to 'empirical' qualification and correction. What is wrong with this kind of analytic framework which identifies one big transformation? The answer is that such a framework is a grossly uninformative basis for any analysis concerned with a concrete problem such as what the poor law or the prison system was doing in the nineteenth century; it is not very helpful to presume that these institutions are implicated in the modern stage of punishment and have been doing much the same thing since the 1830s.

Nevertheless, the over-simple schema of the stages could be qualified and redressed, if the text developed a subtle account of the disciplinary techniques which are the content of the modern stage of punishment. At this point, therefore, it is appropriate to consider the *Discipline and Punish* account of the disciplinary techniques.

The techniques of discipline are of two kinds. First, there are what might be called the analytic techniques for organising the time and motion of the individual and for coordinating individuals into a collective mechanism (Foucault, 1977, pp. 135-69); the bodies caught in Foucauldian power relations must go through endless rifle drills, inside and outside the army. The 'means of training' are a second set of techniques designed to ensure that the individual goes through the time and motion sequences which the analytic techniques prescribe as necessary to efficiency (Foucault, 1977, pp. 170-94). Disciplinary training depends upon 'hierarchical observation' or a view of those who are disciplined. Furthermore, it requires a 'normalising judgment' of the individual's performance in the examination which is the characteristic institution of disciplinary training and correction.

The text maintains that the disciplinary techniques are a thoroughly 'disparate set of tools and methods' (Foucault, 1977, p. 26); the bricks and mortar of a cell system, a printed timetable and a drill procedure cannot be smoothly elided as elements in any one universe. The text also supposes that particular institutions pick and mix the available disciplinary techniques; so the techniques apparently have no natural point of unity in a concrete institution or a particular type of institution (Foucault, 1977, p. 26). Nevertheless, and despite various qualifications, the text supposes that the different techniques do relate and hang together in terms of 'coherence of results' (Foucault, 1977, p. 26). In the case of disciplinary techniques, these results are supposed to be so many politically docile and economically useful bodies; 'the disciplines function increasingly as techniques for making useful individuals' (Foucault, 1977, p. 211).

The problem here is the way in which Foucault discursively identifies the essential disciplinary techniques and assures us of their unity in a three-step procedure. First, the text itemises the different disciplinary techniques; it 'map(s) on a series of examples some of the essential techniques that most easily spread' (Foucault, 1977, p. 139). Second, the text introduces the concept of an 'ideal form' of institution which is an assurance that the fragmented techniques can combine together into an ideal totality. Hence a whole chapter (Foucault, 1977, pp. 195-228) is devoted to the Benthamite panopticon as 'the ideal form' of the disciplinary apparatus. Third, the text tries to show that the totality of disciplinary techniques is practically relevant to the operation of specific modern institutions. Thus, the analysis of disciplinary techniques culminates in a chapter (Foucault, 1977, pp. 231-56) about one modern institution, the prison, which is a 'practical realisation of the ideal form of disciplinary techniques' (Foucault, 1977, p. 249).

These procedures of discursive identification are a reprise of Weberian 'ideal type' analysis. Weber's treatment of the 'protestant ethic' makes the same ascent from a detailed analysis of elements to an ideal form of 'the spirit of capitalism' and then descends to practical realisation in Franklin's *Autobiography*. In Weber or Foucault, the ideal type may be nominally constructed at the end of the analysis of detail, but actually is dominant from the beginning. The ideal type functions as a principle for recognition of practical exemplifications and ensures that the analysis discovers only fragments or approximations of itself. Foucauldian analysis cannot, therefore, recognise or assimilate anything which is different from the unitary combination of techniques to produce coherent results. For this reason, the analysis of techniques of power does not resist, but reinforces, the schematicism about stages of punishment and leads the text towards final hysteria about the disciplinary society and the carceral archipelago.

There can, of course, be no question of empirically refuting Foucault's totalitarian analysis, but it is possible to construct other analyses based on different presuppositions and procedures. The last two chapters' analyses of the poor law after 1834 are hardly exemplary but they do avoid some of Foucault's objectionable procedures and presuppositions and consequently come to very different conclusions. According to Foucault, disciplinary techniques infiltrate all our institutions which rely on surveillance and constant individualising observation, and which institute programmes of training the body with the aim of reforming or modifying behaviour. According to our alternative analyses, the poor law was very different.

In the period 1834 to 1870, most paupers were outdoors, and those on outdoor relief were not affected by new disciplinary techniques but by simple exclusion and the effective refusal of relief to one class of pauper, able-bodied men. New general mixed workhouses were constructed in almost every union, but in their architecture, documentation, and regime, these workhouses were not instruments of disciplinary knowledge. The new hub and spokes structures were not panopticons and in their regimes disciplinary techniques played a blind, repressive role. Generally, official strategy did not positively aim to reform and remake individual paupers; it was presupposed that the working classes could never be reformed to the point where they would prefer honest work to a relief allowance. The aim was negatively to repress pauperism by making indoor relief thoroughly unattractive and making outdoor relief unobtainable for able-bodied men.

The changes of 1834 to 1870 were not a once and for all transformation which fixed the institution in its modern form, because after 1870 more or less everything changed again. These post-1870 changes did not move the institution any nearer to the Foucauldian ideal. To begin with out-relief, treatment that involved a knowledge *of* paupers was only on the agenda after the 1890s. Before this date, the strategy of the crusade had emphasised a knowledge *by* the poor which would put representational obstacles in the way of relief applications and, in practice, the crusade degenerated into more blind repression, which simply excluded all classes from out-relief. Right from 1870, there was an indoors strategy of classification and treatment which was very important in practice by 1900. But the new institutions built on the pavilion system were very unlike panopticons and operated a battery of treatment techniques. Interestingly, the pavilion system was developed for hospital construction and subsequently widely used for workhouses, prisons, asylums, schools, etc. This general change in architectural form may well indicate a broad change in the ends and means of 'discipline' which was being recast in a quasi-clinical form seldom encountered before 1870.

As the last chapter concluded, the poor law after 1870 was an apparatus that intertwined repression, classification, special treatment, and surveillance. It is more like a Barthesian text than a Foucauldian institution. This kind of poor law is a useful reminder of the possibility of complex, contradictory institutions, where diverse techniques are simultaneously used so that everything does not hang together and converge on the one end. Ultimately, Foucault's analysis is unacceptable because it conjures away such complexity.

Introduction

The tables in this appendix rework official statistics on relief practice
in England and Wales from 1800 onwards. For much of this period,
poor relief in Scotland was administered under a different system and
statistics for the United Kingdom are unavailable or meaningless.

An annual series on total expenditure begins in 1812 and continues
under the new poor law. More generally, the form of the available
statistical material changes radically around 1834. The pre-1834 period
was not pre-statistical, but it was dominated by *ad hoc* special returns.
For this reason, the available statistics on the old poor law have been
collected in Section A.

Subsequent sections of this appendix present statistics, as far as
possible, for the whole period from 1840 to 1939. This is not always
easy, because different categories and bases of calculation were used in
the official statistics published by successive central authorities. For
example, the Poor Law Commission on the 1840s published quarterly
totals of the number of paupers relieved while, for the next sixty years,
the Poor Law Board and Local Government Board usually calculated
pauper numbers on a day count basis.

The problems posed by such discontinuities have been dealt with on
an *ad hoc* basis. Major breaks in particular statistical series are indicated
by a heavy horizontal line across a table or by the start of a new table.
The nature of the discontinuity and any ensuing comparability problem
is explained in the relevant footnotes.

The tables have been organised into sections on specific themes.
Sections B and C present the available information on total numbers of
paupers and total expenditure. Sections D, E, F and G then present

statistics on relief to particular classes of paupers: men without work, widows with dependent children, the aged and infirm, and the insane. Section H brings together the available information about one object of expenditure, workhouse construction after 1834.

Graphs have been included at relevant points in some of the sections. A final comparative section has also been added to the statistical appendix because it is difficult to cross-refer between tables in different sections. The summary tables in this Section J show long-term changes in objects of expenditure and the composition of the pauper host.

Totals and sub-totals have been rounded off, therefore totals may not be the exact sum of the sub-totals. All other discrepancies are explained by footnotes.

A full list of the tables and graphs in the appendix is given at the front of this book.

Before 1834, only relief expenditure is covered by a regular annual series; the expenditure statistics from 1812 onwards are presented in Table 4.1. These statistics only yield significant information about relief practice if they are cross-referenced to the other available resources. First, there are the returns for 1802–3 which are summarised in Table 4.2. Second, the Select Committee in 1824 and the Royal Commission in 1832 sent out questions whose answers are tabulated in Tables 4.3 and 4.4.

The 1802–3 returns have been shamefully neglected in recent historical debate. It is worth emphasising therefore that these returns are the most important resources on pre-1834 relief practice. Almost all the parishes in England and Wales returned replies to eight questions about pauper numbers and eight questions about cost of relief. The main problem is that we do not directly know what kind of pauper total was returned; parishes could have returned either an average load figure or a total of all paupers relieved through the year, Easter 1802 to Easter 1803. However, we do know that different places did return the same kind of total because the proportion of paupers occasionally relieved (Table 4.2, col. iv) is remarkably constant.

In 1802–3 the crucial question inquired about the number of paupers who were aged and infirm. By a process of subtraction it is then possible to calculate the number of able-bodied men, women, and children. Table 4.2 (col. vii) gives the crucial result; the able-bodied and dependent children accounted for four out of every five paupers in England and Wales as a whole and in almost every one of the agricultural and industrial counties. For the first and only time before 1834, this gives an approximate measure of the massive involvement of the institution in assisting the male labourer and his dependants.

The questions of 1824 and 1832 inquire about the existence and extent of three distinct modes of relieving the able-bodied labourer: first, child allowances given to the low paid; second, wages paid out of the rates to the underemployed, and third, work or doles paid to the unemployed. Replies were returned by a relatively small sample of parishes whose relief practices were probably representative. Table 4.3 shows that child allowances were nearly universal in 1824 and commonplace in 1832, while payment of wages out of the rates was always less important and by 1832 had declined to marginality. However, the crucial point is that Blaug (1964) is wrong to suppose that this implies relief to the labourer was reduced to a rump of child allowances by 1832. He ignores relief to the unemployed and Table

4.4 shows that 92 per cent of urban places gave money and/or work to the unemployed in 1832.

Table 4.1   Expenditure on poor relief in England and Wales, 1802, 1812–33

	Total poor relief expenditure £000s	Approx. expend. per head of population		Index relief in terms of wheat prices (1802 = 100)
		s.	d.	
	(i)	(ii)		(iii)
1802	4,078	8	11	100
1812	6,676	12	9	90
1813	6,295	11	10	98
1814	5,419	10	0	125
1815	5,725	9	10	149
1816	6,911	12	4	151
1817	7,871	12	1	139
1818	7,517	13	0	148
1819	7,330	12	6	168
1820	6,959	11	8	176
1821	6,359	10	6	194
1822	5,773	9	5	223
1823	5,737	9	2	185
1824	5,787	9	1	155
1825	5,929	9	2	148
1826	6,441	9	10	188
1827	6,298	9	4	184
1828	6,332	9	5	179
1829	6,829	10	0	170
1830	6,799	9	10	182
1831	7,037	10	1	182
1832	6,791	9	7	199
1833	6,317	8	10	

Sources: After Mark Blaug, 'The Myth of the Old Poor Law and the Making of the New', *Journal of Economic History,* vol. 23, no. 2, June 1963, pp. 151–84.

Table 4.2 Abstract of returns for 1802-3[1]

County[2] groups	Number permanently relieved outdoors[3]		Number[3] permanently relieved indoors (adults and children)	Number relieved occasionally[4]	Total relieved (cols i-v)	Total relieved as % of pop.[7]	Non-able-bodied[6]	Able-bodied (adults and children)[8]	Able-bodied as % of total	Permanent indoor paupers as % of total
	Adults	Children								
	(i)	(ii)	(iii)	(iv)	(v)	(vi)	(vii)	(viii)	(ix)	(x)
Agric. counties										
Beds.	2,516	2,014	674	2,072	7,276	11.1	1,172	6,104	83.9	9.3
Berks.	5,620	7,533	1,169	8,266	22,588	20.0	2,872	19,716	87.3	5.2
Bucks.	6,505	6,493	1,260	5,392	19,650	17.7	2,529	17,121	87.1	6.4
Cambs.	3,870	3,164	892	3,368	11,294	12.2	1,579	9,715	86.0	7.9
Essex	11,219	10,737	2,969	13,412	38,337	16.4	4,850	33,487	87.3	7.7
Hereford	4,515	3,419	303	3,542	11,779	12.8	2,083	9,696	82.3	2.6
Herts.	4,197	2,749	1,754	4,649	13,349	13.3	1,890	11,459	85.8	13.1
Hunts.	1,588	1,483	353	1,322	4,746	12.2	611	4,135	87.1	7.4
Lincs.	6,609	5,303	1,112	5,821	18,845	8.8	3,294	15,551	82.5	5.9
Norfolk	13,668	11,004	3,996	14,114	42,782	15.2	7,366	35,416	82.8	9.3
Oxford	6,539	8,055	1,243	6,148	21,985	19.4	2,912	19,073	86.8	5.7
Rutland	498	300	169	393	1,360	8.1	268	1,092	80.3	12.4
Suffolk	8,066	8,096	4,098	15,850	36,110	16.6	4,115	31,995	88.6	11.3
Sussex	9,415	16,947	3,823	6,891	37,076	22.6	3,231	33,845	91.3	10.3
Wilts.	12,500	16,900	1,617	11,111	42,128	22.1	5,219	36,909	87.6	3.8
Agric. group Total:	97,325	104,197	25,432	102,351	329,305	16.1	43,991	285,314	86.6	7.7

[contd. overleaf]

Table 4.2 (cont.)

County[2] groups	Number permanently relieved outdoors[3]		Number[3] permanently relieved indoors (adults and children)	Number relieved occasionally[4]	Total relieved (cols i–v)	Total relieved as % of pop.[7]	Non-able-bodied[6]	Able-bodied (adults and children)[8]	Able-bodied as % of total	Permanent indoor paupers as % of total
	Adults	Children								
	(i)	(ii)	(iii)	(iv)	(v)	(vi)	(vii)	(viii)	(ix)	(x)
Ind. and commerc. counties										
Durham	7,099	4,866	746	2,596	15,307	9.3	3,494	11,813	77.2	4.9
Glos.	11,851	12,299	1,857	10,893	36,900	14.3	5,094	31,806	86.2	5.0
Kent	9,227	10,939	6,387	15,129	41,682	13.1	4,567	37,115	89.0	15.3
Lancs.	14,448	15,858	2,719	13,175	46,200	6.7	6,928	39,272	85.0	5.9
Middx.	12,185	11,037	15,186	24,765	63,173	7.5	8,407	54,766	86.7	24.0
Northumbs.	7,801	3,285	600	2,618	14,304	8.8	4,613	9,691	67.8	4.2
Staffs.	6,829	7,245	1,828	6,608	22,510	9.1	3,863	18,647	82.8	8.1
Surrey	5,173	8,532	5,268	17,167	36,140	13.0	3,720	32,420	89.7	14.6
Warks.	10,624	9,544	1,981	6,416	28,565	13.3	3,922	24,643	86.3	6.9
Yorks. W. Riding	20,149	17,721	2,534	13,961	54,365	9.3	9,867	44,498	81.9	4.7
Indus. group Total:	105,386	101,026	39,106	113,328	359,146	9.5	54,475	304,671	84.8	10.9
England and Wales Total:	336,119	315,150	83,468	305,899[5]	1,040,716	11.4	166,829	873,887	84.0	8.0

Source: Abstract of Returns relative to the Expense and Maintenance of the Poor, BPP, 1803–4, vol. XIII.

Table 4.3   Relief to the low paid and underemployed in 1824 and 1832

| | 1824 | | | 1832 | | |
	Agric. counties	Indus. counties	England and Wales	Agric.[15] counties	Indus.[15] counties	England and Wales
	(i)	(ii)	(iii)	(iv)	(v)	(vi)
Number of districts providing returns[9]	155	95	382	542	395	1,332
% giving any[10] (a) child allowances[11]	95	82	90	69	39	55
(b) Wages out of rates[12]	51	25	41	9	2	7
% giving (a) both forms of relief[13]	51	25	40	8	2	6
(b) neither form of relief[14]	5	18	9	30	60	45

Sources: 1824   Abstract of Returns prepared by order of the Select Committee on Labourers' Wages, BPP, 1825, vol. XIX.
1832   Report of Royal Commission on the Poor Laws, Appendix B1 (pt II) *Answers to Rural Queries* 24, BPP, 1834, vol. XXXI. Appendix B2 (pt III) *Answers to Town Queries* 30, 32, BPP, 1834, vol. XXXVI.

Table 4.4   Relief to the unemployed in urban areas, 1832

	1832
Number of districts providing returns[16]	262
Percentage giving any[17] (a) Money relief	68
(b) Work	60
Percentage giving (a) Both forms of relief	37
(b) Neither form of relief	8

Source: Report of Royal Commission on the Poor Laws, Appendix B2 (pt III) *Answers to Town Queries* 30, 34, 35, BPP, 1834, vol. XXXVI.

Notes (Section A)

1 14,611 parishes or places in England and Wales made returns for the year 20 April 1802 to 12 April 1803.
2 The classification into county groups follows Deane and Cole (1962, p. 103).
3 Schedule question 10 inquired about 'the number of persons relieved from the Poor's Rate permanently throughout that year'. The answers give a total of the permanent indoor and outdoor pensioners of the institution.
4 Schedule question 12 inquired: 'What was the number of persons relieved occasionally in that year?' Parishes may have returned either an average load figure or a total of all paupers relieved and, in the last case, may or may not have made allowance for double-counting of individuals who obtained relief more than once in the year.

   The all pauper total could be two or three times as large as the average load figure. There is no way of directly knowing what kinds of total were returned by the parishes. But there is internal evidence in the returns that the ambiguous question 12 was understood in one sense and that the returns give totals of one kind which are comparable and may be added together without absurdity. The significant point here is that the relation between numbers occasionally relieved (col. iv) and the total number of paupers (col. v) is remarkably consistent on a county by county basis. If, for example, we consider the group of agricultural counties as a whole, then the occasionally relieved account for 31.1 per cent of all paupers relieved; now fewer than thirteen of the fifteen counties in this group have percentages in the range 28 to 37 per cent. The industrial and commercial group of counties is more diverse; nevertheless, paupers 'occasionally relieved' account for 26 to 39 per cent of all paupers in six of the ten counties. Considering both groups of counties as a whole, the industrial group average (31.5 per cent) is almost exactly the same as the agricultural group average.
5 For the years 1813 to 1815 inclusive, the 'Abstract of Returns Relative to the Expense and Maintenance of the Poor' (BPP, 1818, vol. XIX) contains more information on those occasionally relieved. Schedule question 9 in this return inquired about 'the number of parishioners relieved occasionally'. The England and Wales total for 1815 was 423,150 and this group of occasionally relieved parishioners accounted for 45 per cent of the total number of 939,977 paupers.

   These figures show an apparent increase in the relative importance of the group of those occasionally relieved. Therefore it is important to emphasise that the 1813–15 total are not directly comparable with the 1802–3 total of those occasionally relieved. The latter totals exclude relief to non-parishioners who in 1815 made up almost one in five of the million paupers receiving relief.

6 These non-able-bodied persons are those defined by schedule question 13 as 'above sixty years of age or disabled from labour by permanent illness or other infirmity'. Such individuals are, of course, included in the sub-totals in columns i–iv and the total in column v.

7 Population totals are for the census year 1801.

8 The total of able-bodied adults and dependent children has been calculated by subtracting the non-able-bodied in column vii from the all-pauper total in column v.

9 In both 1824 and 1832, the parishes which replied to the questions were grouped into districts. 382 'hundreds' returned replies in 1824, and 1,444 'places' answered in the rural and town questions in the latter half of 1832. See chapter 1 for a discussion of the adequacy of these samples.

The totals tabulated for 1832 exclude the City of London and 122 places which answered issue 2 of the rural questions of 1832. The reasons for this last decision are explained in footnote 11.

10 All these totals were produced by counting the number of places in each sample which answered 'yes' to a question about a specific relief practice. Two points should be noted about the definition of 'yes'.

'Yes' means admitting any relief in a particular form, but does not imply that such relief was necessarily either usual or universal. This relative frequency criterion was chosen because we know from 1802–3 evidence that the relief system was selective in its operation. This criterion also directly follows the qualification 'any' which was used in all the original questions except the question about child allowances in 1824.

'Yes' includes attributed 'yeses' from places which did not directly answer 'yes' but, conceded, in a sentence or a few words describing practice, that some relief was given in this form. Generally, such attributions are not arbitrary but they do require nice judgment in a relatively small number of borderline cases. Therefore all percentages and totals should be regarded as reasonable but approximate estimates.

11 Replies to the following questions were tabulated.
(a) 1824 returns: 'is it usual in your district for married labourers having children to receive assistance from the parish rate?' (question 2).
(b) 1832 rural questions: 'whether any allowance is made from the poor's rate on account of large families?' (question 24, sub-question (a), issue 1 and 3 only).
(c) 1832 town questions: 'is it [i.e. relief] given to any persons wholly employed by individuals on the ground that their wages are insufficient to maintain their children?' (question 32).
It is necessary to emphasise two points about rural question number 24 in 1832.

First, only replies to issue 1 and issue 3 of the rural questions have been tabulated. Issues 1 and 3 were answered by 1,070 places, or 90 per cent of the places answering the rural questions; another

122 places answered issue 2 of these questions. These 122 replies were not tabulated because question 24 was differently worded in issue 2 and did not clearly discriminate and inquire separately about child allowances and payment of wages out of the rates.

Second, no parish ever replied to the question which Mark Blaug (1964, p. 231) represents as question 24: 'have you any, and how many, able-bodied labourers in the employment of individuals, receiving allowance or regular relief from your parish on their own account, or on that of their families?' This question 24 was a composite of the three separate issues and the differently worded questions answered by the parishes. The composite was printed on a fold-out sheet as an aid to the reader of the relevant volume of parliamentary papers.

12 Replies to the following questions were tabulated.
(a) 1824 returns: 'do any labourers in your district, employed by the farmers, receive either the whole or any part of the wages of their labour out of the poor rates?' (question 1).
(b) 1832 rural questions: 'whether any wages paid out of the poor's rate?' (question 24, sub-question (b), issue 1).
No specific question about payment of wages out of the rates was asked in issue 2 of the rural questions or in the town questions. A small number of replies to the town questions mention the practice even though it was not specifically inquired about. These replies have been tabulated but the results should obviously be treated with caution.

The most important point that should be emphasised is that information on this practice of paying wages out of the rates reliably covers only the rural areas in 1824 and 1832. In 1824 the answers are about rural areas because the relevant question asked only about payment of wages out of the rates to those labourers employed by the farmers. In 1832, the town questions omitted a specific query about payment of wages out of the rates.

13 In 1824, 158 places admitted payment of wages out of the rates and 153 of these places also admitted paying child allowances. In 1832, eighty-seven places paid wages out of the rates and seventy-seven also paid child allowances. Thus, payment of wages out of the rates was something extra offered by a proportion (and in 1832 a small proportion) of those paying child allowances. Payment of wages out of the rates was not something offered by a separate group of places distinct from those paying child allowances.

14 For 1832, this total includes all categorical 'noes', plus ambiguous replies. Categorical 'noes' to both forms of relief account for approximately half to two-thirds of the total.

15 Replies to questions have here been distributed by county into the groups of agricultural and industrial counties. The city and county of York have been assigned to the industrial groups. Thus totals given for these groups combine and add together answers to different questions and different sets of questions. The material has been tabulated in this way to preserve comparability with the results of 1802–3 and 1824.

If we consider the 1832 results alone, then the obvious grouping is into rural and town places according to whether the places answered rural or town questions. The table below gives the results of such a tabulation.

1832	Rural	Town
Number of districts providing returns	1070	262
Percentage giving any		
(a) child allowances	59	37
(b) wages out of rates	7	3
Percentage giving		
(a) both forms of relief	7	3
(b) neither form of relief	40	63

16 These are the 262 places that returned replies to the town questions.

It is impossible to say anything about assistance to the unemployed in 1824 or in the rural areas in 1832. Neither the 1824 returns nor the 1832 rural questions asked questions whose answers would disclose the amount of assistance specifically given to the unemployed.

17 The percentage is calculated in exactly the same way as the comparable figure in Table 4.3. For an explanation of the mode of calculation, see footnote 10.

Replies to the following questions in the 1832 schedule of town questions are tabulated.

(a) 'Is allowance or regular relief out of the workhouse given by your parish to any able-bodied mechanics, manufacturers, labourers or servants?' (question 30).

(b) 'Have you any and what mode of employing able-bodied paupers out of the workhouse?' (question 34).

(c) 'Is relief ever, and under what circumstances, given to able-bodied applicants without setting them to work?' (question 35).

Replies to the general question (3) disclose much about able-bodied relief practice, and replies to the two specific questions (34 and 35) should disclose assistance to the unemployed.

Section B   Numbers on relief, 1840-1939

Table 4.5 in this section reworks the official statistics of total numbers
on relief in England and Wales for the years 1840–1939. The only
statistics continuously available for nearly the whole of this period are
day count figures which show the number in receipt of relief on one
day. A mean of one summer day count and one winter day count gives
an average load figure which gives a fair idea of the average number on
relief over the whole year. At least this is so up to 1914, when there
was a pattern of gentle seasonal variation in total numbers on relief.
But the reader should be warned that there were violent short-run
fluctuations in numbers drawing relief in the inter-war period. And, for
any year from 1840 to 1939, the average load total is, of course, much
smaller than the total number of individuals separately assisted through
the year. This last figure was always nearly twice as large (see Section
J) and in the mid-nineteenth century the difference was greater.

From 1849 onwards, the mean figure in the table for each year is
the mean of the number relieved on 1 January of that year and 1 July
of the preceding year. This was the way in which statistics of numbers
on relief were routinely presented in the official publications of the
later nineteenth and early twentieth century. In the form of ratio per
1,000 of population (Table 4.5, col. viii), this figure was the standard
measure of pauperism used in all official and unofficial discussion of
the poor law in this period. A sub-division into 'indoor' and 'outdoor'
relief (Table 4.5, cols i and iii) was also always made because the
distinction between the two types of pauperism was fundamental to
most discussion of the issue: indoor paupers were those relieved within
the workhouse and outdoor paupers those who received a cash
allowance while they continued to live in their own homes. This table,
therefore, does not so much reconstruct as reproduce the basic 1849–
1914 operational measure of pauperism.

Nevertheless, it is not straightforward to obtain a long-run series
because of discrepancies caused by small changes in the procedure for
counting and classifying paupers. The series for the years 1840–1939
has been pieced together from sub-series that are not exactly comparable. The breaks between sub-series are indicated by a horizontal line
across the table. These breaks have been arranged so that they fall
between periods when numbers on relief changed considerably. Thus
anyone, for example, considering the fall in numbers on relief in the
1870s, can turn to a continuous series of comparable figues which
covers the period of change. In any case, the sub-series after 1849 are
nearly comparable. This can be seen from a comparison of the figures

immediately above and below the horizontal lines. Inside the brackets are figures for the first year of the new series calculated on the basis of the previous series. As far as possible, the sources of discrepancy between the series have been identified and are listed in the footnotes which also record minor changes in classification within each series.

Table 4.5   Total numbers on relief in England and Wales, discriminating indoor and outdoor relief, 1840–1939

Year ended March	Indoor		Outdoor		Total (excluding casuals and insane)		Total (all classes)	
	Mean numbers ('000s)	Rates per 1,000 estimated population	Mean numbers ('000s)	Rates per 1,000 estimated population	Mean numbers ('000s)	Rates per 1,000 estimated population	Mean numbers ('000s)	Rates per 1,000 estimated population
	(i)	(ii)	(iii)	(iv)	(v)	(vi)	(vii)	(viii)
1840	169	11	1,030	66			1,200	77
1841	192	12	1,107	70			1,299	82
1842	223	14	1,205	75			1,427	89
1843	239	15	1,301	80			1,539	95
1844	231	14	1,247	76			1,478	90
1845	215	13	1,256	76			1,471	88
1846	200	12	1,132	67			1,332	79
1847	265	16	1,456	85			1,721	101
1848[1]	306	18	1,571	90			1,877	108
1849	134	7.7	955	55.0			1,089	62.7
1850	123	7.0	886	50.4			1,009	57.4
1851	114	6.5	827	46.5			941	53.6
1852	111	6.2	804	44.7			916	50.9
1853	110	6.0	776	42.7			886	48.7
1854	112	6.1	753	40.9			865	47.0
1855	121	6.5	776	41.7			898	48.2
1856	125	6.6	792	42.1			917	48.7
1857	123	6.5	762	40.0			885	46.5
1858	123	6.4	786	40.8			908	47.2
1859[2] {	121	6.2	744	38.2				
{	108	5.5	706	36.3	814	41.8	865	44.4

Table 4.5 (cont.)

Year ended March	Indoor		Outdoor		Total (excluding casuals and insane)		Total (all classes)	
	Mean numbers ('000s)	Rates per 1,000 estimated population	Mean numbers ('000s)	Rates per 1,000 estimated population	Mean numbers ('000s)	Rates per 1,000 estimated population	Mean numbers ('000s)	Rates per 1,000 estimated population
	(i)	(ii)	(iii)	(iv)	(v)	(vi)	(vii)	(viii)
1860	101	5.1	695	35.3	796	40.4	845	42.9
1861	108	5.4	709	35.6	816	41.0	884	44.4
1862	119	5.9	743	36.9	862	42.8	917	45.6
1863	123	6.0	872	42.8	994	48.8	1,079	53.0
1864	120	5.9	844	40.9	965	46.8	1,015	49.2
1865	118	5.7	783	37.5	901	43.2	951	45.6
1866	118	5.6	746	35.3	864	40.9	916	43.3
1867	122	5.7	755	35.3	877	41.0	932	43.5
1868	134	6.2	801	36.9	934	43.1	993	45.8
1869	140	6.4	817	37.2	956	43.6	1,018	46.4
1870	141	6.4	838	37.7	979	44.1	1,033	46.5
1871	140	6.2	843	37.5	984	43.7	1,037	46.1
1872	133	5.8	791	34.7	924	40.5	977	42.9
1873	128	5.5	702	30.4	830	35.9	884	38.3
1874	127	5.4	646	27.6	773	33.0	827	35.3
1875	129	5.5	616	25.9	745	31.4	801	33.8
1876	125	5.2	567	23.6	692	28.8	749	31.2
1877	130	5.4	530	21.7	660	27.1	720	29.5
1878	139	5.6	527	21.4	667	27.0	729	29.5
1879	147	5.9	555	22.1	702	28.0	765	30.6

Table 4.5 (cont.)

Year ended March	Indoor		Outdoor		Total (excluding casuals and insane)		Total (all classes)	
	Mean numbers ('000s)	Rates per 1,000 estimated population	Mean numbers ('000s)	Rates per 1,000 estimated population	Mean numbers ('000s)	Rates per 1,000 estimated population	Mean numbers ('000s)	Rates per 1,000 estimated population
	(i)	(ii)	(iii)	(iv)	(v)	(vi)	(vii)	(viii)
1880	159	6.3	582	22.9	741	29.2	808	31.8
1881	161	6.3	561	21.8	722	28.1	791	30.8
1882	161	6.2	557	21.4	718	27.6	788	30.3
1883	162	6.1	551	20.9	712	27.0	782	29.7
1884	160	6.0	534	20.1	694	26.1	766	28.8
1885	162	6.0	533	19.8	695	25.8	769	28.6
1886	164	6.1	542	19.9	707	26.0	781	28.7
1887	167	6.0	555	20.2	722	26.2	796	28.9
1888	170	6.1	554	19.9	724	26.0	800	28.8
1889	168	6.0	548	19.5	716	25.5	796	28.3
1890	166	5.8	530	18.7	696	24.5	775	27.3
1891	163	5.7	515	17.9	678	23.6	760	26.4
1892	163	5.6	499	17.2	662	22.3	745	25.6
1893	169	5.7	505	17.2	675	22.9	759	25.8
1894	180	6.1	519	17.4	699	23.5	788	26.5
1895	184	6.1	523	17.4	706	23.5	797	26.5
1896	187	6.1	535	17.6	721	23.7	816	26.8
1897	186	6.0	530	17.1	716	23.3	815	26.5
1898	188	6.0	525	16.8	713	22.9	814	26.2
1899	190	6.1	538	17.1	728	23.2	832	26.5

Table 4.5 (cont.)

Year ended March	Indoor		Outdoor		Total (excluding casuals and insane)		Total (all classes)	
	Mean numbers ('000s)	Rates per 1,000 estimated population	Mean numbers ('000s)	Rates per 1,000 estimated population	Mean numbers ('000s)	Rates per 1,000 estimated population	Mean numbers ('000s)	Rates per 1,000 estimated population
	(i)	(ii)	(iii)	(iv)	(v)	(vi)	(vii)	(viii)
1900	188	5.9	500	15.7	689	21.6	797	25.0
1901[3]	186	5.8	489	15.2	676	21.0	781	24.3
	204	6.3	494	15.3	698	21.6	777	24.1
1902	213	6.5	502	15.4	715	21.9	797	24.4
1903	221	6.7	511	15.5	732	22.2	818	24.8
1904	229	6.9	516	15.5	745	22.4	832	25.0
1905	240	7.1	547	16.3	787	23.4	879	26.1
1906	248	7.3	550	16.2	798	23.5	892	26.2
1907[4]	251	7.3	542	15.8	793	23.1	887	25.8
1908	256	7.4	540	15.6	796	23.0	893	25.7
1909	267	7.6	551	15.7	818	23.3	916	26.1
1910	275	7.8	540	15.2	815	23.0	916	25.9
1911	275	7.7	508	14.2	783	21.9	886	24.8
1912	267	7.4	408	11.3	676	18.7	780	21.6
1913	265	7.3	412	11.3	677	18.6	784	21.5
1914	255	7.0	387	10.6	642	17.6	748	20.4
1915[5]	253	6.8	392	10.6	644	17.4	752	20.3
1916	226	6.1	365	9.8	591	15.9	696	18.7
1917	213	5.7	328	8.7	541	14.4	642	17.1
1918	199	5.3	302	8.0	502	13.3	596	15.8
1919	184	4.9	285	7.6	469	12.5	556	14.8

Table 4.5 (cont.)

Year ended March	Indoor		Outdoor		Total (excluding casuals and insane)		Total (all classes)	
	Mean numbers ('000s)	Rates per 1,000 estimated population	Mean numbers ('000s)	Rates per 1,000 estimated population	Mean numbers ('000s)	Rates per 1,000 estimated population	Mean numbers ('000s)	Rates per 1,000 estimated population
	(i)	(ii)	(iii)	(iv)	(v)	(vi)	(vii)	(viii)
1920	181	4.8	298	7.9	479	12.7	563	14.9
1921	193	5.2	347	9.2	540	14.3	627	16.6
1922	209	5.5	1,147	30.3	1,356	35.8	1,449	38.3
1923	214	5.6	1,398	36.6	1,612	42.2	1,710	44.8
1924	215	5.6	1,062	27.7	1,277	33.3	1,379	36.0
1925	213	5.5	915	23.6	1,128	29.1	1,229	31.7
1926	217	5.6	1,011	26.0	1,227	31.6	1,331	34.2
1927	221	5.7	1,735	44.4	1,956	50.1	2,064	52.9
1928	221	5.6	997	25.4	1,218	31.0	1,330	33.9
1929	221	5.6	891	22.6	1,113	28.2	1,228	31.1
1930[6]	217	5.5	850	21.4	1,067	26.9	1,183	29.9
1931	209	5.2	762	19.1	971	24.3	1,090	27.3
1932	196	4.9	859	21.5	1,055	26.4	1,177	29.4
1933	191	4.8	1,087	27.0	1,278	31.8	1,405	34.9
1934	184	4.5	1,154	28.6	1,338	33.1	1,465	36.3
1935	178	4.4	1,223	30.3	1,401	34.7	1,529	37.8
1936[7]	170	4.2	1,175	28.9	1,344	33.1	1,472	36.2
	170	4.2	1,170	29.0	1,340	33.2	1,468	36.3
1937	161	4.0	1,105	27.2	1,266	31.2	1,395	34.4
1938	153	3.8	912	22.3	1,065	26.0	1,195	29.2
1939	149	3.6	928	22.6	1,077	26.3	1,208	29.5

Table 4.5 (cont.)

Sources: 1840–1920   Annual Reports of Poor Law Commission 1840–8, Poor Law Board 1849–70, Local Government Board 1871–1919, Ministry of Health, 1920.

1921–36   18th and 22nd Abstract of Labour Statistics.

1937–9   Ministry of Health Quarterly Returns of Persons in Receipt of Poor Relief.

The most useful long runs of comparable figures are available in the following publications:

1840–7   Poor Law Commission, 14th Annual Report, 1848.

1849–59   Poor Law Board, 11th Annual Report, 1858.

1859–96   Local Government Board, 25th Annual Report, 1896.

1872–1908   Royal Commission on the Poor Laws (1909), Statistical Appendix, vol. XXV (BPP, 1910, vol. LIII).

1896–1920   Ministry of Health, 1st Annual Report, 1920.

The early twentieth-century comparative statements published as parliamentary papers do not contain useful long-run series. For example, Cd 6675 (BPP, 1913, vol. IV) only gives a continuous yearly run from 1905.

P. F. Aschrott, *The English Poor Law System* (1888) offers a series for the years 1849–83.

S. and B. Webb, *English Poor Law History*, pt 2, vol. 2 (1929) has a chapter on English poor law statistics with many useful references.

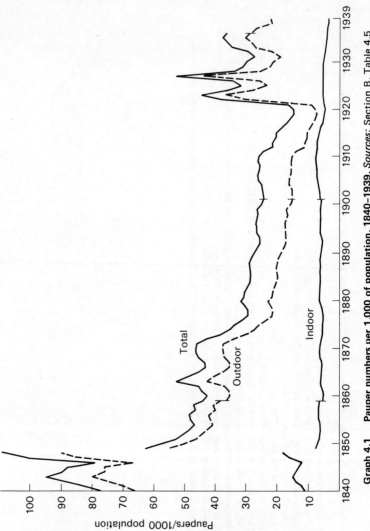

Graph 4.1   Pauper numbers per 1,000 of population, 1840–1939. *Sources:* Section B, Table 4.5

Notes (Section B)

1 Up to 1848, the totals give the number of persons relieved during the first quarter of each year. These totals certainly include some double-counting. From 1849 onwards, the totals are the mean of two day counts of the numbers relieved on 1 January in each year and on 1 July in the previous year. The change in the basis of calculation made a large difference: the day count (all classes) for 1 July 1848 was 893,743, about half the total number relieved during the quarter ended Lady Day, 1848.

   The early figures contain contemporary official estimates of pauperism in parishes which had not been reorganised into poor law unions and therefore did not make statistical returns on the standard forms. This is a significant consideration before the 1850s. In 1850, 16 per cent of the population lived in such parishes, but by 1858, this proportion had fallen to 2 per cent.

2 Up to 1858, the totals in the columns headed 'indoor' and 'outdoor' include all classes of paupers. From 1859, the totals in these columns exclude the insane (wherever domiciled) and casuals. Insane paupers in asylums were fully returned for the first time in 1859 when they were classified as outdoor lunatics.

3 From 1901 the columns headed 'indoor' and 'outdoor' continue to exclude all casuals but now only exclude those insane who were institutionalised in county and borough asylums, registered hospitals, and licensed houses.

   The final column in Table 4.5 (total – all classes) is affected by a change in 1901 in the procedure for counting casuals. From 1901, the count was no longer of casuals relieved at any time during the day, but of casuals relieved over one night. In 1901, on a day count, there were 9,616 casuals and on a night count, 5,516.

4 Changes in the form of the detailed parliamentary returns show that it is probable that paupers maintained in certain non-work-house institutions (e.g. infirmaries) were not always included in the returns before 1907.

5 The last detailed census of persons in receipt of relief on 1 July was taken in 1914. Subsequently, the 'July' figures in the annual mean total are of persons in receipt of relief on a single day at the end of June. Again, subsequently, the number of lunatics in asylums was calculated using the mean of two 1 January figures. This change was not significant because there was no pronounced seasonal variation in the number of lunatics.

6 Under the Mental Treatment Act of 1930, rate-aided patients in mental hospitals were not deemed to be paupers in receipt of relief. In Table 4.5, to maintain comparability, such cases are still included in columns vii and viii after 1930.

7 In 1936, there is a change in the basis for the calculation of the mean. Except for rate-aided patients in asylums, the 1 January figure is replaced by 'a day at the end of December'.

In the final sub-series, another adjustment has been made to maintain comparability. Columns vii and viii for 1936 and subsequent years continue to include persons receiving domiciliary (outdoor) medical relief only, although they were then excluded from the official returns of pauper totals. This group numbered between 10,000 and 25,000 through the inter-war period.

Section C Relief expenditure, 1840-1939

Tables 4.6–4.8 rework the official statistics of expenditure on poor relief in England and Wales for the years 1840–1939. The annual series for the total amount spent on poor relief continues after 1834 (Table 4.6, col. viii; Table 4.7, col. ix). For comparative purposes, this total is again expressed as expenditure per head of population (Table 4.6, col. ix; Table 4.7, col. x). After the 1834 reform, it becomes possible to break down the total and determine how the money is spent. From 1840 onwards, sub-totals give expenditure on in-maintenance and out-relief (Table 4.6, cols i and ii); and from 1853 onwards, the official statistics also separate out the cost of salaries and of servicing the loans which were usually obtained when institutions were constructed (Table 4.6, cols v and iv). Footnotes to the tables have been used throughout to define what was included and excluded under the various sub-heads.

Over the whole period, there are some changes in the practice of allocating expenditure between different sub-heads and these changes are noted in footnotes where relevant. But the expenditure series are not plagued by the recurrent minor discontinuities that affect the numbers series. Instead, there is one major discontinuity right at the end of our period in 1930. The Local Government Act of 1929 abolished the boards of guardians and transferred the administration of the poor law to county and county borough councils. At this point the form of the expenditure series changes and to underline this point a new table (Table 4.7) gives the post-1930 statistics. Total expenditure figures in this table (Table 4.7, col. i) are comparable with earlier totals. But, of the sub-totals, only that dealing with institutional expenditure on maintenance of rate-aided patients in mental hospital (Table 4.7, col. ii) is comparable. The annual series ends in 1936 and for this reason some of the columns could not be continued up to 1939.

All the information in the main series for 1840–1930 (Table 4.6) has been directly abstracted from official sources except for one column in the table which has been calculated. The figures for 'average weekly dole' (Table 4.6, col. x; Table 4.7, col. xi) were obtained by dividing out relief expenditure by the average load of outdoor paupers (see Table 4.5, col. iii). This produces the weekly dole which would have been received by each outdoor pauper *if* all paupers had received the same allowance. Although this assumption is unrealistic, it does give some idea of a typical weekly dole in any period and it also provides a useful comparative measure of the trend of the dole in money terms.

The money that the poor law authorities spent had first to be raised by taxation. Total rateable value (Table 4.6, col. xi; Table 4.7, col. xii) shows the tax base of the institution. A further table (Table 4.8) shows how much of the poor law's expenditure in the nineteenth century was met out of central government grants in aid of poor rates. This table also shows how the poor rates were used to finance activities like highway maintenance and vaccination as well as poor relief.

Again, the main table (Table 4.6) in this section effectively reproduces the nineteenth-century construction of pauperism. Before 1840, the statistics of total cost were the only regularly available measure of pauperism. After 1840, with number and cost measurements available, pauperism became two-dimensional. Almost all nineteenth-century writers presumed that cost and numbers should both be reduced. Thus total cost and expenditure per head of population were critically scrutinised in nearly all official and unofficial discussion. The sub-totals and the detailed distribution of relief expenditure received less attention. This was partly because sub-totals could not provide a simple pauperism measure and partly because all those with a bias in favour of institutionalisation were embarrassed by the increasing cost of the items connected with institutional relief in the last quarter of the nineteenth century.

Table 4.6 Expenditure 1840–1930

Year ended March	Amount expended for the relief of the poor[1] (£000s)								Expenditure[2] per head population	Average[3] weekly dole per outdoor pauper	Value on[10] which rates levied
	In-maintenance[4]	Out-relief[5]	Maintenance[6] of lunatic paupers	Loan charges[7] (principal repaid and interest)	Salaries and[8] rations of officers	Building repairs, furniture, rates, taxes and insurance	Other[9]	Total[1]	(s d)	(s d)	(£m)
	(i)	(ii)	(iii)	(iv)	(v)	(vi)	(vii)	(viii)	(ix)	(x)	(xi)
1840	808	2,931					838	4,577	5 11	1 1¼	
1841	891	2,995					875	4,761	6 0	1 0½	
1842	934	3,091					886	4,911	6 2	0 11¾	
1843	958	3,322					928	5,208	6 5	0 11¾	
1844	834	3,224					919	4,976	6 1	1 0	
1845	845	3,273					923	5,040	6 1	1 0	
1846	804	3,208					942	4,954	5 11	1 1	
1847	899	3,468					932	5,299	6 3	0 11	
1848	1,103	3,853					1,225	6,181	7 1¾	0 11¼	
1849	1,053	3,359					1,381	5,793	6 6½	1 4¼	
1850	914	3,155					1,326	5,395	6 1	1 4½	68
1851	790	2,874					1,299	4,963	5 6½	1 4	—
1852	763	2,808					1,326	4,898	5 5½	1 4	—
1853	763	2,776		198	596		607	4,939	5 6	1 4½	—
1854	925	2,888		205	611		654	5,283	5 8	1 5¾	—
1855	1,094	3,193		211	620		773	5,890	6 3	1 7	72
1856	1,140	3,240		209	633		783	6,004	6 3¾	1 6¾	—
1857	1,089	3,152	378	217	638		425	5,899	6 1¾	1 7	—
1858	1,068	3,117	398	203	638		455	5,879	6 0½	1 6¼	—
1859	955	2,923	413	195	638		435	5,559	5 8¼	(1 6¼) 1 7	—
1860	912	2,863	420	182	645		433	5,455	5 6	1 7	—
1861	1,034	3,012	444	188	660		440	5,779	5 9	1 7½	—
1862	1,133	3,156	482	183	668		454	6,078	6 0	1 7½	—
1863	1,127	3,574	501	176	679		469	6,527	6 4½	1 7	—
1864	1,096	3,466	524	177	696		464	6,423	6 2½	1 7	—

Table 4.6 (cont.)

Year ended March	Amount expended for the relief of the poor[1] (£000s) In-maintenance[4]	Out-relief[5]	Maintenance[6] of lunatic paupers	Loan charges[7] (principal repaid and interest)	Salaries and[8] rations of officers	Building repairs, furniture, rates, taxes and insurance	Other[9]	Total[1]	Expenditure[2] per head population (s d)	Average[3] weekly dole per outdoor pauper (s d)	Value on[10] which rates levied (£m)
	(i)	(ii)	(iii)	(iv)	(v)	(vi)	(vii)	(viii)	(ix)	(x)	(xi)
1865	1,111	3,259	535	175	707		478	6,265	6 0	1 7¼	94
1866	1,189	3,197	566	181	731[11]		576	6,440	6 1¼	1 7¾	–
1867	1,376	3,358	607	186	748		685	6,960	6 6¼	1 8½	–
1868	1,517	3,620	657	208	771		725	7,498	6 11½	1 8¾	–
1869	1,547	3,677	711	205	805		728[12]	7,673(+10)[12]	7 0¾	1 8¾	–
1870	1,503	3,633	723	252	818		715	7,644(–9)	6 11½	1 8	104
1871	1,525	3,664	746	291	838		822	7,887(+12)	6 11¼	1 8	–
1872	1,516	3,584	742	279	871		1,016	8,007(+70)	6 11½	1 9	–
1873	1,549	3,279	781	273	893		917	7,692(+2)	6 7¼	1 9½	–
1874	1,649	3,111	830	272	909		893	7,665(+1)	6 6	1 10¼	–
1875	1,578	2,959	859	267	930		896	7,488(0)	6 3¼	1 10¼	116
1876	1,534	2,761	883	275	943		940	7,336(–1)	6 0¾	1 10½	119
1877	1,614	2,616	911	285	972		1,001	7,400(0)	6 0½	1 10¾	125
1878	1,727	2,622	957	288	997		1,097	7,689(–22)	6 2½	1 11	128
1879	1,721	2,642	986	297	1,023		1,162	7,830(+8)	6 2¾	1 10	131
1880	1,758	2,711	994	319	1,053		1,180	8,015(–2)	6 4	1 9½	134
1881	1,839	2,660	1,034	338	1,069		1,162	8,102(+27)	6 3	1 10	136
1882	1,832	2,626	1,059	351	1,088		1,277	8,232(–20)	6 3¾	1 9¾	140
1883	1,870	2,590	1,098	430	1,118		1,248	8,353(–56)	6 4	1 9¾	141
1884	1,993[13]	2,518	1,143	484[13]	1,298[13]		967[13]	8,403(13)	6 3¼	1 9¾	143
1885	1,922	2,470	1,188	502	1,357		1,053	8,492	6 3	1 9½	146
1886	1,838	2,490	1,175	541	1,332		920	8,296	6 0½	1 9¼	147
1887	1,778	2,528	1,160	567	1,313		830	8,177	5 10½	1 9	149
1888	1,885	2,538	1,168	586	1,342		952	8,441	5 11¾	1 9¼	149
1889	1,863	2,504	1,185	582	1,360		873	8,366	5 10¼	1 9	150

Year ended March	Amount expended for the relief of the poor[1] (£000s)								Expenditure[2] per head population	Average[3] weekly dole per outdoor pauper	Value on[10] which rates levied
	In-maintenance[4]	Out-relief[5]	Maintenance[6] of lunatic paupers	Loan charges[7] (principal repaid and interest)	Salaries and[8] rations of officers	Building repairs, furniture, rates, taxes and insurance	Other[9]	Total[1]	(s d)	(s d)	(£m)
	(i)	(ii)	(iii)	(iv)	(v)	(vi)	(vii)	(viii)	(ix)	(x)	(xi)
1890	1,900	2,454	1,222	605	1,395		859	8,434	5 9¾	1 9¼	150
1891	1,951	2,400	1,285	621	1,453		934	8,643	6 0	1 9½	152
1892	2,044	2,374	1,332	645	1,496		956	8,848	6 1	1 10	156
1893	2,106	2,371	1,393	640	1,567		1,141	9,218	6 3¼	1 9¾	158
1894	2,198	2,461	1,466	677	1,629		1,242	9,674	6 6	1 10	159
1895	2,216	2,531	1,502	698	1,667		1,253	9,867	6 6¾	1 10¼	161
1896	2,254	2,645	1,556	738	1,739		1,283	10,216	6 8¾	1 10¾	163
1897	2,257	2,680	1,643	793	1,782		1,278	10,432	6 9½	1 11¼	166
1898	2,384	2,733	1,692	839	1,880		1,301	10,828	6 11¾	2 0	156
1899	2,462	2,765	1,749	919	1,972		1,421	11,287	7 2¼	1 11¾	160
1900	2,548	2,698	1,820	973	2,095	926	507	11,568	7 3½	2 0¾	164
								12,120	7 6¾	2 1¾	
1901[14]	2,663	2,722	1,874	860	2,036	921	473	11,549	7 2¼	2 1½	168
1902	2,815	2,836	2,045	923	2,159	923	560	12,261	7 6¼	2 2	175
1903	2,921	2,933	2,196	1,006	2,259	964	570	12,848	7 9½	2 2½	179
1904	3,051	2,991	2,287	1,098	2,359	1,068	583	13,369	8 0¼	2 2¾	183
1905	3,077	3,134	2,315	1,133	2,429	1,178	875	13,852	8 2¼	2 2½	187
1906	3,125	3,234	2,329	1,190	2,491	1,065	913	14,036	8 2¾	2 3¼	191
1907	3,074	3,211	2,339	1,228	2,513	1,002	891	13,957	8 1	2 3¼	194
1908	3,221	3,246	2,330	1,214	2,578	1,093	936	14,308	8 2¼	2 3¾	198
1909	3,332	3,345	2,406	1,213	2,632	1,151	977	14,717	8 4	2 4	201
1910	3,358	3,343	2,468	1,223	2,693	1,110	1,018	14,850	8 3¾	2 4½	203
1911	3,474	3,130	2,527	1,210	2,823	1,170	1,044	15,023	8 4¾	2 4½	205
1912	3,451	2,373	2,562	1,209	2,899	1,258	1,051	14,464	8 0	2 2¾	207
1913	3,520	2,459	2,635	1,232	3,012	1,295	1,118	14,936	8 2½	2 3½	209
1914	3,489	2,422	2,731	1,198	3,108	1,309	1,116	15,056	8 2¾	2 4¾	212

Table 4.6 (cont.)

Year ended March	Amount expended for the relief of the poor[1] (£000s) In-maintenance[4]	Out-relief[5]	Maintenance[6] of lunatic paupers	Loan charges[7] (principal repaid and interest)	Salaries and[8] rations of officers	Building repairs, furniture, rates, taxes and insurance	Other[9]	Total[1]	Expenditure[2] per head population (s d)	Average[3] weekly dole per outdoor pauper (s d)	Value on[10] which rates levied (£m)
	(i)	(ii)	(iii)	(iv)	(v)	(vi)	(vii)	(viii)	(ix)	(x)	(xi)
1915	3,605	2,613	2,879	1,264	3,268	1,369	1,146	15,804	8 6	2 6¾	214
1916	3,843	2,719	3,031	1,172	3,376	1,217	1,127	16,086	8 7½	2 9	216
1917	4,075	2,615	3,117	1,338	3,452	1,052	1,192	16,188	8 7½	3 0¾	217
1918	4,439	2,765	3,304	1,085	3,643	1,075	1,163	17,040	9 0¾	3 6¼	219
1919	4,674	3,054	3,472	1,031	4,201	1,205	1,244	18,424	9 10	4 1½	220
1920[15]	5,903	4,109	4,252	988	5,700	1,990	1,089	23,501	12 6½	5 3¾	221
1921	6,809	5,793	6,316	994	7,643	3,100	1,640	31,925	17 0¼	6 5[16]	224
1922	6,809	15,443	7,265	943	8,048	2,927	1,640	42,273	22 3¾	5 2¼	234
1923	5,800	17,910	6,247	892	7,627	2,550	1,546	41,934	21 11¾	4 11	239
1924	5,761	15,066	5,404	785	7,458	2,512	1,459	37,882	19 8¾	5 5½	236
1925	5,902	13,375	5,221	858	7,682	2,837	1,535	36,842	19 0¼	5 7½	242
1926	6,028	15,736	5,508	837	8,023	2,964	1,606	40,083	20 7¼	5 11¾	247
1927	6,332	23,914	6,019	884	8,566	2,851	1,839	49,775	25 5¾	5 1½	256
1928	5,887	15,147	6,133	960	8,691	2,809	1,899	40,919	20 10	5 10	259
1929	5,916	13,471	6,230	1,057	8,889	2,916	1,807	39,671	20 1¼	5 9¾	268
1930	5,968	12,972	6,617	1,053	9,298	3,528	1,815	40,631	20 6¼	5 10½	255[17]

Sources: 1840–1919 As for Section B, Table 4.5. 1920–34 Annual Local Taxation Returns, HMSO. 1935–7 Local Government Financial Statistics, HMSO.

Table 4.7   Expenditure 1930–9

	Institutional relief		Domiciliary relief			Other expenditure not allocated to institutional or domiciliary relief			Total	Expenditure[2] per head population	Average[3] weekly dole for outdoor paupers	Value on[10] which rate levied
	At establishments used for poor law purposes in 1930[18]	Rate aid patients in mental hospital	Other	Out-relief	Other	Salaries of officers	Building, repairs furniture, rates, taxes and insurance	Other[19]		(s d)	(s d)	(£m)
	(i)	(ii)	(iii)	(iv)	(v)	(vi)	(vii)	(viii)	(ix)	(x)	(xi)	(xii)
1930	16,543	6,617	1,116	12,922	1,685	848	153	747	40,631	20 6¾	5 9	255[17]
1931	15,966	6,552	544	11,566	1,640	1,520	201	573	38,561	19 4½	5 10	257
1932	12,997	6,374	1,004	12,667	1,675	1,456	151	492	36,817	18 5	5 8	265
1933	12,654	6,242	833	15,431	1,727	1,431	165	442	38,924	19 4½	5 5¾	270
1934	12,605	6,264	604	16,689	1,863	1,481	176	475	40,155	19 10¾	5 6¾	274
1935	12,707	6,345	631	18,707	2,003	1,508	161	446	42,507	21 0	5 10½	285
1936	12,578	6,590	637	20,254	2,119	1,589	160	452	44,379	21 10	{ 6 7½ 6 7¾	294
1937	—	—	—	19,950	—	—	—	—	44,240	21 8	6 11¼	299
1938	—	—	—	16,829	—	—	—	—	n.a.	—	7 1¼	304
1939	—	—	—	17,973	—	—	—	—	n.a.	—	7 5½	311

Sources: As Table 4.6.

Useful long runs of statistics are to be found in the following:

Total expenditure and expenditure per head population: S. and B. Webb (1926); Royal Commission on the Poor laws (1909), Statistical Appendix, vol. XXV (BPP, 1910, vol. LIII), 'Notes by Professor Smart on the growth of poor law expenditure in England and Wales'.

Itemised expenditure: 1857–83   P. F. Aschrott (1888);
1861–1900   Local Government Board, 30th Annual Report, 1900–1;
1895–1919   Local Government Board, 48th Annual Report, 1918–19.

Rateable value: 1850–1908   Statistical Memorandum relating to Public Health and Social Conditions (BPP, 1909, vol. CI);
1914–39   Rates and Rateable values in England and Wales, 1938–9, HMSO.

Table 4.8   Receipts other than from the poor rates and expenditure on purposes other than relief, 1840–1900

Year ended March	Receipts (£000s)			Expenditure (£000s)				
	From poor rates	In aid[20] of poor rates	Total	Relief and connected purposes[21]	Purposes partly connected with relief[22]	Purposes unconnected with relief[23]	Total	Medical relief only[24]
	(i)	(ii)	(iii)	(iv)	(v)	(vi)	(vii)	(viii)
1813	8,647	–	8,647	6,981	1,313	547	8,841	–
1820	8,720	–	8,720	7,330	664	679	8,673	–
1830	8,111	–	8,111	6,829	605	727	8,161	–
1840	6,015	228	6,243	4,644	517	907	6,067	152
1850	7,270	230	7,500	5,473	390	1,497	7,360	227
1860	7,716	318	8,034	5,516	433	2,127	8,076	236
1870	11,574	470	12,044	7,671	573	3,493	11,738	282
1880	13,034	968	14,002	8,043	691	5,358	14,092	308
1890	15,821	1,967	17,789	8,434	744	8,557	17,735	327
1900[25]	23,047	3,313	26,360	11,568	14,751 (v and vi combined)		26,319	409

Sources: Poor Law Board, 1st, 23rd Annual Reports, 1848, 1870–1. Local Government Board, 10th, 20th, 20 Annual Reports, 1880–1, 1890–1, 1900–1.

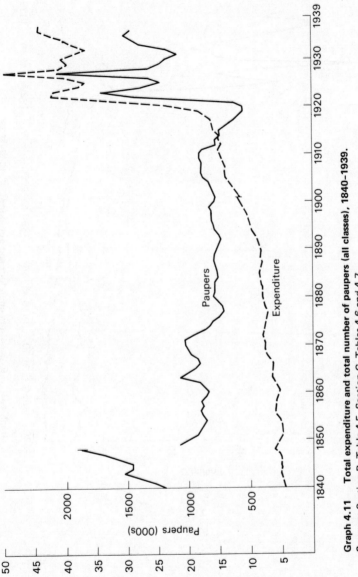

Graph 4.11   Total expenditure and total number of paupers (all classes), 1840–1939.
Sources: Section B, Table 4.5. Section C, Tables 4.6 and 4.7.

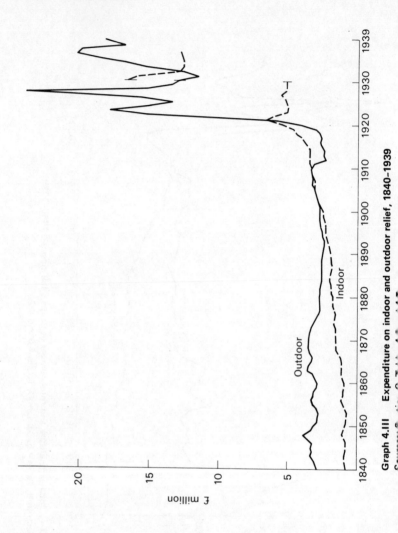

Graph 4.III   Expenditure on indoor and outdoor relief, 1840–1939

Notes (Section C)

1 This total excludes items of expenditure from poor rate receipts which were unconnected or partly connected with the relief of the poor. For the importance of these excluded items, see Table 4.8.

 From 1904, some expenditure is recorded twice, that is, appears in more than one sub-total column. This double-counting has been eliminated from the total which is therefore by a small amount less than the sum of the sub-totals.

2 Available official figures for expenditure per capita differ slightly because different sources use different population estimates for the same year. A more serious problem is the imperfect separation of poor law from non-poor law expenditure in the early nineteenth century.

3 For an explanation of the mode of calculating 'average weekly dole', see the text introducing this section on cost.

4 Includes all expenses of maintenance, treatment, and relief of paupers in workhouses and other poor law establishments (including charges for apprentice fees, outfits, burials, heating, lighting and cleaning, and also cost of maintenance of vagrants in vagrant wards). Excludes cost of building and repairs, furniture, and the salaries, rations and superannuation of officers and servants.

5 Includes cost of relief, in money and kind, given outside poor law establishments, also school fees and expenses for children boarded out. Excludes salaries of officers distributing and administering out-relief.

6 Until 1857 included in 'other' (Table 4.8, col. vii). This is the full sum paid to public or private asylums by boards of guardians without deduction on account of grants from the Exchequer paid through county and borough councils. These grants were first paid in 1874 and amounted to 3 shillings per head by 1900. The costs of maintaining lunatics in asylums included an allowance for staff salaries and asylum running costs. As no such allowance was made for lunatics in workhouses, it is difficult to produce an estimate of over-all expenditure on pauper lunatics.

 The cost of maintenance of imbeciles in the metropolitan asylum district is included under 'in maintenance'.

7 Until 1853 included in 'other' (Table 4.8, col. vii). Until 1883, this sub-total included workhouse loans only and excluded loans for any other purpose.

8 Until 1853 included in 'other' (Table 4.8, col. vii). The total excludes superannuation deducted from salaries under the provision of the Poor Law Officers Superannuation Act of 1896.

9 Until 1853 this sub-total has been calculated by subtraction. From 1857 to 1899 the main items of expenditure here were establishment charges and buildings and repairs not financed from loans.

10 For the years to 1870 inclusive, the figure given is of rateable value at the end of the year. Subsequently the figure is of rateable value at the start of each financial year. From 1898 the figure is of

assessable value as defined by the Agricultural Rates Act 1896, and until 1916 this figure is about £12,000,000 less than the full rateable value. From 1899 the total includes the value of non-rateable government property in respect of which contributions in lieu of rates were received. Such contributions amounted to under £2,000,000 in the 1900s.

11   From 1866 includes superannuation.

12   From 1869 to 1883, the 'other' and 'total' columns include adjustments (in brackets) made for sums received from, or paid to, the Metropolitan Common Poor Fund.

13   From 1884, the contributions made by the metropolitan unions to the managers of the metropolitan asylum district were distributed, as far as practicable, under the appropriate sub-headings.

14   From 1901, this excludes the public health service expenditure of the metropolitan asylum services. In 1901 the sum excluded as 'not properly expenditure on relief' was £571,000.

15   From 1920 expenditure statistics were published in the Annual Local Taxation Returns, where costs of maintenance in institutions controlled by poor law and non-poor law authorities are given separately. In Table 4.6 they have been added together to preserve continuity. Figures (in £000s) for maintenance in non-poor law institutions (not asylums) are 440 in 1920 and 782 in 1930.

16   This figure is distorted by the method of calculation. The sharp increase in outdoor pauperism in the first quarter of 1921 is reflected only in expenditure for that year.

17   The rateable value in October 1929 when rates for the half year then commencing were levied.

18   Partly estimated.

19   Includes interest on temporary loans which amounts to £339,235 in 1930 but thereafter is generally less than £1,000.

20   Includes grants and contributions from relatives.

21   Includes the relatively modest cost of legal proceedings.

22   Includes valuations and legal costs.

23   From 1813 to 1830, this total includes only the police rate. After 1830, such items as registration, vaccination, highways boards, school boards and rural sanitary authorities are gradually introduced.

24   These sums are included in total expenses.

25   Figures in 1900 are not comparable with those for earlier years due to the reorganisation following the Local Government Act 1894 and the Agricultural Rates Act 1896.

Section D Relief to men without work, 1839-1939

This section presents statistics on relief given to men without work for the period 1839-1939. Together with the pre-1834 statistics (Section A), the sequence of tables in this section is crucial to any reconstruction of nineteenth-century pauperism. Specifically, they allow the reader to identify the two massive discontinuities in the late 1830s and in the early 1920s, when there was a decisive change in poor law practice about relief to men without work. The first of these discontinuities in the 1830s has hitherto been invisible to a historiography that has partitioned off the pre-1834 statistics from the post-1834 statistics and even the 1840s statistics from the 1890s statistics. The second discontinuity in the 1920s has not been suppressed, but its definition has suffered from this partitioning.

Table 4.9 lays out the official statistics of the 1840s which usefully discriminated between those unemployed and those underemployed or underpaid. If these statistics on men 'in want of work' are related to the pre-1834 statistics (Section A, Table 4.2) then Table 4.9 shows how relief practice changed dramatically and quickly after 1834. In the 1840s, even with the double-counting inevitable in a quarterly total, the Poor Law Commission could never find more than 43,000 men receiving outdoor relief because of want of work. The total number of men on relief was usually much smaller; the reformed poor law had moved out of large-scale assistance to the unemployed and underemployed which had been the norm before 1834.

Tables 4.10 and 4.11 present the statistics on relief to the unemployed right up to 1914. In outdoor relief, the category of men 'in want of work' is carried over from the earlier statistics, but totals are now calculated on a day count basis. After 1891 an indoor series on 'able-bodied men in health' is available to complement the outdoor series. At the same time, this indoor series introduces an element of exaggeration because, as the footnotes make clear, only a minority of this group was employable. Through the whole period after 1851, the statistics, where available, are presented on an annual basis. When a trade union unemployment percentage is added (Table 4.10, col. ii; Table 4.11, col. vi), this shows how numbers on relief remained small even when unemployment was high at the trough of the regular trade cycle. Between 1861 and 1884, there is a twenty-year gap in the official statistics on relief to those in 'want of work'. This is partly bridged by the special return of 1872 and it is very unlikely, at least in the 1870s, that the poor law deviated from its policy of no relief to the unemployed. Tables 4.10 and 4.11 show that this policy was maintained for seventy years after the great transformation supervised by the Poor Law Commission. In the twenty years before 1914, day counts showed there were never more than 21,000 men (indoors and out) on relief because they were unemployed. Table 4.15 on vagrancy provides an ironic counterpoint: from the 1880s onwards, the poor law often relieved as many or more vagrants than ordinarily unemployed working men.

From the 1880s onwards those in 'want of work' were colloquially known as 'the unemployed' and, from 1926 onwards, the group is identified as such in the official statistics. Table 4.12 gives the numbers receiving relief 'on account of unemployment' from 1921 to 1939. It shows how large numbers of unemployed men – nearly 200,000 in 1922 and 1923 (col. iii) – were relieved by the poor law between the wars. This second transformation cannot be explained simply by reference to high inter-war unemployment rates (Table 4.12, col. iv). As Table 4.13 shows, from mid-1922 onwards, three-quarters or more of the unemployed in Great Britain were drawing state unemployment insurance benefit. And, as Table 4.14 shows, generally only a small minority was claiming poor relief as well as insurance in the 1920s. Paradoxically, before the introduction of state unemployment insurance in 1911, almost none of the unemployed claimed poor relief. But, after the introduction of the unemployment insurance scheme in 1911 and the dilution of the contributory principle in the early 1920s, large numbers of the unemployed did claim poor relief.

It is necessary to be more cautious about relief to strikers since there is not a continuous series covering relief to this group. But, until the early years of this century, the poor law does appear to have opted out of the business of assisting strikers. The available statistics on coal strikes show that in 1893 a six-month coal strike had a negligible effect on numbers on relief. Table 4.16 shows the situation was quite different in 1921 and 1926 when large numbers of strikers obtained relief.

Recent historians, especially Digby (1976), have argued that unemployed and underemployed men were not directly recorded in the relevant official category, because they were relieved outdoors under a variety of pretexts and misrepresented as, for example, sick men. Table 4.17 summarises the relevant evidence for the decade of the 1850s. Moderately large numbers of able-bodied men were relieved on account of their own sickness or sickness in the family, but the pattern of seasonal and cyclical variation rules out the possibility that many of these were underemployed agricultural labourers or unemployed industrial labourers.

Table 4.9   Able-bodied men in 'want of work'[1] relieved outdoors, 1839–46

Number of unions	Quarter ended Lady Day	Able-bodied men relieved outdoors (£000s)				
		On account of want of work	On account of insufficiency of earnings	Other causes not being sickness, accident or infirmity	Total	(iv) as % of all paupers
		(i)	(ii)	(iii)	(iv)	(v)
not given	1839	5.7	8.4	2.5	16.6[2]	—
578	1840	10.4	9.1	2.8	22.3	2.3
578	1841	16.0	8.7	3.2	28.0	2.6
584	1842	21.1	12.5	3.6	37.2	3.1
585	1843	27.5	12.6	3.1	43.2	3.3
585	1844	14.2	9.4	2.5	26.2	2.1
585	1845	11.2	7.9	2.7	21.7	1.7
585	1846	10.6	7.4	2.6	20.6	1.8

Sources: Poor Law Commission, 5th–12th Annual Reports, 1839–46.

Table 4.10   Able-bodied men in 'want of work'[3] relieved outdoors 1849-61, 1872, 1884-90

Number of unions	1 Jan.	Number (000s)	% unemployed in certain trade unions	(i) as % of all paupers
		(i)	(ii)	(iii)
587	1849	17.4	—	1.9
590	1850	9.3	—	1.1
595	1851	5.3	3.9[6]	0.6
597	1852[5]	4.1	6.0	0.5
598	1853	1.6	1.7	0.2
614	1854	3.2	2.9	0.4
620	1855	4.2	5.4	0.5
624	1856	5.0	4.7	0.6
624	1857	3.8	6.0	0.4
629	1858	12.2	11.9	1.3
629	1859	2.5	3.8	0.3
629	1860	1.7	1.9	0.2
629	1861	3.7	5.2	0.4
[4]	1872	2.1	0.9	0.2
	1884	1.3	8.1	0.2
	1885	3.4	9.3	0.4
	1886	4.4	10.2	0.5
	1887	3.5	7.6	0.4
	1888	3.6	4.6	0.4
	1889	2.0	2.1(3.3)	0.2
	1890	0.7	2.1(1.7)	0.1

Sources: (a) cols i, iii
1849-59   Poor Law Board, 11th Annual Report, 1858-9.
1860   Poor Law Board, 12th Annual Report, 1859-60.
1861   Poor Law Board, 13th Annual Report, 1860-1.
1872   BPP, 1872, vol. LI.
1884-90   Royal Commission on the Poor Laws (1909), Statistical Appendix, vol. XXV (BPP, 1910, vol. LIII).
(b) col. ii
Mitchell and Deane (1962).

*Table 4.11   Able-bodied men in 'want of work' and 'in health'
relieved indoors and outdoors, 1891-1914*

	Men ('000s)				(iv) and[10]	Trade[11]	
	Outdoor			Total	estimated	union	(v) as %
		(i) as %		(i) and	dependants	unemployment	of all
1 Jan.	Number[7]	of (iv)	Indoor[9]	(iii)	('000s)	%	paupers
	(i)	(ii)	(iii)	(iv)	(v)	(vi)	(vii)
1891	1.5	17.1	7.3	8.9	35.4	3.0	4.5
1892	0.7	10.0	6.5	7.2	28.9	4.4	3.8
1893	3.0	26.9	8.0	11.0	43.9	10.2	5.6
1894	3.0	23.1	9.9	12.9	51.6	7.9	6.3
1895	2.8	21.1	10.6	13.4	53.7	7.7	6.5
1896	1.1	9.3	10.5	11.6	46.4	4.8	5.5
1897	0.8	7.2	10.2	11.0	44.0	3.1	5.3
1898	0.9	8.2	9.5	10.4	41.4	5.1	4.9
1899	0.5	6.2	7.8	8.3	33.3	2.6	4.1
1900	0.3	3.7	7.7	8.0	32.1	2.3	4.0
1901	0.4	6.0	6.6	7.0	28.0	3.5	3.5
1902	0.6	7.1	7.6	8.1	32.5	4.2	4.0
1903	0.9	10.0	8.3	9.3	37.1	5.0	4.4
1904	1.6	14.2	9.6	11.2	44.7	6.3	5.2
1905	7.9	40.7	11.5	19.3	77.4	7.1	8.4
1906	4.2	25.8	12.2	16.4	65.5	4.5	7.1
1907	2.2	16.3	11.5	13.7	55.0	4.4	6.0
1908	2.7	19.3	11.4	14.1	56.0	5.6	6.1
1909	6.4	30.9	14.2	20.6	82.4	9.1	8.6
1910	3.3	18.0	14.8	18.1	72.2	6.6	7.7
1911	2.7	16.5	13.6	16.2	64.9	5.0	7.3
1912	1.2	8.4	13.1	14.3	57.1	3.1	7.1
1913	1.5[8]	12.1	11.0	12.5	50.0	2.3	6.3
1914	1.6	9.6	9.3	10.3	41.1	2.6	5.4

Sources: (a) col. i
1891–1908   Royal Commission on the Poor Laws (1909), Statistical Appendix,
vol. XXV (BPP, 1910, vol. LIII).
1909–14   Local Government Board, 38th–43rd Annual Reports, 1908-9 to
1913–14.
(b) col. iii
1891–1908   As col. i.
1909–14   Poor Relief Annual Returns (1st Jan.) BPP.
(c) col. vi
1891–1914   British Labour Statistics Historical Abstract.

Table 4.12   Outdoor[12] *relief 'on account of unemployment' 1921–39*

1 Jan.	Total[13] ('000s)	Total per 1,000 population	Men ('000s)	Unemployment[14] among insured workers	(iii) as % of all paupers
	(i)	(ii)	(iii)	(iv)	(v)
1921	37.0	1	9.0	7.8	1.4
1922	744.8	19.7	182.8	17.7	12.2
1923	721.7	18.9	178.6	12.6	11.6
1924	525.1	13.7	128.4	10.5	9.4
1925	326.4	8.4	81.0	10.6	6.7
1926	486.6	12.5	130.1	10.1	9.0
1927	632.1	16.2	175.4	11.7	11.3
1928	449.9	11.4	121.2	9.8	8.9
1929	313.1	7.9	82.8	11.0	6.7
1930	250.1	6.3	66.1	10.9	5.5
1931	155.7	3.9	41.3	19.6	3.7
1932	263.1	6.6	74.5	20.6	5.9
1933	418.2	10.4	122.3	21.5	8.2
1934	424.9	10.5	129.2	17.4	8.5
1935	452.1	11.2	138.8	15.9	8.7
1936	329.9	8.1	105.2	13.9	7.0
1937	241.2	5.9	78.4	11.9	5.6
1938	56.3	1.4	17.9	11.8	1.5
1939	56.3	1.3	17.3	12.7	1.4

Sources: (a) cols i–iii
Poor Relief Annual Returns (1 Jan.) BPP.
(b) col. iv
Abstract of Labour Statistics, *Ministry of Labour Gazette.*

Table 4.13   Proportions of the unemployed assisted by insurance benefit[15] *and poor relief,*[16] *1922-38 (Great Britain)*

Date		Unemployed (excluding dependants)[17]			
		Number receiving		Percentage receiving	
		Insurance benefits ('000s)	Poor relief ('000s)	Insurance benefits	Poor relief
		(i)	(ii)	(iii)	(iv)
1922	June	690	356	45.9	23.7
	Dec.[18]	1,107	239	77.4	17.0
1923	June	1,061	205	83.6	16.3
	Dec.	—	174	—	14.6
1924	June	—	141	—	12.8
	Dec.	1,035	113	82.0	9.0
1925	June	992	117	71.5	8.4
	Dec.	971	162	79.8	13.4
1926[19]	June	1,475	452	84.6	25.9
	Dec.	1,141	264	79.7	18.4
1927	June	825	157	75.6	14.4
	Dec.	943	154	77.9	12.7
1928	June	1,057	120	82.3	9.3
	Dec.	1,092	112	80.6	8.3
1929	June	951	95	79.7	8.0
	Dec.	1,126	94	81.8	6.8
1930	June	1,706	43	89.2	2.2
	Dec.	2,356	59	94.5	2.4
1931	June	2,377	66	87.4	2.4
	Dec.	2,107	101	77.8	3.7
1932	June	2,265	130	78.6	4.5
	Dec.	2,239	168	79.1	5.9
1933	June	1,994	165	78.3	6.5
	Dec.	1,790	192	77.4	8.3
1934	June	1,688	203	77.5	9.3
	Dec.	1,680	222	77.3	10.2
1935	June	1,621	175	77.6	8.4
	Dec.	1,510	173	77.6	8.9
1936	June	1,366	150	76.8	8.4
	Dec.	1,323	144	77.9	8.5
1937	June	1,157	31	81.3	2.2
	Dec.	1,452	30	83.8	1.7
1938	June	1,605	27	85.4	1.4
	Dec.	1,630	28	85.4	1.5

Sources: (a) cols i, iii
Burns (1941), p. 347, Table ii, cols 4 and 7.
(b) col. ii
Burns (1941), p. 360, Table vii, col. 2.
(c) col. iv
Burns (1941), p. 53, Table i, col. 4; and partly calculated from *ibid.*, p. 343, Table i, col. 8 and col. 2.

Table 4.14   Overlap between poor relief and unemployment insurance, 1923-30

Date		Total ('000s)	Receiving poor relief ('000s)	Receiving insurance and poor relief ('000s)	(iii) as % of (i)
		Unemployed insured (excluding dependants)			
		(i)	(ii)	(iii)	(iv)
1923	Nov.	1,250	148 (Dec.)	89.4	7.2
1924	Nov.	1,233	95 (Dec.)	38.8	3.1
1926	April	905	119	34.4	3.8
1927	April	1,045	108	18.8	1.8
1930	Feb.	1,500	57	not known	

Sources: (a) cols i–iii
Witmer (1931), p. 283, Table viii.
(b) col. ii
estimated by allowing 2.4 dependants to each insured person from the Ministry of Health quarterly statements which grouped together the insured persons and their dependants.

Table 4.15   Relief to vagrants,[20] 1849-1939

1 Jan.	Number[21] of vagrants relieved ('000s) (i)	(i) as % of all paupers (ii)	Unemployment[23] % (iii)
1849	7.3	0.8	
1850	3.7	0.4	
1851	3.4	0.4	3.9
1852	1.9	0.2	6.0
1853	1.4	0.2	1.7
1854	1.6	0.2	2.9
1855	1.6	0.2	5.4
1856	1.9	0.2	4.7
1857	2.1	0.2	6.0
1858	2.3	0.3	11.9
1859	2.0	0.2	3.8
1860	1.5	0.2	1.9
1861	1.9	0.2	5.2
1862	2.8	0.3	8.4
1863	4.2	0.4	6.0
1864	3.1	0.3	2.7
1865	3.3	0.3	2.1
1866	4.5	0.5	3.3
1867	5.0	0.5	7.4
1868	6.1	0.6	7.9
1869	7.0	0.7	6.7
1870	5.4	0.6	3.9
1871	3.7	0.3	1.6
1872	3.4	0.3	0.9
1873[22]	3.0	0.3	1.2
1874	3.1	0.4	1.7
1875	2.2	0.3	2.4
1876	3.3	0.4	3.7
1877	4.2	0.6	4.7
1878	5.1	0.7	6.8
1879	4.7	0.6	11.4
1880	5.9	0.7	5.5
1881	6.2	0.8	3.5
1882	5.8	0.7	2.3
1883	4.6	0.6	2.6
1884	4.9	0.6	8.1
1885	4.9	0.6	9.3
1886	5.5	0.7	10.2
1887	5.0	0.6	7.6
1888	5.8	0.7	4.6
1889	7.1	0.9	2.1
1890	5.7	0.7	2.1
1891	5.6	0.7	3.5
1892	7.0	0.9	6.3
1893	7.1	0.9	7.5
1894	9.5	1.2	6.9
1895	10.2	1.2	5.8
1896	13.2	1.6	3.3

1 Jan.	Number[21] of vagrants relieved ('000s)	(i) as % of all paupers	Unemployment[23] %
	(i)	(ii)	(iii)
1897	12.3	1.5	3.3
1898	13.6	1.6	2.8
1899	13.4	1.6	2.0
1900[24]	{ 9.8 / 5.6	1.2 / 0.7	2.5
1901	6.8	0.9	3.3
1902	7.9	1.0	4.0
1903	8.3	1.0	4.7
1904	8.7	1.0	6.0
1905	10.0	1.1	5.0
1906	9.8	1.1	3.6
1907	8.4	0.9	3.7
1908	10.4	1.1	7.8
1909	9.7	1.0	7.7
1910	10.4	1.1	4.7
1911	10.5	1.2	3.0
1912	9.7	1.2	3.2
1913	8.9	1.1	2.1
1914	7.6	1.0	3.3
1915	5.4	0.7	1.1
1916	3.6	0.5	0.4
1917	2.9	0.5	0.7
1918	1.5	0.3	0.8
1919	1.1	0.2	2.4
1920	2.0	0.4	2.4
1921	4.1	0.6	14.8
1922	6.6	0.4	15.2
1923	7.6	0.5	11.6
1924	7.8	0.6	10.9
1925	7.7	0.6	11.2
1926	8.3	0.6	12.7
1927	10.7	0.7	10.6
1928	10.5	0.8	11.2
1929	11.6	0.9	11.0
1930	11.5	1.0	14.6
1931	11.6	1.0	21.5
1932	12.9	1.0	22.5
1933	15.9	1.1	21.3
1934	15.2	1.0	17.7
1935	12.8	0.8	16.4
1936	11.2	0.7	11.3
1937	10.4	0.7	13.3
1938	10.2	0.8	11.3
1939	10.5	0.9	11.7

Sources: (a) cols i, ii
1849–59   Poor Law Board, 11th Annual Report, 1858–9.
1860–1900   Local Government Board, 30th Annual Report, 1900–1.
1900–20   Ministry of Health, 1st Annual Report, 1920.
1920–39   Poor Relief Annual Returns (1 Jan.), BPP, 1938–9, vol. XXI.
(b) col. iii
Mitchell and Deane (1962).

Table 4.16   Coal strikes and the poor law, the 1890s versus the 1920s[25]

Period covered by dispute	Maximum increase in no. of persons on domiciliary relief in directly affected areas		Net increase in the no. of persons on domiciliary relief at same time in England and Wales	
	Number	%	Number	%
1893 June–Nov.	2,270	11	25,489	5
1898 End April–July	43,751	155	32,200	6
1921 1 April–1 July	464,683	373	647,500	144
1926 1 May–drift back late autumn	1,162,592	337	1,266,095	126

Source: Public Record Office, MH57 (94).

Table 4.17   Able-bodied men relieved outdoors on account of sickness or 'urgent necessity', 1849–61

		Causes of relief		Trade union
		Sudden and urgent necessity	Own sickness accident, or infirmity	Family sickness, accident, or infirmity, or a funeral	unemployment annual mean %
		(i)	(ii)	(iii)	(iv)
1849	Jan.	703	25,506	10,996	
	July	506	22,257	8,815	
1850	Jan.	308	22,650	9,071	
	July	201	18,604	6,790	
1851	Jan.	200	19,799	7,489	3.9
	July	190	17,147	6,539	
1852	Jan.	220	17,650	8,801	6.0
	July	102	17,049	6,442	
1853	Jan.	125	17,179	6,476	1.7
	July	81	14,392	5,394	
1854	Jan.	225	17,606	7,431	2.9
	July	133	15,967	6,849	
1855	Jan.	116	17,781	7,587	5.4
	July	97	16,877	6,644	
1856	Jan.	164	18,526	7,579	4.7
	July	78	15,556	6,001	
1857	Jan.	83	17,210	6,835	6.0
	July	117	15,402	6,053	
1858	Jan.	141	19,146	7,820	11.9
	July	78	15,544	5,698	
1859	Jan.	85	17,239	6,335	3.8
	July				
1860	Jan.	94	17,573	6,932	1.9
	July	117	16,116	7,376	
1861	Jan.	168	18,792	8,274	5.2

Sources: cols i–iii
Poor Law Board, 11th–13th Annual Report, 1858–9 to 1860–1.
col. iv
Mitchel and Deane (1962).

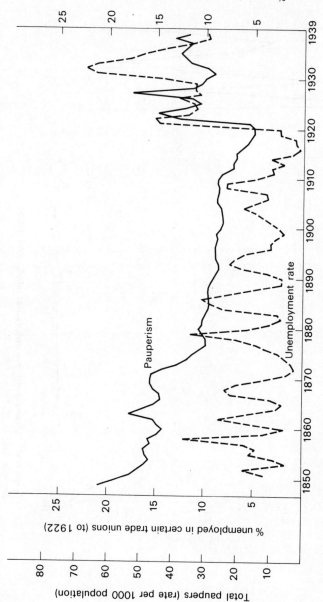

% unemployed among insured workers (from 1922)

% unemployed in certain trade unions (to 1922)

Total paupers (rate per 1000 population)

Pauperism

Unemployment rate

Graph 4.IV   Pauper numbers per 1,000 population versus unemployment rates, 1851–1939
Sources: Section B, Table 4.5. Section D, Table 4.15, col. iii.

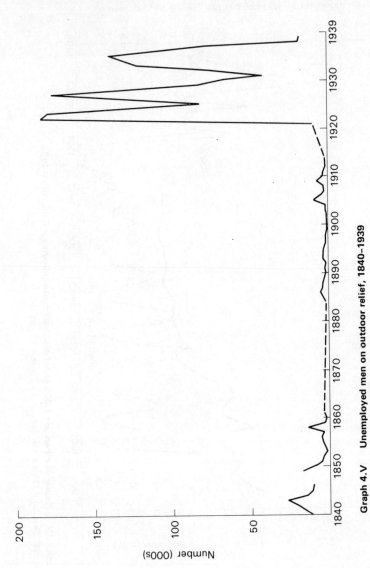

Graph 4.V   Unemployed men on outdoor relief, 1840–1939
Sources: Section D, Tables 4.9–4.12.

Notes (Section D)

1 Those included in Table 4.9 were officially classified as relieved 'on account of want of work, insufficiency of earnings and other causes'. The totals are sub-divided into these categories in columns i, ii and iii.

2 It should be emphasised that these totals are quarterly counts and, unlike the later day count totals, they are swollen by an uncertain amount of double-counting. This makes the relatively low total figures all the more remarkable.

3 Table 4.10 records the able-bodied males relieved outdoors 'on account of want of work and other causes'. Adult able-bodied males were also classified under three other headings: on account of 'sudden and urgent necessity', on account of 'own sickness, accident or infirmity', or on account of 'sickness, accident or infirmity of any of the family' or of a funeral in the family.

4 From 1872 onwards, the returns can be assumed to be complete and cover all unions.

5 A special return from 608 unions (BPP, 1852-3, vol. LXXIV) counted 8,041 persons relieved as 'out of work' and 18,182 relieved 'in aid of wages' during the tenth week of the Christmas quarter, 1852. It is not clear who these 'persons' were. The accompanying notes show that some unions included widows and others did not. The special return of 'persons' is thus substantially less useful than the annual series on 'able-bodied men'.

6 The unemployment percentages given in this column are means for the whole year. For 1889 and 1890, the unemployment percentage at the end of December in the previous year is given in brackets.

7 Totals in this column are completely comparable with, and a direct continuation of, those in Table 4.10, column i.

8 In 1912 the outdoor able-bodied/non-able-bodied classification was abandoned. For 1913 and 1914, the outdoor total is of men relieved on account 'of other causes'. This was one of four sub-headings, the other three being 'own accident or sickness', 'own bodily or mental infirmity', and 'bodily or mental infirmity affecting wife or child'. The 'other causes' total is most closely comparable to the earlier totals given in column i.

9 The totals in this column are of those indoors in institutions and classified as 'in health' rather than 'temporarily disabled'. These totals substantially overstate the numbers of unemployed men relieved in poor law institutions. The category of 'able-bodied and in health' was not officially defined in a rigorous way. Individuals were classified as such at the discretion of workhouse masters who often returned as 'able-bodied' all those who were under sixty and not on a special diet (Royal Commission on the Poor Laws, 1909, evidence Q. 9208). Local Government Board inspectors claimed that only a minority of those classified as 'able-bodied and in health' could have left the workhouse to take up a job (Royal Commission on the Poor Laws, 1909, evidence Q. 4145-7).

10 An estimated total of men and dependants in this column is obtained by multiplying the total of men (col. iii) by four. The results are approximate but probably reasonably accurate. E. M. Burns (1941) used a multiplier of 3.5 for the same purpose in the inter-war period. It would seem sensible to use a slightly higher multiplier for the pre-1914 period to allow for higher fertility among the general labourers who accounted for most of the applications for poor relief because of unemployment.

11 The figures in this column give the percentage unemployed at the end of December in the previous year. The trade unions included are those which paid unemployment benefit. Membership of these unions rose from 167,000 in 1884 to 993,000 in 1914.

12 Virtually all those receiving relief on account of unemployment in the inter-war period were on outdoor relief. The returns of 1927 explicitly state that only a small number of persons received institutional relief on account of unemployment.

13 In 1926 and subsequent years, there were direct counts of those relieved 'on account of unemployment'. From 1922 to 1926, the count was of those 'ordinarily engaged in some regular occupation'. The 1921 figures were official estimates based on the assumption that 90 per cent of 'men on relief in their own homes on account of causes other than sickness, accident or bodily or mental infirmity' were unemployed. This estimate was then multiplied by four to obtain an estimate of the total number of men plus dependants.

14 The unemployment percentages in this column are those for December of the previous year. Because of the way in which the unemployment figures were calculated towards the end of each month, it is the December unemployment percentage which is closer to the 1 January poor relief day count.

15 The totals include those receiving contributory benefits under the insurance scheme proper, and those receiving quasi non-contributory benefits under five supplementary schemes between 1921 and 1937 (uncovenanted benefit, extended benefit, transitional benefit, transitional payment, unemployment assistance). Technically, the total is of the 'number of claims admitted' on one day in the month, except from June 1925 to June 1931, when it is the total of 'claims current' and also includes those with claims under consideration.

16 Only after 1926 do the poor law statistics directly show the number relieved outdoors on account of unemployment. Burns obtained comparable pre-1926 totals by deflating the larger total of persons ordinarily engaged in some regular occupation. It should be noted that Table 4.13 is the only one in the section where the totals are for Great Britain rather than England and Wales.

17 The Ministry of Health poor law statistics only give totals which include dependants. Burns obtained an estimate of numbers of unemployed persons excluding dependants by using a deflator of 3.5 on the Ministry totals.

18 Figures shown for December 1922 and June 1923 relate to November and April of those years.

19 Figures for 1926 show the effects of the general strike and the long continued coal strike of that year.

20 Table 4.15 gives day count totals of homeless, itinerant persons who were mainly single men. In the nineteenth century they were known colloquially as tramps and officially as 'vagrants' or (later) 'casuals'. They should not be confused with what contemporary investigators called casual labourers who were underemployed general labourers hired on an irregular, usually daily, basis.

21 Column i gives the total of those relieved indoors and out. It is worth noting that the majority of vagrants were relieved out of the workhouse until 1857 but that from the early 1870s onwards, the vast majority of vagrants were relieved indoors in a workhouse 'spike'. Figures for certain years are as follows:

1st Jan.	Indoor	Outdoor	1st Jan.	Indoor	Outdoor
1849	1,956	5,308	1875	1,944	281
1850	1,021	2,696	1880	5,347	567
1855	745	811	1855	4,548	318
1860	903	639	1890	5,434	267
1865	2,055	1,284	1895	9,561	601
1870	4,147	1,283	1900	9,723	118

22 Returns are not complete and do not cover all unions until 1873.

23 From 1851 to 1922, the percentage is of unemployed in certain trade unions. From 1923 to 1939, the percentage is of unemployment among insured workers.

24 The day count procedure changes at this point. Before 1900, the count had been of all vagrants receiving relief at any time during the day on 1 January. Subsequently, the count was of vagrants relieved on the night of 1 January. This change eliminated the double-counting of vagrants who received relief from two unions in a single day but at the price of omitting the small number who only received daytime relief.

25 The coal dispute of 1912 was not covered in Table 4.16 which was produced by the Ministry of Health and circulated inside the Ministry but never published. The Annual Report for 1926-7 (p. 116) estimated that the coal dispute of 1912 temporarily added around 50,000 to numbers in receipt of relief.

Section E Children and widows with dependent children on outdoor relief, c. 1850-1939

This section includes one table on all the children who were maintained or assisted by the poor law after 1850 and several tables about the specific group of children who were the dependants of widows.

Table 4.18 presents statistics on the total number of children on the poor law (col. iii), indoors (col. i), and outdoors (col. ii) at five-yearly intervals from 1851. These totals are directly available in the official statistics of an era that idealised age and sex divisions, for example, in its workhouses after 1834. The totals are of limited interest in any modern reconstruction of pauperism, because they lump together children in so many different circumstances. However, the proportion of children to all paupers is significant (Table 4.18, col. iv). Falling percentages here clearly show the institutions' later nineteenth-century movement away from assisting active adults in the child-bearing and rearing years.

The remaining tables in this section deal with those classified in the official statistics as 'widows with dependent children'. The classification was a precise one. In the nineteenth century, out-relief was seldom offered to the separated or unmarried woman with dependent children; thus there is an important difference between 'widows with dependent children' on out-relief and the late twentieth-century group of single-parent families on social security. Even with the exclusion of the disreputable single parent, widows and their children made up between 10 and 20 per cent of all paupers through the nineteenth century (Table 4.19, col. xii; Table 4.20, col. iv). As the tables show, the group was large because the poor law was assisting a substantial minority of all widows in the 20–45 age group (Table 4.20, col. v).

Tables 4.19 and 4.20 present three consecutive series for number of widows and dependent children drawing relief for the years 1840-6, 1849-1912, 1920-32 at yearly intervals except for gaps in the 1860s and 1870s. The series are roughly comparable for reasons explained in the footnotes to each table which indicate the discrepancies. The two later series do not sub-divide the group to show cause of relief because this is no longer recorded in the official statistics after the 1840s. A final table (4.21) takes totals from the three series and calculates the number of dependent children per widow from 1841 to 1931. From this table, it is possible to assess the effect of the 'crusade against out-relief' in the 1870s, on the size of the pauper family unit.

Table 4.18   *Number of children relieved, 1851–1939*

1 Jan.	Number of children relieved ('000s)[1]			(iii) as % of all paupers
	Indoors	Outdoors	Total	
	(i)	(ii)	(iii)	
1851[2]	43.1	276.6	319.7	38.6
1856	44.6	289.8	334.4	38.1
1861	48.2	275.1	323.3	36.2
1866	48.6	277.9	326.5	35.3
1871	55.8	337.4	393.2	36.2
1876	46.3	195.9	242.1	32.2
1881	58.8	214.3	273.1	33.7
1886	57.0	213.7	270.7	33.3
1891	50.8	186.5	237.2	30.4
1896	55.3	184.6	239.8	28.7
1901	51.9	158.2	210.1	26.4
1906	61.2	180.0	241.2	26.2
1911	72.6	183.4	256.0	28.7
1915[3]	69.0	171.3	240.3	31.5
1921	59.8	174.1	233.9	35.2
1926	61.3	242.8	304.7	21.1
1931	53.5	300.4	353.9	31.5
1936	37.7	422.4	460.0	30.6
1939	32.3	261.8	294.1	24.1

Sources: 1851–6   Poor Law Board, 11th annual Report, 1858.
1861–91   Local Government Board, 23rd Annual Report, 1893–4.
1896–1915   Ministry of Health, 1st Annual Report, 1920.
1921–39   Poor Relief Annual Returns (1 Jan.), BPP.

Table 4.19 *Widows with dependent children on outdoor relief, 1840–6*

Number of unions	Quarter ended Lady Day[4]	On account of sickness, accident or infirmity		On account of want of work		On account of insufficiency of earnings		Other causes		Totals			(xi) as % of all paupers
		Adults '000s	Children '000s	Adults '000s	Children '000s	Adults '000s	Children '000s	Adults '000s	Children '000s	Adults '000s	Children '000s	Grand total	
		(i)	(ii)	(iii)	(iv)	(v)	(vi)	(vii)	(viii)	(ix)	(x)	(xi)	(xii)
578	1840	3.1	6.3	2.0	4.7	33.4	87.9	2.1	4.5	40.6	103.4	144.0	14.6
578	1841	3.2	7.0	2.3	5.8	33.1	87.4	1.8	3.8	40.4	104.0	144.4	13.5
584	1842	3.5	8.0	2.8	6.2	34.5	90.5	1.8	4.0	42.6	108.7	151.2	12.5
584	1843	3.4	7.8	3.1	7.6	36.1	94.9	1.7	4.0	44.4	114.3	158.7	12.2
585	1844	4.0	8.8	2.6	6.5	37.6	100.4	1.4	3.3	45.7	119.0	164.7	13.2
585	1845	4.4	9.8	2.9	6.7	38.6	102.0	1.6	3.7	47.5	122.2	169.8	13.6
585	1846	4.6	9.7	2.4	5.6	38.4	101.2	1.4	3.3	46.8	119.7	166.5	14.8

Sources: Poor Law Commission, 6th–12th Annual Reports, 1840–6.

Table 4.20   Able-bodied widows with dependent children under sixteen on outdoor relief, 1849–1932

1 Jan.	Able-bodied widows ('000s)	Dependent children ('000s)	Total (i) and (ii) ('000s)	(iii) as % of all paupers	(i) as % of widows aged 20–45 yrs
	(i)	(ii)	(iii)	(iv)	(v)
1849	51.8	118.3	170.1	18.2	
1850	53.2	126.2	179.3	20.4	
1851	50.6	123.4	174.0	21.0	39.2
1852	47.1	120.0	167.1	20.8	
1853	45.0	115.2	160.2	20.9	
1854	47.2	113.8	161.0	20.0	
1855	49.4	123.4	172.7	20.5	
1856	52.7	125.0	177.6	20.3	
1857	50.4	126.7	177.1	21.0	
1858	52.5	129.4	181.9	20.0	
1859	50.6	126.8	177.4	21.3	
1860	49.1	122.3	171.4	20.1	
1861	50.1	124.4	174.5	19.6	34.6
1872	60.3	154.8	215.1	19.8	36.0
1884	41.5	119.5	160.9	20.7	22.9[5]
1885	40.6	117.1	157.7	20.0	
1886	41.2	119.4	160.6	19.6	
1887	41.8	121.1	162.9	19.8	
1888	41.3	119.0	160.3	19.3	
1889	40.6	117.4	158.1	19.3	
1890	38.4	111.3	149.7	18.9	
1891	37.5	109.2	146.6	18.8	20.7
1892	36.6	107.0	143.6	18.9	
1893	37.1	107.8	144.9	18.5	
1894	38.6	111.2	149.8	18.2	
1895	38.6	119.7	158.3	19.1	
1896	38.8	110.8	149.6	17.9	
1897	37.2	105.6	142.8	17.1	
1898	36.5	103.8	140.3	16.8	
1899	34.6	98.9	133.5	16.3	
1900	33.9	95.8	129.8	16.1	
1901	34.1	97.3	131.4	16.5	18.6
1902	32.3	96.7	129.0	15.8	
1903	34.4	96.8	131.3	15.6	
1904	34.3	95.0	129.2	15.0	
1905	34.8	96.7	131.5	14.2	
1906	34.7	96.8	131.5	14.3	
1907	33.7	93.1	126.7	13.8	
1908	32.7	92.3	125.1	13.5	
1909	33.3	92.5	125.9	13.1	
1910	34.1	94.8	128.9	13.7	
1911	33.9	93.7	127.6	14.3	19.9
1912[6]	34.0	93.5	127.4	17.3	
1920	35.1	88.0	123.0	21.3	
1921	41.5	93.5	135.0	20.3	14.8
1922	50.6	111.5	162.1	10.9	
1923	53.9	121.8	175.8	11.4	
1924	53.4	120.6	174.0	12.7	
1925	53.5	119.9	173.4	14.4	
1926	54.2	120.6	174.8	12.1	
1927[7]	27.5	59.9	87.3	5.6	

Table 4.20 (cont.)

1 Jan.	Able-bodied widows ('000s)	Dependent children ('000s)	Total (i) and (ii) ('000s)	(iii) as % of all paupers	(i) as % of widows aged 20–45 yrs
	(i)	(ii)	(iii)	(iv)	(v)
1928	21.8	49.9	71.6	5.2	
1929	19.8	46.1	65.9	5.3	
1930	19.4	46.3	65.8	5.5	
1931	20.5	47.8	68.3	6.1	10.7
1932	22.5	50.9	73.3	5.8	

Sources: (a) cols i–iv

1849–59   Poor Law Board, 11th Annual Report, 1858–9.

1860   Poor Law Board, 12th Annual Report, 1859–60.

1861   Poor Law Board, 13th Annual Report, 1860–1.

1872   BPP, 1872, vol. LI.

1884–1908   Royal Commission on the Poor Laws (1909), Statistical Appendix, vol. XXV (BPP, 1910, vol. LIII).

1909–12   Local Government Board, 38th–41st Annual Reports, 1908-9 to 1911–12.

1920–32   Poor Relief Annual Returns (1 Jan.) BPP.

(b) col. v

Calculated from census figures and col. i.

Table 4.21   Number of dependent children per widow, 1841–1931

1841	2.6[8]
1851	2.4
1861	2.5
1871	2.6
1884	2.9
1891	2.9
1901	2.9
1911	2.8
1921	2.3
1931	2.3

Sources: Tables 4.19, 4.20, and 4.21 provide the totals used for the calculation.

Notes (Section E)

1 The totals and sub-totals are of children of all classes excluding casuals and, from 1896, the small number of insane in asylums.
2 Only after 1875 do the totals include children in every union in England and Wales.
3 Figures for 1916 are not available.
4 All the totals in Table 4.19 are of those drawing relief in the quarter ended on Lady Day in that year. Double-counting is not a great problem in the case of this group, because widows with dependent children were usually permanent pensioners of the institution in the nineteenth century. Thus the quarterly totals in Table 4.19 are likely to be more or less directly comparable with the later day count totals in Tables 4.20 and 4.21.
5 Using census figures for 1881.
6 After 1912, the count is of widows with dependent children rather than able-bodied widows with dependent children. Practically, the change of category makes no difference.
7 The 50 per cent decrease in totals 1926–7 is due to the introduction of widows' pensions under the Widows' Orphans' and Old Age Contributory Pensions Act 1925.
8 Again, it should be noted that the 1841 totals are quarterly counts and all subsequent totals are day counts. This discrepancy does not seriously affect the comparability of the 1841 figure for reasons explained in footnote 4.

This section deals with the aged, the chronic sick, and the temporarily disabled. These groups are considered jointly in this section because they are dealt with in a series of interrelated categories in the official statistics of the period.

After 1839, the aged and the chronic sick are counted together in one general category. From 1839 to 1846, the 'aged and infirm' are counted together and usefully divided into those 'wholly' and 'partially' unable to work, Table 4.22 presents these statistics of the 1840s. Then for the whole of the period 1849 to 1912, the aged and chronic sick, indoors and out, are categorised together as 'non-able-bodied paupers'. Table 4.23 presents annual totals of the 'non-able-bodied' through the second half of the century. It shows that this general category accounted for up to one half of all paupers (Table 4.23, col. iv).

Any reconstruction of nineteenth-century pauperism has problems about separating out sub-groups such as the aged from this larger general category. The census provides a continuous record of the ages of indoor paupers at decennial intervals through the second half of the century. On this basis, Table 4.24 gives the total number of indoor paupers aged sixty-five and over from 1851 to 1931. But a much larger group of the aged was always outdoors and for this group regular statistics become available only after the special return of 1890. Even after this late date, it is impossible to present one continuous series because the definition of old age in the official statistics varies between sixty-five and seventy years in the inter-war period.

For this reason, the section presents two separate tables on outdoor pauperism of the aged. Table 4.25 gives statistics on those aged sixty-five years and over. It shows the extent of pauperism among the aged at the end of the nineteenth century; on every day count from 1890 to 1906, nearly 40 per cent of all paupers were over sixty-five (Table 4.25, col. vi). Table 4.26 gives statistics on those aged seventy and over. It shows how old-age pensions, which were initially paid only to those in this group, dramatically reduced the numbers of aged on relief after 1911 (Table 4.26, col. ii). This table also indicates how increasing numbers of the old returned in the 1920s to claim poor relief as a supplement to old-age pensions (Table 4.26, col. iii, col. vii). The statistics for the 1930s (Table 4.25, col. vii) show the continuation of this trend.

All the figures on the aged so far considered have been day count figures. Pauperism of the aged acquired a new dimension in the 1890s when special counts were made of the total number of old persons who drew relief at some time during the year. One of the great empirical discoveries of the 1890s was that one in three old persons was included in such a year count. Table 4.27 summarises the results of one of these year counts made in 1892.

If the aged paupers cannot be defined as a distinct group before 1890, then the sick cannot be so defined for another twenty years. Only from 1913 onwards do the official statistics separate out sick paupers from all others. Table 4.30 presents the available statistics for the inter-war period. Before this, from 1849 to 1911, in the era of the able-bodied and non-able-bodied classification, the sick were counted under both these headings. The temporarily sick were returned as (ordinarily) able-bodied and the chronic sick were returned as non-able-bodied. It is impossible to separate out the chronic sick from the aged who were also returned as non-able-bodied.

For this reason, it might be thought that the readily available post-1849 statistics on the number of temporarily sick would be of limited interest. This is not the case. The temporarily sick, as Tables 4.28 and 4.29 show, regularly made up half or more of the men who were returned as able-bodied. Nothing illustrates more clearly the way in which 'able-bodied' was an obfuscating category in the official statistics. The category served to conceal the point that the poor law in the later nineteenth century relieved almost no men who were able-bodied in the common-sense meaning of that term. The annual statistics in Table 4.28 and 4.29 are an essential complement to the statistics on the unemployed in Section D.

Table 4.22   Aged and infirm outdoor paupers, 1840-6[1]

Number of unions	Qtr. ended Lady Day[2]	Wholly unable to work ('000s)	Partially unable to work ('000s)	Total ('000s)	Total as % of all paupers
		(i)	(ii)	(iii)	(iv)
578	1840	166.1	96.8	262.9	26.6
578	1841	170.1	98.3	268.4	25.0
584	1842	171.3	100.4	271.8	22.5
584	1843	180.9	107.9	288.7	22.2
585	1844	186.7	107.7	294.6	23.6
585	1845	191.7	111.0	302.7	24.3
585	1846	189.2	106.2	295.4	26.2

Sources: Poor Law Commission, 6th–12th Annual Reports, 1840–6.

Table 4.23   Adult non-able-bodied paupers (indoor and outdoor), 1849–1912

1 Jan.	Indoor ('000s)	Outdoor ('000s)	Total (i) and (ii) ('000s)	(iii) as % of all paupers
	(i)	(ii)	(iii)	(iv)
1849	36.0	301.5	337.6	35.9
1850	34.7	311.9	346.6	38.9
1851	34.8	315.5	350.3	42.1
1852	34.9	315.5	350.4	43.7
1853	37.3	316.3	353.5	44.3
1854	39.9	317.1	357.1	43.5
1855	41.9	318.7	360.7	42.4
1856	43.1	319.9	363.1	41.4
1857	43.5	321.1	364.6	43.2
1858	49.3	332.9	382.2	40.6
1859	48.2	327.4	375.6	43.6
1860	47.0	328.6	375.6	44.5
1861	51.0	332.6	383.5	43.0
1862	53.8	340.5	394.3	41.7
1863	55.8	359.9	415.7	36.4
1864	55.0	359.7	414.8	41.0
1865	56.4	356.5	412.9	42.4
1866	57.3	348.4	405.8	43.9
1867	59.8	354.3	414.1	43.0
1868	63.3	363.2	426.5	41.0
1869	64.3	370.1	434.5	41.5
1870	67.2	380.5	447.7	41.3
1871	68.5	383.3	451.8	41.6
1872	65.8	368.6	434.4	44.3
1873	66.7	343.3	409.9	46.0
1874	67.0	320.8	387.8	46.6
1875	69.9	310.0	379.8	46.4
1876	69.7	286.8	356.5	47.4
1877	74.6	271.6	346.1	47.3
1878	77.8	265.1	342.9	45.9
1879	83.3	266.3	349.6	43.4
1880	87.8	271.6	359.4	42.6
1881	88.3	268.9	357.2	44.1
1882	88.0	269.6	357.7	44.5
1883	90.8	269.4	360.2	44.8
1884	90.2	261.3	351.5	45.1
1885	92.7	260.1	352.8	44.7
1886	95.2	263.8	359.0	44.2
1887	97.0	270.1	367.1	44.6
1888	99.0	273.9	372.9	44.9
1889	99.7	274.9	374.6	45.8
1890	99.9	274.2	374.1	47.2
1891	98.5	266.7	365.2	46.8
1892	93.0	257.9	350.8	46.1
1893	96.2	258.9	355.1	45.3
1894	101.4	266.8	368.2	44.8

1 Jan.	Indoor ('000s)	Outdoor ('000s)	Total (i) and (ii) ('000s)	(iii) as % of all paupers
	(i)	(ii)	(iii)	(iv)
1895	103.1	274.9	378.0	45.7
1896	104.4	286.9	391.3	46.6
1897	106.1	291.2	397.3	47.8
1898	107.7	292.6	400.3	48.1
1899	108.9	289.9	398.8	48.9
1900	110.6	284.3	394.9	49.2
1901	109.7	278.2	387.9	48.7
1902	116.6	282.9	399.5	48.8
1903	120.4	286.6	407.0	48.4
1904	123.6	290.8	414.3	48.1
1905	128.5	300.0	428.5	46.3
1906	131.8	303.6	435.4	47.3
1907	136.7	306.2	442.9	48.4
1908	138.8	306.0	444.8	48.2
1909	141.2	297.2	438.4	46.0
1910	140.6	280.0	420.6	44.9
1911	140.1	236.0	376.1	42.2
1912	134.3	159.5	293.8	36.6

Sources: 1849–59   Poor Law Board, 11th Annual Report, 1858-9.
1860–71   Local Government Board, 23rd Annual Report, 1893-4.
1872–1908   Royal Commission on the Poor Laws (1909), Statistical Appendix, vol. XXV (BPP, 1910, vol. LIII).
1909–12   Local Government Board, 38th–41st Annual Reports, 1908-9 to 1911–12.

Table 4.24   Aged indoor paupers, 1851–1931

Spring Census Day	Aged 65 yrs and over		
	Number ('000s)	(ii) as % of age group in population	(i) as % of all indoor paupers
	(i)	(ii)	(iii)
1851	25.1[3]	3.0	19.8
1861	29.4	3.2	23.4
1871	38.5	3.6	26.0
1891	59.6	4.3	32.6
1901	76.1	5.0	36.5
1911	82.7	4.4	31.7
1921	61.3	2.7	33.0
1931	60.8	2.1	32.4

Sources: Summary census tables relating to the ages of male and female indoor paupers in England and Wales.

Table 4.25   Outdoor paupers aged sixty-five and over, 1890–1939

1 Jan.	65 yrs and over ('000s)			(iii) as % of all paupers	(i) as % of (iii)	(iii) as % of population 65 yrs and over	% of (iii) in receipt of widows' or old-age pensions
	Indoor	Outdoor	Total (i) and (ii)[4]				
	(i)	(ii)	(iii)	(iv)	(v)	(vi)	(vii)
1890 (1 Aug.)	54.8	190.9	245.7	32.2[5]	22.3	18.0[5]	
1892	63.4	205.0	268.4	38.3	23.6	19.5	
1900	74.6	212.3	286.9	40.1	26.0	19.5	
			(290.9)				
1903 (1 Sep.)	75.2	209.1	284.3	36.1	26.5	18.6	
			(289.8)				
1906 (1 March)	90.1	228.3	318.4	40.0	28.3	19.9	
1928	67.6	134.4	202.7	14.9	33.4	7.3	65.7
1929	68.0	135.1	203.8	16.4	33.4		70.7
1930	66.6	143.4	210.8	17.5	31.6		73.4
1931	65.7	148.3	214.9	19.1	30.6		75.0
1932	63.2	160.7	224.7	17.9	28.1		70.3
1933	62.5	176.3	239.9	16.1	26.1		77.2
1934	61.2	184.3	246.6	16.2	24.8		78.4
1935	62.0	200.5	263.6	16.6	23.5		80.1
1936	61.5	224.5	287.4	19.1	21.4		81.9
1937	61.1	239.6	301.8	21.4	20.2		
1938	60.8	255.1	317.0	26.2	19.2		
1939	59.6	276.4	337.1	27.6	17.7		

Sources: 1890 BPP, 1890–1, vol. LXVIII (Mr Burt's Return).

1892 BPP, 1892, vol. LXVIII (Mr Ritchie's Return).

1900 Local Government Board, 29th Annual Report, 1899–1900.

1903 BPP, 1904, vol. LXXXII.

1906 Royal Commission on the Poor Laws, 1909, Statistical Appendix, vol. XXV (BPP, 1910, vol. LIII).

Table 4.26 Outdoor paupers aged seventy and over, 1890–1930

| 1 Jan. | 70 yrs and over ('000s) | | | (iii) as % of all paupers | (i) as % of (iii) | (iii) as % of population 70 yrs and over | % of (iii) in receipt of widows' or old-age pensions |
| | Indoor | Outdoor | Total (i) and (ii)[4] | | | | |
	(i)	(ii)	(iii)	(iv)	(v)	(vi)	(vii)
1890 (1 Aug.)	38.9	144.5	183.4	24.8	21.2	22.9[6]	
1900	49.4	152.8	202.2	27.9[10]	24.4	22.8	
1903 (1 Sept.)	53.4	156.9	210.3	26.2[7]	25.4	23.7	
1906 (1 March)	61.4	168.1	229.5	28.1	26.8	24.5	
1910	57.7	138.2	195.9	20.9	29.5		
1911	55.3	93.2	148.4	16.6	37.3	13.9	
1912	49.3	9.5	58.9	7.3	83.7		11.6
1913[9]	49.2	8.6	57.8[8]	7.2	85.1		13.6
1914	48.1	8.9	57.0	7.5	84.3		16.2
1915	47.2	8.5	55.7	7.5	84.7		16.7
1919	36.3	6.9	43.2	7.8	84.0		17.6
1920	38.2	8.6	46.8	8.1	81.6		19.9
1921	40.9	11.8	52.7	7.9	77.6	4.0	25.3
1922	42.7	21.3	64.0	4.2	66.7		34.8
1923	43.1	29.5	72.6	4.7	59.4		42.1
1924	43.8	36.6	80.4	5.8	54.5		47.5
1925	44.4	45.1	89.5	7.4	49.6		51.8
1926	45.6	55.8	101.5	7.1	44.9		56.7
1927	46.6	65.5	112.2	7.2	41.5		60.4
1928	46.3	69.9	116.3[11]	8.5	39.8		62.0
1929	46.7	75.1	122.0	9.8	38.3		76.3
1930	45.5	79.8	125.5	10.4	36.3	7.4	83.3

Sources: As Table 4.25.

Table 4.27   Paupers aged sixty-five and over relieved in the twelve months ended Lady Day, 1892

	Number ('000s)	(i) as % of all paupers (in, out, total)	(i) as % of age group in population 1891
	(i)	(ii)	(iii)
Indoor			
Men	68.5	14.9	11.3
Women	45.7	10.0	6.0
Total	114.1	24.9	8.3
Outdoor			
Men	95.1	8.5	15.6
Women	192.6	17.3	25.1
Total	287.8	25.8	21.0
Total			
Men	163.6	10.4	26.9
Women	238.3	15.1	31.1
Total	401.9[12]	25.5	29.3

Sources: Ritchie's Return as tabulated in the Royal Commission on the Aged Poor, BPP, 1895, vol. XIV.

Table 4.28   Temporarily sick able-bodied men[13] *outdoors, 1849-91*

1 Jan.	Number ('000s)	(i) as % of total outdoor able-bodied men
	(i)	(ii)
1849	25.5	46.7
1850	22.7	54.8
1851	19.8	60.3
1852	17.7	61.1
1853	17.2	67.7
1854	17.6	59.2
1855	17.8	59.8
1856	18.5	59.3
1857	17.2	61.7
1858	19.1	48.8
1859	17.2	66.0
1860	17.6	66.9
1861	18.8	60.8
1872	20.2	67.7
1884	9.9	71.1
1885	10.0	61.0
1886	10.7	55.9
1887	11.0	59.5
1888	11.2	58.3
1889	10.3	62.7
1890	10.0	68.1
1891	9.5	63.5

Sources: 1849–59   Poor Law Board, 11th Annual Report, 1858-9.
1860–1   Poor Law Board, 13th, 14th Annual Report, 1860-1, 1861-2.
1872   BPP, 1872, vol. LI.
1884–91   Royal Commission on the Poor Laws (1909), Statistical Appendix, vol. XXV (BPP, 1910, vol. LIII).

Table 4.29   Temporarily sick able-bodied adults,[14] indoors and outdoors, 1891–1912

1 Jan.	Men				Women	
	Indoor		Outdoor		Indoor[16]	
	Number ('000s)	(i) as % of total indoor able-bodied men	Number ('000s)	(iii) as % of total outdoor able-bodied men	Number ('000s)	(v) as % of total indoor able-bodied women
	(i)	(ii)	(iii)	(iv)	(v)	(vi)
1891	6.4	46.6	9.5[15]	73.3	5.9	41.7
1892	9.5	59.4	9.0	64.3	8.1	51.0
1893	10.2	56.0	8.8	55.2	8.0	48.2
1894	11.0	52.6	10.3	56.9	8.3	46.3
1895	11.3	51.7	8.8	54.6	8.7	47.4
1896	12.0	53.3	9.2	63.4	9.0	48.0
1897	11.6	53.2	9.4	67.3	9.0	48.2
1898	12.1	56.0	8.7	65.7	9.6	50.0
1899	12.6	61.8	7.9	68.0	9.9	53.4
1900	13.0	62.8	8.4	69.6	9.3	52.1
1901	12.9	66.3	7.3	69.0	9.8	54.1
1902	13.7	64.4	7.9	67.3	10.7	57.2
1903	14.7	63.7	8.4	63.7	11.1	56.9
1904	15.9	62.3	8.8	61.1	12.1	58.2
1905	17.2	59.9	10.0	44.7	13.0	58.6
1906	18.5	60.3	9.4	51.5	12.8	58.2
1907	18.4	61.5	9.8	59.8	13.2	60.0
1908	17.8	60.9	9.0	55.8	13.1	58.8
1909	19.9	58.3	9.7	45.5	14.0	57.4
1910	20.4	57.9	10.6	56.9	14.5	58.8
1911	20.3	60.0	10.7	57.6	14.7	60.0
1912	19.3	59.7	10.8	64.4	14.0	61.4

Sources: 1891–1908 Royal Commission on the Poor Laws (1909), Statistical Appendix, vol. XXV, (BPP, 1910, vol. LIII).
1909–12 Poor Relief Annual Returns (1 Jan.) BPP.

Table 4.30 *Sick adults,*[17] *1915-39*

1 Jan.	Indoor	Outdoor	Total (i) and (ii)	(iii) as a % of all paupers
	(i)	(ii)	(iii)	(iv)
1915	103.4	139.1	242.5	31.8
1920	77.9	105.0	182.9	31.7
1921	83.9	114.3	198.2	29.9
1922	90.0	145.8	235.9	15.8
1923	94.4	166.4	260.8	17.0
1924	86.6	180.8	267.4	19.5
1925	77.4	212.0	289.4	24.0
1926	79.1	244.9	324.0	22.5
1927	80.4	265.9	346.4	22.4
1928	79.7	269.5	349.1	25.6
1929	79.8	277.5	357.3	28.8
1930	79.3	290.7	370.0	32.9
1931	75.0	292.5	367.5	29.3
1932	65.9	306.7	372.6	29.7
1933	64.5	336.5	400.9	26.9
1934	60.6	350.8	411.4	27.1
1935	58.9	378.0	437.0	27.5
1936	55.3	408.6	463.9	30.8
1937	52.4	421.9	474.2	33.7
1938	51.2	430.7	481.9	39.8
1939	49.5	450.7	500.2	40.9

Sources: Poor Relief Annual Returns (1 Jan.) BPP.

Notes (Section F)

1 The category of 'aged and infirm' is not directly comparable with the subsequent category of 'non-able-bodied' because the latter included only the chronically and permanently infirm.

2 The quarterly figures for the 1840s are not directly comparable with the day count figures given for 1851 and subsequent years in Table 4.23. The difference is significant if the old in the 1840s were not a group of permanent pensioners. For this reason and because, as explained in footnote 1, the categories are different, totals in Table 4.22 (col. iii) and Table 4.23 (col. ii) are not directly comparable.

3 Three points should be made about these totals. First, a large minority of those indoors and aged over sixty-five was very old and and aged over seventy-five. From 1851 to 1921, this minority consistently accounted for just over one-third of the totals in column i.

Second, as might be expected, the institutionalised aged included a larger number of aged men than of aged women. The ratio of men to women was 14:10 in both 1851 and 1931. Third, by the turn of the century many of both sexes were what would now be called geriatric cases. A return of 1903 (BPP, 1904, vol. LXXXII) showed 31,000 men and 27,000 women over the age of sixty and 'unable to satisfactorily take care of themselves'. In percentage terms, 55 per cent of men and 69 per cent of women indoor paupers over the age of sixty fell into this category.

4   Totals for all dates exclude insane in asylums, licensed houses, and registered hospitals. Vagrants are excluded 1890–1906 and are only included in column iii from 1925. The returns for 1899 and 1900 exclude all insane, those, for 1890 and 1903 exclude persons 'constructively on relief'. Figures in brackets for 1900 and 1903 are Royal Commission estimates of 1909 which allow for the different bases of calculation for these years. These estimates have been used to calculate column iv and column vi in Table 4.26.

5   For 1890–1906 and 1930, the totals of population aged seventy years and over are for the nearest census year.

6   In this case, the totals are of estimated population aged sixty-five years and over.

7   As a per cent of all paupers on 1 July.

8   There was a huge decrease in pauperism among the aged between 1906 and 1913. In percentage terms, outdoor pauperism decreased 94.9 per cent, indoor decreased 19.8 per cent, and total pauperism 74.8 per cent. This was a direct result of the Old Age Pensions Act of 1908 which came into operation on 1 January 1909, and the removal of the pauper disqualification clause on 1 January 1911. A total of 122,415 persons in receipt of relief on 31 December 1910, subsequently received old-age pensions and ceased to be chargeable to the poor law during the four weeks ended 28 January 1911 (Cd. 5612, BPP, 1911, vol. LXIX).

9   The day count in this year was on 28 December.

10   It is interesting to compare columns iv in Tables 4.25 and 4.26. In the 1900s just under 30 per cent of paupers were aged seventy or over. In the same period those aged sixty-five or over generally numbered 40 per cent. If one drops the line of division another five years to aged sixty and over, then this takes in a group of around 45 per cent of paupers in the 1900s. This shows very clearly the bias of the institution towards support of the ageing and decrepit as well as the positively geriatric.

There is no table of paupers aged sixty and over in this section because the relevant statistics are only available for three day counts. In these years paupers aged 60–64 years add a further 41,000, 54,000, and 61,000 respectively to the 1890, 1903, and 1906 totals of paupers aged sixty-five and over. On this basis, paupers sixty years and over made up 38.8 per cent of all paupers in 1890 and 46.5 per cent in 1906.

11   If large numbers of old people were already claiming relief (as well as old-age pensions) by the late 1920s, this was not a return to the

pre-1909 situation. As Witmer (1931, p. 607) points out, if the same proportion of the population aged seventy years and over was receiving relief in 1928 as in 1906, the figure in column iii for 1928 would be 400,000, rather than 116,000.

12 This total included 134,535 persons who were receiving medical relief only. That is to say, only two-thirds of this total were receiving a maintenance allowance of some kind from the poor law. This was a point neglected in most of the alarmist and propagandist interpretation of these statistics.

13 Officially these sick able-bodied men were classified as receiving outdoor relief 'on account of their own sickness, accident or infirmity'. Other adult able-bodied males were classified into three groups according to whether they were relieved on account of 'sudden or urgent necessity' or 'sickness, accident or infirmity of any of the family' or 'want of work or other causes'.

14 The classification was of ordinarily able-bodied adults 'sick or temporarily disabled'. All other able-bodied adults were classified as 'in health'.

15 Totals in Table 4.29 (col. iii) are directly comparable with those in Table 4.28 (col. i). All totals in Table 4.30 are completely noncomparable with earlier figures because these later totals include those who in pre-1913 terms would have been classified as nonable-bodied. On 1 January 1912, the non-able-bodied outnumbered the 'sick able-bodied' by a ratio of more than 4:1.

16 There are no outdoor figures for women because the majority of women receiving outdoor relief were dependants and therefore classified not in their own right but as dependants of male heads of family.

17 In this period the official classification was of adults receiving relief 'on account of sickness, accident or bodily infirmity'.

Section G The insane, 1842-1939

Any reconstruction of nineteenth-century pauperism must consider the insane, who made up a rapidly increasing number of paupers and an increasing percentage of the 'pauper host' in the second half of the nineteenth century. In 1842, one in a hundred paupers was categorised as insane, but by 1910, the proportion had risen to one in every eight paupers (Table 4.31, col. ii).

Official statistics also give the numbers of insane maintained in workhouses and in other kinds of institution (Table 4.31, cols iii–vi). From these columns of the table it is possible to trace the rise to predominance of the rate-aided county lunatic asylum.

Table 4.31   Insanity and pauperism, 1842-1939

1 Jan.	Number of insane chargeable to unions ('000s)	(i) as % of all paupers	In county or county borough asylums ('000s)	In registered hospitals or licensed houses ('000s)	In workhouse and metropolitan district asylums ('000s)	With relatives or in lodgings or boarded-out ('000s)
	(i)	(ii)	(iii)	(iv)	(v)	(vi)
1842[1]	13.9	1.1	3.3	2.2	3.8	4.6
1852	21.2	2.6	9.4	2.6	5.1	4.1
1854	24.5	3.0	12.0	1.9	5.7	4.9
1861	32.6	4.5	16.7	1.2	8.5	6.1
1866	40.0	4.3	22.0	1.5	10.0	6.6
1871	48.5	4.5	27.1	1.9	12.2	7.3
1876	55.5	7.4	32.0	1.5	15.5	6.5
1881	63.5	7.8	39.1	1.5	16.8	6.1
1886	70.0	8.6	45.7	1.3	17.2	5.9
1891	76.2	9.8	51.8	1.6	17.0	5.8
1896	85.7	10.2	61.1	1.7	16.9	5.9
1901	96.7	12.1	72.7	1.2	17.1	5.6
1906	109.4	11.9	84.9	1.1	17.7	5.6
1911	119.3	13.4	94.4	0.7	18.7	5.5
1915[2]	144.8	19.0	103.0		36.1	5.7
1921	114.9	17.3	84.3		26.1	4.5
1926	130.1	9.0	96.5		28.3	5.3
1931	144.0	12.8	108.9		29.0	6.1
1936	151.0	10.0	118.0		26.5	6.5
1939	155.0	13.8	123.9		24.6	6.5

Sources: 1842   Poor Law Commission, 10th Annual Report, 1844.
1852   Poor Law Board, 5th Annual Report, 1852.
1854   Poor Law Board, 7th Annual Report, 1854.
1861-1901   Local Government Board, 30th Annual Report, 1900-1.
1906-11   Local Government Board, 43rd Annual Report, 1913-14.
1915-39   Poor Relief Annual Returns (1 Jan.) BPP.

Notes (Section G)

1   There are again problems of comparability about the earlier figures
   in Table 4.31. The earlier returns were not complete. The 1842
   figures, for example, cover 589 unions, while the 1865 figures
   cover 666 unions. More important, the total of all paupers and
   the sub-total of insane paupers were calculated on a different basis
   in 1842 and for that year the percentage (col. ii) must understate
   the proportion of total paupers who were categorised as insane.
       The 1842 sub-total (col. i) is of the number of insane relieved
   during the month of August; later figures give January day counts.
   Furthermore, the 1842 total is of all paupers relieved in the quarter
   ended Lady Day; later totals give the mean of two day counts. In
   1842 occasional applications and thus double-counting would have
   been more significant among the total of all paupers than among
   the sub-total of insane. To a small extent the figure of 1.1 per cent
   in 1842 (col. ii) must understate the fraction of paupers categorised
   as insane.
2   From 1852 onwards, there are no changes in the mode of calculating the total of all paupers and the sub-total of insane paupers
   which significantly affects the comparability of the percentages
   in column ii of the table.
       The only additional point that should be made concerns changes
   in the classification of mentally defective persons receiving relief
   under the provisions of the Mental Deficiency Act 1913. Before
   this Act, the 'insane' had been those classified as 'lunatic' or 'idiot'.
   Subsequent returns subsumed these groups in the broader category
   of those 'suffering from mental infirmity'. Matters were further
   complicated when the indoor and outdoor insane were sub-divided
   into two groups according to whether or not they were certified
   under the Lunacy Acts or the Idiots Acts. These classification
   changes cause some comparability problems in columns v and vi
   of the table.

Section H Construction of workhouses and other institutions, 1835-1914

This section presents statistics on the construction of workhouses and other institutions from 1835 to 1914. Only statistics about expenditure for these purposes are continuously available for the whole period. Table 4.32 presents the annual series on expenditure authorised for the construction of new workhouses and the alteration of existing workhouses. The table shows that large sums were authorised for these purposes throughout the period; the cumulative total authorised was £8,000,000 by 1870 and over £36,000,000 by 1914 (Table 4.32, col. iv).

This result suggests further questions. How many institutions were built after 1834? What kinds of institution were built? When and where did building take place? Answers to these questions are obtained in Tables 4.33 to 4.36 by piecing together information from a variety of resources and by making various calculations and estimates. Sources used are listed at the bottom of each table and footnotes explain the nature of the different calculations and estimates. The pattern of construction was different in the two periods 1835 to 1870 and 1870 to 1914, which will therefore be considered separately in different tables.

1834 to 1870 was the period when the general mixed workhouses were built. Table 4.33(a) calculates the number of poor law unions which built such workhouses. It shows that three out of four unions certainly or very probably built a new union workhouse. Those which did not build, operated converted pre-1834 workhouses; as Table 4.33(b) shows, only a very small number of marginal unions were without workhouses after 1854. Table 4.34 examines differential rates of building in two large groups of urban and rural unions. Although the rural unions built earlier, by 1870, an almost uniformly high proportion in both groups had built new union workhouses.

1870 to 1914 was the period when specialised treatment facilities for particular classes of paupers were provided. Construction took two forms; first, special-purpose blocks were added to pre-1870 general mixed workhouses, and second, specialised institutions were built completely separate from existing workhouses. Table 4.35 estimates the total number of facilities of both kinds which were authorised in the 1870 to 1914 period, and Table 4.36 gives a precise total of the number of specialised institutions in operation by 1908. The tables show that specialised facilities were built in large numbers. Although most of these facilities were additional blocks at existing workhouses, the number of, and the accommodation in, specialised institutions was significant by 1908.

Table 4.37 brings together various fragments on numbers of institutions and available accommodation. The 1776 figures are dubious and all the estimates of available accommodation depend on culturally variable notions about the space and facilities required for paupers. Nevertheless, it is interesting to note that the ratio of institutional accommodation to population remained much the same or even declined through the nineteenth century. The construction programmes after 1834 and after 1870 were about building different kinds of institutions, rather than building more accommodation.

Table 4.32   *Expenditure on workhouse construction,*[1] *1835-1914*

	Annual (£000s)		Cumulative[3] (£000s)	
Year[2]	New workhouses	Alterations of old workhouses	New workhouses	Alterations of old workhouses
	(i)	(ii)	(iii)	(iv)
1836	656	99		
1837	486	81		
1838	548	62		
1839	200	7		
1840	182	19	2,144[4]	
1841	101	49	2,245	
1842	98	33	2,343	
1843	99	22	2,422	
1844	43	46	2,485	
1845	52	19	2,537	
1846	78	62	2,616	
1847	32	14	2,648	
1848	221	56	2,868	
1849	130	53	2,999	
1850	120	26	3,119	
1851	127	15	3,246	
1852	131	11	3,377	
1853	95	16	3,472	
1854	95	27	3,566	
1855	170	29	3,737	
1856	257	6	3,994	773
1857	175	20	4,169	793
1858	119	34	4,288	827
1859	75	15	4,363	842
1860	105	26	4,468	868
1861	69	19	4,520	886
1862	94	7	4,616	875
1863	191	19	4,807	894
1864	141	43	4,949	937
1865	233	16	5,177	953
1866	248	29	5,411	982
1867	145	65	5,556	1,047
1868	452	24	6,008	1,071
1869	459		7,497	
1870	540		8,028	
1871	524		8,545	
1872	330		8,875	
1873	329		9,203	
1874	351		9,555	
1875	484		10,039	

Year[2]	Annual (£000s)		Cumulative[3] (£000s)	
	New workhouses	Alterations of old workhouses	New workhouses	Alterations of old workhouses
	(i)	(ii)	(iii)	(iv)
1876	356			10,395
1877	448			10,792
1878	594			11,386
1879	382			11,768
1880	272			12,040
1881	630			12,670
1882	441			13,111
1883	527			13,638
1884	586			14,224
1885	440			14,664
1886	374			15,037
1887	433			15,470
1888	287			15,758
1889	393			16,150
1890	539			16,689
1891	403			17,092
1892	532			17,623
1893	415			18,039
1894	502			18,543
1895	606			19,148
1896	999			20,147
1897	1,142			21,303
1898	1,769			23,072
1899	1,238			24,310
1900	1,776			26,087
1901	1,729			27,816
1902	975			28,792
1903	1,184			29,976
1904	941			30,917
1905	771			31,688
1906	762			32,450
1907	440			32,889
1908	583			33,472
1909	354			33,826
1910	462			34,289
1911	693			34,982
1913	798			35,780
1914	568			36,347

Sources: Poor Law Commission, 1st–13th Annual Reports, 1835–47.
Poor Law Board, 1st–23rd Annual Reports, 1848 to 1870–1.
Local Government Board, 1st–43rd Annual Reports, 1871–2 to 1913–14.

Table 4.33(a)   New workhouses built, 1834-70

	Unions building workhouses[5]			Total cols (i)–(iii)	Col. (iv) as % of all construction
	Certain[6]	Very probable[7]	Possible[8]		
	(i)	(ii)	(iii)	(iv)	(v)
1834-9	325	6	6	337	52.1
1840-9	40	22	9	71	11.0
1850-9	27	36	9	72	11.1
1860-9	1	28	10	39	6.0
1870		4		4	0.6
Date not known	3[9]	0	22[10]	25	3.9
Others	n.a.	n.a.	n.a.	99[11]	15.3
Total	396	96	56	647	100

Sources: Poor Law Commission, 5th–13th Annual Reports, 1839–47.
Poor Law Board, 1st–23rd Annual Reports, 1848 to 1870-1.
Return of Workhouse Building 1840–58, BPP, 1857-8, vol. XLIX.

Table 4.33(b)   Unions without a workhouse[12]

1854	1870
Great Broughton (Cheshire)	Todmorden (Lancs)
Runcorn (Cheshire)	Builth (Wales)
Camelford (Cornwall)	Lampeter (Wales)
Stratton (Cornwall)	Tregaron (Wales)
Todmorden (Lancs)	
Dulverton (Somerset)	
Hemsworth (Yorks)	
Penistone (Yorks)	
Anglesey (Wales)	
Holyhead (Wales)	
Builth (Wales)	
Lampeter (Wales)	
Tregaron (Wales)	
Conway (Wales)	
Dolgellau (Wales)	
Machynlleth (Wales)	
Presteigne (Wales)	
Rhayader (Wales)	
Total 18 unions	4 unions

Sources: Return of Workhouse Accommodation in 1854, BPP, 1854-5, vol. XLVI.
Poor Law Board, 23rd Annual Report, 1870-1.

Table 4.34   Urban and rural[13] workhouse construction, 1834-70

	Unions building new workhouses			
	Number		Percentage	
	Rural	Urban	Rural	Urban
	(i)	(ii)	(iii)	(iv)
1834-9	106	45	62	30
1840-9	13	29	8	20
1850-9	7	32	4	22
1860-9	3	19	2	13
1870		2		1
Date not known[14]	8	7	5	5
Others[15]	33	13	19	9
Total	170	147	100	100

Sources: As Table 4.33(a).

Table 4.35   Specialised accommodation authorised,[16] 1870-1914

Type of accommodation	Authorisation 1870-1914
Workhouses	70
Infirmaries[17]	384
Cottage/Children's homes[18]	175
Schools	38
For married couples/aged	24
For imbeciles	26
For casuals	255

Sources: Poor Law Board, 23rd Annual Report, 1870-1.
Local Government Board, 1st-43rd Annual Reports, 1871-2 to 1913-14.

Table 4.36   Specialised institutions[19] operating in 1908

	London		England and Wales (excluding London)		All England and Wales	
	Number of institutions	Available accommodation	Number of institutions	Available accommodation	Number of institutions	Available accommodation
	(i)	(ii)	(iii)	(iv)	(v)	(vi)
Separate infirmaries	26	14,669	17	9,090	43	23,759
Sick asylums	4	1,439			4	1,439
District or separate schools	16	7,488	17	3,897	33	11,385
Grouped cottage homes	6	2,822	43	6,692	49	9,514
Children's homes	1	46	12	491	13	537
Receiving homes	16	1,141	4	252	20	1,393
Homes for aged poor	2	603	4	273	6	876
Other specialised instits	1	42	11	1,154	12	1,196
Metropolitan asylums District institutions	22	9,289			22	9,289
Not workhouses	94	37,539	108	21,849	202	59,388
Workhouses	51	40,797	631	199,762	682	240,559
Total	145	78,336	739	221,611	884	299,947

Sources: Royal Commission on the Poor Laws (1909), Statistical Appendix, vol. XXV, (BPP, 1910, vol. LIII).

Table 4.37   Available institutional accommodation and average size of institution 1776, 1854, 1908

Year	Number of institutions	Capacity	(ii) per 1,000 population[20]	Average size workhouse
	(i)	(ii)	(iii)	(iv)
1776	1970 (workhouses)	89,775	12	46
1854	725+ (mostly workhouses + 12 schools)	211,569	12	290
1908	682 (workhouses 201 (not workhouses)	240,559 59,388	9	353

Sources: 1776   Abstract Returns of Expense of Poor 1802–3, BPP, 1803–4, vol. XIII.
1854   Return of Workhouse Accommodation 1854, BPP, 1854–5, vol. XLVI.
1908   Royal Commission on the Poor Laws (1909), Statistical Appendix, vol. XXV (BPP, 1910, vol. LIII).

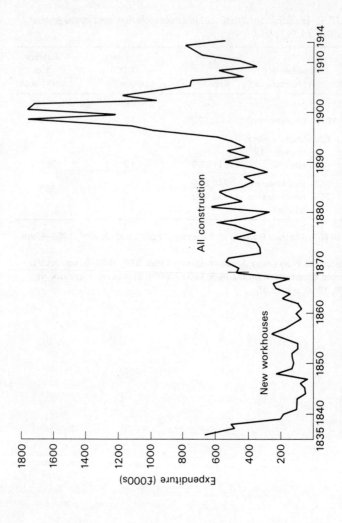

Graph 4.VI   Authorised expenditure on workhouse construction etc., 1835–1914
Sources: Section H, Table 4.32.

Notes (Section H)

1 All totals are of 'authorised expenditure' which is not the same as capital cost actually incurred, because expenditure authorisations may not necessarily be taken up and spent.

   In the first twenty-five years, it is not clear whether expenditure totals consistently include or exclude cost of site and cost of fitting out the shells of workhouses. From 1861 cost of site is specifically included.

   Early totals may also significantly underestimate expenditure because some capital projects were undertaken without proper authorisation. Many newly formed unions had irregular sources of income from, for example, sale of parish workhouses.

   Totals from the 1860s onwards do not include the substantial expenditure of the Metropolitan Asylums Board, the Metropolitan District Sick Asylums, and the District Schools. By 1914, authorised expenditure by these three organisations had amounted to over £7,500,000.

2 Until 1848, although the annual reports do not give specific dates, it is probable that the annual expenditure totals are for the year ending in May.

   From 1849 to 1910 inclusive, the totals record expenditure in a calendar year, while the 1913 and 1914 totals record expenditure in a financial year. This leaves two years when the accounting base was being adjusted: '1848' runs from 1 May 1847 to 31 December 1848; '1911' runs from 1 January 1911 to 31 March 1912.

3 Before 1855 cumulative totals have been calculated by subtraction because such totals are not given in the annual reports. The results are approximate and overestimate actual expenditure since a proportion of authorised expenditure was not taken up and officially rescinded.

   Rescinding also explains why, in subsequent years, the cumulative expenditure totals increase by amounts which are slightly different from the annual figure given in the adjacent column.

4 A cumulative total of £1,598,694 is given in a special return of 'sums expended in the purchase of land, the erection of the buildings and the fitting up of workhouses' to Michaelmas 1840 (BPP, 1841, vol. XXI). The same source gives annual expenditure figures for 1838, 1839, and 1840 as £382,084, £410,492, and £253,179, respectively, in a financial year ending on Lady Day.

   It is not surprising that the annual totals of sums expended are higher than the annual totals of expenditure authorised which probably understates expenditure for the reasons discussed in footnote 1. But it is puzzling that the cumulative totals of 'sums expended' to 1840 is significantly lower than the corresponding total of expenditure authorised.

   There are two possible explanations: either the two series have different starting dates, or one series takes account of rescinded expenditure (see footnote 3). It is not worth worrying over this discrepancy because, as explained in footnote 1, all the early statistics are approximate estimates.

5 A very small number of unions appear from the official records to have built new workhouses more than once in the 1834–1870 period. In such cases only the first workhouse has been recorded in the table. Thus every union can only appear once in Table 4.33 and no double-counting inflates the total number of unions building workhouses.

6 Workhouses are classified as 'certainly constructed' if they appear on one of two *ad hoc* lists. The first list is of workhouses completed and in operation in 1839 and it appears in Appendix D, no. 4, III in the fifth Annual Report of the Poor Law Commission. The second list is a special Return of the Cost of Building of Workhouses 1840 to 1858 (BPP 1857–8, XLIX). This return records not only capital expenditure for each workhouse, but also running costs for food and clothing; it is reasonable to suppose therefore that all the workhouses on the 1858 list were completed and in operation. The 1858 list is known to be incomplete because one in three of the unions returned no information to the central authority.

7 The annual reports of the central authority list sums authorised to be expended on workhouse building and distinguish between 'initial' and 'additional' authorisations made for every workhouse project.

'Very probable' workhouses are those where an initial authorisation was obtained, followed by additional authorisations within five years. If a union returned for an additional authorisation within a few years, it is reasonable to suppose that the initial authorisation had been exhausted on building a workhouse.

8 'Possible' workhouses are those that only appear once in the expenditure series as requiring an 'initial' or (more unusually) an 'additional' authorisation. Most of these workhouses were presumably built out of the initial authorisation. The point is simply that one cannot be sure of this from the expenditure series. In the thirty-four cases where we have an approximate date of construction, the uncertainty could be dispelled by crosschecking against union correspondence held in the Public Record Office. This was not done because the total number of cases was so small as not to justify the effort.

9 These are workhouses that appear on the 1858 list but cannot be traced in the expenditure authorisations from 1840 to 1858. It is therefore not clear when these three workhouses were built within this period.

10 These are workhouses that appear once in an ambiguous way in the authorisations series. The classic example would be a workhouse that required an additional authorisation although no initial authorisation appears earlier in the expenditure series.

11 This is a residual category that includes all the unions which do not appear to have built new workhouses because they do not appear in either of the two lists of new workhouses or in the expenditure authorisations series.

The group comprises sixty-nine unions, which are recorded as having old workhouses in operation in 1839, four unions with no workhouse accommodation in 1870, and twenty-six unions on which no information is available from the sources.

12 Both lists are of unions without a workhouse in operation or in the course of erection. In 1839, thirty-seven unions were listed as 'decline to provide an adequate workhouse'.

13 Unions are classified into urban and rural groups on the basis of Booth's (1894) classification of all unions according to degree of rurality.

The rural group consists of the 170 unions classified as most rural (Groups I–V in Booth's classification). The urban group consists of the 150 non-metropolitan unions classified as most urban (Groups XIV–XVIII in Booth's classification). London unions have been excluded from the urban group, mainly because of practical difficulties about allocating workhouses known to be built among unions of parishes which were only formed relatively late in the period.

14 As in Table 4.33 (a), this category covers ambiguous entries in the available series.

15 This is again a residual category. It includes twenty-eight rural and six urban unions which are recorded as having old workhouses in operation in 1839. Only one union (from the rural group) was listed as having no workhouse accommodation in 1870.

16 The totals in this table have been obtained by working through the expenditure authorisation series covering 'erection enlargement, etc. of workhouses, separate workhouse schools, infirmaries, relief offices etc., and purchase of sites for the same'. These authorisations cover three distinct kinds of construction project; first, the alteration of existing buildings, second, additional blocks of buildings on existing workhouse sites, and third, new institutions on green-field sites. As far as possible, the totals in the table list only the second and third kinds of project, that is, new blocks and new institutions.

However, the information on the projects in the authorisations is often skeletal and it is not always possible to determine whether a particular project involved altering existing buildings or adding new special-purpose blocks. Therefore, the totals of new blocks and new institutions must be approximate. It is also true that any such estimate would show a very large number of specialised blocks and institutions built to accommodate casuals, the sick, and children.

17 This category includes the detached 'infectious wards' built on workhouse sites in the 1870s, the 'pavilions' of the 1890s, and the large city infirmaries built at the turn of the century.

18 This category includes receiving homes.

19 Table 4.36 lists the number of specialised institutions operating in 1908. These would be on separate sites often some distance away from general mixed workhouses. The information on number of institutions and available accommodation was supplied by the poor law inspectors.

The totals in this table do *not* include the special purpose blocks on existing workhouse sites which are included in the totals in Table 4.35.

The total number of non-workhouse institutions given in columns (i) and (v) is one greater than at source. This adjustment was made to correct an apparent discrepancy in the London returns.

20   Estimated population of England and Wales.

      1776   7,300,000
      1854 18,516,000
      1908 35,059,000

The 1854 total is an official estimate which excludes population not covered by the poor law returns.

Section J Summary tables on the poor law, 1802-1939

The tables in this section provide a summary of long-run trends in composition of the 'pauper host' and in objects of expenditure.

Because of the nature of the statistics, it is difficult to make any comparison between old and new poor law. Table 4.38 juxtaposes the 1802-3 year count and some post-1834 statistics on the composition of the pauper host. This comparison shows the increasing importance of the group of aged paupers, but it does not show the change in composition of the able-bodied group and the abolition of relief to unemployed able-bodied men after 1834.

Under the new poor law after 1834, it is possible to make fairly precise long-run comparisons. Tables 4.39 and 4.40 respectively summarise changes in the composition of the pauper host and in objects of expenditure. Table 4.39 shows the abolition of relief to unemployed men under the new poor law. Here the old and the fatherless families were the predominant groups and the insane were increasingly important. Table 4.40 on objects of expenditure indicates the steady pre-1914 decline in the proportion of expenditure spent on out-relief doles. These accounted for nearly two-thirds of relief expenditure in 1840, but for less than one-quarter of such expenditure by 1910. This development was paralleled by a steady rise in the relative importance of all the expenditures connected with indoor relief.

Table 4.38   The old and the new poor law, 1803–1907

	1803 During year ending March		1849 on 1 Jan.		1907 on 1 Jan.		1907 During year ending Sept.[2]	
	Number ('000s)	% of all paupers	Number ('000s)	% of all paupers	Number ('000s)	% of all paupers	Number ('000s)	% of all paupers
	(i)	(ii)	(iii)	(iv)	(v)	(vi)	(vii)	(viii)
Aged and infirm adults	167	16	335.8	35.9	442.9	48.1	} 1,145.1	67.0
Able-bodied adults	} 874	} 84	199.5	21.3	121.3	13.2		
Children			379.2	40.6	231.9	25.2	564.3	33.0
Vagrants			7.3	0.8	15.0	1.6	–	–
Insane			13.0	1.4	110.6	12.0	–	–
Total	1,041		933.3[1]		920.8[1]		1,709.4	
Paupers/100 population	11.4		6.3		2.8		4.9	

Sources: 1803   Abstract of Returns of Expense of Poor, BPP, 1803–4, vol. XIII.
1849   Poor Law Board, 8th Annual Report, 1858.
1907   Local Government Board, 36th Annual Report, 1906–7; BPP, 1908, vol. XCII.

Table 4.39 Composition of the pauper host, 1851–1931[5]

1 Jan.	1851[3]	1861[4]	1872	1884	1891	1901	1911	1922[6]	1931
	(i)	(ii)	(iii)	(iv)	(v)	(vi)	(vii)	(viii)	(ix)
Total numbers ('000s)									
(i) Aged and infirm adults[7]	349.3	383.5	434.4	351.5	365.2	387.9	368.6	235.9	345.8
(ii) Fatherless families[8]	204.5	216.0	246.1	203.0	162.3	148.4	188.8	208.8	133.9
(iii) Insane[9]	14.3	32.9	50.0	68.1	75.6	96.7	118.9	119.0	117.4
(iv) Unemployed men[10]	5.3	3.8	2.1	1.3	8.9	7.0	16.2	182.8	41.3
(v) All others[11]	252.9	256.1	248.8	155.3	168.7	161.5	200.4	746.6	485.5
(vi) Total[12]	829.4	891.9	981.0	779.0	780.5	801.3	891.8	1,493.1	1,123.9
Total as % of population	5.4	4.5	4.2	2.9	2.7	2.5	2.5	3.9	2.8

1 Jan.	1851[3]	1861[4]	1872	1884	1891	1901	1911	1922	1931
Categories as % of all paupers									
(i) Aged and infirm adults	42.1	43.0	44.3	45.1	46.8	48.4	41.3	15.8	30.8
(ii) Fatherless families	24.7	24.2	25.1	26.1	20.8	18.5	21.1	14.0	11.9
(iii) Insane	1.7	3.7	5.1	8.7	9.7	12.1	13.3	8.0	10.4
(iv) Unemployed men	0.6	0.4	0.2	0.2	1.1	0.9	1.8	12.2	3.7
(v) All others	30.5	28.7	25.4	19.9	21.6	20.2	22.5	50.0	43.2

Sources: 1851 Poor Law Board, 11th Annual Report, 1858.
1861 Poor Law Board, 13th Annual Report, 1860–1.
1872 Local Government Board, 2nd Annual Report, 1872–3.
1884 Local Government Board, 14th Annual Report, 1884–5.
1891 Local Government Board, 20th Annual Report, 1890–1.
1901 Local Government Board, 30th Annual Report, 1900–1.
1911 BPP, 1911, vol. LXIX.
1922 BPP, 1922, vol. XVII.
1931 BPP, 1930–1, vol. XXV.

Table 4.40   Objects of expenditure,[13] 1840–1930 (as percentage of all expenditure)

Year ended March	1840 %	1850 %	1860 %	1870 %	1880 %	1890 %	1900 %	1910 %	1920 %	1930 %
	(i)	(ii)	(iii)	(iv)	(v)	(vi)	(vii)	(viii)	(ix)	(x)
In-maintenance	17.8	16.9	16.7	19.7	21.9	22.5	22.0	22.1	24.6	14.5
Out-relief	64.0	58.5	52.5	47.5	33.8	29.1	23.3	22.0	17.1	31.4
Maintenance of lunatic paupers	18.3	24.6	7.7	9.5	12.4	14.5	15.7	16.2	17.7	16.0
Loan charges			3.3	3.3	4.0	7.2	8.4	8.0	4.1	2.6
Salaries			11.8	10.7	13.1	16.5	18.1	17.7	23.7	22.5
Other			7.9	9.4	14.7	10.2	12.4	14.0	12.8	13.0
	100%	100%	100%	100%	100%	100%	100%	100%	100%	100%
Total (£000s)	=4,577	=5,395	=5,455	=7,644	=8,015	=8,434	=11,568	=14,850	=23,501	=40,631

Sources: As Section C, Table 4.8

Notes (Section J)

1 These are net totals that exclude a relatively small number of persons double-counted in the sub-totals, because they were in receipt of both indoor and outdoor relief on the same day.

2 This total excludes insane in asylums and vagrants.

3 There is a discrepancy at source between the official gross total (831,430) and the sum of the individual categories (826,335). All percentages have been calculated using the latter total.

4 Returns on 'causes of relief' for outdoor able-bodied paupers were received from only 629 unions. These figures have been marginally increased to obtain estimates which are directly comparable with the indoor and other outdoor figures returned from 646 unions.

5 Returns are not complete and do not cover all of England and Wales until 1872.

6 1922 was chosen instead of 1921, because 1922 is the first year in which the poor law supported large numbers of unemployed men, as it subsequently did throughout the inter-war period.

7 1851–1911 totals are of 'not able-bodied'. 1922 and 1931 totals are of those relieved 'on account of sickness, accident, or bodily infirmity'.

8 1851 to 1901 totals are of outdoor relief only. 1911 and 1931 totals cover indoor and outdoor relief.

The category includes able-bodied widows (alias widows with dependent children, in 1922 and 1931); wives deserted by husbands, prisoners' and soldiers' wives; single mothers; and the dependent children of all these groups.

The sizeable group of orphans – about 40,000 throughout the period – has been excluded from the category because of problems about inconsistencies in the long-run count.

9 1851–1911 totals are of 'insane' and the 1851 total is incomplete since it does not record all pauper lunatics in asylums. 1911 to 1931 totals are of those relieved 'on account of mental infirmity'. All totals cover indoor and outdoor relief.

10 1851–84 totals are of outdoor able-bodied men relieved 'on account of want of work or other causes'. 1891 to 1911 totals continue to count men outdoors in this category but also include indoor able-bodied men 'in health' (as opposed to 'temporarily disabled'). 1922 and 1931 totals are of men outdoors relieved on account of unemployment.

11 This category includes orphans, casuals, children of non-able-bodied adults, and the small group of able-bodied not included in any of the earlier categories.

12 These are net totals and exclude the small number of individuals double-counted in more than one sub-total.

13 See the footnote to Table 4.6 for detailed reference to what was included and excluded in the various categories.

Part two

Social investigations

Low Wages was published and *London Labour* first appeared in book form, Mayhew also published a history of the Mormons. The most important of the texts ignored by historiography is the *Great World of London*, alias *The Criminal Prisons of London* (Mayhew and Binny, 1862). This began as a new part-work which appeared in 1856. Like the earlier part-works, it was abandoned unfinished. The completed section deals almost exclusively with criminal London, one sub-division of the 'great world'. Mayhew's publishers then reprinted the part numbers in book form under the title *The Criminal Prisons of London*. Mayhew's collaborator Binny was commissioned to bring the part-work material to some kind of conclusion and simply added 150 pages of his own to finish off the treatment of criminal prisons. This text is excluded from the historiographic canon, but contemporaries made no such division. Thus, Mayhew's publishers in their catalogue, bound with the 1861–2 four-volume edition of *London Labour,* described the *Criminal Prisons* book as the 'companion volume to the preceding'. The *Criminal Prisons* book could be a missing fifth volume of *London Labour*.

If historiography operates an unreasonable restriction of reference in its construction of a textual canon, it even more blatantly restricts reference within the canon when specific readings of Mayhew are being constructed. Different historiographic readings of Mayhew are based upon appeal to different texts. Claims that Mayhew is trivial refer to the 1861–2 edition of *London Labour*. This text is the basis for the traditional condemnation of Mayhew as an undisciplined journalist with an overdeveloped taste for colourful detail. Himmelfarb (1973) has recently modified this judgment and defined Mayhew as an ideologist. Revisionists have never directly challenged such condemnations of *London Labour,* but have found other texts to praise. Claims that Mayhew is highly serious refer to the earlier serious texts, with the *Morning Chronicle* letters as the key empirical text and the 'Answers' column and the part-work on low wages as the key theoretical texts. This is the early work that Thompson and Yeo (1971) rediscovered and claimed as a serious discourse about poverty. Samuel (1973) has subsequently claimed the early work propounds a theory of exploitation.

The restriction of reference to parts of the canon is all the more unfortunate because the internal divisions and boundaries within the canon are uncertain. The serial publications are openly chaotic. Different projects overlap, and none of them reaches a conclusion where a task defined at the beginning has been accomplished; the part-works simply stop, sometimes in mid-sentence. There is even uncertainty about where the book *London Labour* ends, when different editions make different selections from the original serial material and some incorporate additional material. The 1851 *London Labour* book was a simple binding up of the part-work into two volumes, complete with the original part numbers in the margin. Some copies of this edition included the treatment of prostitution, others did not. Subsequent editions in 1861 and 1861-2 contained new and recycled material - mainly on street folk - so that three volumes were now required. Mayhew's publishers could not decide what to do with the material on prostitution. The 1861 (Griffin & Co.) three-volume edition omitted this material; the 1861-2 (Griffin, Bohn) four-volume edition included the original material on prostitution in a fourth volume which also incorporated essays by various contributors on thieves, swindlers, and beggars.

These historiographic restrictions of reference and substantive disagreements among historians define a series of questions about the relations between, and content of, Mayhew's texts. A first series of questions concerns the relation between the texts. How do the various serial and book publications relate? Are they parts of one project, or are there breaks? If so, what kinds of breaks are there between the texts? More specifically, what is the relation between the first *Morning Chronicle* project of investigating manufacturing trades and the second *London Labour* project of investigating street folk? How does the theoretical treatment of *Low Wages* connect with the empirical *Morning Chronicle* material? How does the treatment of institutions in *Criminal Prisons* relate to the earlier treatment of manufacturing trades and street people? A second series of questions concerns the content of the different texts. Are the *Morning Chronicle* letters a poverty survey, as Thompson and Yeo argue? Or does the early work provide a theory of exploitation, as Samuel argues? And, if these historians are wrong about the *Morning Chronicle* letters and the economic theory, what are they about and how are they held together? Is the concern with street folk in *London Labour* as trivial or as merely ideological as historiography makes out? Does the difference of thematic content in *Criminal Prisons* justify its separation from the rest of Mayhew's work?

When these questions have been answered, almost all current historiographic claims can be dismissed. Historiography is wrong about the relations and non-relations between Mayhew's texts, and is also wrong about the substantive content of them. Specifically, it will also be argued that all existing accounts of Mayhew apply inappropriate evaluative criteria. It is wrong to use the presence or absence of a unitary object of poverty in the *Morning Chronicle* letters as a measure of seriousness, just as it is wrong to use the imperfectly controlled detail of *London Labour* as a measure of triviality. If Mayhew's texts are on the edge of modernity, it is not because the *Morning Chronicle* letters are a discourse on poverty. It is the non-unitary and uncontrolled quality of the discourse in *London Labour* which defines the modernity of Mayhew's texts.

Method

A methodological credo is always present and always the same in all Mayhew's texts, in the *Morning Chronicle* letters, in *London Labour,* and in *Criminal Prisons.* Early or late, Mayhew had a grand philosopher's notion of method: choose a subject matter, any subject matter, and the universal method would provide procedures for acquiring, organising, and using knowledge. He accepted the traditional philosophical alibi for this breathtaking claim; the one method was safe because it was a rationalisation of the procedures of the natural sciences. Mayhew's aim was to extend this method to social phenomena; 'I made up my mind to deal with human nature as a natural philosopher or a chemist deals with any material object' (Mayhew, 1850, p. 6). He conceived the natural scientific method to be a dual one of induction and classification.

Mayhew was a strident inductivist. He presented himself at the time of the *Morning Chronicle* letters as someone who was applying the 'laws of inductive philosophy' to the subject matter of political economy which had hitherto languished in deductive error (Mayhew, 1850, p. 6). On account of its deductive character, political economy was always typed as a 'pseudo-science' ('Answers', 19 June 1851). Although deduction might be a mode of using knowledge, induction was 'the mode of acquiring it' (Mayhew, 1861-2, vol. 4, p. 2). Theory in the inductive sense was 'a large collection of facts' (Mayhew, 1861-2, vol. 4, p. 2). Thus Mayhew could announce quite seriously at the beginning of the *Morning Chronicle* letters, 'my vocation is to collect facts and to register opinions' (*Morning Chronicle,* letter II, Thompson and Yeo, 1971, p. 105). The work of collecting facts was modest, but the theoretical prospects were glittering:

> Mr. Mayhew is . . . a mere collector of facts, endeavouring
> to discover the several phenomena of labour with a view of
> arriving ultimately at the laws and circumstances affecting
> and controlling the operation and rewards of the labourer
> ('Answers', no. 10, 15 February 1851).

Classification was the methodological complement of inductive empiricism: 'what the generalisation of events is to the ascertainment of natural laws; the generalisation of things is to the discovery of natural systems' (Mayhew, 1861-2, vol. 4, p. 4). Mayhew regarded himself not only as an inductive empiricist but also as a classifier because 'of all scientific processes, the classification of the various phenomena in connection with a given subject is perhaps the most important' (Mayhew, 1861-2, vol. 4, p. 4; see also, *Morning Chronicle,* letter LII). Thus in the taxonomic reflections of the fourth volume of *London*

Labour, there was to be a central place for the classification of occupations. Mayhew's aim was:

> to distribute under one or other of these four (classificatory)
> categories the diverse modes of living peculiar to the
> members of our own community, and so to enunciate for
> the first time, the natural history, as it were, of the industry
> and idleness of Great Britain in the nineteenth century
> (Mayhew, 1861-2, vol. 4, p. 4).

In Mayhew the procedures of induction and classification were to methodise the work. But the question of the unity of his work cannot be settled by reference to these precepts. To begin with, it is easier said than done to deliver a discourse constructed in the image of a methodological credo. The texts did try to construct a discourse according to Mayhew's methodological precepts; inductive and taxonomic effort runs through the texts from the *Morning Chronicle* letters to the book on *Criminal Prisons.* However, far from organising the work, Mayhew's methodological precepts become an active disorganising principle.

This has been obscured by the Thompson and Yeo claims (1971, pp. 45 and 51) that Mayhew was a 'systematic empirical sociologist'. Mayhew's texts never used any of the systematic empiricist techniques for resolving association into plausible causal connections between empirical variables. Mill's (1843) *System of Logic* proposed four methods of inductive experimental inquiry: the methods of agreement, of difference, of residues, and of concomitant variation. But these were completely absent from Mayhew's texts which can therefore be described as unsystematic empiricism.

The absence of systematic empiricist techniques did not prevent Mayhew from instituting inductive tests. Little tests about the effects of institutions are scattered across his texts. The *Morning Chronicle* letters tested to see whether the ragged schools had made any impression on juvenile crime (*Morning Chronicle,* letters XLIII-V). *Criminal Prisons* tested to see whether the 'separate system' of permanent isolation of the prisoner in his cell produced a higher rate of lunacy (Mayhew and Binny, 1862, p. 103). Apart from such tests about the effects of institutions, there was also a general interest in the concomitants of social phenomena like crime. Both *London Labour* and *Criminal Prisons* presented a mass of maps and tables relating different variables to criminality (Mayhew, 1861-2, vol. 4, pp. 451-504). This was done so that induction might render crime and vice more intelligible:

> We must, in order to arrive at a comprehensive knowledge
> of its antecedents, consequences and concomitants, con-
> template as large a number of facts as possible in as many

different relations as the statistical records of the country
will admit of our doing (Mayhew, 1861–2, vol. 4, p. 3).

Without techniques for resolving association into cause, however,
the results were chronically uncertain. This is illustrated by the reply of
the secretary of the Ragged Schools Union (*Morning Chronicle*, 22
April 1850). He queried the rationale of Mayhew's test; given that the
ragged schools were not reformatories for criminals, it was unreasonable
to test for their effects upon juvenile crime. Furthermore, he showed
that the connection of ragged schools with increasing juvenile crime
was thoroughly precarious; Mayhew assumed a secular increase of
juvenile crime, but the pattern was one of random fluctuations, most
of which could be removed by five-year averages, while any increase in
juvenile crime after 1847 was most probably caused by legal changes
which made committal easier. More generally, where the texts examined
the concomitants of social phenomena like crime, Mayhew's results
were so chaotic that they discredited themselves. It was totally impossible to sort out causes and thus Mayhew's conclusions about the
correlates of crime were entirely negative; crime did not positively
relate to ignorance, density of population, wealth, pauperism, vagrancy,
drunkenness, or breach of the Sabbath. The cause of criminality could
only be identified by making the mighty and non-inductive leap to the
conclusion that, if criminality did not relate to these variables, then the
criminals must be 'that portion of our society who have not yet conformed to civilized habits' (Mayhew and Binny, 1862, p. 384).

If the results were so uncertain, Mayhew's texts could not constitute
theory in the methodologically approved inductive manner. What Yeo
calls 'the subtle interplay between fact and hypothesis' (Thompson
and Yeo, 1971, p. 70), is a figment of her imagination. When induction
produced only uncertainty about the connection between the 'facts',
then formal theory in the sense of determinative connection had to be
introduced as a deductive *deus ex machina*. This is classically the case
with the deductive economic theory of low wages in the 'Answers to
Correspondents' column or the *Low Wages* part-work. Mayhew claimed
this theory was speculation 'perhaps based on a greater number of
phenomena than any economist has as yet personally obtained'
('Answers', no. 16, 29 March 1851). But the theory is deductive rather
than inductive; it departs, not from the facts about low wages, but
from abstract definitions of capital and such like. Much the same point
can be made about *London Labour*'s use of the mid-Victorian ethnology
of Pritchard and Smith (Mayhew, 1861–2, vol. 1, pp. 1–2). The 'hypothesis' of wandering tribes does not arise from the facts, but is added
as a kind of interpretative garnish to the facts.

It is possible to turn now to the role of classification in Mayhew's
texts. This classifactory concern is unfamiliar, because a historiography

concerned with precursors and anticipations of a discourse on poverty is much more interested in Mayhew's empiricism than in his taxonomy. It is symptomatic that neither the Thompson and Yeo (1971) nor the Humphreys (1971) selections from the *Morning Chronicle* reprint the letter which is concerned with classification (*Morning Chronicle*, letter LII). To counter this neglect, we must reinstate Mayhew's classifications in their proper place as an everpresent framework. First the classifications will be described and then their role in the discourse will be examined. The texts develop working and programmatic classifications which will now be considered in turn.

Working classifications were typically simple general divisions which were developed and further sub-divided on an *ad hoc* basis as the work proceeded. The *Morning Chronicle* letters began by proposing a division of the metropolitan poor 'according as they will work, they can't work and they won't work' (*Morning Chronicle*, letter I). Those that will work were examined and, some ten letters later, sub-divided into those that make, do and sell, or 'artisans', 'labourers' and 'hucksters' (*Morning Chronicle*, letter XII). When the series was more than half-way through, a further series of discriminations was proposed (*Morning Chronicle*, letter LII). Artisans or skilled labourers were now to be sub-divided 'according to the material upon which they worked'. At the same time another class of those that worked was discriminated: a broad service class of 'servants' was to include clerks and shopmen as well as domestic servants.

London Labour's working classification of the street folk began where the *Morning Chronicle* classification of 'hucksters' left off. Right at the start of *London Labour*'s first volume, street folk were classified into six distinct 'genera': street sellers, street buyers, street finders, street performers, street artisans, and street pedlars (Mayhew, 1861-2, vol. 1, p. 3). Three of these genera had already been announced in the *Morning Chronicle* (letter LII). Mayhew's *London Labour* further sub-divided the genera on a principle already enunciated in the *Morning Chronicle* (letter XIII). The first three genera of street sellers, buyers, and finders were to be sub-divided according to the object bought, sold and found, while the last three genera were to be sub-divided according to the character or place of performance or service (Mayhew, 1861-2, vol. 1, pp. 3-4).

The other occupational groups considered in Mayhew's tests – prostitutes and criminals – were also scrupulously classified. In *London Labour*, different types of prostitute were classified according to place of residence or business (Mayhew, 1861-2, vol. 4, p. 213). The same text proposed a classification of crimes and criminals (Mayhew, 1861-2, vol. 4, pp. 30-1) which was then developed in *Criminal Prisons* (Mayhew and Binny, 1862, pp. 87-90). Habitual criminals were classified according to the mode in which they obtained their living:

cracksman, drummer, mobsman, sneaksman, and shofulman. *Criminal Prisons* also offered a classification of prison regimes into five different types: the classification of prisoners, the silent associated system, the separate system, the fixed system, and the mark system (Mayhew and Binny, 1862, p. 97).

The divisions so far considered are working divisions; they provide a set of empty boxes into which material is sorted. Mayhew apologised in the *Morning Chronicle* (letter II, letter XII) for erratic movement between occupations, but the texts did obey his own classificatory rules. The classification suggested a grouping of artisans according to object worked upon; and the *Morning Chronicle* letters dealt with a group of trades that worked upon a restricted range of materials – leather, cloth, and woodworking trades accounted for thirty of the thirty-three *Morning Chronicle* letters on manufacturing trades. There was even a certain order in the *Morning Chronicle* treatment of unskilled and service workers who were united in terms of what they did and where they worked. The unskilled workers loaded or unloaded goods on the waterside as dock labourers, ballast heavers, coal whippers, and so forth. The service workers were mainly employed in sea or land transport. *London Labour*'s treatment of street folk was even more strikingly in accord with the classificatory proposals. Except for a few diversions into the consideration of ethnic groups like the Jews and the Irish, the street folk were treated exhaustively and serially in the order of the classification. The book, like the classification, considered in turn: street sellers, street buyers, and the other 'genera'. Each 'genus' is then considered in the way the classification proposed; street sellers, for example, were sub-divided according to the object sold.

Beyond the working divisions that define what Mayhew wrote are the programmatic divisions which define an encyclopedic discourse that Mayhew never finished writing. The departure point for the encyclopedia was the sub-division of the poor into three groups at the beginning of the *Morning Chronicle* letters. This sub-division was taken up again in the sub-title of *London Labour* as a 'cyclopaedia of the condition and earnings of those that will work, those that cannot work and those that will not work'. The encyclopedia was planned in detail in the programmatic classifications that Mayhew inserted into the fourth volume of *London Labour* and into the *Great World* part-work.

London Labour added a fourth group of 'those that need not work', and thereby produced a programmatic classification which covered the whole population (Mayhew, 1861-2, vol. 4, p. 3). Each of the four classes was then sub-divided (Mayhew, 1861-2, vol. 4, pp. 12-27). For example, the 'need not work' class was sub-divided according to whether income was derived from rent, dividends, yearly stipends, and so forth (Mayhew, 1861-2, vol. 4, p. 27). In much modified form, the working classifications were incorporated as details in the larger design of the programmatic classification. Thus artisans or skilled labourers were now to be classified, not according to the material worked upon, but, 'according as they pursue some mechanical or chemical occupation' (Mayhew, 1861-2, vol. 4, p. 11). Moreover, the make, do and sell division of 'those who will work' was reformulated as a division into enrichers, auxiliaries, benefactors, and servitors (Mayhew, 1861-2, vol. 4, p. 12). To complicate matters further, the endpapers of the first part of the *Great World* announced a second programmatic classification which was completely different from *all* the earlier classifications. Here the whole population – working class and non-working class – was to be treated in twenty-nine occupational sections: legal London, medical London, religious London, commercial London and so forth.

The introduction of the programmatic classification only produces confusion. *London Labour*'s working classification is in many ways contradicted by the fourth volume's programmatic classification. Subsequently, the *Great World* simply added another and quite different programmatic classification. But it is important not to get distracted by the discrepancies. All the classifications, early and late, working and programmatic, encounter similar problems.

Mayhew clearly identified the immediate difficulties of classifying occupations:

> the branches of industry are so multifarious, the divisions of
> labour so minute and manifold, that it seems at first almost
> impossible to reduce them to any system (Mayhew, 1861-
> 2, vol. 4, p. 4; see also, *Morning Chronicle*, letter LII).

None of his classifications achieves this reduction; they are all descriptive and unanalytic reinscriptions of detail. This is true, for example, of the classification of artisans, whether by material worked upon, or by mechanical or chemical operation. It is also true of the classification of street sellers by object sold. These are not classifications but lists. One does not wish to condemn this descriptiveness in the name of some classificatory norm and argue that Mayhew's classifications should have been different and more analytic. The point is that because these classifications are descriptive, certain consequences follow. With artisans the number of different materials worked upon, or of mechanical operations, was very large, as was the number of separate articles sold by street sellers. The lists thus specified more boxes than could easily be filled. Classification might have provided a framework where the significant could be economically and exhaustively discussed. Lists only made the discourse interminable.

All Mayhew's texts demonstrated that getting to the end of the list was an endless Sisyphean task. Eighty letters in the *Morning Chronicle* dealt with only a fraction of the London manufacturing trades. Even in areas of concentrated effort, such as textile trades, the coverage was not exhaustive. The 'Answers' (no. 4) column listed twenty-three trades of makers-up of textile materials; only five of these trades were ever covered in the *Morning Chronicle*. The shirt makers, the embroiderers, the bed and mattress makers, the artificial flower makers, and fourteen other groups remained to be dealt with. *London Labour* did deal exhaustively with the street folk, but took four weighty volumes to cover this 'comparatively small and obscure portion of the community' (*Great World*, pt 1, end cover). On Mayhew's own calculations the street folk were around 2½ per cent of the population (Mayhew, 1861-2, vol. 2, p. 1). At this rate, if the rest of London's population was to receive similar attention, 160 volumes would be necessary to cover the whole population. The arithmetic is even more spectacular for the *Great World* project. The part-work was retitled *Criminal Prisons* when republished in book form, because 550 out of the book's 630 pages were devoted to the criminal prisons and criminals of London. These were two out of a total of twenty-four sub-headings given under the general heading of 'legal London' which was one of twenty general headings. If each general heading had been developed until it had twenty-four sub-headings and if all the sub-headings had been treated like the two in *Criminal Prisons*, then 300 companion volumes, each of 650 pages, would have been necessary to complete the project.

Seldom can anyone have put his trust in method and been so confounded as Mayhew. In all his texts, induction and classification did not so much produce as oppose any kind of project definition. For the dual method was an active disorganising principle spreading uncertainty and interminability. The texts had to try and get things together in spite of induction and classification. Facts and theory would have to be acquired and organised around some different basis; strategically, in the interests of economy, some set of discursive priorities would have to be articulated. If Mayhew's discourse had to be built around non-methodological principles, the rest of this chapter will be concerned with whether and how this was achieved. The question of the unity of Mayhew's texts remains to be settled.

Morning Chronicle letters

The *Morning Chronicle* letters inquired serially into a number of different trades. It is possible to begin to define the inquiry by answering two questions: first, what trades were selected out of the multiplicity of separate trades defined in the occupational classification; and second, what questions were asked when a trade was being investigated?

To begin with the first question, there was always some principle for selecting trades, and at the beginning of the *Morning Chronicle* inquiry, the principle was absolutely straightforward: Mayhew promised an inquiry into low wages. His intention was 'to devote myself primarily to the consideration of that class of poor whose privations seemed to be due to the insufficiency of their wages' (*Morning Chronicle*, letter II; Thompson and Yeo, 1971, p. 104). The letters therefore began by selecting trades with low wages. The Spitalfields weavers were an obvious starting point because they were 'notorious for their privations' (*Morning Chronicle*, letter II; Thompson and Yeo, 1971, p. 104). Three groups of the low paid – Spitalfield weavers, dock labourers, and slop clothing workers – accounted for nine out of the first fifteen letters. But the investigation of low-wage trades lasted for little more than a dozen letters, because the basis for selecting manufacturing trades shifted in mid-investigation.

Letter sixteen on tailoring observed that the trade was divided into two sections: an honourable trade where garments were made up by skilled union labour working at standard rates on the retailers' premises, and a dishonourable trade where retailers bought in garments from sweaters who employed non-union labour at sub-standard rates (*Morning Chronicle*, letter XVI; Thompson and Yeo, 1971, p. 182). The inquiry was now reoriented towards trades with a dual-sector structure. For, albeit under different names, the dual-sector structure was found elsewhere in a variety of trades. Hatters, boot and shoe-makers, carpenters, joiners and cabinet makers (*Morning Chronicle*, letters XXXII, LX, LXI, LXIC, LXXVII; Thompson and Yeo, 1971, pp. 234, 339, 346, 373, 445) all worked in dual-sector trades. Here, typically one-tenth of the workers, 'the aristocracy of the trade', was in the unionised high-wage honourable sector and the remaining nine-tenths were in the non-union low-wage dishonourable sector (*Morning Chronicle*, letter LXIV; Thompson and Yeo, 1971, pp. 372-3).

When the series of letters ended, the treatment of dual-sector manu-facturing trades took up more space than anything else. Manufacturing trades were described in thirty-two out of eighty letters, or nearly half of the total number. Unskilled labourers and service workers were relatively neglected; even together, the two groups accounted for many fewer letters. More than three-quarters of the letters on manufacturing trades were about dual-sector trades. Garment, footwear and wood-working trades, organised on a dual-sector basis, accounted for twenty-five of the thirty-two letters devoted to manufacturing trades. The *Morning Chronicle* letters are not about one thing, but they concentrate on manufacturing trades and these trades are preponderantly dual-sector trades. The contrast with *London Labour*'s later investigation of street folk is obvious.

It is now possible to turn and consider what questions were asked when trades were investigated. At the beginning of the investigation, everything was very simple. The questions were about low wages because, as Mayhew announced, 'the proprietors of the *Morning Chronicle* have undertaken to obtain for the first time in this country, an account of the earnings of the workpeople in the Metropolis' (*Morning Chronicle*, letter IX; Thompson and Yeo, 1971, p. 165). In this case, the investigator needed only to ask some basic questions about pay, and to make sure that respondents were not 'extreme cases' (*Morning Chronicle*, letter VII; Thompson and Yeo, 1971, p. 127). Beyond this, Mayhew tried to obtain the opinions of the workpeople about the causes of low wages. As he explained in his second letter (*Morning Chronicle*, letter II; Thompson and Yeo, 1971, p. 105):

> In my inquiry I have sought to obtain information from
> the artisans of Spitalfields upon two points in particular. I
> was desirous to ascertain from the workmen themselves,
> not only the average rate of wages received by them, but
> also to hear their opinion as to the cause of the depreciation
> in the value of their labour.

When the inquiry turned to the dual-sector trades, the questions changed. There were new questions about the conditions in, and organisation of, the two sections. When an all-purpose schedule of queries for trade investigations was finally formulated in the 'Answers' column (no. 48), the wages information was to be sub-divided into two categories 'fair' and 'unfair', and informants were to provide a profile of 'the badly paid trade' with descriptions of its history, labour force, middle men, and employers. Above all, the issue was the interrelation between the honourable and dishonourable trades. When Mayhew convened a public meeting of tailors, the first of the stated 'objects of the meeting' was 'to learn whether, and how, the slop trade influences the regular and honourable tailoring trade' (*Morning Chornicle*, letter XVII; Thompson and Yeo, 1971, p. 198). With these new concerns, the business of investigating trades became altogether more complicated. In low-wage trades, it was sufficient to avoid extreme cases. In dual-sector trades, Mayhew had to obtain separately for each sector a sample of workers representative of those engaged in different branches of a trade and also representative of those with different chances of employment (*Morning Chronicle*, letter XVI; Thompson and Yeo, 1971, p. 184).

Nevertheless Mayhew still found time to record the opinions of artisans. He recorded, for example, that tailors blamed a decline of wages on the introduction of piece-work (*Morning Chronicle*, letter XVII; Thompson and Yeo, 1971, p. 200), and shoe-makers blamed a decline of wages on the absence of protection (*Morning Chronicle*, letter XXXII; Thompson and Yeo, 1971, p. 235). Such opinions show a restriction of reference in the *Morning Chronicle* questions, which were not concerned with broader cultural arrangements as *London Labour*'s questions would be. The letters included only abbreviated 'descriptions of modes of life and habits, politics, religion, literature and amusements of the trade' ('Answers', no. 48). Even the biographies featured in the *Morning Chronicle* are not so much lives as statements of a trade history. The questions in the investigation of the manu-facturing trades were simply about trade matters.

The discussion so far should establish the elementary difference of subject matter which separates the *Morning Chronicle* letters from what came after. It cannot define the peculiar character of the letters on dual-sector trades because this character is defined by the nature of the treatment rather than the subject matter.

Radical historiography has praised Mayhew's treatment of dual-sector trades as an analysis of the unacceptable face of mid-Victorian capitalism. Samuel claims that Mayhew had a 'theoretical grasp of the *system* which they [the sweaters] personified' (Samuel, 1973, p. 52) and Yeo claims that Mayhew was able to see 'poverty . . . as the pro-duct of an economic system' (Thompson and Yeo, 1971, p. 88). It is therefore worth insisting that the later questions about the organisation of, and conditions in, dual-sector trades were questions which an artisan could have formulated. The categories of the *Morning Chronicle* analysis were those of the artisans themselves. In particular, the central conceptual division between honourable and dishonourable trades was an everyday one for the workers themselves. Mayhew's questions were only cues or prompts which triggered a pre-existing artisan analysis.

The treatment of artisan opinions is even more interesting and will further establish what a small distance there is between the *Morning Chronicle* analysis and the artisans. The letters not only collected artisan opinions, but also endorsed them as significant and serious. This is an interesting indicator. Such uninformed opinion would have no status in a multiplicity of other discourses. Why should an artisan be able to identify correctly the causes of a fall in wages? The answer in this case is straightforward. The opinions of aristocratic artisans in the honourable sectors of the trades are not being critically recorded but uncritically assimilated as the investigation's own conclusions. This can be shown by looking at indicators of the assimilation of artisan opinions, such as the enthusiasm for the respectable artisan's mode of life and the enthusiasm for trade societies.

Historians are virtually unanimous in noticing with approval that Mayhew's discourse avoids applying the standards of bourgeois respectability to the working class (Thompson and Yeo, 1971, p. 46; Himmelfarb, 1973, p. 722; Humphreys, 1971, p. xvi). Indeed they are so busy congratulating Mayhew on escaping bourgeois respectability, that they fail to notice that these texts completely endorse proletarian respectability. The letters eulogised the skilled artisans who lived as respectable working men should. They praised the cultural refinement of artisans like wood carvers whose trade society admitted employers and employed, and maintained a library for the benefit of members; 'those who wish to be impressed with the social advantages of a fairly-paid class of mechanics should attend a meeting of the Wood-carvers Society' (*Morning Chronicle*, letter LXV; Thompson and Yeo, 1971, p. 376). Positive approval for their comfortable domesticity shines through all the descriptions of the honourable artisans' homes where,

> you have the warm, red glow of polished mahogany
> furniture; a clean carpet covers the floor; a few engravings
> in neat frames hang against the papered wall; and book-
> shelves or a bookcase have their appropriate furniture. Very
> white and bright coloured pot ornaments, with sometimes a
> few roses in a small vase, are reflected in the mirror over the
> mantleshelf (*Morning Chronicle*, letter LXIII; Thompson
> and Yeo, 1971, p. 196).

If Mayhew here was unlike Booth and Rowntree in his refusal of bourgeois standards in all forms, he was also unlike Booth and Rowntree in his uncritical endorsement of proletarian respectability, which Booth and Rowntree condemned as empty domesticity.

Consequently, the *Morning Chronicle* letters came near to disparaging the disreputable as so many nineteenth-century social investigations did. The dishonourable artisan was always unfavourably compared with the honourable artisan, as when the letters claimed that in tailoring 'the honourable part of the trade are really intelligent artisans, while the slopworkers are generally almost brutified with their incessant toil, wretched pay, miserable food and filthy homes' (*Morning Chronicle*, letter XVII; Thompson and Yeo, 1971, p. 196). The difference in Mayhew's discourse was that the dishonourable artisan escaped straightforward condemnation of the conventional kind, because the letters identified a guiltier party. With the same enthusiasm as many of his artisan informants, Mayhew scapegoated the small master in the dishonourable trade. Such masters were characterised as 'those who care only for themselves and seek to grow rich by underselling their fellow-tradesmen as well as by underpaying the workmen in their employ' (*Morning Chronicle*, letter LX; Thompson and Yeo, 1971, p. 339). The sweater, the chamber master, the garret master, the strapping shop owner, all small working masters, were abused as the cause of every evil in the honourable and dishonourable trades.

The enthusiasm for trade societies is as significant as the endorsement of proletarian respectability or the scapegoating of small masters. On the subject of unionism, the letters read as though produced by a public relations officer for the trade societies (*Morning Chronicle,* letter LXV; Thompson and Yeo, 1971, pp. 377–9). Trade societies did not exist to obtain an exorbitant rate of wages from their employers; the standard rate of wages was agreed between employers and employees who were 'as strongly opposed to strikes as a means of upholding them, as the public themselves'. Moreover, friendly society functions were as, or more, important than wage-rate maintaining functions; the trade societies supported their own sick and aged and thus saved poor law expenditure, so that 'every ratepayer in the kingdom' benefited. Thus, the activities of trade societies were altogether benign and even benefited the (middle class) 'public'. On the intra-working-class role of trade societies, the letters were completely silent. It was taken for granted that only 'honourable' workers belonged to trade societies; 'it is the fact of belonging to some such society which invariably distinguishes the better class of workmen from the worse' (*Morning Chronicle,* letter LXV; Thompson and Yeo, 1971, p. 378). The letters endlessly considered conditions in, and relations between, honourable and dishonourable sections of the trades, but it somehow escaped notice that trade societies were key institutions for the protection of a small minority of skilled workers. At this important point the letters could not concede that there was a relation between honourable and dishonourable trades.

In conclusion, then, it can be said that the *Morning Chronicle* letters did not analyse but rhetorically deprecated 'the tendency of the cheap slop trade to destroy not only the able artisan, but the honourable tradesman, and to substitute for employer and employed, cheats, children and criminals' (*Morning Chronicle,* letter XXXVI; Thompson and Yeo, 1971, p. 271). This is a nice irony when, in his methodological credo, Mayhew was an inductivist committed to strict neutrality. He promised that the labour question would be investigated 'without reference to any particular prejudice, theory, party or policy' (Mayhew, 1850, p. 6); but the *Morning Chronicle* letters worked by breaking this promise. They are held together by a presiding artisan consciousness, prejudice, theory and all. This is not so much a negative fault, as part of the positive identity of the texts; the *Morning Chronicle* letters tell the story of the trades from the point of view of an honourable artisan. Ultimately, it is this voice rather than the subject matter that establishes the difference of the *Morning Chronicle* letters.

The voice and point of view are not a disembodied discursive effect, they are supported by the appearance of an authorial figure in these letters. This figure is not the human subject Mayhew who is long dead and no doubt had as little identity and stability as the rest of us. The figure is the discursive creature Mayhew who is alive in the *Morning Chronicle* letters, in whose reference he achieves identity and stability. Mayhew, as text effect, is here enlisted on the side of the honourable

artisans and the letters represent the moment of his quixotic identification with, and as, artisan consciousness.

Thompson and Yeo, the rediscoverers of the *Morning Chronicle*
letters, present a rather different reading of the achievement of a human
subject. Booth and Rowntree are usually credited with the first
empirical investigations of poverty at the end of the nineteenth
century. Yeo would give the credit to Mayhew in the mid-nineteenth
century; she claims 'it was Henry Mayhew as metropolitan commissioner
for the *Morning Chronicle* who set out to conduct the first empirical
survey into poverty *as such*' (Thompson and Yeo, 1971, p. 52).
Mayhew defined his project in his first letter as 'examining into the
condition of the poor of London' (*Morning Chronicle,* letter I;
Thompson and Yeo, 1971, p. 102). He also introduced 'the poverty
line in embryonic form' in the same letter when he defined the poor as
'those persons whose incomes are insufficient for the satisfaction of
their wants' (*Morning Chronicle,* letter I; Thompson and Yeo, 1971,
p. 102). Apart from this, Yeo emphasises Mayhew's questions; he is
praised for instituting the first social survey which asks questions about
wages, hours, and regularity of employment (Thompson and Yeo,
1971, pp. 53-4). Mayhew's conclusions about cause are also praised
for their modernity; he posited a relationship between poverty and
low wages to methodise the work (Thompson and Yeo, 1971, p. 55)
and thus could see 'poverty in the round as the product of an economic
system' (Thompson and Yeo, 1971, p. 88).

Thompson and Yeo are not alone in their obsession with anticipation and precursors. Razzell, for example, has subsequently claimed
that, in the *Morning Chronicle,* Mayhew described the nineteenth-
century equivalent of Lockwood's privatised worker and that Mayhew
anticipated the subsequent sociological distinction between 'rough'
and 'respectable' workers. The search for discursive precursors and
anticipations may be popular, but it nevertheless always faces certain
general problems. History in the future anterior, the story of what was
to be, is never convincing because it is so uninformative: nothing really
happens because everything is there in the beginning in underdeveloped
form. Such historiography is also completely unable to characterise
anything except modernity: the non-modern does not exist except as
a blank or negative. Finally, the identification of precursors is usually
achieved by the violent rearrangement of discursive reference into one
approved configuration. When these general points have been made, it is
only necessary to demonstrate first, the carelessness of Yeo's search for
a precursor and second, the implausibility of the letters as a poverty
survey.

Thompson and Yeo never specify criteria which define a poverty
survey. If the criteria are insufficiently explicit, almost any text can be
presented as a poverty survey. Any criticism must begin by proposing

its own criteria. Choice of criteria is simplified because Yeo insists that Mayhew's discourse is not simply a discourse about poverty but an 'empirical survey into poverty *as such*' (Thompson and Yeo, 1971, p. 54). She explicitly develops the comparison with Booth and Rowntree. Criteria for a poverty survey are complicated when, as will be shown in later chapters on Booth and Rowntree, the poverty survey is not always the same. Nevertheless, three criteria can be suggested. First, the investigation has to cover a defined population, usually selected on the basis of physical location or occupation. Second, the investigation has to specify a poverty line, an expenditure or consumption standard below which individuals are in poverty. Third, the investigation must obtain data on incomes and earnings so that individuals can be placed above or below the poverty line. These three criteria are jointly necessary for the calculation of a percentage of the population in poverty and this calculation is the minimal defining characteristic of the poverty survey.

On these criteria, the *Morning Chronicle* letters are not a poverty survey. They did ask questions about wages and thus meet one criterion, but they do not meet the other two criteria. As Yeo concedes (Thompson and Yeo, 1971, p. 54), Mayhew never calculated a poverty line. After asserting in the first letter that the poor were those with wants greater than incomes, Mayhew showed no further interest in the question of defining minimum necessary income. Furthermore, in poverty survey terms, the occupations covered were a nonsensical population. The letters neglected or ignored what Mayhew calculated to be the largest occupational groupings, the 168,000 domestic servants and the 50,000 labourers (*Morning Chronicle*, letter XXXII; Thompson and Yeo, 1971, p. 228). Instead the letters concentrated on manufacturing trades like the 25,000 tailors and the 18,000 carpenters and joiners (*Morning Chronicle*, letter XXXII; Thompson and Yeo, 1971, p. 228); but they did not cover all the trades, nor did Mayhew ever claim that those trades he did cover were representative of the whole.

The texts simply do not fit Thompson and Yeo's reading. This is something of an achievement when, as will be shown in the next chapter on Engels, a number of different readings can usually find justification in any moderately polysemic text. Matters are made worse when the discrepancy between reading and text is hidden by a self-deluding optimism about what the texts say. As has been shown, Yeo cites Mayhew's statements of intent and project definition to support her argument that the letters are about poverty. She fails to notice that in these passages Mayhew himself never used the term poverty, but always the conventional mid-nineteenth-century term 'the poor'. And, in the end, everything becomes totally circular. The presupposition that the discourse is about poverty establishes further indicators that the discourse is about poverty. One such indicator is the letters' supposed analysis of the causes of poverty.

By presenting texts that are not a poverty survey as a poverty survey, all Thompson and Yeo have done is to make the texts unintelligible and inexplicable. Here it is salutary to compare the alternative reading of the *Morning Chronicle* letters proposed in this section. The letters' concern with wages must be unintelligible to Thompson and Yeo, because the data collected is wasted in poverty survey terms when it never connects with a poverty line. However, the concern becomes intelligible on this chapter's alternative reading; for an artisan consciousness, recording wages, hours, and conditions of work could be an end in itself. It is the same story with regard to Mayhew's sampling procedures which for Thompson and Yeo must be so puzzling, because the procedures were careful within each trade, but non-existent between trades, so that the letters never obtained the poverty survey's necessary guarantee of representativeness. On the alternative reading, everything falls into place. If the *Morning Chronicle* project was an examination of dual-sector trades, all Mayhew had to do was to restrict himself to trades with this pattern of organisation; broader considerations of representativeness were irrelevant. Finally, the letters' movement between occupations must be unintelligible to Thompson and Yeo because it does not produce a poverty survey population. However, if the letters are held together by artisan consciousness, the concentration on dual-sector trades becomes intelligible; the honourable trade was a congenial object, and the threat from the dishonourable trade was *the* crisis. Thus, at every point where Mayhew is unintelligible to Thompson and Yeo, this chapter's alternative reading can make sense of his procedures.

The reading suggested here can also make sense of the ending of the series of letters. If the *Morning Chronicle* letters manifest a trade consciousness, they also demonstrate the limits of such consciousness. The *Morning Chronicle* investigation did not add up to anything but endless repetition; the investigation did not progress analytically after the sixteenth letter, where the notion of a dual-sector trade was introduced. After that, the same structure was discovered in every trade. Such an investigation could not be brought to a conclusion, it could only be abandoned. And this was what happened. When publication of the *Morning Chronicle* letters ceased, Mayhew turned to two new projects, a theoretical treatment of low wages and an empirical investigation of street folk. These two projects will now be considered in turn.

The theory of low wages

Mayhew began to consider the theory of low wages in some of the later *Morning Chronicle* letters and in his speech to the tailors (Mayhew, 1850). The theoretical treatment of low wages was then developed in the 'Answers' column on the endpapers of the *London Labour* part-work and in a separate part-work entitled *Low Wages* (Mayhew, 1850). In the most literal way, this theory came between two empirical projects – the investigation of the manufacturing trades in the *Morning Chronicle* and the investigation of street folk in *London Labour*. It has already been argued, in the section on Mayhew's method, that his economic theory is not, and cannot be, inductively derived from the facts. In this case it is reasonable to begin by considering the status of Mayhew's economic theory as a deductive system. Questions of this sort are traditionally asked of any body of economic theory.

The theory did develop some interesting and even important concepts. For example, the concept of 'supersubsistence' was a real conceptual innovation which introduced the notion of time into political economy's atemporal notions of the wage labourer's subsistence. Mayhew conceded that short-run subsistence was largely determined by the cost of food (Mayhew, 1851, pp. 16-17); but he argued that in the long run a different 'supersubsistence' criterion should be applied because here, the minimum was 'such a rate of remuneration as will maintain not only the labourer himself when working, and also when unable to work, but support his family and admit of the care and education of his children' (Mayhew, 1851, p. 11). This concept allowed an identification of the social consequences of low wages. If wages were reduced to the level of present subsistence, then the capitalist had transferred long-run subsistence costs to the community:

> wages are cut down to a bare subsistence point so that the
> workpeople are obliged when ill, old, or out of work, to
> apply for parish relief – that is to say, the slop masters
> reduce the wages down to the *present* subsistence of the
> labourer, and transfer his future keep to the community in
> general (Mayhew, 1851, p. 17).

Mayhew should be remembered for conceptual innovations like supersubsistence which he did make, rather than for innovations like the poverty line which he never made. But conceptual innovation should not distract the reader from paying attention to the over-all deductive systematicity of Mayhew's economic theory.

The initial question was whether the 'law of supply and demand' applied to wage determination. This question was provoked by Mayhew's observation of anomalies in the honourable and dishonourable sectors of trades where wages had declined, although the number of workers was constant and the amount of work had not decreased (*Morning Chronicle*, letter LXIII; Thompson and Yeo, 1971, pp. 362-3). The existence of the anomalies was completely dependent upon a

statement of the law of supply and demand in Aunt Sally form whereby wages depended upon the collision of a quantum of work and a
body of labourers:

> According to the law of supply and demand, the decrease
> of workmen should have given rise to a proportionate
> increase in the wages, provided there was no corresponding
> diminution in the quantity of work to be done (*Morning
> Chronicle,* letter LXIII; Thompson and Yeo, 1971, p. 360).

In this statement of the anomaly, the question of effective demand
and supply at particular price levels was not considered at all.

Mayhew's counter-theory explained away the 'anomaly' with the
aid of some supplementary assumptions about the shape of, and shifts
in, the demand and supply curves for labour. It was presumed that the
demand curve for labour would continually shift downwards, as
employers competed among themselves and used lower wages as a
means of cost reduction. Every artisan trade with small masters illustrated this proposition (*Morning Chronicle,* letter LXIII; Thompson
and Yeo, 1971, p. 363). There was no consolation or compensation in
extended demand if final product prices fell. Mayhew was thoroughly
pessimistic about the prospects of increased demand for most industrial
products; 'a reduction of price ... cannot, in *many cases*, be followed
by an increase of demand' ('Answers', no. 16; see also 'Answers', no. 30,
and Mayhew, 1851, pp. 28-30). On the side of supply, it was assumed
that the supply of labour was never diminished by wage reductions
because workers sought always to maintain a conventional income level;
'any reduction in the rate of remuneration for labour causes the work-
man to do precisely that quantity of extra work which will make up his
wages to the same extent as formerly' (Mayhew, 1851, pp. 27-8).

These assumptions did no more and no less than specify a special
case of the law of determination of wages by supply and demand. But,
this was not obvious because Mayhew's exposition of the counter-
theory was completely chaotic. *Low Wages,* scheduled to run for
twenty-five parts, ceased publication after four numbers had been
published. Mayhew here never got further than preliminary skirmishing
with political economy. Not surprisingly, therefore, Thompson locates
'Mayhew's most systematic thoughts' in the 'Answers' column
(Thompson and Yeo, 1971, p. 44). However, the exposition in that
column was a matter of hit and run, start and stop. For example, the
numbers immediately preceding number twenty-two had featured a
running exposition of a few concepts and connections each week. Then
the economic theory vanished from the column for six numbers, and,
when it returned, it was developed in the form of replies to correspondents on particular points.

Given this chaotic exposition, it was possible to present the special case as a complete alternative to the explanation of wages in terms of supply and demand. Thus Mayhew claimed to have discovered a new law: 'overwork makes under-pay'. This was universally true because the special case assumptions vanished in the statement of the new law; 'any system of labour which tends to make the members of a craft produce a greater quantity of work than usual, tends at the same time to overpopulate the trade as certainly as an increase of workmen' (*Morning Chronicle*, letter LXVI; Thompson and Yeo, 1971, p. 385). By this stage, Mayhew had reached the point where his explanation of low wages was a set of speculative assumptions masquerading as an alternative theory.

Considered as a deductive system, Mayhew's economics is negligible, naïve, and incoherent. But it would be beside the point simply to condemn Mayhew's theory as a system which falls short of the standards of deductive rigour established in, for example, Ricardian or Marxist economic theory. It is altogether more profitable to ask: what is the pertinence of Mayhew's economic theory? Even if the theory is not a satisfactory deductive system, it nevertheless is something other than uninstructive error. The theoretical treatment of low wages reinforces the *Morning Chronicle*'s empirical material on manufacturing trades. The deductive non-system can and does further express the artisan consciousness which is what holds the *Morning Chronicle* letters together.

In the *Morning Chronicle* letters, the artisan manufacturing trade provided the empirical frame of reference. With a few exceptions such as the sawyers, the letters considered craft groups in artisan trades where technology was not changing rapidly and where a skilled artisan typically laboured in a small workshop with the aid of a few hand tools. These were not the heroically transformed trades of the textbook Industrial Revolution. This frame of reference was carried over into the economic theory of *Low Wages*. Mayhew's economic theory mentioned, but did not treat at length, trades where increases of output arose from the introduction of new machines or methods of production ('Answers', no. 22). On the other hand, a significant part of his analysis was devoted to itemising the devices that made overwork possible in an artisan trade with a given technology: in the honourable trade there was the institution of piece-work and in the dishonourable trade, division of labour and scamping of detail allowed increased output with the aid of semi-skilled helpers ('Answers', no. 22; see also, Mayhew, 1851, pp. 15-20).

Mayhew provides the economic theory of the artisan manufacturing trade as surely as Marshall provides the economic theory of the Lancashire cotton firm. However, Mayhew's economic theory goes beyond a simple reinscription of what is already there in the *Morning Chronicle* empirical material. For this economic theory does not simply express artisan consciousness, it also articulates that consciousness in two ways. First, and most obviously, theory universalised the particular grievance. Artisans disliked particular forms of overwork. Mayhew's economic theory culminated, as we have seen, in the discovery of the universal law 'overwork makes under-pay'. Second, and more subtly, the economic theory allowed Mayhew to distance himself from the immediate concerns of the artisans and to develop a strategic analysis. Thus Mayhew's theory contained serious sections on the future prospects of the artisan under the industrial system and on solutions for the crisis in the artisan manufacturing trades. Here Mayhew is something other than the artisan impersonator of the *Morning Chronicle* letters.

Mayhew's economics 'proved' that the prospects of the artisan under the industrial system were dismal. Every development in the system directly harmed the worker because every development entailed the expansion of some kind of capital fund at the expense of the subsistence fund from which the labourer was paid ('Answers', nos 18-20). More sophisticated distribution required a larger distribution fund ('Answers', no. 20). Greater 'economy of labour', that is, greater labour productivity, required a larger material fund ('Answers', no. 22). Any expansion of production also directly required a larger material fund ('Answers', no. 22), while an increase of mechanisation required a larger sinking fund ('Answers', no. 56). Mayhew's total hostility to machinery is especially noteworthy. He claimed to have established that 'it was physically impossible that machinery in the abstract could benefit the labourer' ('Answers', no. 58). In this way, Mayhew's economics articulated a theoretical Luddism.

Mayhew's economics also articulated pre-socialist solutions for society's problems. He recommended 'production by association' whereby the association of workers would combine the functions of capitalist and labourer in one person ('Answers', no. 28). Where this was not possible, he favoured a regulation of wages according to the 'equitable system' (Mayhew, 1851, pp. 36-51). Here, both labourers and capitalist were to receive a fair share of the produce. Wages were to be set according to the gap between the cost of the raw material and the wholesale price of the finished product (Mayhew, 1851, p. 38, 'Answers', no. 42). It was not clear how the capitalist's own reward was to be calculated, but the capitalist could and should have a fair reward (Mayhew, 1851, pp. 15 and 38). In this case there would be a reconciliation of interests under the equitable system where,

> you make the interest of the employer and the employed
> one and the same (whereas, at present they are diametrically
> opposed), and so you destroy all that bitter enmity
> between classes which is now ready at any moment to burst

forth into physical fury. It wants but this fusion of interests to wed the two great classes of this country – the savers and the workers – into one united family (Mayhew, 1851, p. 42).

In this way, Mayhew's economics allowed him to articulate a vision of ultimate harmony.

In conclusion, the relation of the economic theory to the *Morning Chronicle* material is straightforward. Mayhew's economic theory is unitary with the earlier empirical material in that both express an artisan consciousness. However, the economic theory is more advanced because it seeks to articulate and develop that consciousness. The project in the economic theory is serious but definitely pre-socialist. Unfortunately, this is not clear in the Thompson and Yeo selections from *Low Wages* since these editors do not reprint the section on the equitable wage system (Mayhew, 1851, pp. 36–51). This opens the way for attempts to enlist this pre-socialist Luddite economic theorist as a precursor of Marx. Samuel has recently argued that Mayhew developed a 'theory of exploitation' which anticipated Marx's theory in that it attributed low wages to the drive for surplus value and poverty to capitalist super-profit (Samuel, 1973, p. 51). On the basis of this chapter's reading, Samuel's argument about the theory in the early work must be rejected. It is not simply that Marx's economic theory was infinitely better developed as a system. Marx did not write from the viewpoint of the aristocratic respectable artisan but tried theoretically to constitute the minimum necessary for identification of the working-class interest. Mayhew simply assimilated and articulated the world taken for granted by the aristocratic artisan.

London Labour and the street folk

The first sixty-three numbers of the *London Labour* part-work were reprinted in the first three volumes of the *London Labour* book. This work has an elementary thematic unity that distinguishes it from what went before: the first three volumes of *London Labour* examine a distinct and different group of 'those that will work'. All Mayhew's subsequent work was about 'those that will not work' according to his programmatic classification. Following up the part-work on prostitution, Mayhew's collaborators, Hemyng, Binny and Halliday, produced essays on prostitutes, thieves, beggars, and swindlers for the fourth volume of the 1861–2 edition of *London Labour*. And later the *Great World* part-work and the *Criminal Prisons* book of 1862 were to examine the institutions in which another class of 'non-workers' was confined.

The *Morning Chronicle* letters had concentrated upon artisans in manufacturing trades with a dual-sector structure. But in *London Labour*, this group was definitely dropped although the third volume was padded out with recycled material from the *Morning Chronicle* articles and this material accounted for the whole of the last half of the third volume. Mayhew reprinted descriptions of labourers on the waterfront and in transport; coalwhippers, dock labourers, and hackney cabmen were all covered. For good measure, the *Morning Chronicle* treatment of low lodging houses, vagrancy, and homelessness was also thrown in. But the material on artisans which had dominated the *Morning Chronicle* letters was not reprinted. A meagre ten pages on 'garret masters' (Mayhew, 1861-2, vol. 3, pp. 221-30) condensed some of the *Morning Chronicle* conclusions about dishonourable trades.

The first three volumes of *London Labour* selected a new group of 'those who will work' from the classification. The title page promised, and the volumes delivered, a treatment of 'the London street folk comprising street sellers, street buyers, street finders, street performers, street artisans, and street labourers'. On Mayhew's own estimate these groups accounted for some 50,000 men, women, and children - around one-fortieth of London's population (Mayhew, 1861-2, vol. 1, p. 6). Numerically, the group of street folk was dominated by the street traders, 'sellers' and 'buyers' who accounted for four-fifths of all street folk (Mayhew, 1861-2, vol. 2, p. 1). The coster sellers, who bought at the wholesale 'green' and 'fish' markets, alone accounted for some 30,000 (Mayhew, 1861-2, vol. 2, p. 1). *London Labour*'s treatment of street folk showed much the same emphasis with more than one and a half volumes devoted to an examination of street traders. Thus the first volume of *London Labour* was largely a serial examination of street sellers of fish, fruit, vegetables, game, poultry, rabbits, butter, cheese and eggs, trees, shrubs, flowers, roots, seed and branches, green stuff, eatables and drinkables, stationery, literature, fine arts, and manufactured articles.

The question now is whether the difference of subject in *London Labour* is associated with a difference of treatment. Formally, a certain similarity of treatment connects the *Morning Chronicle* letters and *London Labour*. Both texts offer a representation of a social group after a conversation between two subjects, Mayhew and the group. In *London Labour*, Mayhew carried on talking to the poor as he had in the *Morning Chronicle*. The street folk were Mayhew's most important single source of information, and he included tens of thousands of words of direct *reportage* of what the poor said. He described *London Labour* as the first 'attempt to publish the history of a people, from the lips of the people themselves' (Mayhew, 1861-2, vol. 1, p. xv).

The problem was how the representation of the new social group was to be managed. In the *Morning Chronicle,* the representation was managed by assimilating the viewpoint of the artisans, but *London Labour* was different, for in this text there was no such identification with the object group. A variety of indices show that *London Labour* did not adopt the viewpoint of the street folk; to demonstrate this point the devaluation of the opinions of street folk, and the use of theory, can be considered.

The *Morning Chronicle* letters had cherished the opinions of manufacturing artisans, but *London Labour* devalued the opinions of street folk about their trade and its history. The opinions of casual rubbish carters provoked the generalisation that, 'it is rarely that labouring men can advance any feasible reason for the changes in their trade' (Mayhew, 1861-2, vol. 2, p. 336). And while Mayhew had been infinitely credulous of artisan claims that things were getting worse, he was thoroughly sceptical of similar claims made by street traders; 'that these men hold such opinions must be accounted for mainly by the increase of their numbers, of which I have before spoken and from their general ignorance' (Mayhew, 1861-2, vol. 1, pp. 84-5). *London Labour* was careful to bring out the ignorance of street people by the use of 'vox pop' against them. Questions about religion, current affairs and general knowledge nicely established the ignorance of the poor, like the mud lark who,

> thought he was a Christian, but he didn't know what a
> Christian was. . . . London was England, and England, he
> said, was in London, but he couldn't tell in what part (May-
> hew, 1861-2, vol. 2, p. 156).

In passages like these, a certain fastidious disdain replaces the identification of the *Morning Chronicle* letters.

In the *Morning Chronicle*, theory was an articulation and justification of the views of the artisans, but in *London Labour,* theory was a means of condemning the street folk as parasites. As economic theory was used to explain overwork and low wages in artisan trades, so anthropological theory was used to explain the existence of the street folk. The reference here was to the mid-Victorian ethnology of Pritchard and Smith which divided all races into two groups, wanderers and settlers, who were distinct in physical, moral, and intellectual characteristics. Here *London Labour* did not try to construct a radical alternative theory, but simple endorsed the conventional wisdom of ethnology and identified the street folk as the wandering tribe in the midst of a civilised nation (Mayhew, 1861-2, vol. 1, pp. 1-2). This identification is all the more striking because the borrowed ethnological theory directly condemned the wanderers as undesirable parasites. The wandering tribes were presented as 'preying upon'

(Mayhew, 1871-2, vol. 1, p. 1) settled tribes and 'possessing nothing but what they acquired by depredation from the industrious, provident, and civilized portion of the community' (Mayhew, 1861-2, vol. 1, p. 2). The wanderers were also credited with a long list of undesirable lower-class characteristics: 'want of providence', 'repugnance to regular and continuous labour', 'inability to perceive consequences ever so slightly removed from immediate apprehension', and so forth (Mayhew, 1861-2, vol. 1, pp. 2-3).

The street folk were not therefore represented from their own point of view. Perhaps the street folk were too disreputable for that option to be directly open. Did the text then develop another distinctive point of view upon which the representation might depend? Certainly there was no problem about inflexible reluctance to change earlier positions. This is illustrated by the fate of the *Morning Chronicle* diagnosis of the social problem.

The whole diagnosis of the social problem was transformed by the change of object of investigation from artisan trades to street folk. In a number of cases, Mayhew's opinions changed completely. Thus in the *Morning Chronicle,* Mayhew had reported artisan protectionist views and subsequently in the 'Answers' column he developed a rabid protectionism of his own; 'facts have proved that as fast as food is cheapened, so will the lowest grades of labour be' ('Answers', no. 34; see also, 'Answers', no. 44). But in the body of the text *London Labour,* Mayhew became completely agnostic about the effects of the repeal of the Corn Laws:

> Hence it becomes almost impossible, I repeat, to tell
> whether the increasing difficulty that the poor experience
> in living by their labour, is a consequence or merely a com-
> comitant of the repeal of the Corn Laws. . . . I candidly
> confess that I am as yet without the means of coming to
> any conclusion on this part of the subject (Mayhew, 1861-
> 2, vol. 2, p. 229).

Even the *Morning Chronicle* analysis of low wages was effectively buried. When *London Labour* dealt with low wages, the cause of over-work and the solution of equitable wages were both buried in long lists of other possible causes and solutions (Mayhew, 1861-2, vol. 2, pp. 254-6, 301). For example, on the remedies for low wages, the equit-able system figured as a sub-division of one of sixteen major proposals ranging from 'the establishment of a standard rate of remuneration for labour' to 'cultivation of a higher moral and Christian character among the people'. Furthermore, in *London Labour* there was no longer any master evil such as low wages which required a master remedy. Thus *London Labour* advanced a diverse range of reform proposals such as the segregation of street traders into 'poor men's markets' (Mayhew, 1861-2, vol. 2, p. 4), the abolition of low lodging houses (Mayhew, 1861-2, vol. 1, p. 408), the abolition of the payment of wages in public houses (Mayhew, 1861-2, vol. 3, pp. 285-6), and the introduction of the street orderly system to replace pauper street cleansing (Mayhew, 1861-2, vol. 2, p. 259). In *London Labour,* the social problem is broken into pieces and dispersed.

London Labour's diffuse and agnostic analysis of the social problem reflected a chronic ambivalence about the street people which was manifested in a characteristic three-step sequence. The first step was the assertion that the condition of the street folk was a scandal and a disgrace,

> when the religious, moral and intellectual degradation of a
> great majority of these fifty-thousand people is impressed
> upon us, it becomes positively appalling to contemplate the
> vast amount of vice, ignorance and want, existing in these
> days in the very heart of our land. The public have but to
> read the following plain unvarnished account of the habits,
> amusements, dealings, education, politics and religion of
> the London costermongers in the nineteenth century, and
> then to say whether they think it safe - even if it be thought
> fit - to allow men, women and children to continue in such
> a state (Mayhew, 1861-2, vol. 1, p. 6).

The threat to public order and political stability was emphasised by the explicit identification of the costers as a part of the 'dangerous classes' (Mayhew, 1861-2, vol. 1, p. 22) who were 'nearly all' Chartists: 'I am assured that in the case of a political riot every "coster" would seize his policeman' (Mayhew, 1861-2, vol. 1, p. 20).

In a second step, the text took an environmental view of the causes of the degradation of large numbers of street folk; all those 'bred to the streets must bear about them the moral impress of the gutter' (Mayhew, 1861-2, vol. 1, p. 320). It is important here not to get distracted into considering Mayhew's environmentalism as a progressive element in his discourse. In *London Labour,* environmentalism is a moment in the text's chronic ambivalence about the street people. It is the bridge that allows the text to have it all ways. After environmentalism has been introduced, the text can become sympathetic towards the street folk who had originally been defined as part of the 'dangerous classes'. The important thing is to recover the different moments of this movement, not to seize upon one of them.

The third step was sympathy which characteristically took the form of warnings about the Pharisaism of harsh judgments of the poor. The reader was endlessly reminded that,

we who have been appointed to another state, are, by the
grace of God, what we are, and from no special merit of
our own, to which, in the arrogance of our self-conceit, we
are too prone to attribute the social and moral differences
of our nature (Mayhew, 1861-2, vol. 1, p. 320).

The less fortunate could look forward to some consolation in the next
world because 'after the atonement of their long suffering, they will
make as good angels as the best of us' (Mayhew, 1861-2, vol. 3, p. 429).
The implication was that, here and now, the more fortunate were to
blame:

we are the culpable parties in these matters. That they poor
things should do as they do is but human nature - but that
we should allow them to remain thus destitute of every
blessing vouchsafed to ourselves . . . gives to the zeal of our
Christianity a strong savour of the chicanery of Cant
(Mayhew, 1861-2, vol. 1, p. 43).

The three elements - condemnation, environmentalism, and sympathy
- often follow in quick succession as in *London Labour*'s general
verdict on the 30,000 coster sellers of fish, fruit, and vegetables
(Mayhew, 1861-2, vol. 1, p. 101). And, in one case, the reverse transition from compassionate friend to alarmist propagandist required only
a semicolon:

To revile the street people is stark folly. Their ignorance is
no demerit to them, even as it is no merit to us to know the
little that we do. If we really wish the people better, let us,
I say again, do for them what others have done for us, and
without which (humiliating as it may be to our pride) we
should most assuredly have been as they are. It is the continued forgetfulness of this truth - a truth which our
wretched self-conceit is constantly driving from our minds
- that prevents our stirring to improve the condition of
these poor people; though, if we knew but the whole of the
facts concerning them, and their sufferings and feelings, our
very fears alone for the safety of the state would be
sufficient to make us do something in their behalf. I am
quite satisfied, from all I have seen, that there are thousands
in this great metropolis ready to rush forth, on the least
evidence of a rising of the people, to commit the most savage
and revolting excesses (Mayhew, 1861-2, vol. 2, p. 4).

London Labour's point of view about the street folk was not always the same, it could change wildly in mid-sentence. When the text did not have one point of view, it could not represent the street folk from this point of view. There is no identification of this kind holding the text together. At the same time, the illusion of a presiding consciousness and a unitary authorial figure vanish from the text. These differences fundamentally distinguish *London Labour* from the *Morning Chronicle* letters. The question now is whether *London Labour* manages some kind of project definition which will hold things together in a different kind of way.

London Labour did try to deliver a kind of empirical ethnology which is distinct from the theoretical ethnology Mayhew borrowed from Pritchard and Smith. In the empirical ethnology the street people were to be described as an exotic race rather than, as in the theoretical ethnology, identified as a wandering tribe. In the empirical ethnology everything should hang together; balanced generalisations should cohere and be supported by corroborating statistics and detail. The problem is that *London Labour* did provide all these ingredients of a descriptive ethnology and the text then went on to provide so much more that the discourse ended up radically disordered. This can be demonstrated by considering in turn the descriptive generalisations, the statistics, and the detail.

London Labour offered impeccable descriptive generalisations about the street people. The text provided a carefully balanced 'general view of the numbers, characters, habits, tastes, amusements, language, opinions, earnings and vicissitudes of the London costermongers' (Mayhew, 1861-2, vol. 1, pp. 61-2). It described the Chartist politics of costermongers, their preference for common-law marriage, their religious indifference, their rhyming slang, their counterfeit weights and measures, and much else. Such generalisations, however, take up only the first sixty pages of the first volume of *London Labour* and almost everything in these opening pages is challenged by assertions and emphases in the next couple of thousand pages. This can be illustrated by considering the text's subversion of its own generalisations about the social origins of street folk and about sex and marriage among street folk.

On *London Labour*'s own generalisations about social origin, the street folk were predominantly either an hereditary group or the poorest of the poor. For example, of coster sellers of fruit, fish and vegetables,

one half of the entire class are costermongers proper, that is to say, the calling with them is hereditary, and perhaps has been so for many generations; while the other half is composed of three-eighths Irish, and one-eighth mechanics, tradesmen and Jews (Mayhew, 1861-2, vol. 1, p. 7).

But these generalisations were challenged by the street sellers' biographies subsequently presented. The biographies were no longer, as in the *Morning Chronicle*, trade histories. They were now lives, dramatic renditions of personal history 'here given as it was spoken' (Mayhew, 1861-2, vol. 1, p. 46). In *London Labour*, the lives written up in the text were selected and reworked for melodramatic ends. Bold characters, pathos and 'human interest' were now chosen.

Inevitably therefore, in the lives of the street folk the relative frequency of different social origins was adjusted. Thus, in the biographies we meet a disproportionate number of costers who had sunk on to the streets from a respectable, comfortable position. When he was treating fish sellers and their lives, Mayhew managed to get four sunken respectables on to eight pages of the text; a former gentleman fish seller, a servant left without a character because his master had gone abroad, an old woman who had seen (unspecified) better days, and a periwinkle seller who had been a pattern maker (Mayhew, 1861-2, vol. 1, pp. 68-76). It was appropriate that when Mayhew held a public meeting of street sellers, where 'the costermongers were the great majority present', three of the five speakers who rated more than a few lines in the subsequent account were distressed gentlefolk; a country auctioneer's son, a classical scholar who was the son of an infantry captain, and an Anglican clergyman who was now selling stenographic cards in the street (Mayhew, 1861-2, vol. 1, p. 102). This treatment of origins in the biographies is not ethnology but melodrama, the literary indulgence of all those who run to see accidents.

It is worth observing that the policy of satisfying such morbid voyeurism affected more than the text's treatment of social origins. *London Labour* generally concentrated on pathetic cases. Many of the star performers in the lives were handicapped, like the crippled seller of nutmeg graters who dragged himself around on his stumps (Mayhew, 1861-2, vol. 1, pp. 329-33). Others achieved literary immortality through uttering a few artless pathetic lines, like the watercress girl who said, 'No, I never see any children crying - it's no use' (Mayhew, 1861-2, vol. 1, p. 151). And the pathos suffused more than the lives. This was epitomised by the scene-setting when Mayhew visited an asylum for the 'houseless poor'. Inevitably, there was a queue of homeless outside and it was not only winter but there was 'ice and snow in the streets' and the bleak stinging wind blowing through their rags' (Mayhew, 1861-2, vol. 3, p. 417).

London Labour's generalisations about sex and marriage among street people suffered much the same fate as its generalisations about social origins. From the text's generalisations, stable monogamy was the norm among street people. Costers were by far the largest group of street people and, although they did not formally marry, their sexual arrangements were stable and monogamous. The women ' "in anything like good times" . . . were rigidly faithful to their husbands or paramours' (Mayhew, 1861-2, vol. 1, p. 20). It was also noted that 'the unmarried separate as seldom as the married' (Mayhew, 1861-2, vol. 1, p. 21). When so few married, illegitimacy was high, but ' "chance children" as they are called, or children unrecognised by any father, are rare among the young women of the costermongers' (Mayhew, 1861-2, vol. 1, p. 21). These generalisations were challenged by the text's subsequent fixation upon indecency and sexual promiscuity.

From the amount of space given to these topics it might be supposed that casual promiscuity was the norm among street folk. The coster adolescents' cheap dances and low music halls - 'penny hops' and 'penny gaffs' - were reported with horror and in detail, *double entendres* and all. Mayhew implied that such institutions depraved and corrupted children who had 'their tastes trained to libidinism long before puberty at the penny concert, and their passions inflamed with the unrestrained intercourse of the two-penny hops' (Mayhew, 1861-2, vol. 1, p. 101). At this point the stolid monogamy of the costers was quite forgotten. The other way in which Mayhew undermined his own generalisations about monogamy, was by concentrating on sub-groups who were sexually promiscuous. Hence the text's concern with low lodging houses where juveniles of different sexes might share one bed. *London Labour* insisted that 'it is impossible to present to the reader, in full particularity, the records of the vice practised' (Mayhew, 1861-2, vol. 1, p. 256). But some of Mayhew's informants were gratifyingly explicit:

We lay packed on a full night, a dozen boys and girls squeedged into one bed. That was very often the case - some at the foot, and some at the top - boys and girls all mixed. I can't go into all the particulars, but whatever could take place in words or acts between boys and girls did take place, and in the midst of the others (Mayhew, 1861-2, vol. 1, p. 413).

This is not an ethnology of the sexual mores of street folk. It is dirty journalism, the British Sunday newspaper mix of rhetorical condemnation and salacious detail.

London Labour's descriptive generalisations should have been supported by statistics and corroborating detail, but both the statistics and the detail get out of control in this text. They end up, not corroborating the generalisations, but subverting the mode of empirical ethnological inquiry that the generalisations represent. This can be shown by considering the statistics and the detail in turn.

Statistics were an essential quantitative adjunct to qualitative descriptive generalisations. And *London Labour* did offer careful estimates of all the key magnitudes in the inquiry. The text calculated that there were 50,000 street people, three-quarters of whom were street sellers (Mayhew, 1861-2, vol. 1, pp. 3 and 6). It also included careful estimates of other groups who were also treated in *London Labour*. There were some 200 low lodging houses with some 10,000 individuals regularly sleeping in them (Mayhew, 1861-2, vol. 1, pp. 252-3). Or again, there were 20,000 dock labourers, 7,000 of whom were thrown out of work by an east wind (Mayhew, 1861-2, vol. 4, pp. 271-2). As for the exaggerated estimate of the number of prostitutes, in this case, one of Mayhew's collaborators chose the highest of a series of estimates.

Generally, in the first three volumes of *London Labour,* the problem was not that the key statistics were wrong, but that the text did not stop giving statistics. Thus it contained interminable lists of the capital and income of different classes of street folk. For example, the reader could learn of the capital of London's rat catchers:

20 belts at 3s. 6d. each; 25 cages at 1s. each; 25 pair of
ferrets at 2s. 6d. per pair; keep for 25 pair of ferrets, at 4d.
per pair weekly (Mayhew, 1861-2, vol. 1, p. 287).

The statistics got out of control and broke away from the canons of significance and representativeness which should in an empirical ethnological inquiry have determined their deployment. These statistics suggest a different project, an antiquarian project where every statistic has value and must be written into the record and preserved for posterity.

The detail too should have been a source of verisimilitude, an assurance that *London Labour*'s descriptive ethnological generalisations were not fictitious. This again miscarried because the text piled up more and more particulars of an inconsequential sort. Thus when Mayhew, as part of the inquiry into low lodging houses, convened a meeting of young thieves, he obtained particulars of first occupation, place of birth, number of years thieving, and so forth. But he also obtained a marvellously inconsequential list of the articles first stolen by these thieves:

six rabbits, silk shawl from home, a pair of shoes, a Dutch
cheese, a few shillings from home, a coat and trousers, a
bullock's heart, four tubs of copper, fifteen and sixpence
from master, two handkerchiefs, half a quartern loaf; a set
of tools worth £3, clothes from a warehouse worth £22, a
Cheshire cheese, a pair of carriage lamps, some handkerchiefs, five shillings, some turnips, watch chain and seals, a
sheep, three and sixpence and an invalid's chair (Mayhew,
1861-2, vol. 3, p. 317).

Here again the text abandons ethnology for antiquarianism.

In the end, the detail in *London Labour* became quite surrealist. Such was the case when the text retailed the folk tale about the beggar who kept old meat inside his shirt and then was eaten alive by the maggots (Mayhew, 1861-2, vol. 3, p. 27). This is a tale to cherish alongside more modern folk tales about Kit-e-Kat tins outside Chinese restaurants and about the bee in the bouffant hair-do. Then again there was the whole treatment of bug and rat destroyers. The high spot here was the 'rat catcher by appointment to the Queen', Jack Black, also known as 'the Battersea otter' because he was an accomplished hand fisherman in the Thames (Mayhew, 1861-2, vol. 3, pp. 11-20). Or, best of all, there was the *absolutely true* story of eminent Victorians who paid ransoms for the return of their dogs from professional dog kidnappers (Mayhew, 1861-2, vol. 2, pp. 48-9). There was a list of kidnap victims such as Sir F. Burdett, the Duchess of Sutherland, Mr R. Peel, and the Bishop of Ely. More than this, there was a discussion which brought out how the authorities were hampered in their pursuit of the malefactors in the early 1840s, because dog stealing was not then an indictable criminal offence. Here the reader was finally consoled with the vigour and resourcefulness of the authorities; the kidnapper of the Duke of Beaufort's dog could not be punished for stealing the dog but he was transported for stealing the collar. With detail like this, *London Labour* leaves ethnology behind and enters the world of the Goon Show and Monty Python.

In conclusion, at every point in the development of descriptive generalisations, statistics and detail, this text deviates from the empirical ethnological path. *London Labour* is not held together by the realisations of any such project. If the attempt to produce a descriptive ethnology failed because the text was endlessly distracted, what are we to make of the distraction? Are the deviations from the ethnological path deviations from the only serious project defined in *London Labour*? Or, more neutrally, was the text simply wasted because it chased after too many different projects? Does this pattern of deviation justify the general historiographic dismissal of *London Labour* as a trivial text?

The deviations do not justify any such verdict because the quality of Mayhew's *London Labour* does not depend on whether the text realises any one of its projects. The quality of the text is defined by the relation between a multiplicity of different, half-realised projects. In this section, the account of the text's deviation from descriptive ethnology has shown a series of different projects in cross-section. There is the melodramatic project of concentrating on certain dramatic and pathetic events in a life. There is the dirty journalism always present when *London Labour* considers the sexual. There is the antiquarian project when every detail and statistic must be conserved. The common denominator is that these projects are all realist projects of one sort or another in the minimal sense that each would naturalise an unproblematical reality. But *London Labour* does not support one realist project or convention and, therefore, produces a paradoxical effect. Because the text subscribes to so many different realisms, it denaturalises them all. Descriptive ethnology, melodrama, dirty journalism and antiquarianism individually might have been able to establish themselves as the proper way to present reality and how it really was. Collectively jostling each other, they render each other's pretensions quite ridiculous. Through subscribing to so many realisms, the text makes the identity of realism, of all realisms, as pastiche or *trompe l'œil* only too obvious.

In our appreciation of this effect, let us not forget that like all the best anti-realist texts from Tristram Shandy onwards, *London Labour* is hilariously funny. The discussion of dog kidnapping or of vermin destroyers 'by appointment' makes one laugh out loud. Perhaps Mayhew on this account comes closest to Fourier who, on Barthes's reading, is always doing something discursively inappropriate at the expensive of the bourgeois proprieties and pomposities (Barthes, 1971). Is it surprising that academic readers should seek to categorise *London Labour* as a less subversive text? This is the strategy in the three separate accounts of *London Labour*; in the conventional dismissal of the text as journalism, in the Yeo and Humphreys definition of the text as anthropology, and in the Himmelfarb definition of the text as ideology. All three readings in different ways deny the text's subversiveness.

Historians have usually been thoroughly condescending about *London Labour*. Harrison's verdict is typical. He claims that 'Mayhew fails at the outset to define the problem that he is seeking to solve; nor does he outline any consistent scheme of investigation'. He then concludes that *London Labour* is 'a very ill-constructed work whose defects amply justify Ruth Glass's complaint that "there is no theme; by and large there is description without selection or analysis" ' (Harrison, 1967, p. 638). Nor do the revisionists necessarily challenge this verdict. Thompson is concerned only to establish that the *Morning Chronicle* articles are serious social analysis. After this moment of glory, Thompson supposes there was a retreat from seriousness:

as he comes to the end of 1851 . . . whatever the reasons,
the Mayhew of the *Morning Chronicle* was already beginning to recede and the somewhat quainter but also more
dramatic and more readable Mayhew of the London street
folk was taking his place (Thompson and Yeo, 1971, p. 45).

Such condescension is the result of carelessness and prejudice. It is simply a careless misreading to suppose that the text is completely chaotic. The text is disordered but this disorder is a positive feature that produces certain definite anti-realist effects. Moreover, the hostility to the text's choice of the street folk as object, and the hostility to the treatment of that object, is pure prejudice. It is hardly possible to characterise discursive objects as intrinsically serious or trivial; a discourse about a fraction of the working class is not necessarily inferior to a discourse about the whole working class. The historiographic refusal of *London Labour*'s treatment of the street folk is indeed nicely ironic when that treatment puts in question the banal representational presuppositions which are commonplace in historiography. The deficiencies here are not in *London Labour,* but in the conventional historiographic notion of what constitutes serious social analysis.

Not all the revisionists who have rediscovered the *Morning Chronicle* letters are completely prepared to endorse the traditional verdict upon *London Labour.* Thus Yeo and Humphreys have sought to claim Mayhew as an anthropologist. Yeo claims that in the analysis of the costers, Mayhew described 'a group whose lives were based on a code of shared meanings as different from that of other London workmen as from respectable middle class Englishmen' (Thompson and Yeo, 1971, p. 86). *London Labour* is thus an analysis of a sub-culture without an explicitly formulated concept of a sub-culture. More generally, but on similar lines, Humphreys invokes the comparison with Oscar Lewis: Mayhew's work is an elucidation of what Oscar Lewis calls 'the culture of poverty' (Humphreys, 1971, p. xviii).

Such an appreciation of *London Labour* is, however, little better than the first dismissal. To begin with, it is equally careless. The street folk are defined in Mayhew's classification as an occupational grouping rather than a cultural grouping; and the unitary cultural identity of the street folk is always precarious when the theoretical and descriptive ethnology is challenged by so much else in the discourse. This is exactly the key point of difference between Lewis and *London Labour.* Lewis's 'culture of poverty' is a typological definition of poverty which defines the condition in terms of character and situation: poverty here is a list of the characteristics of the poor. Apart from being circular, the typological definition of Lewis opens on to assumptions about essential individual and social identity. These assumptions are now anachronistic in any modern discourse, and *London Labour* is sufficiently modern to undermine them by subscribing to so many different realisms. The practical effect of the different assumptions is that in *La Vida* or *The Children of Sanchez* Lewis writes the most banal kind of realist novel, while in *London Labour* Mayhew produces a kind of realist *'texte limite'*, carrying transgression against realism as far as it can go within realism's own field.

The ultimate misreading is provided by Himmelfarb (1973). She claims that Mayhew's texts identified the street folk with the labouring poor and thus promoted an ideological perception of the poor. *London Labour* 'had the conceptual effect of pauperizing the poor by first creating the most distinctive, most dramatic image of the lowest class, and then imposing that image upon the lower classes as a whole' (Himmelfarb, 1973, p. 726). She argues that 'the same image of the poor' (Himmelfarb, 1973, p. 726) recurs in the work of Mayhew's contemporaries; the Blue Books, for example, tended 'to emphasise the worst conditions of the lowliest poor' (Himmelfarb, 1973, p. 718). Such misperceptions were even necessary to Mayhew and his contemporaries. Such kind of recognition in a dual-subject structure may be a crucial prerequisite for thought and action:

> One is reminded of the master-slave relationship described
> by Hegel, in which each partner can find self-consciousness
> only through the consciousness, the recognition of, the
> other (Himmelfarb, 1973, p. 730).

Mayhew figures here as a kind of primitive ethno-methodologist.

London Labour does not, however, promote an identification of the street people with the poor. Again and again the text insisted that its object group was the street folk. Other mid-Victorian investigations, like the Statistical Society surveys, were equally specific in terms of object group or problem or type of investigation. It is, at the least, uninformative to tie all this together as a 'concern with the lowliest poor'. And categorically, there has never been any historiographic misconception about the object group of *London Labour*; the concern with street folk has traditionally been one of the grounds for historiographic complaint about the text. There is great ambiguity in *London Labour*'s treatment of the street people, but this arises from an uncertain point of view on the street people and the text's endorsement of a multiplicity of separate realist projects. The Himmelfarb reading completely inverts the effect produced by this ambiguity. *London Labour* does not promote an ideological recognition; it interdicts an easy ideological recognition of the street people.

Prostitutes and criminal prisons

The material on prostitution is conventionally admitted by historiography as the final fourth volume of the definitive 1861–2 version of *London Labour*. The 'fifth volume' on *Criminal Prisons* is conventionally separated from *London Labour* as part of a different project. This chapter argues against such a division of Mayhew's texts. It has just been shown that the first three volumes of *London Labour* should be bracketed together as anti-realist. It will now be shown that the fourth and 'fifth' volumes should be bracketed, because the treatment of prostitutes and of criminal prisons reinstated a presiding consciousness and one simple project definition. This can be demonstrated by considering point of view and project definition in the two later texts.

London Labour did have a consistent point of view about prostitutes: it was against them. Prostitution was not just another job, but a kind of moral degradation involving,

> the surrendering of a woman's virtue in a manner that excites *our moral disgust*. The offensiveness of the act of unchastity to the moral taste or sense constitutes the very essence of prostitution; and it is this moral offensiveness which often makes the licensed intercourse of the sexes, as in the marriage of a young girl to an old man, for the sake of his money, as much an act of prostitution as even the grossest libertinism (Mayhew, 1861-2, vol. 4, p. 36).

If prostitutes were objects of condemnation, the contrast with the earlier treatment of street folk is obvious: only the 'professional vagrants' of the casual wards aroused such hostility in the earlier volumes of *London Labour* (Mayhew, 1861-2, vol. 3, p. 397). Street folk had strained the sympathy earlier shown to artisans, but prostitutes were beyond the pale.

Mayhew's texts did not directly become more advanced as his sympathy for the object group waned. The fourth volume on prostitution represented a retreat rather than an advance on the first three volumes of *London Labour*. The key difference is that the fourth volume treatment of prostitutes reinstated one simple project. The prostitutes were the excuse for a piece of dirty journalism which mixed condemnation and prurient detail. Illustrations of scantily dressed exotic or fallen women were interleaved with the text; and the text itself proceeded in the style of the preliminary survey of sexual customs through the ages. For Mayhew's collaborator, this survey was an excuse for a lot of anecdotes about such institutions as the Physical Club of Moscow:

> the object of which exhibited, perhaps, more depravity of manners than could be found in any other part of the world, except among the Areois of the Pacific. . . . At stated intervals the members of the club assembled at a large house, where, in a magnificent saloon, brilliantly lighted up, they indulged in every kind of licentious amusements, inflaming themselves with strong potations, and preparing for the

hideous orgies that were to follow. Suddenly all the candles
were put out, each man chose a companion, and a scene of
indescribable debauch ensued (*London Labour*, vol. 4, p.
160).

As one among several other contradictory projects in the first three
volumes of *London Labour,* the dirty journalism helps to secure an
anti-realist effect. But where, as in the treatment of prostitution, the
dirty journalism excludes every other project definition, the result is
tiresome Victorian soft porn.

Criminal Prisons is about a new and different kind of object. For
the first time Mayhew leaves behind occupational groups and examines
institutions. The book was entitled *Criminal Prisons* - not 'Criminal
Prisoners'. The working classification was no longer of the population
covered but of different institutional regimes - separate, silent associated,
and so forth. Nevertheless, the treatment of criminal prisons is like the
treatment of prostitutes since it also relies on one point of view and a
single project definition.

Criminals were more sympathetically treated than prostitutes. The
old tricks to induce sympathy are all used. There was scene-setting
when Mayhew visited the convict nursery at Brixton and the convict
burial ground at Woolwich. At the latter, it was suitably enough over-
cast and raining so that the text could claim the burial ground as 'one
of the dreariest spots we had ever seen'. 'There but for the grace of
God' was the inevitable reaction when Mayhew contemplated the
prisoners in Pentonville Chapel:

what vast difference in the eyes of the All-wise and Just can
there be between us and these same 'miserable offenders'
whom we, in the earthly arrogance of our hearts, have
learnt to loathe. . . . If we are a little better than they, is it
not simply because we have been a great deal more favoured
than they? (Mayhew and Binny, 1862, pp. 165-6).

Some of the casual observations on different penal regimes were also
apparently tender-hearted as when the text suggested society must
'abandon all systems of silence and isolation (for convicts) as utterly
incompatible with the very foundation of social economy' (Mayhew
and Binny, 1862, p. 108).

Nevertheless there are limits to this sympathy and *Criminal Prisons*
displays an underlying steely firmness. The text does not take the
prisoner's part; Mayhew is no more a radical criminologist than a
pioneer analyst of poverty. For example, there was no objection in
principle to the separate system where, as at Pentonville, a prisoner
slept, lived and worked in solitary confinement in one cell, except for

exercise which was taken with a hood over the head, and chapel where each prisoner was confined in a separate box. This system was praised as 'an eminent improvement upon the old classified system of our prisons, and more particularly upon that more ancient system of indiscriminate intercourse among criminals' (Mayhew and Binny, 1862, p. 328). The text's reservations about the separate system concerned the increased insanity produced by this system; at Pentonville the lunacy rate was twice the national average. *Criminal Prisons* concluded that, 'were it not for this terrible drawback, it must be admitted that the separate system is the best of all existing modes of penal discipline' (Mayhew and Binny, 1862, p. 168). The prisoners were objects for reformation and every consideration of sympathy was subordinated to that consideration.

It is hardly surprising that *Criminal Prisons* features a new kind of authorial figure who maximises the distance between himself and the object social group considered – the convicts. Thus Mayhew went out of his way to side with authority. For example, he positively eulogised the judiciary:

> if there be one class in whose iron integrity every English-
> man has the most steadfast faith . . . it is the class to whom
> the high privilege of dispensing justice among us has been
> intrusted (Mayhew and Binny, 1862, p. 77).

The text also carefully established Mayhew's status as a kind of semi-official visitor. The authorised tour of inspection was nicely suggested by a sketch of Mayhew's trip to each prison, his conducted tour of the premises and observation of the daily round, and his final thanks to the prison officers for their courtesy. Negatively, it was significant that *Criminal Prisons* completely dropped the procedure of talking to the object group: Mayhew observed carefully, but he did not talk with the prisoners. This eliminated even the possibility of representing the convicts from their own point of view. *Criminal Prisons* offered a view of the prisoners from above, from the point of view of disciplinary and corrective authority.

The project definition was completely coherent with this point of view. The project of *Criminal Prisons* was to provide practical suggestions which would make prisons into more effective reformatories. Mayhew's analysis here was completely within the circle of orthodox penological assumptions. The function of prisons was to deter and reform, and the problem was that existing prisons did neither; 'our treatment of criminals neither deters nor reforms' (Mayhew and Binny, 1862, p. 107). The solution to this problem was more prisons and different prisons.

Thus *Criminal Prisons* made a detailed critique of existing institutional regimes, criticising everything that hindered the reform of prisoners. For example, sending prisoners to the hulks was criticised because free association and heavy labour as a punishment would not reform. On the same grounds, the text opposed useless labour in any prison regime, and especially the treadmill, 'an instrument which is especially adapted to render labour inordinately repulsive by making it inordinately useless' (Mayhew and Binny, 1862, p. 275). Positively, the text made two practical suggestions for changes of regime. First, the prisoner's labour should be motivated by a system of rewards; all food above a punishment diet of bread and water was 'to be proportionate to the amount of labour done' (Mayhew and Binny, 1862, p. 302). This would prepare the prisoner for the essentially just world outside prison where reward was proportionate to effort (Mayhew and Binny, 1862, pp. 351-2). Second, the prisoners were to be prevented from discussing 'common or depraved subjects' by a general regime of silence while their minds would be turned towards higher things by a public reading from an edifying text as they toiled silently in the prison work-room.

If the treatment of street traders in the first three volumes of *London Labour* had taken Mayhew to the edge of bourgeois consciousness, his subsequent treatment of prostitutes in the fourth volume of *London Labour* and the book on *Criminal Prisons* brought him back from the edge. And he was not brought back as the *Morning Chronicle*'s impersonator of artisans, but as the grubby journalist of sex and the would-be penological authority.

Mayhew was enthusiastic about unity as an intellectual or visual value:

> as the intellect experiences a special delight in being able to
> comprehend all the minute particulars of a subject under
> one associate whole, and to perceive the previous confusion
> of the diverse details assume the form and order of a
> perspicuous unity; so does the eye love to see the country or
> the town, which it usually knows only as a series of dis-
> jointed parts – as abstract fields, hills, rivers, parks, streets,
> gardens or churches – become all combined, like the
> coloured fragments of the kaleidoscope, into one harmon-
> ious and varied scene (Mayhew and Binny, 1862, p. 7).

Both the *Morning Chronicle* articles and the *Great World* part-work began with a view of London from the top of St Paul's. And, in all the texts considered in this chapter, London was the ultimate intellectual object whose diverse details and disjointed parts were to be reconciled into a unity.

Mayhew's classificatory ambition was to treat *all* of London. But he ended up treating *parts* of London – the artisan trades in the *Morning*

Chronicle, the street folk in *London Labour,* the criminal prisons in the *Great World.* He never arrived at an integration of those parts; there were too many changes of point of view and project definition within and between the different parts. Mayhew wanted to establish the unity of London but ended up with London broken into pieces. The way in which he managed this breaking up defines Mayhew's position in social investigation as the realist who stumbled into the subversion of realism. His masterpiece on this count is *London Labour,* where the anti-realism is got inside one text. Elsewhere it subsists spectrally in the discrepancies within the series of texts.

By these means Mayhew subverts so many worlds taken for granted. His texts are therefore profitable reading(s) for a historiography on the edge of rejecting the academic verities. More generally, Mayhew's achievement in social investigation is a negative one whose importance must ultimately depend on the possibility of more positive achievements. A cautious verdict would be that the breaking of identification in Mayhew must rate highly if the comparison is made with the tedious and self-deluding making of identification in Booth and Rowntree.

May, 1978

Engels

6

From one treatment of the workers and non-workers in London, we now turn to another contemporary treatment of the workers in Manchester and other parts. The material in Mayhew's *London Labour* was first published in 1849-50 and Engels's text *The Condition of the Working Class in England* (Engels, 1975) was first published in German in 1845. Although these two texts will be compared, this chapter is not simply an exercise in comparison. It tries to go further and develop the argument of the previous chapter, in particular by making explicit an alternative concept of reading and of text.

Nevertheless this chapter is not all formal propositions and abstract theory of discourse. Most of it is devoted to concrete arguments about the *Condition,* which should practically demonstrate the nature and effects of the reconceptualisation proposed here. From the other side, theoretically it is a question of constituting the minimum necessary to produce an alternative reading of the *Condition.*

A critical consideration of the existing readings of the *Condition* provides the point of departure. The first section identifies and criticises the shared presuppositions of readings of the *Condition* made by the historians Hobsbawm (1968, 1969), Henderson and Chaloner (1958), and the literary critic Marcus (1974). It will also consider the readings of Marx and Engels's texts of the 1840s made by the French Marxist Althusser (1969).

(Mis) readings of Engels

This first section begins by considering the readings of the *Condition* proposed by Engels's English-speaking friends and enemies. The

argument is that, although there are violent disagreements in this literature, these disagreements rest upon an underlying consensus about the
nature of the discourse.

Manifestly, the right- and left-wing historians disagree about this
text. Their conclusions now and always have been quite different. On
the right, Henderson and Chaloner conclude that Engels in 1844 'was
no historian' or 'can hardly be taken seriously as a historian', because
'the way in which Engels handled his material falls below generally
accepted standards of scholarship' (Henderson and Chaloner, 1958, p.
xx). On the left, Hobsbawm comes to exactly the opposite conclusion
in his alternative introduction to the text: 'by all sensible standards the
Condition is an excellently documented work handled with a sound
grasp of evidence' (Hobsbawm, 1969, p. 16).

The left and right historians have fought the war of Engels's footnotes (Henderson and Chaloner, 1958; Henderson, 1976; Hobsbawm,
1968; Hobsbawm, 1969). Henderson and Chaloner (1958) originally
charged Engels with a whole series of improprieties in the use of
evidence. Engels regularly produced 'garbled' quotations, tended not
to weigh his evidence for authoritativeness, used anachronistic evidence,
and suppressed awkward facts (Henderson and Chaloner, 1958, pp.
viii, xx, xxv). Hobsbawm's defence was that the total number of
improprieties was small and that most of them were trivial and did not
undermine Engels's argument (Hobsbawm, 1968, pp. 100, 109-10). In
a second offensive, Henderson (1976) in his biography of Engels
changes the emphasis in his attack. He now emphasises the issue of bias
rather than factual accuracy; 'it is in the selection and interpretation of
the facts that Engels was at fault' (Henderson, 1976, p. 70). Even if
Engels's description is reliable in most important respects, it is not
impartial or comprehensive or at any rate sufficiently Olympian.
Engels suffers from an incapacitating bias against the middle classes
generally and capitalist employers in particular (Henderson, 1976, pp.
48-9, 71-2). On this issue, Hobsbawm observes that Engels does introduce some qualifications (Hobsbawm, 1969, p. 16).

At this point the historian would ask which conclusion is correct. It
is altogether more important to establish the underlying agreement of
the left and right. Henderson, Chaloner and Hobsbawm are only providing different answers to an agreed question. As Henderson and
Chaloner put it, the question is whether the *Condition* is 'an unbiased
and authoritative account of social conditions in England in the 1840s'
(Henderson and Chaloner, 1958, p. xxii). Hobsbawm's formulation in
his rival editor's introduction is similar: 'how far is Engels's description
of the British working class in 1844 reliable and comprehensive?'
(Hobsbawm, 1969, p. 15).

Underlying this agreement about the proper question is a shared
assumption about the identity of the discourse. Both left and right

historians recognise a familiar genre of discourse. The presupposition of a debate about Engels's scholarship is that Engels is writing empirical history about the 'facts'. It is this presupposition that makes it possible to judge Engels as though he were a professional colleague and to discuss whether the *Condition* attains the standard required of academic historiography. The nature of this genre of discourse is unproblematic. It stems from a confrontation between the subject (Engels) and the real object (Manchester in 1844), a confrontation that is either directly a matter of personal experience or mediated through the 'sources'. The text as an account of social conditions in England in 1844 is a result of this confrontation. Whatever their disagreements, the historians are agreed about the genre of discourse in the *Condition* and about the nature of such discourse.

Ostensibly, there is a huge gulf between the reading of the *Condition* made by the historians and the reading made by Marcus, the literary critic. The facts get short shrift in the Marcus book. For example, it is irrelevant whether optimists or pessimists are factually correct about the consequences of the Industrial Revolution: 'what is at issue is the existential character of various historians and social theorists' (Marcus, 1974, p. 159). By this standard, Engels is a significant figure because he responds imaginatively to urban industrial England. The *Condition* provides a reading of the city, which has hitherto been illegible and unintelligible (Marcus, 1974, p. 98). This reading is an imaginative *'tour de force'*: 'I know of no representation of an individual city before this that achieves such an intimate creative hold upon its living subject' (Marcus, 1974, pp. 198-9).

But what really are the differences that separate Marcus from the historians? Marcus recognises a different genre of discourse. For Marcus, the *Condition* exemplifies *verstehen,* an interpretative understanding of the real exemplified by literature, but also including history, most of philosophy, and the social sciences (Marcus, 1974, p. 139). The *Condition* is literature or like literature. Hence Engels's response to the city can be compared with the responses of Wordsworth, Dickens, and other literary figures. However, the nature of this interpretative discourse is familiar. Marcus supposes the subject (Engels) faces an object (reality) and produces a 'representation of an industrial city' (Marcus, 1974, p. 199).

Thus, underlying the apparent differences in the English-speaking literature on the *Condition,* there is general agreement on the nature of the discourse. This agreement has certain practical implications. To begin with, it ensures there is a strong affinity between Marcus's praise and Henderson and Chaloner's disparagement of the *Condition.* Imagination for Marcus means that the subject (Engels) has experiences and produces a reading 'not only accessory to these experiences but constitutive of them as well' (Marcus, 1974, p. 101). It is interesting to counterpose the Henderson and Chaloner (1958, p. xxiv) accusations:

> He did not pretend to be an impartial observer. He selected
> facts which strengthened his indictment of the middle
> classes and he suppressed or tried to explain away any
> evidence which did not support his thesis of the innate
> wickedness of the bourgeoisie.

The correspondence between the terms of praise and blame is un-surprising given the common representational definition of the nature of the *Condition*'s discourse. On such a definition, imagination and bias are closely related; imagination is bias made into a discursive virtue. This conclusion points to the futility of invoking imagination or bias as critical considerations.

More importantly the agreement on the nature of discourse defines a certain field of the visible and the invisible. Certain issues become pertinent and are debated in the literature on the *Condition*, while other issues are ignored. To illustrate this, two examples can be considered: first, the question of Engels's personal history and second, the question of theoretical system in the text. On these two issues, it is possible to show that the area of the visible and the invisible is substantially the same in all the readings of the *Condition* so far considered.

If discourse is the result of a human subject's confrontation with a real object, then it is highly pertinent to consider the question of the personal history, motivations, and intentions of the subject Engels. Thus Henderson and Chaloner explain that Engels's bias has psychological conditions. They present Engels as Jimmy Porter: 'he was a young man in a bad temper' (Henderson and Chaloner, 1958, p. xxx). From a defensive position, Hobsbawm makes the conservative academic response and argues that such considerations are irrelevant or redundant. Fury about the condition of the working class was a reasonable response: 'Why then bring in Engels's family rows?' (Hobsbawm, 1968, p. 113). But they will be brought in, given the current literature's definition of the place of the subject in the production of the text. And Marcus nicely illustrates this. Although Marcus disapproves of Henderson and Chaloner's vulgarities, he himself wishes to reserve a place for personal motivation and a whole chapter of his book is devoted to psycho-history (Marcus, 1974, pp. 67-130).

If discourse is the result of a subject's confrontations with a real object, then any kind of theoretical system is unimportant, whether the subject Engels is scholarly, biased, or imaginative. Thus, in their original exchange, Henderson, Chaloner and Hobsbawm were silent about any theoretical system. Facts alone were considered by these historians who debated exclusively whether these facts were correct, properly selected, and interpreted. There are, however, more subtle ways of devaluing

theory than by simply ignoring it. Hobsbawm's later contribution to
the historian's debate and the Marcus book illustrate two such subtler
tactics. In his introduction to the *Condition*, Hobsbawm acknowledges
theory but devalues it by treating it as a matter of anticipations. The
Condition is a precursor of a mature 'Marxist method', and it antici-
pates later use of the concept 'industrial revolution' in economic
history and subsequent social scientific analysis of 'capitalist indus-
trialization and urbanization' (Hobsbawm, 1969, p. 12). Marcus's
tactic for devaluing theory is rather different: he simply treats theory as
secondary to experience. He admits the *Condition* did apply 'Hegel's
system' (Marcus, 1974, p. 178), but this is conceded only so that 'the
courage and intelligence of a young foreign intellectual' can be promoted to a primary role in the genesis of the imaginative *'tour de force'*
(Marcus, 1974, pp. 198-9).

There is nothing inevitable about this neglect or devaluation of
theory. So far, only a narrow literature has been considered – the
English-speaking readings of this one text, the *Condition*. But there
are other readings of the work produced by the young Marx and
Engels in the 1840s, the period that is conventionally held to be dominated by Marx's 1844 *Economic and Philosophical Manuscripts* (Marx,
1970). Many of these readings of the young Marx and Engels conceptualise discourse differently, in that they emphasise the dominance
of theoretical system. *For Marx*, by Althusser, will be considered as an
example of this kind of reading. This collection of essays has since
been disowned by Althusser and in French terms, it is already a curiosity
of the formalist, structuralist 1960s. But, in Anglo-American terms,
these essays are still current. Since Kuhn introduced the notion of
'paradigm', it has become increasingly fashionable in English history
of ideas to analyse structures and systems of ideas rather than elements.
For Marx provides a pertinent and rigorous statement of the text as
theoretical structure position. This can now be analysed and criticised.

For Marx started from an explicit reflection about the nature of
reading, of text, and of theoretical knowledge as a form of production.
For Marx criticises orthodox history of ideas, because its mode of
reading analytically abstracts elements of the text (Althusser, 1969,
pp. 56-7). Such readings are arbitrary: everything depends upon, and
is limited by, the initial choice of the grid which reads the elements
(Althusser, 1969, p. 60). *For Marx* proposes an alternative mode of
reading which is concerned with a totality rather than with elements
of the text. This totality is an absent structure unifying and underlying
all the elements present in the text. In Althusserian terminology this is
the 'problematic' or 'the typical systematic structure unifying all the
elements of thought' (Althusser, 1969, p. 67). The existence of the
underlying structure of problematic is established by reference to
indicators that are present in the text; it is a matter of scrutinising the

conceptual terminology (Althusser, 1969, p. 45) and, more decisively, working out the relation between the concepts (Althusser, 1969, p. 159).

On this basis, *For Marx* argues that Marx's texts of the 1840-4 period are in a humanist problematic. This is a structure defined by the presence within it of a theoretical subject (man) (Althusser, 1969, pp. 34-6, 233-6). In this period, only the essence of the anthropological subject changes. From 1840-2, Marx is in a Kantian-Fichtean humanist problematic where the essence of man is freedom and reason (Althusser, 1969, pp. 34, 233-4). From 1842-5, Marx is in a Feuerbachian humanist problematic where the essence of man is 'communalist', concrete intersubjectivity and species being (Althusser, 1969, p. 225). Nor does Marx's philosophy of this period break with this kind of structure. In the 1842-5 period, Marx appropriates Feuerbach's epistemological empiricism as well as his substantive humanism. Philosophically, Feuerbach simply inverts or reverses Hegel and makes the real into the prime-mover or subject in the Feuerbachian philosophical system (Althusser, 1969, pp. 76 and 186). It is the same subject-dominated structure which recurs in Marx's epistemological and substantive positions.

In *For Marx*, Marx's break with this structure is dated from 1845. The break is made when Marx founds a new double discourse, historical materialism, or the scientific theory of history and dialectical materialism or the new Marxist philosophy implicit in the scientific discourse upon history. *For Marx* concedes that the break with humanism in the mid-1840s was not immediate and total. In 1845, the *German Ideology* and the *Theses on Feuerbach* are 'works of the break' which ambiguously introduce the new problematic in the negative critical form of a polemic against his erstwhile positions (Althusser, 1969, pp. 34 and 36), and the works of the next twelve years are classified as 'transitional' (Althusser, 1969, p. 34).

A final caution should be added. Althusser in the 1960s writes at length about the texts of Marx and Engels in the 1840s but he does not specifically discuss the *Condition*. Thus, the Althusserian humanist reading is a potential reading of the *Condition*. It is not a reading executed or authorised by Althusser himself, but Althusser does detect humanism everywhere in Marx's text of the 1840s. Marx applies and extends Feuerbachian humanism to religion (*The Essence of Christianity*), to politics (*On the Jewish Question*, the *1843 Manuscript*), and to history and political economy (*the 1844 Manuscripts*) (Althusser, 1969, pp. 46, 68-9, 136). There is, in principle, no difficulty about detecting a humanist problematic in a text like the *Condition* which is not directly a theoretical exposition. And, in practice, it is easy to find conceptual indicators of an underlying humanist problematic in the *Condition*; as a reading later in this chapter will show, the text contains many references to a subject (man). It is therefore worth analysing the nature of the Althusserian reading of the texts of the 1840s and the way in which this reading differs from the English-speaking readings of the *Condition*.

Marx and Engels's pre-1845 discourse is part of a genre of discourse or, more exactly, discourses. *For Marx* detects humanist problematics elsewhere outside the young Marx's work, in all previous bourgeois theories of knowledge, of society and political economy (Althusser, 1969, p. 228). In these different theoretical domains only the content of the human essence and the identity of the subject changes, since, in a general sense, all bourgeois knowledge depends on 'a problematic of *human nature* (or the essence of man)' (Althusser, 1969, p. 227). The problematic remains the same because the structural relation persists through all the changes in the identity of the essence.

If humanism is the nearly universal, pre-scientific genre of discourse, it is radically different from the genres of discourse taken for granted by the *Condition*'s English-speaking readers. *For Marx* brackets together many discourses in the same genre and it defines the nature of the genre differently, because the representational nature of discourse is denied. After an early flirtation with the notion of ideology as deformation of a real external referent (Althusser, 1969, p. 67), these essays present humanist discourse as non-representational. Thus there can no longer be any question of a real subject (Engels) representing a real object. In *For Marx*, the subject becomes a theoretical term inside discourse which defines its discourse's internal theoretical structure.

In the Althusserian reading, just as surely as in the case of the other readings, the definition of the genre and nature of the discourse delineates a certain field of the visible and invisible. In several respects the visible and invisible are simply reversed. This can be demonstrated by reference to the two issues already considered; the question of the author's personal history and the question of theoretical system in the text. In *For Marx*, theoretical system is primary and determinant of what can appear in the text and thus, theoretical system is virtually the only thing worth consideration. Indeed the system is intricated in a process of theoretical production which ends up more or less autonomous and running by itself (Althusser, 1969, pp. 183-6). And as theoretical system in a process of theoretical production is promoted, so the author is demoted by *For Marx*. The author is no longer the constitutive subject; in the Althusserian scheme of things, the author ends up merely an operator in, or a support of, a process of theoretical production. The essays are totally silent about Marx and Engels's family rows or sexual partners. In *For Marx*, all this is irrelevant.

Immediately, the Althusserian reading represents the world turned upside down. It appears to reject almost everything taken for granted in the English-speaking readings. Nevertheless, certain fundamental presuppositions unite the English readings of the *Condition* as representation and the Althusserian reading of the texts of the 1840s as theoretical system. At the level of these presuppositions, both parties share a common concept of the nature of reading and of discourse. All the readings so far considered subscribe to what can be called the double transparency assumption; they assume first, a transparency of the one reading to the text and second, a transparency of the text to its other.

First, all the readings considered assume the transparency of their one reading to the text. This is not a matter of explicit claim, but of significant silence in orthodox historiography and literary criticism. There are never any loose ends or at least never any loose ends that seriously embarrass the reading. By implication, the one reading exhausts significance in the text. There is never the possibility that the text escapes, or is more than, or is other than, the categorisation as representative history or imaginative literature, as the case may be. Hence we have straight-faced debates - as between Henderson and Hobsbawm - which treat the text as an unproblematic referent and suppose that enough footnotes to this referent will settle the matter. In orthodox historiography, this is the stock presuppostion that launched 10,000 articles. Althusser does not really dissent from all this. He only proposes more and different rules for obtaining the one true structure by referring to indicators on the textual surface. Indeed he takes up a more extreme position and promotes his own reading to a quasi-scientific status at the expense of all others. In Althusser, there is one 'symptomatic' reading which discloses the problematic and exhausts significance so completely that all other readings are erroneous misconstruction of the indicators present in the text.

Second, all the readings considered insist upon the transparency of the text to its other. For, although the text is directly the object of the reading, in all the readings so far considered, the text is ultimately not the referent. The ultimate referent is the text's other which is reality in the case of the text's English readings, and theoretical system in the case of the Althusserian reading. The historians all insist that the only proper relation of the text to its other is that where the text corresponds to reality. Marcus insists that the only proper relation is where a text responds to reality so as to render it intelligible. Anything that does not meet these transparency criteria is a bad text - inaccurate or biased for the historians and dull for Marcus. But at least these readers do concede the possibility that the text does not correspond or respond to reality in the appropriate way. This is more than Althusser does. In *For Marx*'s scheme of things, there is no possibility of a discrepancy between the text (surface) and its other (underlying theoretical system). The only possible arrangement is where a text displays the surface indicators corresponding to one specific absent problematic. This proposal is made all the more fierce by the repeated insistence that there is basically only one ideological structure, that is, humanism, or at least a subject-dominated structure. Between the text and its other, in Althusser, there is a necessary relation of expression and that which is expressed is always the same.

All the readings so far considered are thus united by the double transparency assumption. They presume a relation of representation or expression between three terms, the reading, the text, and the other. In the rest of this chapter, the possibility of such a relation of expression is denied and criticised in the name of an alternative concept of discourse which can be formally stated in the form of nine dogmatic theses, the first five of which concern reading and the last four of which concern the text.

1 All readings involve artificial construction of a text.
2 Reading is a process of naming and constructing chains of reference.
3 It is usually possible to construct more than one chain of reference in a text.
4 Relationships of representation and expression do not normally arise within or between readings: one chain of reference is not reducible to another.
5 There are vertical relations between the different chains of reference: relations of dislocation can be as important as relations of solidarity between the readings.
6 The text is the readings which have and can be made; chains of reference lead away from these readings to something else which is always another text.
7 The text is not always the same; the text is only the same as long as it is constructed in the same way; change the readings and the old text vanishes.
8 The text exists in a surround of reference or intertext; to change the intertext is to change the identity of the text itself.
9 The character or quality of a text is determined by the relations between the readings which provisionally define an open-ended structuration rather than a determinate closed structure.

Formally, there is a certain similarity between the concept of text in these theses and the concept of text in *S/Z* or *Le Plaisir du Texte* by Barthes (1970, 1973). But this chapter does not propose anything like the Barthesian 'codes' (proairetic, hermeneutic, etc.) which are formulated in *S/Z* so that the analysis can tackle the particular problem of the character of realist narrative. Furthermore, this chapter does not depend upon a binary opposition between two kinds of text, the modern and the non-modern, or, in Barthesian terms, 'scriptible' and 'lisible'. Thus the concept of text active in this chapter is not positively Barthesian.

The alternative concept has a negative and differential identity in relation to the double transparency assumption which is rejected. It is worth extablishing how and why this is so. To begin with, it is important to be clear about the implications of refusing a relation of transparency between the text and its non-textual other. Texts are not necessarily books because books are not the only things which can be read. As a practical demonstration of this point, the first half of this book provides a reading of an institution, the nineteenth-century poor law. If the definition of text is broadened in this way, the relations surrounding a text can be very complex. But a text does not and cannot have another which is non-text.

It is not clear how the 'reality' of representational history or literary criticism might get into or behind the text. The chains of reference like footnotes lead from one text to another text and beyond to infinity. There is no referent behind the paper, only an infinite reference to other texts. This is a modest enough conclusion, but its anti-representational implications will still be scandalous in orthodox historiography. It is being proposed, for example, that Engels's 'Manchester' is not a real city nor a representation of that city, but a discursive figure in a text. Without the provocative example, we might say that the 'real' is another discursive construct and that this point is equally pertinent whether one reads structuration in a text by Engels or in an institution like the nineteenth-century poor law. Differently constructed realities may have an almost infinite capacity to naturalise themselves for a short time in particular areas of knowledge; but reflection upon representation, as in this book, or subversion of representation, as in *London Labour,* must denaturalise such constructs.

Equally, the text does not and cannot have an other which is an absent system. It has been argued elsewhere (Williams, 1977) that Althusser's pursuit of such a system only produces internal problems in his discourse; the problematic is a simple system of relations which are a kind of referent such as Althusser condemns in other modes of reading. On the alternative account of text and reading, the problems are more fundamental. No system can become the sole object of analysis because that would deny the polysemy of discourse. Textual systems are possible objects for readings, if systems are chains of reference with clearly defined internal relations and boundaries. But systems cannot be privileged objects, since there is no reason why all readings should start and stop at the boundaries of such systems. In any case, textual systems are often broken-backed, either because of internal problems or because they are challenged and subverted by other reference; the appendix to this chapter develops this point in an analysis of 'humanism'.

Just as it denies the relation of text to other, so the alternative account denies the relation of one reading to text. There cannot be a relation of transparency between the one reading and any text, because a text is not usually exhausted by one reading: there is usually something more to be read, another chain of reference to be constructed. Reading should conceptualise the variable nature and extent of this polysemy. The notion that the text has a readable essence must be discarded, because the text neither is, nor contains, a primal referent. Thus it is not something to which different readers can appeal for justification as in the historiographic debate between Hobsbawm and Henderson. The text is something for whose (re)construction each reader must take responsibility. This is another modest enough conclusion and proposal whose anti-representational implications will still be scandalous in orthodox historiography: the text has only a provisional character that lasts as long as it is constructed in a particular way and inserted in the same intertext.

All this has implications for the way in which texts are evaluated and for what is substituted in place of the crude 'success' and 'failure' labels of the readings so far considered. If the text no longer has an essence of the sort supposed by these readings, the quality of the text cannot be defined by its fulfilment of one project like the representational project of the English readings, nor can the quality of the text be defined by its realisation of one theoretical system like the problematic of the Althusserian reading. The final thesis suggests that the quality of a text can perhaps be defined in an interim way in terms of the structuration established by relations of solidarity and dislocation along and between chains of reference.

Three chains of reference in the *Condition*

At this stage, it is possible to turn to the Engels text and demonstrate all these points. The demonstration will first try to clinch the point that the text is not exhausted by one reading. It will do this by deploying three alternative readings, by constructing three chains of reference in the text. The first reading will be concerned with the process of naming, by which the text colours-in class identities with the bourgeoisie as villains and the proletariat as victims. The second reading will be concerned with the text's empiricist reference, and the third with the text's humanist reference. The second and third readings deliberately reconstruct humanist and empiricist reference which is misconstructed in the misreadings already criticised. It would have been easy to proliferate readings and to forget that the *Condition* ever referred to representation or humanism. Constructing these particular chains of reference forces us to confront the possibility of humanist and representational readings of the text, and to pose questions about the nature and place of the *Condition*'s empiricism and humanism.

To begin with the first reading, the *Condition* identifies the bourgeoisie as the responsible villains and the proletarians as the victims of the social process. As Engels says in his 1846 postscript:

I attached especial importance to proving how completely justified the proletariat was in waging this struggle, and to rebutting the English bourgeoisie's fine phrases by means of their ugly deeds (Engels, 1975, p. 585).

The identification of class villains and victims is worked out on at least three separate levels: the ethical–juridical level, the socio-political level, and the historico-economic level. These three levels will now be considered in turn.

At the juridical level the text is concerned with the legal or moral responsibility of the bourgeoisie. The *Condition* considers whether their conduct is legal or ethical. At this level, structure of society is treated as a given; the term 'bourgeois' is used more or less interchangeably with the term 'society' in this indictment. The bourgeoisie collectively are charged with social murder and Engels plays the part of prosecuting counsel:

I have now to prove that society in England daily and hourly commits what the working men's organs, with perfect correctness characterise as social murder, that it has placed the workers under conditions in which they can neither retain health nor live long (Engels, 1975, p. 394).

The crux of the prosecution case is that the bourgeoisie *knows*; it has foreknowledge of the effects of its conduct upon the working class. Foreknowledge is crucial because, if the bourgeoisie knows not what it does, then the charge should be manslaughter rather than murder:

When one individual inflicts bodily injury upon another, such injury that death results, we call the deed manslaughter; when the assailant knew in advance that the injury would be fatal, we call his deed murder. But when society places hundreds of proletarians in such a position that they inevitably meet a too early and an unnatural death ... knows these thousands of victims must perish, and yet permits these conditions to remain, its deed is murder just as surely as the deed of the single individual (Engels, 1975, p. 393).

At the political level, the text is concerned with the political responsibility of the bourgeoisie. The starting point here is an explicit political theory. In society, there is a 'ruling power' which is 'the class which at present holds social and political control' (Engels, 1975, p. 393) and in England this ruling class is the 'bourgeoisie' (Engels, 1975, p. 593). This English bourgeoisie does not discharge its political obligations but uses the state as an instrument of class power. This is demonstrated by considering 'the manner in which the bourgeoisie as a party, as the power of the state, conducts itself towards the proletariat' (Engels, 1975, p. 567). This conduct is a matter of class legislation in parliament and of class bias in the administration of the law by justices of the peace. The post-1834 poor law is identified as the key indicator which formulates the bourgeoisie's 'conception of its duties towards the proletariat' (Engels, 1975, p. 577). Here the bourgeoisie 'acts *in corpore* as the ruling power' against those proletarians who, for whatever reason, are unable to support themselves (Engels, 1975, p. 578). Politically, the bourgeoisie is thoroughly irresponsible and it is blind; this class worries not at all about the imminent dissolution of a society already divided into two hostile groups (Engels, 1975, p. 427).

At the historico-economic level, the text is concerned with the historical and economic effect of the bourgeoisie. The *Condition*'s economic analysis provides the concept of a production process and this is intricated with a historical analysis of the variability of these production arrangements. In this sphere, the behaviour of the bourgeoisie is neither murderous nor politically irresponsible. At the historico-economic level, the behaviour of the bourgeoisie is economically selfish. Ironically, the bourgeoisie is criticised for that rational economic hedonism which is necessary, in orthodox economics from Smith onwards, if everything is to be for the best. Love of money or gain is the dominant motive in a middle class which 'knows no bliss save that of rapid gain, no pain save that of losing gold' (Engels, 1975, pp. 562-3). The inter-class implication is that the bourgeois 'cannot comprehend that he holds any other relation to the operatives than that of purchase and sale' (Engels, 1975, p. 563). The economy, therefore, is the sphere of competition between self-interested individuals and especially of unequal competition between classes when the bourgeoisie has a monopoly of the means of existence (Engels, 1975, p. 376). The central principle of the economic system is competition that determines wages, produces surplus population, and periodical crisis (Engels, 1975, pp. 374-81). Competition is equally the motor of historical changes like the Industrial Revolution (Engels, 1975, p. 375).

There is, however, more to the *Condition* at this level than a radical twist on apologetic economics about competition and the 'hidden hand'. The text resisted the ahistorical approach of political economy and sketched an analysis of several different historical states of the economic system – slavery, serfdom, and wage labour. There is only an ambivalent progress between these states as the text demonstrates by comparing the wage labourer, the serf, and the slave. A detailed nine-point comparison of the English labourer of 1845 and the Saxon serf of 1145 (Engels, 1975, pp. 473–4) on the whole favours the 'open, honest servitude' of 1145 with the caveat that there had been some progress in that the principle of freedom was formally affirmed by 1845. The other invidious comparison is between the English wage labourer of 1845 and the North American slave of 1845 (Engels, 1975, pp. 379–80, 467–8). Unlike the slave, the factory hand who is bought piecemeal, and with the semblance of freedom, must perform on command.

This first reading establishes that there are more things and different things than historiography, literary criticism, or Althusserianism imagines in the text. At the same time, it is easy to construct a chain of representational reference in the *Condition,* just as it is easy to construct a chain of humanist reference. In a second and third reading, these chains can now be traced.

The text can very easily be read as representational when the *Condition* constantly promises neutral sounding and apparently empirical investigations; the text will investigate what sort of people the workers are, the influence of the great towns upon the proletariat, and how society rewards the worker in terms of dwelling, clothing, and food (Engels, 1975, pp. 392, 327, 331). Here are clear definitions of a representational project. These investigations will have the classic empiricist function of correcting theory. The 1844 preface to the first German edition of the *Condition* claims 'a knowledge of proletarian conditions is absolutely necessary to be able to provide solid ground for socialist theories' (Engels, 1975, p. 302). In particular, this knowledge is identified as the necessary corrective for German communism which supposedly derives, more than any other, from 'theoretical premises', especially 'the Feuerbachian dissolution of Hegelian speculation' (Engels, 1975, p. 303).

In retrospect, however, Engels acknowledged the active role of these 'theoretical premises' in the text. In the 1892 postscript, he distances himself from 'the general theoretical standpoint of this book', claiming 'this book exhibits everywhere the traces of the descent of modern socialism from one of its ancestors, German philosophy' (Henderson and Chaloner, 1958, pp. 363–4). References to humanism in the *Condition* can easily be discovered, so that humanism can be read in the text. There are certainly references to a subject (man) and essence of man assumptions. The *Condition* presupposes a *Homo faber* who finds his essential realisation through productive labour; 'voluntary, productive activity is the highest enjoyment known to us' (Engels, 1975, p. 415). As voluntary work has a capacity for satisfying, so involuntary wage labour for capital has a capacity for frustrating man (Engels, 1975, p. 415). Moreover, these references to the essence of man are not a matter of occasional ornament or optional extra. An active human subject, *Homo faber*, is presupposed in much of the substantive analysis of the mid-nineteenth-century economy and in many of the political positions.

Consider, for example, the analysis of private property and competition in the economy. In the *Condition*, property is the crucial determinant of social division, against which all other privileges vanish (Engels, 1975, p. 562). Private property attains this privilege because it drives a wedge between the subject (*Homo faber*) and the object in which he finds his realisation, except where it is taken away from him as the property of another. Or again, there is the privilege of the principle of competition which is invoked recurrently in the analysis as the expression of 'the battle of all against all which rules in modern civil society' (Engels, 1975, p. 375). Competition attains this privilege because of the prior assumption that there is an identity of all human interests which become opposed in competition. The text's political positions and postures are equally marked by humanism. The *Condition* begins with a dedication that is notable for its humanist tone. Here Engels salutes the working classes of Great Britain as 'men, members of the great and universal family of mankind' (Engels, 1975, p. 298). More significantly, there is the whole definition of communism in the *Condition* as a movement which 'is a question of humanity and not of the workers alone' (Engels, 1975, pp. 581-2). Communism is a movement which is in some ways above and beyond class struggle, because it seeks the inauguration of an era of human fulfilment.

The three readings outlined in the last few pages provide a vindication of the alternative concept of reading and of text rather than consolation for the misreadings. First, and most obviously, on this basis the transparency of any one reading to the text must be rejected. When three alternative readings are laid out, there are already, and fatally, two readings too many for any such transparency to be sustainable. Second, if three such disparate readings can find support in the text, this must show the futility of appeals to the text as some kind of primal referent. Furthermore, the obvious explanation for a multiplicity of possible readings is that the individual readings construct chains of reference in the text as supposed in this chapter's alternative concept of reading. Third, the final reading admits references to humanism, but the appendix to this chapter shows that these references in the *Condition*, or the other texts of Marx and Engels in the 1840s, do not add up to a humanist structure of the kind which Althusser called a problematic. So the *Condition* does not have an other of the Althusserian kind.

The readings do not add up

If three or more readings of the text can be constructed, the question must be whether and how the chains of reference add up. This is an issue of some importance. If the text is the sum of the separate chains of reference, there is ultimately a definite textual structure in which the readings of representation, humanism, and class identity are all reconciled. And, if the text is some kind of master structure, the errors of Althusserianism are not being resolved, they are only being refined. For, in this case, the one structure thesis evicted at the level of the reading returns at the level of the text.

The first point here must be that the three alternative readings are different from one another. The areas of the visible and the intelligible do not coincide in these readings any more than in the misreadings originally considered. Because of this, one reading can be used to render explicable that which is inexplicable on another reading of the text.

Consider, for example, the *Condition*'s borrowed analyses and positions and stock attitudes. On any representational reading, there is much here which is inexplicable. Engels did not simply plagiarise as Henderson alleges (e.g. Henderson, 1976, pp. 49 and 69). The *Condition* always modifies the analysis and twists the stock attitudes which it borrows. The text modified Gaskell's notion of a pre-industrial golden age; pre-industrial life was not idyllic when the workers were ' "toiling machines" who lived in a condition of silent vegetation' (Engels, 1975, p. 309). Again, the text twists the stock mid-nineteenth-century notion that factory work damages family life because of its effects upon male and female role division; in the *Condition*, these consequences of role reversal demonstrate only that the original roles were unhealthy (Engels, 1975, pp. 435-9). These puzzling reservations and qualifications become intelligible on a humanist reading. The Industrial Revolution represents a kind of progress beyond the pre-industrial stage because it has moved society nearer towards its destination of human realisation (Engels, 1975, p. 309). And the text has critical reservations about the pre-industrial male/female role division, because it supposes this depended upon private interest and possession (Engels, 1975, p. 439). In this second example, as in the first, what is inexplicable on a representational reading becomes explicable on a humanist reading.

The class identity reading again alters the field of the visible. This can be demonstrated by considering the text's handling of evidence which is another puzzle for a representational reading. Henderson is wrong when he claims that Engels relies heavily on left-wing sources like the Chartist *Northern Star* (Henderson, 1976, p. 70). As Hobsbawm recognises, Engels relies wherever possible on right-wing sources (Hobsbawm, 1969, p. 16) like the *Manchester Guardian* and the

Liverpool Mercury (e.g. Engels, 1975, p. 370). But no representational reading can work out the rationale of this reference rightwards, because the *Condition*'s use of sources does not connect to some general historiographic, representational duty to establish how it really was by critical reflection upon the sources.

However, the *Condition*'s deployment of evidence is explicable at the juridical level: Engels, the prosecuting counsel, has to make the charge stick. First, this requires great care about the bias and reliability of discursive witnesses. Engels is highly sensitive to bias; with some honest exceptions (Engels, 1975, p. 366), he notes that liberals chose to emphasise rural distress and conservatives chose to emphasise urban distress (Engels, 1975, p. 304). Engels is equally careful to assess the reliability of his witnesses. Gaskell is honest, but confuses the whole working class with mill hands (Engels, 1975, p. 366), while the 1832 Tory report on factories is a farrago of leading questions and misleading answers. But the effective prosecuting counsel has to be more than simply critical of the available witnesses if he is to secure a conviction when the defendant feigns innocence. The bourgeoisie knows its guilt but is unable to admit it; 'the bourgeoisie will not confess, even to itself, that the workers are in distress because it, the property-holding, manufacturing class must bear the moral responsibility for this distress' (Engels, 1975, p. 322; see also p. 434). In this case, the prosecuting counsel calls a particular kind of discursive witness. Engels's explicit and articulate preference (Engels, 1975, p. 304) is for official documents and liberal sources. These sources can establish the element of foreknowledge which is crucial if Engels is going to make the murder charge stick at the juridical level. The bourgeoisie 'cannot complain if, after the official and non-official testimony here cited which must be known to it, I broadly accuse it of social murder' (Engels, 1975, p. 407).

If the readings are so different in what and how they comprehend or do not comprehend, how can they be added together? There is one possibility: each of the different readings may add a mite of intelligibility so that the *Condition* is some kind of structure produced by supplementation in which the readings of representation, humanism and class identity all add something. To deal with this possibility, it is necessary to pose in more general terms the question of the relations and non-relations between the chains of reference in the readings so far considered – class identity, representation, and humanism.

There certainly are some points of intersection between the chains of reference. First, there are some relations of positive cross-reference between chains of reference. For example, from humanism to the ethico-political level, there is a cross-reference; the *Condition* insists that class law is not simply a reflex of bourgeois political irresponsibility and claims bourgeois law is necessary because of the existence of the propertyless (Engels, 1975, p. 567). Elsewhere, there are relations of direct overlap where chains of reference intersect. Competition, for example, is both the expression of the humanist war of all against all and the motor of the historical process at the historico-economic level (Engels, 1975, p. 375). It would indeed by surprising if there were not occasional relations of overlap and cross-reference between the chains. The question is whether the relations go beyond this. Are there simple positive relations of solidarity between the readings? This would be the case, for example, if the humanist assumptions about man's essence are so much input for an altogether more complex analysis of class identity, villains, and victims.

Such a reconciliation is impossible because the three chains of reference are incapable of entering into stable positive relations with one another. For example, to consider the representational chain of reference, the *Condition*'s project of a representational empirical investigation is underdeveloped. It promises too much and too little, just like the man who goes into the police station and says 'I will tell you everything'. The project only acquires an identity when the text moves on to something other than methodology and general statement about type of investigation. This something other is in no way derivable from the proclamations at this level. Furthermore, this something other in the *Condition* appears to be thoroughly contradictory, especially in the case of the humanist reference. This text's humanism is, at least in aspiration, a general theoretical position that renders empirical investigation redundant; the basic human identity is never in question before, during or after any empirical investigation. To complicate matters, the *Condition*'s particular humanism cannot be stably connected up to anything else because, as is argued in the appendix to this chapter, it is a broken-backed system. If there are no fixed identities to connect with, it is hard to see how this reading can enter into relations of a stable sort.

The identification of class villains and victims may be more straight-forwardly a matter of theme than the other two readings, but it cannot be connected easily with the other readings. The identification of class villains and victims conflicts jars with any kind of neutral representational project; how can *all* the bourgeoisie and *all* the proletariat be identified so confidently with particular roles? At the same time, the identification of class villains and victims deals in an identification that is not derivable from Feuerbach or from the Marxist humanist critique of political economy, and indeed is strictly unsustainable within these analyses. In humanist terms, there cannot be class villains and victims in the here and now. As is admitted at the beginning of the fourth chapter of the *Condition,* competition must take place not only between, but also within, groups of the propertied and propertyless. In the *Condition,* there is not a specific and peculiar inter-class relation like the extraction of surplus value. Wage labourers, the class of the propertyless, cannot have a corner in alienation. Nor indeed can there be two classes in the humanist hereafter. The human realisation of communism is as much for the unjust as the just, the propertied as the propertyless. Class identities conflict with the humanist project as much as with the representational project.

In sum, the relation between the readings is not one of smooth supplementation, but of contention, disconnection, and dissonance. There can be no question of a textual master structure when the readings contend with, and challenge each other, in a number of different ways. Dislocation is here more important than solidarity. The *Condition* is a quarrelsome text; it is not a unitary whole but plural, polysemic, and dispersed.

Such a reconceptualisation of the nature of the text threatens existing evaluations of the *Condition*. All our misreaders, whether historians, literary critics, or academic Marxists, have an evaluative obsession. The text that they misconstruct is endlessly inspected to see whether it is worthy of praise or blame. The evaluative obsession arises because the individual misreadings include criteria of discursive success or failure which are often, though by no means always, of an epistemological legislative sort. This is most clear in Althusser's epistemological legislation.

Althusser in the 1960s is a philosopher who is sceptical about the problematisation of knowledge in orthodox epistemology, but does not renounce legislative prescription about the possible and impossible forms of knowledge. In a familiar way, discourses are divided into two groups, sciences and ideologies, possible and impossible forms of knowledge. The evaluative connotations are obvious and the project is familiar in English-speaking philosophy of science. *For Marx* simply proposes demarcation criteria different from those about representation and empirical content which are favoured in English-speaking prescriptive methodology. In Althusser, the status of a discourse is to be decided according to whether it displays the process with a subject structure characteristic of ideologies.

Generally, Althusser's demarcation criteria are caught up in problems about their own vacuity and impossibility. The division of discourses is uninformative if almost everything under the sun is organised into one of two enormous categories. *For Marx*'s concession that there are many different ideologies and sciences is purely formal, when all the discourses in each category have essentially the same structure defined by the presence or absence of a subject. There is also the problem that the criteria judge discourses according to the presence of characteristics which are imaginary in the sense that they cannot easily be read in many discourses. As the appendix to this chapter argues, a text like the *Condition* does not contain a subject-centred structure of the sort necessary for an Althusserian decision on its ideological status. *For Marx*'s demarcation criteria only generate the insoluble problems of 1960s Althusserianism.

Specifically, with regard to Marx's or Engels's texts of the 1840s, the Althusserian criteria encourage an unreasonable devaluation of these texts. The one division and two big categories approach produces a comparative statics view of Marx's development which counterposes Young Marx and Old Marx, before and after. Young Marx and Engels, or more exactly the texts of the 1840s, are devalued as immature, inferior, and ideological. Althusserian comparative static analysis even has an alibi for dealing with the disorderliness which is such a characteristic of the texts of the 1840s. In texts like the *German Ideology*, this disorderliness is a symptom of confusion and a lack of clarity which is later resolved brilliantly by Old Marx. Here disorderliness is conceded but devalued by treating it as a symptom of transition.

The notions of immature Marxism and transitional text are the legacy of the 1960s Althusserian criteria of evaluation. They are categories that prevent any kind of analysis of the texts of the 1840s. That way lies only a triumphalist reading of *Capital* as, for example, the text where the necessary existence of relations of exploitation securely establishes class villains and victims. This is the final insult to texts like the *Condition* which deserve better than condescension about their naïveté and confusions. It is lamentable that non-Althusserians have also been hooked on the comparative static analysis of Young Marx and Old Marx. They only alter the specification of the break or continuity between the two figures of Young Marx and Old Marx. And it is to counter all this that the present argument leans so far the other way. The treatment of Mayhew, Booth, or Rowntree, makes reference to all their work. But in the treatment of Marx and Engels, reference has been deliberately restricted to the texts of the 1840s in order to try and say something about the 'humanism' of those years. The other chapters of the book construct an intertext of non-Marxist texts within which the *Condition* has its individuality. This is done to avoid the comparative static analysis which *For Marx* epitomises and promotes.

The criticism of Althusser's directly epistemological project will only confirm the prejudices of many English readers about French philosophers. Therefore, it is important to insist that those historians who provide the most common-sense English misreadings of the *Condition* are not philosophically innocent. These historians have assimilated the evaluative criteria of positivist epistemology: a discourse can only be virtuous if its 'interpretation' is fair, and such interpretation must ultimately depend on the support of accurate and representative 'facts'. But this is naïve when the text is not exhausted by one reading and when by shifting between readings it is possible radically to change the standards of interpretative fairness and the definition of the proper fact to interpretation relation. All the evaluations of historiography can be erased or reversed by shifting between readings of the *Condition*; as the following examples will show, when the reading changes, discursive vice is often transformed into discursive virtue.

The *Condition*'s treatment of bourgeois and proletarian responsibility for the condition of the proletariat is an interesting case of fairness and unfairness. The bourgeoisie is always held responsible for outrages against the working class while the proletariat is never responsible for its own misbehaviour. Industrial injuries and coal-mining accidents, howsoever caused (Engels, 1975, pp. 456-7, 537-8), are 'injuries undergone in the service and through the fault of the bourgeoisie' (Engels, 1975, p. 457). The text pursues this connection relentlessly and even extenuates the reckless worker:

If adults are reckless, they must be mere overgrown children on a plane of intelligence which does not enable them to appreciate the danger in its full scope; and who is to blame for this but the bourgeoisie which keeps them in a condition in which their intelligence cannot develop? (Engels, 1975, p. 456).

It is such an environmental argument which is always used to excuse the behaviour of the poor. For example,

Drunkenness has ceased to be a vice for which the victims can be held responsible, it becomes a phenomenon, the necessary inevitable effect of certain conditions upon an object possessed of no volition in relation to these conditions (Engels, 1975, p. 401).

Sexual licence, wasteful expenditure of temporarily high wages, and even pauperism under the old poor law are similarly explained (Engels, 1975, pp. 413, 423, 572).

In orthodox historiography, this is only legible as interpretative double standard and fault. Thus Hobsbawm is virtually silent on the issue, while Henderson exults in the bias of an author for whom the bourgeoisie could do no right (Henderson, 1976, pp. 71-2). Defence is impossible and attack is easy, because both historians are enmeshed in orthodox historiographic definitions of interpretative unfairness. But, at the political level of the class identity reading, the fault vanishes. Here there is no question of a double standard because the politically inexcusable dereliction of duty by the bourgeoisie licenses any working-class reaction. More exactly, that dereliction of duty amounts to a declaration of war. Society is involved in civil war which is, as the Oxford dictionary says, a political condition of dispute between parts of a nation, conducted by armed force and suspending ordinary relations. In the *Condition,* the operation of the state, actions in the political sphere and, beyond this, large areas of class behaviour are viewed in this light. The clearest illustration of this is the text's treatment of explosion, incendiarism, physical attacks, and other working-class outrages against bourgeois property and persons (Engels, 1975, pp. 508–13). The *Condition* does not condemn such actions but justifies them as part of 'social war'. This, for example, is how the text rationalises unionism:

> In war the injury of one party is the benefit of the other,
> and since the working men are on a war footing towards
> their employers, they do merely what the great potentates
> do when they get into a quarrel (Engels, 1975, p. 510).

It is not surprising that a few pages later, the text maintains that attacks on property exemplify the courage of the working class.

Standards of interpretative unfairness can be turned upside down in other instances. Consider, for example, the *Condition's* condemnation of all types of industrial work. The text does not simply condemn the ill-effects of heavy manual labour as wasting; it also condemns specialisation and the division of labour which reduces work to 'some paltry mechanical manipulation' (Engels, 1975, p. 415), and asserts that steam power in factories only introduces the 'unmeaning and monotonous' work of machine-minding (Engels, 1975, pp. 415, 447, 466). Orthodox historiography can only be sceptical about such blanket condemnation which is usually regarded as an index of interpretative bias. But for a humanist reading, no such conclusion is possible. Indeed, the blanket condemnation can be seen as the index of a rigorous humanism; the workers are still alienated even when they are not visibly ill-treated by their employers.

In orthodox historiography, factual accuracy is even more sacrosanct than standards of interpretative fairness. Thus, Henderson and Hobsbawm evaluate the cases and examples in the *Condition* on the assumption that their accuracy and representativeness is crucial to the success of the discourse. These historians adopt an implicit refutationism: if the text gets the examples absolutely wrong, or even gets the relative frequency of key events wrong, then that discredits the discourse. These historians have assimilated the notions of factual proof and refutation promoted by, and necessary to, positivist epistemology; discursive identifications must be decisively challenged or confirmed by the empirical facts. The key weakness of this position is that the textual relation between discursive identifications and examples does not necessarily conform to this philosophic model. The possibility and profitability of putting everything into refutationist form has been disputed in the first half of this book. Here, it is enough to show concretely that the relation between discursive identification and examples in the *Condition* can easily be constructed in a different way.

At this historico-economic level, in the class identity reading, the cases and examples *act out* a pre-existing discursive identification; 'illustrates' is too weak a word for this relation at the historico-economic level where discursive identities are *dramatised*. Consider, for example, the way in which the great towns dramatise social isolation in a society which has universalised competition at an economic level. The 'unfeeling isolation of each in his private interest' is dramatised by the crowds of a city like London:

> And however much one may be aware that this isolation of
> the individual, this narrow self-seeking, is the fundamental
> principle of our society everywhere, it is nowhere so shame-
> lessly barefaced, so self-conscious as just here in the crowd-
> ing of the great city. The dissolution of mankind into
> monads, of which each one has a separate principle, the
> world of atoms, is here carried to its utmost extreme
> (Engels, 1975, p. 329).

It is altogether appropriate that the great towns are constructed on a 'hypocritical plan' of ecological segregation and isolation (Engels, 1975, p. 349). Even on their journeys through working-class districts, the lines of petit bourgeois shops along the main roads shield 'everything which might affront the eye and the nerves of the bourgeoisie' in Manchester (Engels, 1975, p. 349). In so far as cases and examples act out theoretical identities in this way, any fuss about the accuracy and representativeness of these examples is irrelevant.

To supplement this point, here are two examples of the irrelevance of relative frequency considerations. First, there is the question of the *jus primae noctis* of the factory owner. As Engels makes clear, the *jus primae noctis* is not so much a fact as a formal right attached to a position; 'the fact that not all manufacturers use their power, does not in the least change the position of the girls' (Engels, 1975, pp. 441-2). The relative frequency of sexual relations between factory owners and factory girls does not exhaust the significance of the behaviour, especially when Engels has explicitly discounted the importance of the number of pairs of bloodstained sheets. The *jus primae noctis* is a sexual relation that dramatically acts out a social relation of servitude. On the other hand, the trade union strike is an instance of a dramatic acting out of a social identity. Trade unionism is privileged in the *Condition* as an attempt by the workers to put an end to competition among themselves. The text supposes, however, that strikes for higher wages or better conditions are usually unsuccessful because they cannot suspend the operation of the laws of supply and demand in the labour market (Engels, 1975, pp. 505-7). But the failure of strikes does not exhaust their significance. When strikes are an acting out of human identity and an assertion of human dignity, it is irrelevant how many working days are lost to secure a given change in the wage rate. The notion of acting out is nicely caught by the notion of strikes as manifestos; 'they are pronunciamentoes of single branches of industry that these too have joined the labour movement' (Engels, 1975, p. 512).

By shifting between readings, it is possible to undercut completely the evaluative terms of the historians' debate. Moreover, it should be clear from these examples that it is not simply a question of rejecting the historians' evaluation or Althusser's evaluation. When the criteria of evaluation can always be changed by shifting between readings, we must reject all evaluation of the text in the name of one reading. At this point, perhaps the safest conclusion is that the proper task of reading is to render the text intelligible rather than pass judgment; to say not how good or bad a text is, but simply that is the way it is. But there is an evaluative dimension to reading and some sort of evaluative riposte to historiography is required. Here the starting point has to be the nature of the structuration in the text disclosed and defined by several readings. This structuration provides an object for evaluation, at least where, as in the *Condition* or *London Labour,* the text is moderately polysemic and can easily be read in more than one way.

If one considers structuration, then polysemy and dislocation are the *Condition*'s redeeming qualities. On the basis of the three readings constructed, the text's merits do not lie in the avoidance of error. On our construction, the text is caught in a kind of humanism and in a representational delusion. But the *Condition* is not exhausted by a few elementary impossibilities, and that is the difference of the text from its (mis)readings. Take away representation and the historians are left arguing over nothing; take away representation and there is a whole lot left in the *Condition.* Perhaps the good text is not the text that avoids elementary error but that which is not exhausted by elementary errors. But this notion must be handled carefully. The discourses of Hobsbawm and Marcus are nearly univocal while that of Engels is polyphonic; but it is not the case that many readings and voices necessarily produce a richness that cannot be attained by one voice. There is more to the merits of the *Condition* than a simple multiplicity of voices in discourse.

It is at this point that the difference between the *Condition* and *London Labour* fits in. In *London Labour,* there is a multiplicity of voices which produces an anti-realist effect. But this effect is perhaps less important than modernist literature and its commentary discourses would have us believe. There is always a suspicion that anti-realism is about aesthetic effects which divert but do not intellectually sustain.

From this point of view, there is an important difference between Mayhew and Engels, just as there is between Fourier and Marx. In the *Condition,* the relation, or strictly, the non-relation, between the voices directly challenges many of the theoretical presuppositions of commentators and readers – whether historians, literary critics, or academic Marxists.

The *Condition* puts these presuppositions in question by the contradictoriness of its workings. It is a text that aspires to represent reality and yet is marked at every step by a theoretical system which turns out not to be a system. It is a text that presupposes a general human essence and at the same time is desperately concerned to establish class identities. It is all a matter of so many conflicting identifications which cannot all be right. Discourse cannot be representational and theoretical, at least when the empirical/theoretical relation is a matter of dramatisation, and there are no stable identities in the humanist theory. Society cannot be both a human and a class society; the critical effect follows from the contradictory identifications. The world is full of texts that opt for one kind of identification or another – discourse is representational, the proletariat are victims, or whatever. It is the easy way. The unsettling critical effect of the *Condition* is that it will not accept and develop one identification. On the three readings, the text's disorderliness is critically holding open two areas, two sets of problems. Area one is the theory of discourse now coming into existence as we probe the inadequacies of supposing discourse is either representational or a theoretical system. Area two is the area of politics: the conflict between general human identity and class identity at the interface between philosophies of conservatism and liberalism and theories of socialism and communism. It would be absurd to expect the *Condition* in the 1840s (or *Capital* in the 1860s) to provide exemplary solutions to problems in these areas which we are unable to solve. Meanwhile, until we resolve or re-pose a few of these problems, the *Condition* is a modern text, perhaps the only serious modern text considered in this book.

January, 1978

Appendix   The *Condition* has no other

This appendix argues that the references to humanism in the *Condition* do not define a structure of the kind which *For Marx* calls a humanist problematic. To demonstrate this, it is necessary to return to Feuerbach's texts of the early 1840s and to Marx's and Engels's texts of 1843-4. The issue is whether one subject-centred structure underlies these texts.

It is important to avoid being distracted by *For Marx*'s misidentification of the subject in these discourses. According to Althusser, both the Marx/Engels and Feuerbach texts presuppose a communal inter-subjective essence of man. But, as this appendix will show, none of these texts presupposes such an essence and its associated subject; the Marx/Engels texts presupposes *Homo faber,* a subject with an essence distinct from Feuerbach's subject, the sensuous real being. This Althusserian misidentification of the subject is not really of great importance, because an orthodox 1960s Althusserian could rectify the misidentification, and easily restate and reconcile the different human-isms of the 1840s texts. The restatement would emphasise that speculative philosophy's thinking man is critically dissolved into Feuerbach's sensuous man or the Marx/Engels worker-man while, all the time, nothing really happens because the one subject-centred structure survives all the dissolutions. Such a restatement would main-tain the two main Althusserian propositions about the Marx/Engels text of 1844 and their relation to Feuerbach's texts. The first of these Althusserian propositions is that all the texts have an other which is a structure: a closed internally satisfactory system of relations departing from formal definitions of the key terms. The second Althusserian pro-position is that it is essentially the same subject-centred structure of relations which recurs in Marx/Engels, Feuerbach, and all the dis-courses they criticise; only the identity of the occupant of the subject's place within the structure changes. It is these two main propositions that must be challenged by a detailed examination of the humanism of Feuerbach, Marx, and Engels.

To begin with Feuerbach's humanist critique of religion, the *Essence of Christianity* discusses theology, or the reflection of religion upon itself, and concludes 'the true sense of Theology is Anthropology' (Feuerbach, 1854, p. 14). The divine being is the human being freed from the limits of individual man and made objective (Feuerbach, 1854, p. 65). Thus in God, the human individual only contemplates human nature in general, and in this sense man is the substance of religion (Feuerbach, 1854, pp. 13-14). Religion therefore rests on a funda-mental confusion and the text goes on to explain the mechanics of this confusion. Religion turns the predicate or essence of the subject, man, into an independent existence (Feuerbach, 1854, pp. 18 and 22) called God, in which the Christian recognises his own predicates and receives them back. In non-technical vocabulary, the process of confusion is one whereby man's nature is projected from man to God and then received back again by man. The text likens the process to the circulation of blood through arteries and veins (Feuerbach, 1854, p. 30).

There is also a Feuerbachian critique of speculative philosophy articulated most clearly in the *Preliminary Theses* of 1842 and the *Principles* of 1843. The *Theses* open with the assertion that 'theology itself is the secret of speculative philosophy' (in Feuerbach, 1972, p. 192) because, from Spinoza to Hegel, speculative philosophy sets up an analogue to the divine being in the form of its 'Absolute' which is the essence of reason (ibid., p. 178). In a preliminary way, speculative philosophy is a critical reform of theology because it 'places the divine being back into this world' as subject of history rather than object of worship (Feuerbach, 1972, p. 180). But speculative philosophy is confused about the identity of the subject. In Feuerbach's texts, the true subject is identified as 'being', alias 'the real and whole being of man' (ibid., p. 239) and the predicate/essence of 'being' was 'thought' (ibid., p. 168). The argument is that speculative philosophy turns this predicate/essence into an independent existence which in Hegel's case is transcendent thought, that is, 'the thought of man posited outside man' (ibid., p. 156).

This is Feuerbach's critical humanism as it would be recognised in all Althusserian restatement and as it is recognised in so many academic accounts of humanism. It is, however, only half of Feuerbach's humanism. The other and unknown half of his humanism is a careful and coherent attempt to establish the rationality of, and necessity for, the one critical operation whereby the true subject is established and the false subject discovered.

The *Essence of Christianity* calls this critical operation 'translation' (Feuerbach, 1854, p. v). It involves a movement from imagination to reality: 'I change the object as it is in the imagination into the object as it is in reality' (Feuerbach, 1854, p. xii). Imagination is the sphere of the discursive overlay where words 'have the effect of a narcotic on man, imprison him under the power of the imagination' (Feuerbach, 1854, p. 77). Thus critical translation involves movement from the discursive signifier to the real signified. The lesson of the whole business is quite straightforward:

> We should not, as is the case in theology and speculative
> philosophy, make real beings and things into arbitrary signs,
> vehicles, symbols, or predicates of a distinct transcendent
> absolute, i.e., abstract being (Feuerbach, 1854, p. xiii).

Given this Feuerbachian theory of signification, the criticised discourse must be in the realm of imagination, as are religion and philosophy. Religion is a form of knowledge in the imagination which is unfavourably compared with knowledge obtained through perception of the senses; in religion, the consciousness of object is not distinguishable from consciousness of self, the object is within, rather than outside, man, and the object is selected rather than indifferent (Feuerbach, 1854, p. 12). Such a type of knowledge in imagination exhibits a peculiar closure and circularity in the subject–object relation:

And here may be applied without any limitation the proposition: the object of any subject is nothing else than the subject's own nature taken objectively (Feuerbach, 1854, p. 12).

A rather different argument is used to attack philosophy, but this discussion is just as firmly relegated to the realm of knowledge in the imagination. In conceptualising reason, man mistakenly believes that he is dealing with an object in the realm of the senses, rather than in the realm of imagination,

as a being affected by external things he is accustomed always to distinguish the object from the conception of it. And here he applies the same process to the conception of reason, thus, for an existence in reason, in thought, substituting an existence in space and time, from which he had, nevertheless previously abstracted it (Feuerbach, 1854, p. 36).

When this misconception is discovered, speculative philosophy simply joins the other impossible discourses in the realm of knowledge in the imagination.

Conversely, Feuerbach's own critical discourse has to be in the realm of knowledge obtained through perceptions of the senses. Hence, the new philosophy outlined in *The Principles of the Philosophy of the Future* (in Feuerbach, 1972, pp. 177-264) is insistent in its sensuous materialism. It departs from the principle 'I am a real and sensuous being' (ibid., p. 277), and takes sensuous knowledge rather than thinking as its datum: '*indubitable* and *immediately certain* is only that which is the *object of the senses* of perception and feeling' (ibid., p. 228). Subsequent commentators have often been nonplussed by the seriousness with which Feuerbach takes sight, digestion and all as 'organs of philosophy' (ibid., p. 137). Althusser himself regards this kind of empiricism as an epistemological solecism. But the emphasis is neither eccentric nor naïve, given Feuerbach's theory of signification.

This emphasis on sensuous knowledge is an attempt to provide the necessary basis for a truly critical philosophical discourse in the realm of knowledge of the senses.

The critical discourse is set up on the right side of a theory of signification and a reality/imagination divide which condemns the criticised discourse. Only on these conditions can the new philosophy renounce speculation and attain its true dignity as 'the knowledge of what is' (ibid., p. 161). In this way, Feuerbach's texts internally secure 'translation' and substitution of the true essence and subject. If a once-and-for-all critical dissolution is possible and necessary in Feuerbach, it depends on a 'substructural' level and a theory of signification which is ignored by commentators concerned solely with a humanist 'structure' of subject and object. In this case, when the humanist structure can be referred to another substructural level, Feuerbach provides a poor example of the supposedly classical humanist structure. The Feuerbachian texts do not have an 'other' of the structural type which Althusser presumes to exist beneath all humanist texts. The remaining question must be whether there is any such 'other' in the texts of Marx and Engels.

In 1844 Marx and Engels develop a humanist critique of political economy. Marx in the *Economic and Philosophical Manuscripts* departs from a subject (man) whose essence is productive labour. The process of economic production is a two-term, subject and object, affair: the subject man is a natural being whose species life activity is production (Marx, 1970, p. 113); and whose object is nature or the sensuous external world necessary for production and belonging to man's labour (Marx, 1970, p. 109). Equally clearly, the *Manuscripts* rely on the notion of the movement of predicate between subject and object. Human realisation is achieved in production whereby the predicate, the essence of the subject (man), passes into the object laboured upon, which becomes an objectification of himself – something that confirms and realises his identity (Marx, 1970, p. 140). Alienation occurs where work, that is, the realisation of man, becomes a means to an end. Alienation is the result of the intervention of private property driving a wedge between subject and object, the human and the natural (Marx, 1970, pp. 108–12). There is also a criticism of other discourses for mis-identification of essence and subject. In Hegelian philosophy, the subject is the Idea and the essence 'abstractly mental' labour, and in political economy, the subject is private property and the essence 'abstract labour' (Marx, 1970, pp. 71–2, 120, 128, 178, 188).

Engels's 1844 *Outlines of a Critique of Political Economy* (Marx, 1970, pp. 197–226) propounds a humanism that is almost identical to that of the *Economic and Philosophical Manuscripts*. Engels's text advances a humanist theory of production. The two elements of production turn out to be the subject (man) and the object (nature) (Marx,

1970, p. 208). A predicate transferable between subject and object is again presupposed. In the humanist analysis of the *Outlines* the alienating consequences of private property are a 'split of production into two opposing sides – the natural and the human' (Marx, 1970, p. 212). The terms of Engels's critique of political economy are again humanist. The errors of political economy are partiality and inversion (Marx, 1970, pp. 197 and 207); these are the classic errors of a discourse that mistakes subject and essence. It is this same Marx/Engels humanism that recurs in the *Condition*, as already outlined in the third alternative reading of this chapter; in Engels's texts of 1844-5 a *Homo faber* is frustrated by private property.

Such is the officially recognised humanism of Marx and Engels. On this basis, in a general descriptive sense, Marx and Engels are, like Feuerbach, humanists substituting the true subject for the false subject. But there is a significant difference at the substructural level, because Marx and Engels do not appropriate the Feuerbachian theory of signification which is the substructure of Feuerbach's critical humanism. Equally, Marx and Engels do not line up the critical and criticised discourses on either side of an imagination/reality division. It is true that in the first of the 1845 *Theses on Feuerbach,* Marx goes on to espouse a materialism more radical than Feuerbach's, a materialism of 'sensuous activity' rather than sensuous contemplation (Marx–Engels, 1968, p. 28). But that is yet to come, and the aphoristic assertion of such a position cannot retrospectively rationalise the 1844 critique of political economy as a discourse. It is also true that Marx, in the *Economic and Philosophical Manuscripts,* did establish an opposition between the alienation of consciousness and the alienation of real life. The opposition is, however, only set up to devalue the alienation of consciousness, to claim the alienation of real life as more important and the proper object of analysis. In the 1844 critique of political economy by Marx and Engels, the issue at stake is simply how this alienation of real life is to be handled discursively. In this case, Marx and Engels simply substitute their preferred form of analysis for political economy's analysis, with *both* analyses identified as theoretical discourses purporting to refer to, and explain, external objects/the alienation of real life. The critical and criticised discourses are now both in the one realm where they refer to reality.

Consequently, in the Marx and Engels texts, the critical discourse's identification of the true subject and essence, and the discourse's relation to misidentification of the subject and essence is set up differently and unstably. In the Marxism of 1844, political economy's unsatisfactory treatment of the alienation of real life is simply denounced in the name of Marx's alternative treatment of that alienation. This involves a critical shift between humanisms: from an essence of abstract (wage) labour and a subject (private property) in political economy to an essence of labour and a subject (*Homo faber*) in Marx's alternative analysis. Marx and Engels make this 'translation' and then accuse political economy of being mystified because it has chosen the wrong subject and essence. At this point, the texts have not made the one possible and necessary substitution. The accusation of confusion, once made, can be applied to any and all discourses referring to reality and relying on the subject. A vertiginous prospect opens up. In Marx and Engels the infinite process of substituting the subject cannot legitimately be cut short after one substitution, with the claim that the one true subject is now identified. Rigorously, from Marx and Engels's one substitution, we are led to an infinity of possible substitutions of the subject.

Marx and Engels's texts dispense with the substructural underpinning of Feuerbachianism. But, paradoxically, that does not mean their humanism approaches the Althusserian structural ideal because, without the substructure, the relation of the identity of the true subject to false subject is set up differently and unstably. If there is not a stable identity for the occupants of the subject and object places in Marx and Engels's texts, their humanism is not so much a system or structure as an unstable moment in a potential movement of 'translations' to infinity.

In conclusion, Feuerbach's humanism is unlike that of Marx and Engels, and neither humanism contains a structure of the approved sort. There are doubtless many more different humanisms just around the corner. Meanwhile, it is clear that there is no universal structure that is extended, transferred, and applied, as Althusser and so many analysts of humanism suppose. It is also clear that Marx and Engels's particular humanism does not add up to a stable structure or system of any kind: texts like the *Condition* do not have an other in the Althusserian sense. This was the conclusion promised at the beginning of this section. It should also now be possible to see a more general point. The whole argument about Feuerbach, Engels, and Marx must surely demonstrate the futility of pursuing one structure and relating everything in a text to it. This point is worth making because it is plausible to suppose, as *For Marx* does, that much reading miscarries because it abstracts elements, and the solution is to find the absent structure which unifies the different elements. It should now be clear that this is no solution, because to pursue one structure is to deny the polysemy and multiplicity which are constitutive of texts. All reading must be concerned with elements; 'good' and 'bad' readings are separated only by the way in which they construct and connect elements. Re-reading is about reconceptualising the nature and connection of the different elements so that polysemy and multiplicity are not denied.

Booth

7

In 1889, Charles Booth published the first volume of *Life and Labour of the People in London*. When publication was completed in 1903, the text comprised seventeen volumes, including a one-volume conclusion and three separate multi-volume series on poverty, industry, and religious influences (Booth, 1902-3). The scale of the text is quite intimidating, but it cannot be said that historians have been intimidated. In *Life and Labour*, they search for one familiar form and content; their question is whether the text is an empirical investigation about poverty or unemployment. Three readings of *Life and Labour* will be used to demonstrate that historians disagree only about the answer to this question. The Simeys (Simey and Simey, 1960) in their biography of Booth tried to claim *Life and Labour* as a moderately successful empirical investigation of poverty. The revisionist work of Brown (1968) and Stedman Jones (1971) challenges this verdict.

The general thesis of this chapter is that the historiographic question about the form and content of *Life and Labour* is misconceived and that the historiographic answers are misleading. As this chapter's alternative reading will demonstrate, the form of the text is classificatory. It is therefore unprofitable to debate whether the text realises some general form of empirical investigation. In terms of content, the alternative reading will demonstrate, first, that the text is not simply about poverty or some such master-theme and, second, that reference to poverty or unemployment cannot be abstracted from a longer chain of reference. In *Life and Labour*, reference does not converge on to historiography's chosen themes and this chapter's alternative reading will try to recover the divergent character of the chains of reference around poverty and unemployment.

Historians have been obsessed with the question of whether *Life and*

Labour can be enrolled as a precursor of modern social investigation of poverty. Ironically, they have completely ignored another Booth text, the *Aged Poor* (1894), which uses the methods of systematic empiricism to investigate pauperism. The *Aged Poor* is discussed in an appendix to this chapter.

General form

This section examines the form of *Life and Labour*'s investigation. It begins by considering existing historiographic readings of the text's form by the Simeys, Stedman Jones, and Brown. The section then goes on to present an alternative reading of form which emphasises the role of taxonomy and classification.

The Simeys characterise Booth as an empirical social investigator and they even claim that he is a 'great sociologist' (Simey and Simey, 1960, p. 247). They justify this claim by referring to the form of *Life and Labour*, which approaches the ideal form of scientific investigation. There is one true scientific method involving movement between fact and theory in a virtuous circle. The natural sciences exemplify this method and the resulting form of discourse (Simey and Simey, 1960, p. 242). Before *Life and Labour*, social analysis had been 'cut . . . off from its empirical roots and dependent upon *a priori* speculation and deductive reasoning' (Simey and Simey, 1960, p. 252). *Life and Labour*, or at least the poverty series volumes, tried to 'place a firm foundation of evidence under theories relating to social structure and behaviour, as had already been accomplished more than two centuries before in the natural sciences' (Simey and Simey, 1960, p. 254). In these terms, the poverty series was a qualified success despite breakdowns in the fact to theory circuit which allowed in proposals for segregating the poor in labour colonies (Simey and Simey, 1960, p. 195), and despite an inadequate theoretical framework which led to the accumulation of 'vast numbers of facts' (Simey and Simey, 1960, p. 196). For the Simeys, the other relevant methodological consideration is the investigator's attitude. The proper scientific attitude is to suppress value judgments; Booth creditably tried to do this although he was not always successful. For example, a bias against socialism can be detected in his work, but at least his survey results conflicted with, and therefore were not governed by, his preconceptions and desires (Simey and Simey, 1960, p. 191).

Brown (1968) represents revisionism within the same general framework as the Simeys. He accepts the same ideal form of value free empirical scientificity, but places *Life and Labour* farther away from the ideal form. *Life and Labour* made a careful empirical study of all the available evidence, especially statistical, on the causes of poverty

(Brown, 1968, p. 360), but the investigation's empiricism was corrupted because of a failure on the part of the investigator. Booth 'was less conscious of his assumptions than he might have been' (Brown, 1968, p. 353). The assumptions that particularly exercise Brown are those which involve 'moral judgments' about the poor (Brown, 1968, p. 352). In these respects, Booth is typical of late nineteenth-century social investigators like the Webbs and Beveridge, who were unaware of the 'preconceptions which they brought to their social investigations and which influenced the results they obtained' (Brown, 1968, p. 350). Brown's hero is Rowntree, who 'consciously tried to avoid any un-favourable judgment of those living in poverty' (Brown, 1968, p. 350).

Stedman Jones introduces a different, Althusserian framework for describing and evaluating the form of Booth's text. The general form of Booth's text is now ideological; *Life and Labour* is theoretical ideology unified by an underlying theoretical problematic. Categorically, the discourse is not in the scientific form. From the Althusserian point of view, the task is to understand the theoretical conditions of a necessary ideological failure. *Life and Labour* is different from, but not an advance on, earlier ideology. The text represents only a moment in a movement from one ideological problematic to another, specifically from the demoralisation problematic of the 1860s to the degeneration problematic of the 1880s.

There is, however, less difference between Stedman Jones and the Simeys than there appears to be. The Stedman Jones description and evaluation of the form of ideological discourse is simply the Simey description and evaluation turned upside down. Stedman Jones (1971, p. 16) takes up an early, and not very radical, Althusserian definition of ideology as something which distorts a real referent:

A comparison of the problems posed by the ideologue (his problematic) with the *real problems* posed for the ideologue by his time, makes possible a demonstration of the truly ideological element of the ideology, that is, what characterizes ideology as such, its *deformation*. So it is not the *interiority of the problematic* which constitutes its essence but its relation to real problems: *the problematic of an* ideology cannot be demonstrated without *relating* and *submitting* it to the real problems to which its de-formed enunciation gives a false answer.

For Stedman Jones, the one vicious form of investigation is empiricism, the bad abstraction that distorts the referent. For the Simeys, the one virtuous form of investigation is empirical investigation, the good abstraction that moves in a fact to theory circuit.

In conclusion, beneath the historiographic product differentiation, there is a strong tendency towards very limited differences about the general form of Booth's text. The Simeys and Brown read the same empirical investigation and only assess its success differently. Stedman Jones's empiricist ideology is not dissimilar.

If *Life and Labour* is always the same, it is easily inserted into a series of similar empirical investigations. The textbooks bracket Booth's London survey with Rowntree's later York survey as the two pioneering empirical investigations of poverty. The monographs introduce a cross-reference to Rowntree and debate to what extent Rowntree's survey was more successful. Equally, precursors of Booth's empirical investigation can and have been fabricated, as in Cullen's analysis of the Statistical Society surveys of the 1830s and the 1840s (Cullen, 1975). These earlier surveys were empirical 'enquiries . . . to reveal to the public by means of "facts" the condition of the population' (Cullen, 1975, p. 146). Their unsuccess is analysed in a familiar way: the Statistical Society surveys were loaded with assumptions and 'major conclusions . . . were anticipated and preconceived' (Cullen, 1975, p. 146). In form, every kind of empirical investigation turns out to be much the same.

Such a conclusion is disappointingly uninformative. More radically, it can be argued that historiography's analysis of the Booth text and of the other texts has completely miscarried. To establish this point, it is necessary to identify what has gone wrong. The basic problem is that in the readings already considered, empiricist epistemology provides a set of categories that dominate historiographic analysis of the texts of social investigation. This epistemology constructs how *Life and Labour* works, because it provides the concepts of the key operations and components of the text: 'fact', 'hypothesis', 'theory', and 'test'. The first half of this book showed how empiricism increasingly provides a rationale for, and model of, current historiographic investigation of the past. We can now see that empiricism also supplies a grid for reading and evaluating past social investigation. This second pretension is as unacceptable as the first which has already been demolished. Specifically, there are two main reasons why empiricist epistemology should not play a grid role in readings of past social investigations. First, the raw materials of social investigation are never 'facts', because these raw materials always have a more specific identity which generally has significant repercussions within the investigation. Second, empiricist epistemology recognises, and approves, only one way of processing raw materials, that is, by 'testing'. But the processing of raw materials can be undertaken in many different ways and the design of investigative projects is much more mutable than empiricism supposes. These general, abstract points will now be illustrated by a reading of *Life and Labour*, which will consider in turn raw materials and the processing of them.

The investigation in *Life and Labour* depended on two kinds of raw materials: first, official statistics on overcrowding, birth rates, death rates, occupations, etc.; and second, information supplied by those set in administrative authority over the poor. In this respect, there was a break between the industry series and the poverty series. The treatment of overcrowding in the later industry series relied heavily upon official statistics after material from the 1891 *Census* had been released to Booth. The earlier poverty series relied on information supplied by those set in administrative authority over the poor. The original household classification of those in poverty depended upon information supplied by the school board visitors. Some three to four years later ('Poverty', vol. 2, p. 230), these results were revised and reworked as a street classification for the second volume of the poverty series, with the aid of additional information supplied by school teachers, Anglican clergy, agents of the Charity Organisation Society, poor law relieving officers, and police constables ('Poverty', vol. 2, pp. 16-17). At the end of the investigation, the street classification was finally revised with the aid of policemen ('Religion', vol. 1, p. 6). It is the reliance on this type of information that defines one of the peculiarities of Booth's investigation; Booth talked to those set in administrative authority over the poor while Mayhew talked to the poor and Rowntree let the concepts do the talking.

The specific identity of the raw materials is important because it had significant effects upon the investigation. The information supplied by the school board visitors, who were the main informants on poverty, necessarily did not cover the whole population. *Life and Labour* claimed that these officers attained a breadth of view which was denied to agencies dealing with distress ('Poverty', vol. 1, p. 147), but it was obstinately true that their view was circumscribed by their administrative responsibilities as 'whippers-in' for compulsory schooling. The school board visitors only directly knew those families with schoolchildren, a group amounting to between half and two-thirds of the population ('Poverty', vol. 1, p. 26). Doubtless, they only knew well the much smaller group of families who failed to send their children to school regularly.

The condition of families with schoolchildren was hardly representative of the whole population, because children were an economic liability – at least until the eldest child began to earn. This point was conceded at the end of the industry series where the text described what was later conceptualised as life-cycle poverty ('Industry', vol. 5, pp. 321-3). Nevertheless, in calculating the percentage in poverty or in various sub-groups of the poor, Booth explicitly assumed that the condition of those with schoolchildren was representative of the whole: 'I have, however, assumed, that as is the condition of the tested part . . . so is the condition of the whole population' ('Poverty', vol. 1, p. 5; see also, 'Poverty', vol. 2, p. 16). This procedure was defended with the argument that it was better to overstate rather than understate poverty ('Poverty', vol. 1, p. 5). The effect was that all Booth's measurements of poverty and of sub-groups among the poor contained an uncertain margin of overstatement.

The processing of raw materials is a complicated issue because it raises questions about methodological aspirations and substantive achievements. There is often a disjuncture between the methodological credo and what is actually done in a text, which is not necessarily in accord with the prescriptions of one or any methodology. Some of these complications can be illustrated by reference to *Life and Labour*.

At the level of epistemological credo, Booth subscribed in a naïvely empiricist way to the importance of accumulating facts and suppressing bias. But this credo does not appear to have much connection with what is done in the text. In any case, there is more than one methodological strand in the text. A chapter of the first volume of the poverty series was devoted to an analysis of family expenditure patterns ('Poverty', vol. 1, pp. 133–46). This was in accord with Booth's credo that the statistics of the extensive method were profoundly uninstructive unless complemented by a Le Play type of intensive investigation into family lives. Booth (1896, p. 11) later observed that without such intensive investigation,

> the most imposing statistical array would be comparatively
> barren of teaching, because lacking the material needed to
> place the unit of the household in the framing of home, of
> training, of individual environment, of habit, of influence
> and of character that its proper comprehension would
> demand.

Although a programmatic empiricism and a Le Play type 'intensive method' may have complicated matters, one 'method' was practically dominant from the beginning of the poverty series to the end of the industry series. Classification may not be overdeveloped in Booth's methodological credo, but when it came to understanding or explaining anything, *Life and Labour* almost always began by classifying the raw material. Thus, classification provided a framework for the whole investigation. To be more exact, in the poverty and industry series, six successive classifications provided a matrix for the investigation. In this sense *Life and Labour*'s discourse was taxonomic in form. This point can be illustrated by outlining the six major classifications of life and labour in the order in which they are presented in the first nine volumes.

1   The household classification

Volume one of the poverty series offered a household classification, which had been previewed in Booth's earlier articles. A pilot study of Tower Hamlets (Booth, 1887) already used the classificatory system of the first volume of the poverty series. The household classification dealt with London district by district. In the first part of the volume, the prime object of concern was east London but later sections dealt comparatively with central, north, and south London. School board visitors supplied the information for the inquiry. The units for classification were the individual households which were divided by sections and classes ('Poverty', vol. 1, pp. 34-5): they were divided into thirty-nine 'sections', according to the 'character of employment' of the head of family; and they were divided into eight classes A to H according to the 'means and position' of the head of family.

The first six sections ('Poverty', vol. 1, p. 34) divided 'ordinary' unskilled labour according to period of hire, type and regularity of work, and wage level:

1 'lowest class, loafers, etc.'
2 'casual day-to-day labour'
3 'irregular labour'
4 'regular work, low pay'
5 'regular work, ordinary pay'
6 'foremen and responsible work'

Labour in the remaining sections was classified according to specific competence and industrial attachment: for example, section seven was building trades artisans and section eight was furniture trade artisans.

The other division is the class division into eight classes ('Poverty', vol. 1, p. 33) as follows:

A 'the lowest class of occasional labourers, loafers and semi-criminals'
B 'casual earnings – very poor'
C 'intermittent earnings'
D 'small regular earnings' 'together the poor'
E 'regular standard earnings – above the line of poverty'
F 'higher class labour'
G 'lower middle class'
H 'upper middle class'

The results of the household classification were about classes and sections. The conclusions of volume one were partly about the size of the different classes in the East End of London. Booth demonstrated the insignificance of the disorderly class A which made up under 1.5 per cent of population and the worrying size of class B, the casual earners who made up over 10 per cent of population ('Poverty', vol. 1, pp. 37-44). A revisionist historiography, preoccupied with Booth's adverse value judgments of class B, has emphasised the class division. Against this, it must be insisted that volume one's conclusions also concerned employment sections and the interrelation between classes and sections. For example, because class and section divisions did not co-incide, it was possible to calculate the recruitment of classes from sections. Thus, less than half of class B were casual labourers and other sections contributed significantly when 10 per cent of class B were building and furniture artisans and another 10 per cent were female-headed families with young children ('Poverty', vol. 1, p. 40).

2   The street classification

Volume two of the poverty series offered a second classification, the street classification. There are significant differences between the first and second classifications which are blurred in historiography. The information for the inquiry was again supplied by school board visitors, but the second classification reviewed London as a whole rather than by district and the unit for classification was the street rather than the household. This change was made to lighten the load of work when London as a whole was being considered ('Poverty', vol. 2, p. 3). Never-theless, the change had significant repercussions. The employment classification and cross-reference had to be dropped because, unlike heads of households, streets could not be assigned to employment sections ('Poverty', vol. 2, p. 3). At the same time, the class grouping had to be simplified. Classes C and D, the irregular and the low paid, had to be bracketed and presented as one group because the separation of the irregular from the low paid required data on unemployment which was not calculated on a street basis ('Poverty', vol. 2, pp. 20-1).

London's working-class streets were thus assigned to four class groups ('Poverty', vol. 2, p. 20):

A   'the lowest class - occasional labourers, loafers and semi-criminals'

B   'the very poor - casual labour, hand-to-mouth existence, chronic want'

C, D   'the poor - including alike those whose earnings are small, because of irregularity of employment, and those whose work, though regular, is ill-paid'

E, F   'the regularly employed and fairly paid working class of all grades'

This classification was again slightly modified by the introduction of a hybrid 'mixed with poverty' category when the results were represented on a London street map. Seven shades of colour were used on the map to indicate the general condition of the inhabitants of each street ('Poverty', vol. 2, pp. 40-1).

black	'the lowest grade'	A
dark blue	'very poor'	B
light blue	'standard poverty'	C, D
purple	'mixed with poverty'	C, D, + E, F, perhaps B
pink	'working-class comfort'	E, F

red   'well-to-do'
yellow   'wealthy'

With the employment cross-reference removed, and the class groupings simplified, there was a much stronger emphasis on the dividing line between poverty and comfort. The result was the conclusion about London as a whole for which *Life and Labour* is still best remembered: 30.7 per cent of London's population lived in poverty and 69.3 per cent in comfort ('Poverty', vol. 2, p. 22). This is the result that is preserved in all the older textbooks on the welfare state.

3   The schoolchildren classification

Volume three of the poverty series presented a third classification, the classification of schoolchildren. If historiography blurs the first two *Life and Labour* classifications, it virtually ignores the third classification; this is the forgotten poverty classification. The information for the inquiry was supplied by school teachers ('Poverty', vol. 3, p. 195). Individuals were no longer classified; children were not individually assigned into a category as households and streets had been. This inquiry obtained 'general statements from the school teachers about the condition of children in their school classes' ('Poverty', vol. 3, p. 201). Furthermore, only a sample of schools returned such statements ('Poverty', vol. 3, p. 196). As for groups, children were assigned to the simplified classes that had already been used in the street classification ('Poverty', vol. 3, p. 200):

A   'lowest class'
B   'very poor'
C + D   'poverty'
E + F   'comfort'

The results of the schoolchildren classification were thus directly comparable with the results of the immediately preceding street classification. But the result of the schoolchildren classification was significantly different and deserves to be remembered. According to the schoolchildren classification, 45 per cent of London's population were in poverty ('Poverty', vol. 3, p. 200).

4   The overcrowding classification

Volume one of the industry series introduced a new and completely different classification of social condition in terms of 'rooms occupied' or 'servants kept'. 1891 census information on crowding provided the basis for this new classification ('Industry', vol. 1, pp. 1–2). Individuals and households were both classified so that the results could be expressed as a percentage of total population or a percentage of households. The whole population was divided according to the number of rooms occupied or servants kept. The working class divided into six classes according to number of persons per room and number of rooms occupied. Thus, the working class living independently in households was classified ('Industry', vol. 1, p. 9) as follows:

1 + 2	3 or more persons per room
3	2–3 persons per room
4	1–2 persons per room
5	less than 1 person per room
6	occupying more than four rooms

Classes one to four were bracketed as 'lower class' and classes five and six were bracketed as 'central class' ('Industry', vol. 1, pp. 2–3). An 'upper class' of servant-keepers was sub-divided into classes, from a to h, according to number of persons served by each servant. The results concerned the size of the various sub-groups, especially classes one to three, who were overcrowded according to a criterion of more than two persons per room. On this basis, 31.5 per cent of London's population was crowded and 68.5 per cent was not crowded.

5   The trades classification

Volume one of the industry series took up again the question of classification by employment which had been dropped at the end of the first volume of the poverty series. The poverty series division into thirty-nine employment sections had adopted a curious dual principle of classification; some London workers were classified according to hiring or wage level and others were classified according to industrial attachment. Comparison and cross-reference from London to national employment patterns was impossible when the census, as far as possible, classified workers solely by industrial attachment. For comparative purposes, one of Booth's Statistical Society articles had used a modified census framework (Booth, 1888, pp. 305–8). The trades classification in the first volume of the industry series marked a final reconciliation with census categories and principles of classification.

The basis for the trades classification in the industry series was provided by 1891 census information on occupations. Both the individual and the family were classified under a double system of enumeration ('Industry', vol. 1, p. 25): under 'system A', all occupied persons were classified according to occupation; under 'system B', each family was classified according to the employment status of its head. Trades and occupations were divided into eighty-nine sections along a primary, secondary, and tertiary axis as in the census. Thus sections one to nine covered building and included nine occupations: architects, builders, masons, bricklayers, carpenters, plasterers, painters, plumbers, and gas-fitters ('Industry', vol. 1, p. 24). The results were the familiar census-type conclusions about numbers engaged in particular employments with the refinement that Booth counted both families and individuals.

6 The earning classification

For the first time, Booth obtained and published data on wages in the industry series. This information was the basis for one more classification – the earnings classification. The wage data were obtained in 1893, four years after the publication of the poverty series. Wherever possible, data were obtained on actual earnings in an average week from 'the best class of firms' in each trade ('Industry', vol. 1, p. 27). This was supplemented by Board of Trade returns for 1886-7 which covered wages for a full week's work, but, even with this supplementation, there remained gaps in the information. For each trade where data were available, earnings were divided into bands such as 'under twenty shillings', 'twenty to twenty-five shillings', and so forth. The results concerned absolute and relative numbers in a particular trade within each band. Thus ('Industry', vol. 1, p. 165) 2.5 per cent of building trades workers earned less than 20 shillings per week and 8 per cent earned between 20 and 25 shillings per week. Given the deficiencies of the available data, there was no possibility of generalisation about the wages of the whole working-class population.

In *Life and Labour*, the population of London is endlessly divided by one classification after another. A running commentary on the six classifications has already indicated many points where a historiography which is concerned with 'facts', 'theory', and 'value judgments' has misrepresented some of the classifications and ignored others. More generally, historiography has completely missed the point about the strategic role of classificatory frameworks in *Life and Labour*. In an article that appeared after this chapter had been drafted, Hennock (1976) does place some emphasis on Booth's classifications. But he misrepresents the role of classification in *Life and Labour* for two reasons. First, Hennock identifies the text *Life and Labour* with the original two-volume edition of 1889, rather than the definitive seventeen-volume edition of 1902-3. In effect, he reads only the first two volumes of the poverty series and therefore considers only two of Booth's six classifications. Second, Hennock presents classificatory organisation as a general property present in all statistical material; in Booth's work 'as with any set of figures, it is the classification that matters' (Hennock, 1976, p. 75; see also pp. 72-3). This misses the point about the way in which classification defines the particular form of Booth's discourse.

Even if Hennock's claims about the universal importance of classification are rejected, the reconceptualisations proposed in various chapters of this book could easily create misunderstanding about the general importance of classification in nineteenth-century social investigation and institutional practice. Classification is a theme that has already appeared in several chapters. The last chapter showed that, even if Mayhew never filled the empty boxes, classifications of one sort or another were important in all his investigations. Furthermore, in the first half of this book, the analysis of the poor law after 1870 showed that classification and treatment of paupers was a strand in pre-1914 relief practice. An incipient Foucauldianism might be detected in all this. Does not the argument about social investigations lead to the identification of a nineteenth-century classificatory *episteme*? If the analysis of relief practice is added, does not the argument lead towards the discovery of a classificatory strategy which unites knowledge and power?

Foucauldian analysis has already been critcised. Such analysis extracts one level from, or more exactly, constructs one level in, discourse or institutional practice and then takes this as an object for investigation. The decisive objection to this is that, whatever formal concessions it may make, the Foucauldian analysis denies plurality and divergence in the operation of texts and institutions. It ends up eliminating differences that should be conceptualised. Generally, the analyses proposed in various chapters of this book are not of the Foucauldian type and do not lead to the Foucauldian destination. Classification may be a theme in Victorian social investigation and poor law practice, but it is articulated and worked out in different ways. The analyses in different chapters recover these differences as much as, or more than, the common theme.

With this general point established, it is possible and necessary to return to the particular issue of *Life and Labour* and nineteenth-century social investigation. A Foucauldian approach would be particularly disastrous here. This section attacks the notion that *Life and Labour* is part of a series of texts which can usefully be conceptualised as similar, more or less successful, 'empirical investigations'. It would obviously not resolve anything simply to re-label the series of texts as classificatory investigations. But this kind of label change can only be avoided by establishing differences between various classificatory investigations. So, at this point, the individuality of *Life and Labour*'s investigation will be established by differentiating it from the Statistical Society surveys of the 1840s which were also classificatory. The Statistical Society *Journal* published seven surveys of a similar kind between 1838 and 1848 (Heywood, 1838; Fripp, 1839; Manchester Statistical Society, 1839; London Statistical Society, 1840; Manchester Statistical Society, 1842; Weld, 1843; London Statistical Society, 1848).

The raw materials for these surveys were the replies to a 'schedule of queries' which was completed after house-to-house inquiry by a paid agent. Individual queries concerned particular issues like water supply, number of beds, or books. The queries came in thematic clusters defining areas of concern such as domestic circumstances, bodily health, and moral condition. A completed schedule was a kind of sequential check-list for describing the relationship of each family in a parish to its material and moral environment. The schedule of queries was always substantially the same in the social surveys of the 1830s and the 1840s, although there were differences of detail, as when one survey would consider newspapers read as well as the books in working-class homes. Processing of raw materials was equally stereotyped in all the surveys of the 1830s and 1840s. The classic end result of a Statistical Society survey was a synopsis in tabular form with an accompanying text giving only a brief commentary upon the figures. Up to twenty individual tables summarised responses to the more important queries. Thus, the Bristol survey (Fripp, 1839, p. 371) dealt with books in working-class homes as follows:

	Number	%
Families having religious books (Bible or prayer book or both)	3,430	57.4
Families having other books or tracts or parts of the same	947	15.8
Families not having any books or tracts, including two not ascertained	1,604	26.5

In the Statistical Society surveys there was endless tabular enumeration, but there was almost no cross-reference between the different tables. Thus, in the Bristol survey, it was possible to consult tables on education, and to determine the proportion of children attending school (Fripp, 1839, p. 373). However, the tables on education were not connected or cross-referenced to other tables on occupation or religious denomination and it was impossible to determine how school attendance varied with, for example, parental occupation.

Life and Labour is obviously different from the Statistical Society surveys in terms of raw materials and processing. The replies to queries of the 1840s are unlike *Life and Labour's* official statistics or the information supplied by those set in administrative authority over the poor. The tabular enumerations are unlike *Life and Labour's* more analytic classifications. The difference about the connection of different results is not so obvious, but perhaps more important. Except in the 1848 Saint George in the East parish survey, the Statistical Society tables were unconnected. *Life and Labour* obsessively pursued connections of one sort or another between different classifications.

Life and Labour's first interconnection established an explanatory cross-reference between different classifications of how people lived and worked. This was the purpose of the double division by classes and by employment sections, in the household classification in the first volume of the poverty series. The text never relinquished this project. The industry series interrelated on a trade-by-trade basis, first, a classification of earnings, and second, a classification of overcrowding which was used as a proxy for social condition and style of life ('Industry', vol. 5, p. 14). *Life and Labour*'s second interconnection established a corroborative cross-reference between the independently obtained results of different classifications. Here, the prime exhibit was the correspondence between the results of the overcrowding classification, with 31.5 per cent crowded and the results of the street classification, with 30.7 per cent in poverty ('Industry', vol. 1, p. 10). The text argued for a 'startling similarity of results' obtained by the new classification to those shown in the original classification ('Industry', vol. 1, p. 10).

Ultimately, in the final volume of *Life and Labour*, the significant results from the different classifications were brought together in an attempt to show a general pattern of joint variation. The centrepiece was the 'table of districts arranged in order of social conditions' ('Conclusion', p. 17), which showed that the rank order of fifty London districts was not so very different whether poverty, crowding, birth rate, or death rate was considered. The point about joint variation was reinforced graphically by a 'chart showing comparative social condition of London in 50 districts as tested by poverty and crowding, combined with birth and death rates' ('Conclusion', p. 18). Other things being equal, a poor district was also an overcrowded district where many early marriages would produce a high birth rate, and then a high death rate as many of the births were culled by high infant mortality. The joint variation is such that the final column of Booth's table is a 'combined order'. At this point right at the end of the work, interconnection produces a final multi-dimensional composite measure of social conditions.

In the Statistical Society surveys an absence of connection limited the discoveries which could be made in, or the use which could be made of, the surveys. The 1840s survey was simply a rag-bag holding an assortment of results on various issues. It is not surprising that these surveys had a short discursive life when they had no advantage over the economical alternative of collecting statistics on individual issues as and when required. Forty years later, by emphasising interconnection Booth made the social survey viable as an investigative form. There were distinct advantages in a survey which tackled several issues simultaneously in a classificatory way so that different results could explicate and corroborate each other.

If new interconnections made the survey form viable, they did not make the survey into a thoroughly virtuous mode of social investigation. Paradoxically, the immediate reason for this was that *Life and Labour* overdid the demonstration of interrelation, corroboration, and joint variation of the classifications. The question of corroboration between classifications nicely illustrates the way in which the text secured an impression of agreement by dubious means.

The crucial cross-check was between the results of the street classification and those of the schoolchildren classification. These two classifications used exactly the same class categories, with the population independently assigned to class groups on the basis of two different opinions, the school board visitors' opinion in the street classification, and the school teachers' opinion in the schoolchildren classification. The two opinions did not agree; the school teachers put half as many again into groups A to D as did the school board visitors. There was a large discrepancy between 45.0 per cent of the population in poverty, according to the school teachers, and 30.7 per cent in poverty, according to the school board visitors ('Poverty', vol. 3, p. 200). The text tried but could not satisfactorily explain this discrepancy ('Poverty', vol. 3, pp. 200–1) when there was no good reason why all the sources of error in the schoolchildren classification should have invariably operated in one direction, leading to an exaggeration of the numbers in poverty.

By the opening section of the final volume, the text had conveniently forgotten the crucial cross-check and the discrepant result. It chose instead to discuss the results which apparently did corroborate each other: the results of the street classification by classes, the overcrowding classification by number of persons per room, and the earnings classification into income bands. By coincidence, the percentage crowded two or more to a room came to within 0.8 per cent of the percentage in poverty in classes A to D. However, this was hardly firm corroboration because the crowding criterion was conventional and, if it had been set higher or lower than two per room, it would have taken in a different percentage. The text simply showed that if a two per room criterion of crowding was used, this cut off 30 per cent of the population. Coincidentally, the street classification showed exactly the same percentage were in poverty. Where coincidence did not occur, there is a strong suspicion that the dividing lines were rigged to produce spurious corroboration. In the street classification, Booth had defined the income level of the 30 per cent in classes A to D as 18 to 21 shillings per week for a moderate family ('Poverty', vol. 1, p. 33; vol. 2, p. 40). When data on earnings were finally collected, however, less than 30 per cent were found to be earning 21 shillings or less per week. To remove the discrepancy, the income line was adjusted upwards in an *ad hoc* way to 'nominal earnings' of from 25 to 30 shillings ('Industry', vol. 5, p. 15). *Life and Labour* had some good arguments for adjusting the line upwards to allow for irregularity and wages lower than those returned. Nevertheless, these adjustments cannot be trusted when they are always made to remove discrepancies.

The corroborations are spurious and this is ultimately as much of a burden for Booth's survey as non-connection was for earlier social surveys. The aim here is not to abuse Booth. The point about the interconnecting classifications and their spuriousness is made to establish the specificity of the form of Booth's discourse. Praise and blame is, of course, an obsession in orthodox historiographic readings of *Life and Labour*. It will now be argued that, if Booth is blamed in the conventional empiricist terms our understanding of the text is limited.

In the historiographic readings outlined at the beginning of this section, empiricist epistemology does more than provide a set of concepts for describing the key operations and components of discourse as 'theory', 'text', 'fact', and so forth. This epistemology also provides a set of criteria for evaluating discourses. First, the virtuous discourse is that which moves through the operations of theoretical testing which are supposed to exist in empiricist epistemology. Second, the virtuous discourse is that in which value judgments are suppressed. Both criteria must be rejected. It has already been argued in the first half of this book that the operation of testing is not rational in its own terms, that is, testing does not produce probable or certain knowledge about causal connection. It therefore does not matter whether any discourse jumps through the hoops specified by Popper or Carnap. As for value freedom, the next chapter will discuss this issue and will argue both generally, and with specific reference to Rowntree's work, that value free discourse is either a chimera or a fraud.

Here, it is only necessary to make a simple supplementary point about Booth's supposed 'value judgments'. As we have seen, historiography condemns Booth's value judgments about the different classes which were discriminated in the original household classification and then carried over, in simplified form, into the street and schoolchildren classifications. These judgments, especially the adverse judgments of class B, are deprecated and treated as lapses. Against this, it will now be argued that these value judgments are part and parcel of the text and necessary at certain points in the classificatory analysis.

The principle(s) of classification are a general problem in all classificatory discourses. *Life and Labour* was no exception. The text struggled painfully to find a basis for the household classification division into classes. Some divisions came easily; in the case of pariah groups like 'the savages' in class A or 'the leisure class' in class B, *Life and Labour* simply appropriates definitions of social problem groups which were conventional by the 1880s. It is significant that Booth used the notion of a residuum in one of his papers which pre-dated the London survey; there was 'a natural deposit in great towns of those who are too helpless to get away' (Booth, 1886, p. 331). But *Life and Labour*'s class schema went beyond such conventional discriminations to make more complicated and novel discriminations between six classes from A to F. The key point here is that the six classes were not discriminated according to one master classificatory principle, but according to at least three different principles. *Life and Labour* argued that the six classes were distinct: first, according to their situation in the labour market, second, according to their domestic economy, and third, according to their moral character.

Initially, when the A to F classification was enunciated, the individual classes were distinguished according to their place in the labour market or, more exactly, according to regularity of employment and wage level. Lives at this stage hardly figured except in so far as they interacted with labour. Thus class D of small regular wage earners was characterised ('Poverty', vol. 1, pp. 49-50) as follows:

As a general rule these men have a hard struggle to make ends meet, but they are, as a body, decent steady men, paying their way and bringing up their children respectably.
The work they do demands little skill or intelligence.

Later chapters of the first volume increasingly emphasised that the lives of the various classes were distinct. In a first supplementary investigation of differences between the classes, family expenditure patterns were analysed ('Poverty', vol. 1, pp. 133-46). The aim was to show that each class had a separate expenditure pattern. Class B was distinguished by its characteristic domestic economy. This was a marginal class whose income was absorbed by necessary expenditure so that food had to be stinted and rent unpaid if clothes and household things were to be bought.

In a second and final attempt to redefine the distinctness of the classes, the text presented the results of a 'participant observation' investigation. Booth lived as a lodger with classes B, C, D and E, 'shared the lives of the people' ('Poverty', vol. 1, p. 158), and thus obtained new information about domestic economy - food, clothing, household accommodation, furnishings, and occupations of wives and children were all fairly systematically recorded. Class B was again characterised in terms of its domestic economy. This class lived in 'miserable and unsavoury' homes whose outward and visible sign was the window which was broken or patched and dirty with never a respectable curtain ('Industry', vol. 5, p. 326). The staple food of class B was bread and, as for clothing, 'this class may almost be distinguished by its deplorable boots' ('Industry', vol. 5, p. 327). Above this level, there were several different domestic economies. For example, in Class D the people were creditably dressed and houseproud and puddings a regular institution, while in class E, meat and vegetables appeared every day, people showed skill in their cookery and the clothes were new rather than second-hand.

On the basis of personal experience, lodger Booth was also able to give every district class a testimonial, a kind of moral characterisation. This is where the historians' favourite quotation about class B fits in:

'the most prevailing characteristic is incompetence which may be due to age or illness, but is often aggravated by indulgence in alcohol' ('Industry', vol. 5, p. 325). This was a kind of adverse character reference. And 'they are most likely incapable of permanent improvement' was the referee's ultimate put down ('Industry', vol. 5, p. 326). When different classes got different testimonials, each class was as distinct in terms of moral character as in domestic economy.

In conclusion, *Life and Labour*'s classifications were not Linnaean; the first volume division into classes was not based on variation in an *a priori* selected, analytically defined set of features like the number of stamens and styles. Differences in 'manner of life' were introduced as part of an attempt to vindicate the original labour divisions and the classificatory divisions became dependent on descriptive and evaluative material rather than simple variation of analytic features. This was the way the class division worked and it would be absurd to deprecate the evaluative material. The value judgments were not an indulgence or lapse, since they had a positive function in justifying the division of classes. If the 'value judgments' were excised, the division into classes would be correspondingly difficult to sustain.

Specific content

In considering the thematic content of *Life and Labour,* this section will begin by looking at the accounts of the text's content provided by the Simeys, Brown, and Stedman Jones.

In the historiographical readings of *Life and Labour*'s content, there is, again, surface disagreement and underlying agreement. To begin with, all the historians ask one basic question of the text: does *Life and Labour* anticipate the virtuous modern definition of the nature of the social problem, its environmental causes, and collectivist solutions? Historians obtain different answers to this question by concentrating on different themes and different classificatory divisions in *Life and Labour.*

For the Simeys, *Life and Labour*'s problem was poverty in the modern sense of the term. Poverty was 'the central objective of his inquiry' (Simey and Simey, 1960, p. 3), whose master question was: 'why were there poor people in a relatively rich society?' (Simey and Simey, 1960, p. 197). Booth's intention was 'to demonstrate once and for all that the incidence of poverty could be measured with some precision' (Simey and Simey, 1960, p. 178). His great achievement here was the introduction of the concept of the poverty line (Simey and Simey, 1960, p. 184). The crucial division therefore cut off 30 per cent of population, in classes A to D, as those who were in poverty. The corollary of a shift in problem was a shift in cause away from character and towards environment. For the Simeys, the key index of this shift was the table in the poverty series which showed questions of employment to be the dominant cause of poverty (Simey and Simey, 1960, pp. 4 and 181). The text even reached a second series of hypotheses that 'embodied the more complicated generalisation that poverty could be regarded as a facet of the structure of society'. At the same time, although Booth himself was never a whole-hearted collectivist, the new analysis of the social problem opened up the possibility of a collective solution to the problems of poverty, initially through old-age pensions (Simey and Simey, 1960, p. 190).

Brown obtains a different and less modern Booth, by concentrating on a different theme, Booth's analysis of unemployment. The Simeys incidentally concede the failure of Booth's analysis of unemployment. Brown simply examines this failure in greater detail. The argument is that *Life and Labour* did not reach a modern definition, explanation, or solution of the social problem of unemployment. The text never isolated fluctuations in the total volume of employment as a cause of unemployment but remained fixated on 'its permanent presence as a result of the competition for work at the lowest social levels' (Brown, 1968, p. 359). Unitary with this failure to reach a modern problem definition was a continuing stress on 'character' in the explanation of poverty. Brown stresses the adverse descriptions of the poor and emphasises that *Life and Labour* only introduced an environmental explanation of their character deficiency; 'it was their environment and especially their constant struggle for work not personal viciousness nor moral frailty which had degraded' (Brown, 1968, p. 353). Again the text's collectivism is seen as unitary with its problem definition. Booth proposed the entire removal of his class B, some 10 per cent of the population, into labour colonies. This was neither retrograde nor aberrant, given Booth's moralistic problem definition; 'Booth's solution to general poverty is understandable in the light of his description of the poor' (Brown, 1968, p. 353).

Stedman Jones obtains a different and less modern Booth by concentrating attention on a different classificatory division. For the Simeys, the key division cuts off classes A to D, the bottom 30 per cent of population. For Stedman Jones, the key division cuts off classes A and B, the bottom 10 per cent of population. In *Life and Labour*, 'the real problem' was the nature and condition of the casual labourers in class B (Stedman Jones, 1971, p. 306). Booth's work in the 'degeneration problematic' was preoccupied with a type of chronic poverty that is not a modern concern. Stedman Jones sets up character/environment and individualism/collectivism transitions of the sort supposed by Brown. Thus, moral considerations about character were still invoked to explain poverty; with the shift to degeneration, 'the traditional distinction between the deserving and the undeserving remained a central tenet of middle-class philosophy' (Stedman Jones, 1971, p. 285). The novelty was that the deficiencies of the undeserving were now seen to be a result of the 'urban environment' (Stedman Jones, 1971, pp. 313–4). At the same time, the collectivism of Booth and his contemporaries was of an 1880s type. Stedman Jones notes Booth's proposal for labour colonies for the bottom 10 per cent, and assistance such as non-contributory old-age pensions for those above. The basic idea was to draw 'a clearer distinction . . . between the "true" working class and the casual residuum so as to preserve the existing social system' (Stedman Jones, 1971, p. 301).

The historiographic accounts of the specific content of *Life and Labour* raise almost as many issues as the historiographic accounts of general form. To begin with, the radical divorce of form and content is in itself dubious. The divorce is necessary to historiography because its discourse analysis operates with a cosmic category of empirical form which is always the same, and of content which is always different, and thus establishes the individuality of the different discourses. On any more subtle reading of Booth's investigation, the radical divorce of form and content collapses. This chapter only accepts the division as an expository device. The taxonomic material already considered is not contentless form, and the themes considered in the remainder of this chapter are defined by the divisions along, and the interconnections among, the axes of classification. But, for purposes of exposition, it is convenient to pursue historiography's errors by considering the material as 'form' so as to dispose of Booth's 'empirical method' and then separately to consider 'content' in terms of chains of reference around the concept of poverty.

Historiography's questions about this content are, as we have seen, questions about Booth's anticipation of, or difference from, modern concepts and problem definitions. The earlier discussion of Mayhew should have already made the point that such questions are usually unprofitable. The criticism in this section will be more specifically concerned with how historians can produce an answer to their questions about anticipation. How can a historian decide that the text is about the 30 per cent in poverty, or about the 10 per cent in chronic poverty? Or again, how can a historian decide that unemployment is a separable aspect of the text? These decisions depend on certain conventional procedures for constructing textual reference. Underlying such procedures for constructing reference are certain assumptions about the organisation of reference in texts. The basic assumption is that textual reference is organised in a convergent way. Within the field of this basic assumption, there are different positions about the extent of convergence and therefore about the internal organisation of the text. If reference is organised in a convergent way through the whole text, the text becomes one object-centred unity. If, more modestly, reference is organised in a convergent way in parts of texts, the text becomes a collection of modules or smaller unities.

The object and module variants on the basic assumption are classically represented by the Simeys and Brown. On the Simeys' account of the poverty series, reference converges on to a central concept of poverty and the 30 per cent measurement. This implies that the text is an object-centred unity. Brown avoids such an assumption by choosing to discuss one thematic 'aspect' of *Life and Labour*. This choice presupposes that reference to unemployment is a kind of module within the text. Stedman Jones represents exactly the same position as the Simeys; he reads *Life and Labour* as an object-centred unity where reference converges on to chronic poverty and the 10 per cent measurement. This revisionist emphasis has become the new orthodoxy in the last few years. According to Hennock's (1976, p. 75) recent article, the division at the 10 per cent point,

> formed the most crucial conceptual device of the whole work. It enabled him [Booth] to provide an analysis of what he considered to be the greatest cause of poverty in London, that is, casual and irregular employment, and to suggest a remedy.

This question shows how recent revisionism has moved the supposed centre of the text and uncritically presupposes that the text does have a centre which has been misidentified.

The conservatism of Stedman Jones on this point is neither an accident nor lapse from Althusserianism. The Stedman Jones demoralisation and degeneration problematics are not subject-centred structures of the sort that Althusser discerned in high theory. However, the Stedman Jones problematics are object-centred unities and, in that respect, orthodoxly Althusserian. Predictably, Stedman Jones reiterates the orthodox Althusserian criticism of the history of ideas for one-sided abstraction of elements: 'looking forward to the welfare state', an earlier generation of historians selected the modern elements in collectivist proposals, old-age pensions rather than labour colonies (Stedman Jones, 1971, p. 313). Equally predictably, Stedman Jones is silent about the organisation of the Althusserian totality. In so far as this totality is an object-centred unity, Althusser formalised the assumption of the history of ideas about the organisation of textual reference.

Against this it must be argued that textual reference is always, or sometimes, organised on divergent lines. The radical position would be that divergence is constitutive of textual reference, just as polysemy is. The cautious position would be that divergent or convergent organisations of reference are both possible and that reading should situate individual texts between these ideal poles. It is not necessary to resolve this general difference of position before reading *Life and Labour*. At least in this one text, *Life and Labour*, reference does not converge on to a master object and is not organised into neat modular unities. This thesis can be vindicated by presenting an alternative reading of *Life and Labour*. Like every other the alternative reading has to cut off reference at some point; the text is never exhausted. But this alternative reading tries to make the cuts in a different way so that the organisation of reference in the text is not pre-judged. This alternative would concretely establish the violence of the historiographic pre-judgment whereby reference which does not converge on the historian's chosen problem of X is rearranged into convergence, or eliminated from the reading, or treated as an index of original failure in the text.

Several problem groups and social problems are defined by the developing classificatory frameworks of *Life and Labour*. This is only what might be expected from the discussion of 'form' in the previous section; put in another way, the frameworks specified by successive classifications define a limited play of polysemy.

The alternative reading can begin by considering the way in which the first volume's household classification placed four distinct groups, A, B, C and D, below the poverty line. A and B established definitions of the social problem as something other than poverty. The existence of class A involved the problem of disorder and fears that 'the hordes of barbarians . . . issuing from their slums, will one day overwhelm modern civilization' ('Poverty', vol. 1, p. 39). The existence of class B involved the problem of pauperism; class B is 'the material from which paupers are made' ('Poverty', vol. 1, p. 176). A worrying tenth of East London's population was 'incapable of independent existence' up to the standard required. As for results, the first volume conclusions were more about the size of individual classes (and employment sections) than about the A to D classes aggregated to make a total in poverty. Indeed, there was radical uncertainty about what classes should be added together to make up the social problem group. Classes A to D added together made up a four-class problem group which accounted for 35 per cent of East End population 'in poverty sinking to want' ('Poverty', vol. 1, p. 62). The classes did not, however, have to be added together in this way. This is nicely illustrated in Booth's 1888 paper which previewed the volume-one results. After first bracketing A to D, Booth immediately went on to exclude class A; 'we have classes B, C and D as containing the true problem of poverty' (Booth, 1888, p. 293). This produced a three-class social problem group, in size rather less than 35 per cent of population. And in the ensuing discussion of the paper, Booth did not protest about a proposal to exclude class D (those in regular work at low wages) from the social problem group. This would have produced a different three-class social problem group, in size rather less than 20 per cent of population (Booth, 1888, pp. 334 and 339). The conclusion is obvious: it would be absurd to claim that any one division or definition of problem group was central to volume one.

If the first volume of the poverty series was not about an object called poverty, the second volume was apparently rather different. In volume two of the poverty series, with the change to the street classification, the loss of reference to employment sections and the simplification of the class system, a privileged poverty line began to emerge. This second volume finally produced the famous figure of 30 per cent of London's population in poverty ('Poverty', vol. 2, p. 30). Later in the work, 30 per cent was the figure and the division that Booth remembered and reinforced with his subsequent calculations.

Nevertheless, the second volume of the poverty series did not mark the point of arrival at an object called poverty around which reference was subsequently organised. Poverty could not play the part of object in the later volumes of *Life and Labour* for two reasons: first, *Life and Labour*'s concept and measurement of poverty was too insubstantial to act as any kind of centre; and second, the text veered away to discuss something other than poverty by a process which may be called translation. These points will now be examined and developed in turn and the concept of poverty will be discussed first.

From 1887 onwards, in connection with the London survey project, Booth produced a series of definitions of poverty that were apparently individually substantial and mutually consistent. Ostensibly, the definitions had an operational dimension which allowed a series of comparable measures of poverty. The best known of these definitions came at the beginning ('Poverty', vol. 1, p. 33) of the first volume of the poverty series:

> By the word 'poor' I mean to describe those who have a sufficiently regular though bare income such as 18–21 shillings per week for a moderate family, and by 'very poor' those who from any cause fall much below this standard. The 'poor' are those whose means may be sufficient but are barely sufficient for decent independent life; the very poor those whose means are insufficient for this according to the usual standard of life in this country. My 'poor' may be described as living under a struggle to obtain the necessaries of life and make both ends meet, while the very poor live in a state of chronic want. It may be their own fault that this is so; that is another question; my first business is simply with the numbers who, from whatever cause, do live under conditions of poverty and destitution.

Some six classifications later, a final multi-dimensional version of a poverty definition-cum-calculation was offered at the end ('Industry', vol. 5, p. 324) of the industry series:

> The result of all our inquiries make it reasonably sure that one-third of the population are on or about the line of poverty or below it, having at most an income which at one time with another averages 21s. or 22s. for a small family (or up to 25s. or 26s. for one of a large size) and in many cases falling much below this level. . . . [This] group, who are practically those who are living two or more persons to each room occupied, contains our classes A, B, C and D. . . . Of the [group] . . . many are pinched by want and all live in poverty, if poverty be defined as having no surplus.

However, it is easy to dissipate the appearance of solidity, consistency, and smooth operationalisation in these definitions. This will now be done by considering in turn *Life and Labour*'s treatment of the income criterion, secondary poverty and the 'appearance of the home'.

In its definitions and measurements of poverty, *Life and Labour* was apparently using an income standard to define the poor. The 1887 article definition and the first volume of the poverty series definition ('Poverty', vol. 1, p. 33) proposed a standard of 18 to 21 shillings per week for a 'moderate' family. By the end of the industry series ('Industry', vol. 5, p. 324), the standard had been modified to 21 to 22 shillings per week for a 'small' family. The difference was of some significance when so many standard unskilled wages were at this time about one pound per week. More seriously, if measurement rather than definition is considered, at the operational level the income standard simply vanished. In the first volume household classification measurements of classes A to D, any income criterion could only be approximate because no wages data were obtained until 1893, four years after the first volume of the poverty series was published. Of course, it was the second volume of the poverty series and the street classification which supplied the well-remembered conclusion that 30 per cent were in poverty. An income criterion could not have been used at all here because detailed information about the occupations of the inhabitants of the streets was not recorded in the relevant schedules ('Poverty', vol. 2, pp. 4–15). It is thus not clear whether poverty for Booth involves an income criterion – definitionally it does, operationally it does not.

The inconsistencies did not simply concern the use of an income criterion. Booth vacillated in his treatment of what Rowntree was later to conceptualise as secondary poverty. The 1887 article definition excluded some of those in secondary poverty who spent large earnings on drink; 'cases of large earnings spent in drink are intended to be excluded as not properly belonging to the poor, but the results of ordinary habits of extravagance in drink in inducing poverty are not considered any more than those of other forms of want of thrift' (Booth, 1887, p. 328). The second volume of the poverty series took a different position and did not then exclude from the ranks of the poor the 'man who spends ten or fifteen shillings in drink one week' ('Poverty', vol. 2, p. 18), a sum that was around twice the 6 shillings or so that the average working-class family spent on drink. By this point the investigation's policy was to 'disregard the follies past or present which bring poverty in their train' ('Poverty', vol. 2, p. 19). How the original decision or its modification affected the measurement of poverty is anyone's guess.

The role of 'appearance of the home' as a criterion is equally unclear. The 1887 article definition of poverty proposed that appearance of the home be used as a criterion of poverty where income was unknown; 'as it is not always possible to ascertain the exact income, the classification is also based on the general appearance of the home' (Booth, 1887, p. 328). In the first volume's definition of poverty, this criterion is apparently dropped; certainly there is no mention of it in the formal definition of poverty. But, when the industry series had developed an overcrowding classification based on official statistics, it was alleged that the earlier household and street classifications had been based on 'opinions' about 'apparent poverty':

> The original classification has the advantage of being
> directly aimed at poverty . . . but was based on opinion
> only – that is, on the impression made on the minds of the
> school board visitors and others by what they had seen or
> heard as to the position in the scale of comfort of the
> people amongst whom they lived and worked ('Industry',
> vol. 1, p. 11).

As for measurement, all that can be said is that the role of an appearance criterion is uncertain except in the street classification of the second volume of the poverty series, where appearance is the only basis on which streets could have been assigned into categories.

No single set of criteria was used to define and measure poverty from beginning to end of *Life and Labour*. At any point in the investigation, it was usually not clear what criteria were being used to establish the poverty of an individual or group. *Life and Labour*'s concept of poverty and its operational measurements were thus inconsistent and insubstantial. This conclusion does not condemn the text; in a preliminary way it establishes what is done in the text. The definitions and measurement of poverty are directly too weak to establish a discursive object called poverty.

In any case, ultimately the concept and measurement of poverty at the 'centre' of the work was irrelevant, because the text veered off to discuss something other than poverty. In an operation of translation, particular problems like poverty or unemployment were explained by setting up chains of reference so that one initial problem definition was translated into another. *Life and Labour* itself insisted on the necessity for such translations; in discussing poverty, its causes and remedies, the text observed:

> The immediate explanation of poverty is usually very simple: no savings; no opportunity of remunerative work; inadequate pay; inability or unwillingness to do the work that offers; reckless expenditure – such are the causes of which one thinks. But in seeking remedies it is rather for *causae causarum* that we must look ('Industry', vol. 5, p. 308).

At the same time, 'translation' is an inexplicit notion of the kind of chain of reference that Booth set up. Characteristically, the text did not make a direct translation substituting equivalent terms from a second order which was the equal of the first, nor did it undertake a hermeneutic deciphering like Feuerbach's from the surface to the hidden meaning in a second and more fundamental order. The movement of reference involved a complex three-step movement whereby an initial making and breaking of reference was followed by a remaking of reference. This can be illustrated by taking some examples of three-step movements in the definition and analysis of the nature and causes of society's problems. Two specific examples follow: first the treatment of poverty and unemployment; and second, the treatment of poverty and industry.

In *Life and Labour*'s treatment of poverty and employment, the first step was a making of reference from poverty to unemployment in the famous first-volume tables on the causes of poverty in 4,000 cases known to school board visitors ('Poverty', vol. 1, pp. 146-9). Three possible causes of poverty were considered: 'employment' which covered lack of work and low pay, 'habit' which covered idleness, drink or thriftlessness, and 'circumstance' which covered sickness and large family. The tables showed that more than half the 'great poverty' and more than two-thirds the 'poverty' was attributable to questions of employment. This was an important connection though not of course a great empirical discovery, given the way in which those in poverty were initially defined in the sections and classes as those who were irregularly employed or earning low wages.

The second step was a decisive breaking of reference. *Life and Labour*'s conclusion about the importance of employment as a cause of poverty was deradicalised and cancelled by the explanation of unemployment which immediately followed the tables. Unemployment was referred to personal 'incapacity' for work or 'personal disability' ('Poverty', vol. 1, p. 149); see also 'Industry', vol. 5, p. 317. As the text claims,

> Incapacity [for work] of two sorts is no doubt common:
> that which leads especially to low pay and that which leads
> especially to irregularity of employment. There are those
> who never learn to do anything well on the one hand and
> those who cannot get up in the morning on the other
> ('Poverty', vol. 1, p. 149).

The unemployed were then simply identified with the incapacitated:

> The unemployed are as a class a selection of the unfit, and,
> on the whole, those most in want are the most unfit. This is
> the crux of the position ('Poverty', vol. 1, p. 150).

The low wage problem was similarly dealt with in the industry series where those on low wages were identified as those who made an insignificant contribution to the world; 'when they are paid very little or are unable to earn anything at all, it is fully probable that what they contribute to the service of the world is no less insignificant' ('Industry', vol. 5, p. 309). Thus, in a second step, unemployment and low wages were devalued; they were identified as symptoms which would not ultimately explain poverty.

The real cause of poverty lay elsewhere and the third step was to advance an alternative explanation. Positively, the text explained away poverty by referring it to intra-working-class competition:

> To the rich the very poor are a sentimental interest; to the
> poor they are a crushing load. The poverty of the poor is
> mainly the result of the competition of the very poor
> ('Poverty', vol. 1, p. 154).

Life and Labour advanced a millstone explanation of poverty and the millstone was class B:

> The disease from which society suffers is the unrestricted
> competition of the needy and the helpless. . . . It is class B
> that is *du trop*. The competition of B drags down C and D
> and that of C and D hangs heavily upon E ('Poverty', vol. 1,
> pp. 162-3).

This kind of three-step making, breaking, and remaking of reference in the treatment of unemployment was repeated in the treatment of poverty and industry, where the first step was a making of reference from poverty to industry. Poverty was connected to industry as a disturbing anomaly. The point was made explicitly in the industry series: 'where there is industry there ought to be no poverty' ('Industry', vol. 5, p. 293).

The second step was a breaking of reference whereby 'modern industry' was exonerated from responsibility for society's ills. The text went to some trouble to conceptualise the technical and financial characteristics of 'modern industry' ('Industry', vol. 5, pp. 169-70). Technically, modern industry was identified with division of labour, continuously extending use of machinery, and general complexity of organisation. Financially, modern industry was identified with a changed relation between supply and demand, with trades attempting to anticipate or create demand. Then came the necessary anti-climax: these characteristics 'cannot be said to be in themselves responsible for the connection of poverty with industry' ('Industry', vol. 5, p. 70).

The poverty series had prepared the way for this conclusion by its treatment of the employment-connected evils of 'sweating' and casual labour. Sweating was dismissed as a popular notion which jumbled together an assortment of particular evils. It could not be identified with any specific kind of industrial system or organisational structure; 'there is no industrial system co-extensive with the evils complained of' ('Poverty', vol. 4, p. 330). Casual labour had to be admitted as an economic institution, but it was then devalued as an irrational excrescence on the industrial system. Whatever the deluded employer of casual labour might think, casual labour was of advantage to nothing or nobody ('Poverty', vol. 1, pp. 152-3). When sweating and casual labour had effectively been devalued as non-existent or irrational, it is not surprising that the industry series did not make the connection between poverty and modern industry.

The third step with poverty and modern industry was to advance an alternative explanation. This explanation partly took the form of a redefinition of what was to be explained. Thus the text argued that part of what modern industry was blamed for was not really pathological at all; the trade cycle, for example, was likened to 'the orderly beating of a heart causing the blood to circulate' ('Industry', vol. 5, p. 73). The other line of argument was that anomalies like poverty were so many necessary evils, part and parcel of progress as competition spurred on economic agents:

The heightened struggle for existence, with its ups and downs of commercial inflation and contraction, causes more evils than we have mentioned. They are however all compatible with a rising standard of comfort and a greater

diffusion of wealth. Competition is a force that drives un-
ceasingly ('Industry', vol. 5, p. 82).

These 'translations' have been treated at some length because they
are fairly complex and because they are important, not least because
they must finally scupper the existing historiographic accounts of the
status and relation between different themes in Booth's *Life and
Labour*. The discourse is not about an object called 'poverty' or
'chronic poverty', because the text is always taking off for another
theme along some chain of reference; the translations in our examples
are away from poverty which is the point from which things diverge,
rather than the centre on which they converge. Moreover, unemployment cannot be treated as an abstractable theme because it exists
between other themes; in the example considered, unemployment is
sandwiched between poverty and competition. Furthermore, insofar as
the poverty and industry series move to any one space, that space is
outside the field of poverty as constructed by historiography; recurrently, in these examples, the making and breaking and remaking of
reference moves Booth towards a characteristic quasi-destination of
competition.

It is now possible to define *Life and Labour* by making the cross-
reference back to the Engels and Mayhew texts. The present analysis
of *Life and Labour* deliberately echoes the analyses of the last two
chapters. Translation refers us back to the Engels translations of the
identity of the subject. Three-step movements refer us back to the
prevarications of Mayhew, the master of ambiguity. Such cross-references
should make it clear that Booth's text is different.

There is a quality of prevarication in *Life and Labour*, which
accounts for the text's chronic uncertainty about what had been discovered, when it came to the summing up at the end of the poverty and
industry series ('Poverty', vol. 1, pp. 172-8; 'Industry', vol. 5, pp. 337-
8). It also accounts for the ease with which historians like the Simeys
could fabricate a progressive Booth, while historians like Brown, a few
years later, could fabricate a reactionary Booth. From the examples
cited, it is easy to see how Booth could be credited with explaining
poverty in terms of environment and/or character. At the same time,
the uncertainty of identification is limited, because the ambiguities are
characteristically resolved in a conservative way. Translation in *Life
and Labour* took the form of cancelling reference. In explaining
poverty, the text made radical connections to the operations of the
economy and then these possibilities were devalued or explained away
by additional reference. Put in another way, it could be said that the
translations allowed the text to move from a variety of initially hetero-
geneous problems and explanations towards a homogeneous space
where competition rules and everything is for the best.

Problems of identification are thus resolved in the direction of a banality which ultimately threatens to erase the distinctions and discriminations which the text has so painstakingly established. By the end of the industry series, competition had been stressed so strongly that this great classificatory text was disregarding any division of the population into classes and trades. The conclusion to the final volume of the industry series preferred to 'discard trades or groups of trades, classes or groups of classes, and think of the whole population simply as individuals or as families, each and all fighting for themselves and for those who belong to them, the good battle of life' ('Industry', vol. 5, p. 336). The text was then able to state its 'main conclusion': 'life presents itself as full of chances and success depends mainly on the power to grasp and make use of opportunities as they occur' ('Industry', vol. 5, p. 336). If the text got anywhere at the end of the poverty and industry series, it was to the space of an anodyne headmasterly vision of atomistic social competition where you get out what you put in. It was the insufferable school prize-day stuff about how the race is to the swift and riches to men of understanding and the rest of us must endeavour to be more deserving.

Finally, it is necessary to add a caution that competition is only a quasi-destination in *Life and Labour*; it is not a final destination on to which all textual reference converges. Reference moves on and around competition so that this theme is a link in a chain that has no ascertainable beginning or end. It is easy to change the cut-off point and to find a different quasi-destination in the text. Thus, our reading concerned with *Life and Labour*'s definitions of the social problem has disclosed a quasi-destination of competition. It can be shown, however, that another reading, concerned with *Life and Labour*'s solutions for the social problem, discloses a different quasi-destination.

Booth's most familiar solutions are the proposal for old-age pensions made at the same time as *Life and Labour* was being written and the proposal for labour colonies made in *Life and Labour* ('Poverty', vol. 1, p. 154). The first proposal is emphasised by the Simeys and the second by Brown. We should not be distracted by the benevolence of old-age pensions or by the 'sober authoritarianism' of labour colonies; Booth was not a prototype 1930s Fabian or Fascist. The key point is that labour colonies and old-age pensions had much the same status for Booth as regulating the banks for Friedman; they were strategic interventions that made other intervention unnecessary. The *Life and Labour* treatment of solutions was notable for the remorselessness with which it moved towards the conclusion that the state could generally do very little. The state should steer clear of regulating the volume of employment or the dangerous business of providing municipal housing ('Industry', vol. 5, p. 316; 'Conclusion', p. 190). At most, the state might provide improved transport facilities to ease suburbanisation of the overcrowded ('Conclusion', p. 185). All the state could properly do about 'sweating' was to improve the regulatory structure and make the owners of house property legally liable if improper conditions prevailed ('Conclusion', p. 209). Apart from these modest proposals, *Life and Labour* offered only personal solutions and uplift. For example, in line with the text's moral productivity theory of wage determination, the cure for low wages was greater serviceableness. Individually or collectively, the low paid could only attain higher wages by making themselves more deserving; 'it is only by giving his best services that any man is in a position to insist upon his full reward' ('Conclusion', p. 314). Again and again, the text's destination was a tired philosophical conservatism that doubted the possibility of collective action. As Booth said about sweating, 'I see no safe policy but laisser-faire' ('Poverty', vol. 4, p. 344).

It would be possible to go beyond the text's conservatism, as it has been possible to go beyond competition. However, at this point one more demonstration should not be necessary. Booth's is a discourse with quasi-destinations, not terminal destinations of the sort presupposed by historiography. This allows us to generalise the earlier conclusions about the non-object 'poverty' and the non-abstractable theme 'unemployment'. Booth's discourse is not about an object because it does not have the requisite pattern of convergence on to a centre; and more radically, given the peculiar character of Booth's discourse, it is not legitimate to treat any one single theme as an abstractable entity.

The quasi-destinations are also important in defining the ultimately paradoxical quality of Booth's discourse. *Life and Labour* is not only much longer than any other text analysed in these chapters, it is also mechanically more complex. However, all this discursive complexity does not get the text very far, because *Life and Labour* embraces congenial banality at every quasi-destination. As we have seen with competition, at the end of the poverty and industry series the quasi-destinations are so strongly emphasised that they tend to interfere with, and even undermine, the previous analysis. In any case, the quasi-destinations could have been reached without the preliminary of nine volumes of analysis and empirical investigation; greater economy should be possible in a text which tells an audience what they already know or want to hear. All the analyses of texts in the second half of this book do emphasise that it is the textual journey, rather than the arrival, that matters. It is for this reason that the analysis of *Life and Labour* has recovered so much textual reference which occurs before the quasi-destinations are reached. Nevertheless, the length and complexity of Booth's text is out of all proportion to the triviality of the results and quasi-destinations.

In this sense, *Life and Labour* must be judged an unsuccess. The text is, however, more than a historical curiosity since the nature of its unsuccess is now familiar in the publications of major social science research projects funded by official research councils, private foundations, and government departments. Here again we encounter the same disproportion between scale of publication and triviality of results. *Life and Labour* Booth should be enrolled as the prototype manager of such major projects, the very model of a 'distinguished social scientist'.

October, 1977

Appendix   Booth and pauperism

Historiographic discussion has been preoccupied with Booth's *Life and Labour* and it has completely neglected Booth's text the *Aged Poor* which was published in 1894. This emphasis is unjustifiable when historiography situates Booth's work in some kind of transition from pauperism to poverty. *Life and Labour* cannot easily be fitted into such a transition; the last chapter argued that *Life and Labour* cannot profitably be identified as the text which discovered (or failed to discover) poverty by empirical investigation. However, the *Aged Poor* can easily be fitted into such a transition; it is difficult not to identify the *Aged Poor* as one of two or three texts (see also, Hunter, 1894) which damaged important presuppositions of the contemporary pauperism analysis by means of modern empiricist techniques. This appendix is written to establish these points.

The problem of pauperism was reinterpreted in the 1890s. In the 1880s, official statistics had shown that a gratifyingly small and diminishing percentage of the population, under 3 per cent on a day count basis, were drawing relief (see Statistical appendix, Table 4.5, col. viii). As long as the official statistics continued to count the aged and infirm paupers together as 'non-able-bodied', then the extent of pauperism among the aged was necessarily obscure. In the 1890s, new kinds of official statistics directly showed that, on any one day, 20 per cent of the over-sixty-five age group were drawing relief (Statistical appendix, Table 4.25, col. iv) and, over a twelve-month period, nearly 30 per cent of this age group drew poor relief (Statistical appendix, Table 4.27, col. iii).

These official discoveries were corroborated by the results of unofficial social investigations, such as Booth's inquiry into the causes of pauperism in three unions which was published in its final form in 1892 as *Pauperism and the Endowment of Old Age*. Booth's text prevaricated about 'underlying causes' and the possible role of drink (Booth, 1892a, pp. 136, 139, 140), but its tabulation directly showed the predominance of old age and sickness among the 'principal causes' of pauperism. In the Stepney poor law union, for example, old age was the 'principal cause' of dependence on the poor law in 33 per cent of cases and sickness was a principal cause in a further 27 per cent of cases (Booth, 1892a, p. 10).

In this way, contemporaries of the 1890s 'discovered' the composition of the pauper host and the elementary implications of this composition. After fifty years, the specific refusal of relief to able-bodied men and a more general withdrawal of assistance had reduced the pauper host to a rump, and the aged were then the most important single group among those who continued to draw relief. The discoveries of social investigation often concern elementary differences which are so 'obvious' that they have not hitherto been problematised. Thus Booth's 1892 text, *Pauperism and the Endowment of Old Age,* could present pauperism among the old as a disturbing problem that required the radical solution of universal, non-contributory, old-age pensions.

At this time, the payment of poor law out-relief doles to the aged was opposed by the central bureaucracy of the Local Government Board and by much articulate opinion which supposed that out-relief doles increased pauperism among the aged. Booth's pension scheme could not be construed as an extension of this existing system of doles; poor law out-relief to the elderly was to be abolished when old-age pensions were introduced. Nevertheless, his pension scheme could be construed as a new (non-poor law) system of out-relief doles which would dramatically increase the amount of dependence on the state and thus, in a broad sense, the amount of pauperism among the elderly.

In this context of new discoveries and old fears about pauperism, Booth's 1894 text on *The Aged Poor* is important, first, because it directly confronted contemporary presuppositions about the relation between pauperism and relief practice, and, second, because it confronted these presuppositions in a very modern way. The text did not begin formally by stating that a hypothesis would be tested. Part one was, however, concerned to evaluate an implicit hypothesis: offering the workhouse, or attaching severe conditions to out-relief, should reduce the numbers on relief so that, *ceteris paribus,* poor law unions implementing such relief policies should have smaller numbers of old persons on relief. In evaluating this hypothesis, the text did not use the formal statistical apparatus for dealing with association: correlation coefficients, significance, and so forth. But part one was preoccupied with the relation of association between two variables, relief practice and numbers on relief; the centrepiece here was an informal empiricist test of this relation and thus of the implicit hypothesis.

The 1894 text classified relief practices into six distinct 'policy' types ranged along a continuum between two poles. At one extreme (policy A), out-relief was freely used to assist the old who were in poverty and at the other extreme (policy D), out-relief was effectively refused. Intermediate policies (AB, B, BC, C) offered out-relief subject to increasingly stringent conditions about the character of the applicant, proof of destitution, and contributions from relations. Poor law unions were then circularised and asked to describe their relief practice with regard to the aged. Replies were received from nearly half the 600 poor law unions, and these disclosed substantial local variation in relief practice; policies of all six types were represented in Booth's sample.

The unions were sorted into groups according to policy type, and official statistics were used to calculate the proportion of those aged over sixty-five drawing poor relief in the different policy groups.

One table (see Table 7.1) summarised Booth's 1894 results about the relation between relief practice and numbers of the aged on relief.

Table 7.1   Percentage of old in receipt of relief on year count basis v. policy of administration (omitting London unions)

Policy type	Number of unions in group	(a) on indoor relief	(b) on outdoor relief	(c) on medical relief	(d) total drawing relief in all forms
			Percentages of the old		
A	22	6½	18½	1	26
AB	90	5	21	1	27
B	103	5½	22	2	29½
BC	28	6	16½	2	24½
C	15	17½	12	3	32½
D	5	6	3½	1½	11

The results did not show that the workhouse was ineffective as a means of reducing pauperism; the virtual refusal of out-relief (policy D) was associated with remarkably small numbers on relief. But conditional out-relief did not promote independence among the old; if severe conditions were attached to out-relief (policy C) the result was a reduction of out-relief numbers associated with a rise in indoor numbers. Furthermore, unconditional out-relief allowances did not promote greater dependence; freely available out-relief (policy A) was not associated with abnormally large numbers on relief.

These test results undermined conventional presuppositions about the relation between pauperism and relief practice; as Booth concluded, 'the figures shook the basis of the official case, as it might be called, against out-relief to a very considerable extent' (Booth, 1894, p. 424). Discursively, these results opened the way for a reappraisal of poor law out-relief which Booth finally described as 'the least unsuccessful portion of the present poor law relief to the aged' (Booth, 1894, p. 422). Indirectly, these results encouraged schemes like old-age pensions which involved giving the poor money on a new and more systematic basis. Because of its results, the crucial test in *The Aged Poor* is important in any transition from pauperism to poverty.

Nevertheless, Booth's crucial test of 1894 was hardly a triumph. The composition of the pauper host in the 1890s limited the scope of such a test and consequently the possible damage to any pauperism analysis. It was not possible to test the relation of different relief policies to pauperism among unemployed able-bodied men because there were negligible numbers of such men on relief. Furthermore, the very modernity of Booth's informal test procedure created its own problems and limited the actual damage to any pauperism analysis; empiricism of this sort is, as was argued in the first half of this book, always open to sceptical objection. Contemporaries, like Loch of the Charity Organisation Society, were quick to criticise Booth's text which was vulnerable on grounds of imperfect classification and control.

To consider classification first of all, the six-box policy schema made precise discriminations, but it is not clear whether the practices of different unions were, or could be, reliably sorted into one or other of the classificatory boxes. As the text (Booth, 1894, p. 7) admitted,

> in many unions there is a mixture of these rules (defining
> policy types); in some the rules are irregularly observed and
> others do not profess to have any rule, but deal with each
> case as at the time seems best.

The problems about control are even more acute. There must be a suspicion that some unidentified variable explains the negative test results about the unsuccess of conditional out-relief policies. The text itself comes close to identifying this variable as poverty. Policy C of allowing out-relief subject to strict conditions produced the worst result in terms of total pauperism; the text's explanation was 'that this policy is rarely adopted except in poverty-stricken urban unions' (Booth, 1894, p. 20). But, much to Booth's regret (1894, p. 104), the variation of poverty around the country could not be measured and therefore this variable could not be controlled.

Booth should be remembered not as the man who discovered poverty, but as the man who diminished pauperism. This unheroic empiricist feat was a prelude to Rowntree's less than triumphant modern analysis of poverty which will be considered in chapter 8.

Rowntree

In historiography, Seebohm Rowntree's 1901 text *Poverty* marks the point of arrival at the modern social problem of poverty and its associated collectivist solutions. This chapter argues against this conventional verdict on *Poverty,* which is only possible if reference in the 1901 text is unacceptably rearranged into convergent patterns, and if supplementary reference is cut off to preserve the appearance of a modern unity. As always, the anti-historiographic task is to recover the plural and divergent character of the text, and the first section of this chapter attempts this recovery.

The rest of this chapter considers a characteristic pattern of restriction of reference in *Poverty* and in some of Rowntree's other texts, including his second poverty survey (Rowntree, 1942). Positively, it will be argued that, early or late, Rowntree's texts are technicist in that they attempt to demarcate a privileged sphere in social investigation where matters can be settled by reference to a technical calculus. It will also be argued that Rowntree's technicism encounters insuperable internal problems. Generally, therefore, Rowntree's texts of social investigation do not represent a virtuous modern analysis of the social problem.

Poverty/poverties

Historians unanimously praise Rowntree's first York social survey whose results were summarised in *Poverty,* published in 1901. All agree that the text provides a virtuous empirical analysis of poverty.

The biography of Rowntree by Asa Briggs (1961) contains the most extended statement of this position. Briggs describes *Poverty* as 'the

most important book that Rowntree ever wrote' (Briggs, 1961, p. 18).
This text is praised in certain stereotyped terms. It gives the results of
an empirical investigation of York in 1899 which was necessary because
Rowntree 'wanted facts not doctrines' (Briggs, 1961, p. 29). The 'central
questions' of the investigation were about poverty (Briggs, 1961, p. 29),
and the results were a great success because, at the methodological level,
Rowntree devised 'effective methods for measuring material poverty'
(Briggs, 1961, p. 327). Furthermore, the *Poverty* text had a progressive
effect, since it defined a problem of poverty which required modern
collectivist solutions. As Briggs (1961, pp. 41–2, 45) argues, for Rowntree and others, the corollary of the *Poverty* analysis was the new-style
social reform; 'the conclusions Rowntree had reached were used to justify
the demand for a new and more active Liberalism and the introduction
of welfare measures such as old-age pensions' (Briggs, 1961, p. 45).

Such judgments still dominate the current historiographic description
and evaluation of Rowntree. They have been strengthened by the
recent revisionism about Booth which establishes a crucial discontinuity between *Life and Labour* and *Poverty*. In his biography of
Rowntree, Briggs claimed a continuity between the two texts; Booth
inaugurated an analysis of poverty which Rowntree refined when he
distinguished primary and secondary poverty and described life-cycle
poverty (Briggs, 1961, pp. 33, 40–1). The revisionists establish a discontinuity between the two texts by praising one and disparaging the
other in certain stereotyped terms. Brown favourably compares Rowntree with Booth, who hopelessly mixed factual detail and moral
judgment; Rowntree consciously tried to avoid any 'unfavourable
judgment on those living in poverty' (Brown, 1968, p. 352). Hennock
sets up a similar comparison and argues that Rowntree's novel 'use of
his survey as a means of testing a hypothesis marks a . . . theoretical
breakthrough' (Hennock, 1976, p. 91).

This section opposes such historiographic description and evaluation
of *Poverty*. It will now be argued that the historiographic description
of the text is misconceived, because the text is about pover*ties* not
poverty, and the evaluation is misconceived because it considers whether
the text realises imaginary virtues. These errors can be attributed to
now familiar offences against past social investigation. Historiographic
description miscarries since it violently rearranges reference into convergent patterns. Historiographic evaluation miscarries since it uncritically endorses the categories and criteria of empiricist epistemology.
Apart from identifying and criticising these errors, this section advances
a positive alternative characterisation of *Poverty* which identifies a certain
restriction of reference in this text as technicist. This opens the way for
an alternative evaluation because this technicism seeks to justify itself
on its own peculiar evaluative terrain. The question in this case is how
does the discourse measure up against its own criteria?

To begin with a familiar point, two different kinds of poverty were defined in the 1901 text. Primary poverty was defined as the condition of those 'families whose total earnings are insufficient to obtain the minimum necessaries for the maintenance of merely physical efficiency' (Rowntree, 1913, p. xix). Secondary poverty was the condition of those 'families whose total earnings would be sufficient for the maintenance of physical efficiency were it not that some portion of them is absorbed by other expenditure, either useful or wasteful' (Rowntree, 1913, p. xix). Total poverty was simply the sum of primary and secondary poverty. Historiography assumes that Rowntree was here discriminating different kinds or parts of the one unitary object called poverty. As every textbook says, Rowntree found that nearly 30 per cent of York's total population lived in poverty - 10 per cent in primary poverty and 20 per cent in secondary poverty. But the arithmetical simplicity of this statement conceals more than it reveals. The concealed point is that here we have different poverties inhabiting qualitatively different universes, because there were quite distinct investigations of two poverties which were defined and measured in radically different ways.

Neither of these two kinds of poverty was called secondary poverty, for secondary poverty was the simple shadow of two other definitions and measurements. Definitionally, secondary poverty was the shadow of primary poverty. It was a kind of discursive *alter ego*; poverty other than primary poverty defining itself against its other as an income sufficient for the maintenance of physical efficiency were it not for diversion. In measurement terms, secondary poverty was even more of a shadow. Secondary poverty indeed was not directly measured at all. The 20 per cent in secondary poverty result was obtained as a residual after subtracting a measure of primary poverty from a measure of total poverty. Rowntree (1913, p. 149) himself explained the procedure in the following way:

> I have been able to arrive at a fair estimate of the total
> number of persons living in poverty in York. From this
> total number I subtracted the number of those ascertained
> to be living in 'primary' poverty; the difference represents
> those living in 'secondary' poverty.

Ten from thirty leaves twenty is all the investigation secondary poverty gets. So the question becomes: what is the difference between Rowntree's investigations of total poverty and primary poverty?

To begin with total poverty, this involved the investigation of appearances. One hired investigator visited every house in York. As Rowntree (1913, pp. 148-9) explained:

The investigator, in the course of his house-to-house visitation, noted down the households where there were evidences of poverty, i.e. obvious want and squalor. Direct information was often obtained from neighbours, or from a member of the household concerned, to the effect that the father or mother was a heavy drinker; in other cases the pinched faces of the ragged children told their own tale of poverty and privation.

Judging in this way, partly by appearance and partly from information given, I have been able to arrive at a fair estimate of the total number of persons living in poverty in York.

A household was classified as poor therefore on two criteria. The first criterion was 'appearance': a household was poor if there was the appearance of want or squalor. The second criterion was 'information given' on the one topic of drinking habits: a household was classified as poor if there was direct evidence of drinking or if the householder admitted, or a neighbour alleged, that money was being spent on drink. On this basis, it was concluded that nearly 30 per cent of the total city population was in poverty.

The treatment of total and secondary poverty was not only impressionistic, it was also brief: after thirty pages on primary poverty, secondary and total poverty were treated in three pages. There was nothing very much to say or explain about total poverty. The concept was not even worth a formal definition. Apart from brevity, a quality of thinness differentiated the definition of total poverty implicit in the investigation. The investigation reduced the condition of poverty to the appearance of a clean and tidy home and a bit of information about drinking habits. This investigation of total poverty only operationalised stock responses to the working class – coals in the bath and all that. It is quite amazing that the historians's hero should turn out to be the promoter of such a mean little concept.

To turn now to primary poverty, this was a quite different investigation which operationalised 'efficiency'. In the 1901 definition of primary poverty, efficiency considerations determined where the poverty line was drawn. That much is easy. But, what does efficiency mean here?

The Briggs biography of Rowntree does not analyse the meaning of the term, but a monograph by Searle (1971) does offer an articulate definition of the concept of efficiency as an object in political discourse. 'National efficiency' or 'efficiency' is supposedly a dominating political catch cry of the Edwardian period – something analogous to participation or devolution in the 1970s (Searle, 1971, p. 1). This slogan is credited with a 'definite meaning' of a now familiar unitary type. Searle characterises efficiency as a series of qualifying elements, such as positions about the machinery of government or attitudes about the role of the businessman or expert in politics. These elements are supposed to be arranged around, or merge into a centre of admiration for the German model. As Searle (1971, p. 54) argues:

If one were to sum up its meaning in a single sentence, one might describe the 'National Efficiency' ideology as an attempt to discredit the habits, beliefs and institutions that put the British at a handicap with foreigners and to commend instead a social organisation that more closely followed the German model.

In this way, Searle constructs 'efficiency' as a kind of centred discursive object.

But 'efficiency' is not one conceptual unity of any sort. Our aim should be to understand that different references to efficiency can be deployed in various ways in different texts or even in the same text. The Rowntree text illustrates this point perfectly when *Poverty* deployed two distinct concepts of efficiency in different ways.

(National) efficiency appears in the up-beat concluding paragraphs of two chapters of *Poverty* (Rowntree, 1913, pp. 261-2, 307-8) where it was asserted resoundingly that Britain's commercial success depended upon efficiency. As Rowntree (1913, p. 308) concluded,

If adequate nourishment be necessary to efficiency, the highest commercial success will be impossible so long as large numbers even of the most sober and industrious of the labouring classes receive but three-fourths of the necessary amount of food.

In these chapter conclusions, efficiency was part of a series of more or less obligatory gestures towards larger problems and structures which were not directly confronted in a local study of one problem. At the margins of the text, Rowntree made nearly gratuitous reference to the larger life of the world.

(Physical) efficiency was used in an altogether more restricted way in the definition and calculation of primary poverty. Here Edwardian nutritional theory was the crux. Contemporary nutritional theory allowed the calculation of what was minimally necessary to maintain physical efficiency; a labouring man required 3,500 calories per day, including 125 grams of protein to avoid the dangers of 'threadbare tissues' (Rowntree, 1913, pp. 119-129, 268-70, 286-7). In this way, a specific kind of scientific theory was to provide the cutting edge in the calculation of minima. This reference to scientific theory allowed the investigation of a new kind of poverty, primary poverty, and it was therefore of key importance in the text. Unlike Mayhew who talked to the poor, or Booth who talked to those set in administrative authority over the poor, when it came to primary poverty Rowntree let some highly specific concepts do the talking.

If this notion of efficiency in the definition of primary poverty fitted with anything, it was not with a general field called efficiency, nor with the text's up-beat chapter conclusions. It fitted better with the cognate bit of scientism about overcrowding. Rowntree went beyond the contemporary official definition of overcrowding as more than two persons per room. Contemporary scientific theory allowed the calculation of the minimum amount of air space necessary; the Huxley standard suggested a minimum of 800 cubic feet of space for each man. This allowed the text to define a new kind of overcrowding which was all a matter of the air space necessary if each individual was 'to be supplied with respiratory air in a fair state of purity' (Rowntree, 1913, pp. 208–14).

The text was not simply proposing a definition of a new kind of poverty; the definition was associated with a new investigation and measurement of poverty. The 10 per cent in primary poverty figure was obtained by bringing together two separate calculations, the earnings calculation and the minimal expenditure calculation. Data on wage rates were obtained directly from employers whose rates were adjusted for hours worked to obtain available earnings (Rowntree, 1913, pp. 37 and 52). Families could therefore be ranged along an axis of continuous variation between low and high incomes. As a matter of convenience, working-class families were sorted into income groups or bands named A to D along the continuous axis (Rowntree, 1913, p. 57). Such a classification did not of course say anything directly about the nature or extent of any kind of poverty. To say anything about primary poverty, it was necessary to calculate a minimal expenditure standard, and a line below which families were in primary poverty. The 1901 text costed three items to arrive at this standard: food, house rent, and 'household sundries' which covered clothing, light, and fuel (Rowntree, 1913, pp. 119–42). When expenditure allowances for the three items were added up, the result was 'the minimum weekly expenditure upon which physical efficiency can be maintained', and at 1899 prices for a family of five, this sum was 21 shillings and 8 pence (Rowntree, 1913, p. 351). The expenditure standard was then placed against the income axis and on this basis, it was possible to conclude that 9.91 per cent of York's total population was in primary poverty (Rowntree, 1913, pp. 143–4).

Enough has now been said to establish the fundamental distinctness of the definitions and investigations of total and primary poverty. The 1901 text is a discourse on poverties, not poverty. To establish the distinctness of these poverties is to establish the absurdity of crediting Rowntree with one unitary object, the absurdity of making reference converge in this way. The point is worth making but it is excessively formalist unless it is supplemented by some further positive character-isation of the particularity of Rowntree's discourse about poverties. Our starting point here can be the observation that, if reference does diverge, there is also a striking pattern of restriction of reference in this text.

To begin with, the field of causes of, and influences upon, poverty was markedly restricted. The definition of primary poverty was associ-ated with a restriction in the field of possible causes. Where the con-dition was defined as earnings 'insufficient to obtain the minimum necessaries', drink and gambling were necessarily excluded. The causal field was narrowed down to low wages, and absence, sickness, or un-employment of a wage earner. In this restricted field, the text was able to calculate exactly the relative importance of the different causes and to discover that low wages caused over half the primary poverty (Rown-tree, 1913, p. 153). In line with the abbreviated treatment of secondary poverty, the causes of such poverty got *en passant* treatment where drink was briefly cited as 'the predominant factor' (Rowntree, 1913, p. 176). The treatment of influences upon the working class showed another kind of restriction. Material on public houses, education and Christian churches was not incorporated into the main body of the text, instead, it was relegated to an appendix at the end (Rowntree, 1913, p. 362 *et seq.*). This study of influences was undertaken with the restricted aim of allowing 'the reader to form an independent judgment as to how far the conditions in York may be taken as fairly representative of those which obtain in other provincial towns' (Rowntree, 1913, p. xx).

This point about the restriction of reference in Rowntree's *Poverty* emerges more clearly if we make the cross-reference to Booth's *Life and Labour* treatment of the causes of, and influences upon, poverty. *Life and Labour* worried over what did or did not cause poverty and treated influences at great length in the third series of volumes on religious influences. *Poverty* contained or segregated such awkward topics in short sections on the periphery of the main text. The text itself treated in an extended way only those issues, such as the causes of primary poverty, which had been reconceptualised so that precise calculations were possible.

When it came to possible solutions for the problems disclosed, *Poverty* did not so much restrict reference as prohibit it. The 1901 text contained virtually nothing by way of policy proposals for remedying the poverties it analysed. This position was maintained right to the end of the text (Rowntree, 1913, pp. 360-1):

There is surely need for a greater concentration of thought
by the nation upon the well being of its people, for no
civilization can be sound or stable which has at its base this
mass of stunted human life . . .

The object of the writer, however, has been to state facts
rather than suggest remedies. He desires, nevertheless, to
express his belief that however difficult the path of social
progress may be, a way of advance will open out before
patient and penetrating thought if inspired by a true human
sympathy.

The dark shadow of the Malthusian philosophy has
passed away and no view of the ultimate scheme of things
would now be accepted under which multitudes of men and
women are doomed by inevitable law to a struggle for
existence so severe as necessarily to cripple or destroy the
higher parts of their nature.

There the text ends; the problem was serious, solutions could and must
be found, but *Poverty* never disclosed what they might be. The discussion at the end of this section will show that the Edwardian Rowntree
could and did formulate a range of policy proposals for dealing with
poverty and employment; in other texts, Rowntree did appear as the
advocate of particular policy proposals. These were omitted from
Poverty because this text cast its author in a different role as the actuary
of social reform who calculated the extent and nature of social
morbidity and injury. The advocacy of particular reform prescriptions
would simply obstruct the playing of this role. All that could properly
be done in a poverty survey was to estimate the cost and effects of
particular proposals. Thus, the second and subsequent editions of
Poverty included a treatment of the likely effect of old-age pensions
upon poverty (Rowntree, 1913, pp. 436-44).

After all this restriction and prohibition, *Poverty* was left with the
ambition to get the concepts and the arithmetic right. This ambition
went along with a demarcation of two spheres, the 'scientific' and the
'ethical'. The distinction was implicit in *Poverty,* and it was made
explicit in two later Rowntree studies which calculated a primary
poverty line for Belgium and for agricultural labourers in England
(Rowntree, 1911; Rowntree and Kendall, 1913). Both texts identified
the minimum expenditure calculation as a matter of strictly 'economic
considerations' where 'scientific data' allowed a compelling statement
of the minimum necessary expenditure and thus of minimum necessary
income. Outside and beyond this sphere, there was room in a second
sphere for 'ethical considerations' and 'personal opinions'. As Rowntree's text on the English agricultural labourer explained, beyond the
essential items allowed for in his minimum budget 'we enter a region

of controversy where personal opinions must take the place of scientific data' (Rowntree and Kendall, 1913, p. 30). As Rowntree's text on the land question and Belgium made clear (Rowntree, 1911, p. 399), the minimum expenditure calculation was designed to put primary poverty in the sphere of the strictly economic:

> The writer wishes to make it clear that he fixes the mini-
> mum at so low a point not because he feels that this
> standard of life should be imposed upon any section of the
> community, but because, after physical efficiency has been
> provided for, the margin to be allowed for the other needs
> of humanity is determined by ethical rather than economic
> considerations.

In *Poverty*, as in these later texts, the aim was to analyse scientifically an economic condition of primary poverty which did not raise ethical considerations. It is in this context that we must place Rowntree's description of his investigation as 'a contribution to the knowledge of facts in relation to poverty'. Earlier texts by Booth or Mayhew had made much the same general promise but had not delivered 'facts' in Rowntree's restricted way. This pattern of restriction in *Poverty* has a name. It is technicism, the attempt to demarcate a privileged sphere where matters can be settled simply by reference to a technical calculus.

With *Poverty* characterised in this way, it is possible to turn to the evaluation of the text. We will begin by clearing away the obstacles created by the existing evaluative judgments of historians. It is now apparent that Rowntree's technicism meets its shadow in the historio-graphic evaluations by Briggs or Brown. *Poverty* seeks to demarcate the scientific and the ethical, while current historiography identifies the separation of fact and value as the basis of virtuous social investigation. To be more exact, the historiographic position is a clumsy caricature of *Poverty*'s position. Historiography assumes that the smaller the number of value judgments, the better is the text. But, according to its own methodological norms, *Poverty* was not obliged to forswear value judgments, the text was only obliged to exclude value judgments from the sphere of scientific calculation. However, the more important point is that even a perfect symmetry between the positions of the investiga-tion and its critics would not make historiography's judgment any more acceptable.

The fact and value opposition is by now a tired one. Inter-war German positivists, like Popper, were the last philosophers who seriously accepted the existence of 'facts' and their facts were linguistic basic statements rather than unproblematic pieces of information. It has been argued that such a linguistic and relative to theory notion of an empirical basis leads Popper only to relativism rather than a rational process of theory testing (Williams, 1975, pp. 311–28). On a slightly different tack, the first half of this book argued that the Popperian concept of a linguistic empirical basis is impossibly conservative in this post-Saussurean age. Apart from this, the impossibility of value-controlled or value-free knowledge is established in the general sociological rejections of such positions. The elimination of value judgments is an ideal that can never be realised and a discourse which seeks to avoid value judgments is itself committed to a founding value judgment against value judgments. In this case, it is not simply doubtful whether it is rational to control values in the pursuit of factual knowledge, the whole fact versus value opposition should be laid to rest.

If these kinds of arguments seem to be general and epistemological, there are other more concrete objections to any evaluation of *Poverty* according to whether it suppresses value judgments. As we have already seen in the case of Booth's *Life and Labour*, the historian's obsession with disparaging abstracted value judgments is developed at the expense of any analysis of how these features fit into the structuration of the text.

The point can be illustrated by considering the example of *Poverty*'s deprecation of lower-class culture and the moral tone of working-class life. This was how the text (Rowntree, 1913, pp. 25–6) characterised the Hungate slum area of York:

> it is . . . large enough to exhibit the chief characteristics of
> slum life – the reckless expenditure of money as soon as
> obtained, with the aggravated want at other times; the
> rowdy Saturday night, the Monday morning pilgrimage to
> the pawn shop, and especially the love for the district, and
> disinclination to move to better surroundings which, com-
> bined with an indifference to the higher aims of life, are the
> despair of so many social workers.

Such characterisation was not an aberration. Elsewhere, for example, the text claimed that workers in income class D, with thirty shillings a week or more, might be above the poverty line but were 'shut out to a great extent from the larger life and the higher interests' (Rowntree, 1913, pp. 106–7).

It would be beside the point to isolate and label such judgments as lapses. What should be noted is that these judgments show a supple-mentary concern with the moral and spiritual life of the working classes which runs like a thread through all Rowntree's texts. Here, the spiritual life was always the ultimate object of attack in, and pre-condition for, successful social reform. Rowntree's essay on gambling argued that 'the solution of the gambling evil, as of many other social evils, will never be permanently effected without a great deepening in the moral and spiritual life of the nation' (Rowntree, 1905, p. 188). In testing this spiritual life, the leisure time activities of the British working class had a litmus-paper quality. It was from this point of view that Rowntree examined drink and gambling before 1914; Seebohm Rowntree edited a collection of essays on gambling (Rowntree, 1905) and his father Joseph Rowntree wrote the standard Edwardian manual on temperance (Rowntree and Sherwell, 1899). After 1918, this interest in leisure was carried over into the second and third York poverty surveys which devoted increasing amounts of space to the mass entertainments which had supplanted drink and the public house (Rowntree, 1942; Rowntree and Lavers, 1951). Rowntree's technicism was never developed to the point where it eclipsed this concern with the moral life.

If historiography misses such important points, it should be clear that it is unprofitable to praise or damn texts according to naïve epistemological criteria. Past social investigation cannot be judged by those historians who are the residuary legatees of a bankrupt positivism. It is hardly possible to suspend evaluative judgment when most characterisations of how texts work have an evaluative dimension. So an alternative evaluation of Rowntree's text will now be presented. If the text *Poverty* is technicist, it can be questioned on the evaluative ground which it stakes out for itself. All technicism seeks to justify and rationalise itself in terms of the 'hardness' of its calculations, because it is the precision of the results that justifies the restrictions. How hard and precise are *Poverty*'s results?

Before concentrating on the primary poverty calculation, the total poverty calculation can be briefly considered. As has already been explained, the investigation found that 30 per cent lived in poverty on the basis of 'appearances' and 'information given'. This measure of total poverty was not so much imprecise as reckless. As a contemporary critic calculated, if the house-to-house investigation took seven months, then the one investigator would have had to make an average of sixty-two visits per working day (Bosanquet, 1903, p. 12). And large assumptions were necessary before 'appearances' could serve as an indicator of poverty. Some families would display misleading appearances because they lived squalidly out of custom, while others would keep up 'clean and tidy houses' although they were poor. *Poverty* simply and heroically assumed that these two 'sources of error to a large degree cancel each other' (Rowntree, 1913, pp. 149–50). It is surprising to find the historian's hero making such a calculation of total poverty.

Nevertheless, the impressionism about total poverty did not ultimately matter, since it was the primary poverty calculation that was crucial to Rowntree's technicism and this calculation, as we have seen, was quite different. The percentage in primary poverty was calculated by bringing together two sets of hard data, on earnings, and on the minimum expenditure necessary for the maintenance of physical efficiency. The earnings data were incontrovertible; the wage rates were accurate and properly adjusted to obtain earnings (Rowntree, 1903, pp. 12–13). The critical questions must therefore concern Rowntree's construction of a 'low estimate of the minimum expenditure necessary for the maintenance of physical efficiency' by adding together estimates for food, house rent, and sundries.

The food part of this estimate appears to involve the kind of theoretical calculation that was called operationalisation in the first half of this book. Nutritional theory appeared to determine the results, in that this theory specified a minimum which was then costed to obtain the minimum necessary expenditure on food. As with all out-of-date operationalisation, the most obvious problem concerns the obsolete theory used. The nutritional theory of 1899 took account neither of vitamins nor of the usability of different proteins which is a function of their amino-acid patterns (Moore Lappé, 1975, pp. 61–85). But the obsolete theory is less of a problem than might appear. Subsequent changes in nutritional theory may undermine the detail of *Poverty*'s calculation, but they cannot undermine the general nature of the calculation. The serious problems concern the nature of the calculation which, contrary to appearances, was not operationalisation. Nutritional theory did not determine where *Poverty* drew the expenditure line for food because this theory did not, and does not, have an operational dimension of the sort required.

To begin with, the calculation required experimental data on the amount of nutriment required for 'physical efficiency'. *Poverty*'s supporting evidence was partly a matter of anecdote about well-fed labourers in American brickyards, and of 'homely illustration' about a horse fed on hay rather than corn. In 1899 or later, it was possible to cite some experimental studies of the caloric intake required per day to sustain work of a given severity without weight loss or complaint (Rowntree, 1919, pp. 70–80). But these were studies of experimental subjects in closed institutions, like prison or barracks, where conditions were artificial because the institution standardised heating, clothing, sanitation, and personal cleanliness. There were no comparable experimental studies of working-class subjects living independent existences under variable conditions of their own choosing. This left the obvious possibility that, outside closed institutions, food intake might not always be the main determinant of physical efficiency; housing and environmental conditions, for example, might be just as important.

Poverty tried to plug this gap in the argument with a lengthy analysis of variations in welfare among the independent York working class (Rowntree, 1913, pp. 182–305). In this social group, greater private income and expenditure was associated with higher standards of housing, health, and diet; ill-paid unskilled labourers were worse housed, less healthy, and more poorly fed. Clearly, there was a cross-section relation in this one urban community which apparently vindicated *Poverty*'s thesis that 'the wages paid for unskilled labour in York are insufficient to provide food, shelter, and clothing adequate to maintain a family of moderate size in a state of bare physical efficiency' (Rowntree, 1913, p. 166). But a broader comparison of different urban and rural districts did not so directly corroborate the *Poverty* thesis, and this point was admitted in Rowntree's subsequent texts. The text on the agricultural labourer presented official statistics on urban and rural health, which showed that, before 1914, death and disease rates were lower in the countryside even though agricultural wages were typically lower than the urban wages which *Poverty* had condemned as insufficient for efficiency (Rowntree and Kendall, 1913, pp. 13-14). A later text accepted the obvious explanation of this anomaly; favourable environmental considerations in the countryside outweighed the adverse effects of lower wages (Rowntree, 1919, pp. 155-6). The concession significantly weakened Rowntree's arguments about York, and rendered questionable the whole focus on poverty as a personal income and private consumption condition.

Even if income bought food, and food intake determined efficiency, this would not have been the end of *Poverty*'s problems. The nutritional theory could only lay down natural minima required for efficient labour – so many thousand calories and a minimum intake of protein, vitamins, or whatever. But food cannot be socially consumed in this way, material and cultural considerations determine selection, combination, and preparation of foodstuffs. *Poverty* recognised this and drew up a dietary so that a natural requirement of 3,500 calories might be culturally satisfied. At this point, things became rather complicated. In the dietary, some concessions were made to cultural considerations of palatability. The diet of the poor was not to be all boiled potatoes and brown lentils, but the primary poverty dietary was not based on what the independent working class actually ate. For example, the dietary explicitly excluded fresh butcher's meat (Rowntree, 1913, p. 131). On the other hand, when it came to pricing the commodity basket, the text went all the way to actual behaviour. In costing the dietary, *Poverty* incorporated 'realistic prices' allowing the poor to buy in smaller quantities at higher prices (Rowntree, 1913, p. 135). The implications of all this are twofold: first, by the time the dietary – a cultural section of foods satisfying the nutritional requirements – has been specified and costed, then the nutritional theory is no longer determinant; second, a particular pattern of concessions to culture determines the expenditure level deemed minimally necessary and this level can be varied according to the concessions made.

The problems multiplied when it came to non-food expenditure. Here *Poverty* was unable to specify any natural minima, and for all non-food expenditure, the text simply made wildly variable concessions to culture. The concession to cultural behaviour was absolute in the case of house rents where *Poverty* simply took actual rents paid by the poor (Rowntree, 1913, p. 138). The concession to behaviour was more cautious in the case of expenditure on clothing and fuel where decent minimum expenditures were calculated with the aid of working-class informants. In other respects, no concession to behaviour was made at all (Rowntree, 1913, p. 138). This was most remarkable in the case of drink. *Poverty* accepted that, on average, drink took six shillings per week out of a family income, at a time when a standard unskilled wage was around a pound a week. But in the primary poverty budget, nothing was allowed for expenditure on drink. Furthermore, in the nutritional calculations, no calories were obtained from drink, although, in a beer-drinking town like York, the six shillings would, at the price of two pence per pint (Rowntree and Sherwell, 1899, pp. 439-40, 603-7), have bought thirty-five pints per family per week, or around 7,000 calories per family per week, on the assumption that this beer's calorific value was similar to that of the modern product.

Poverty zigzagged wildly and incoherently between natural and cultural poles in its specification of minimum necessary expenditure. There was no reason to prefer this zigzag to others which would have produced higher or lower necessary expenditure totals, depending on the pattern of concessions to culture. Thus, the primary poverty line was arbitrary and could be moved upwards or downwards according to taste. When the results could be rigged to establish anything or nothing, primary poverty was a fraud in its own scientistic terms about minimum level consonant with efficiency. This verdict opens up the possibility of a sophisticated defence of *Poverty*: even if the crucial calculation was bogus, it was made in a good cause. This argument will now be considered.

Historiography generally assumes that the *Poverty* text was progressive since it defined a modern problem of poverty. Briggs cites Rowntree's reply to a critic: 'nothing can be gained by closing our eyes to the fact that there is in this country a large section of the community whose income is insufficient for the purposes of physical efficiency and whose lives are *necessarily* stunted' (Rowntree, 1903, pp. 28-9). On this view, primary poverty is a dramatic reinterpretation and specification of the distinction between the deserving and the undeserving. Those in primary poverty were imperatively deserving because they were unable to maintain physical efficiency. Furthermore, as Briggs (1961, pp. 41-2, 45) argues, for Rowntree and others, the corollary of the *Poverty* analysis was the new-style social reform; 'the conclusions Rowntree had reached were used to justify a new and more active

Liberalism and the introduction of welfare measures such as old-age pensions' (Briggs, 1961, p. 45).

This account cannot be accepted. Generally, technicist calculations are not stably tied to any one kind of problem definition and solution. The founding restriction of reference introduces a certain subsequent potential for mobility. Once the technicist calculation has been made, it becomes just so much arithmetic which can be copied out and inserted in a variety of other analyses. Specifically, it will now be argued that before 1914 Rowntree's technicist measure of primary poverty did not coexist with 'modern' social problem definitions and their collectivist solutions. The contrary arguments of Briggs and others depend on the procedure of cutting off supplementary reference in *Poverty*, and in Rowntree's other pre-1914 texts, so as to preserve the appearance of modernity.

The primary poverty calculation in *Poverty* directly identified a low-wage problem. As the text concluded in a now famous passage, 'the wages paid for unskilled labour in York are insufficient to provide food, shelter and clothing adequate to maintain a family of five in a state of bare physical efficiency' (Rowntree, 1913, p. 166). From this discovery it was possible to draw a variety of inferences about the nature of, and solutions for, the social problem. In historiography's terms of reference, these inferences could just as easily be 'reactionary' as 'progressive'. This is perfectly illustrated by the curious case of Seebohm Rowntree's father, Joseph Rowntree, who invented the minimum efficiency calculation.

Historiography has always assumed that the minimum expenditure calculation first appeared in Seebohm Rowntree's 1901 text *Poverty*. But the famous calculation first appeared two years earlier in Joseph Rowntree's text, *The Temperance Problem* (Rowntree and Sherwell, 1899, pp. 30–43, 446–53). In *Temperance*, the minimum expenditure consonant with efficiency calculation was rather crude: the nutritional authorities were of an earlier generation; proteins, fats and carbohydrates were not clearly identified as interchangeable sources of calorific value; the 'bare existence diet' was worse specified in terms of dietary composition and price data; necessities other than food were treated in a rough and ready way. None the less, all the basic procedures and items are there. Rowntree's father did stop just short of inventing primary poverty; *Temperance* did not add up the expenditure items to produce a total sum of minimum necessary expenditure, nor did the text offer detailed information about the actual earnings of a population. It was simply regarded as self-evident that the minimum expenditures itemised would in total absorb at least an unskilled wage.

All this is not written to initiate a debate on sources and influences. It does not really matter whether *Temperance* was first with the minimum calculation; what matters is how the text used the minimum calculation. In this text, the calculation did not establish a poverty problem, it established the necessity for temperance. From a consideration of the cost of a minimum efficiency diet, and on the assumption that drink was nutritionally worthless (Rowntree and Sherwell, 1899, p. 21), *Temperance* (Rowntree and Sherwell, 1899, p. 36) concluded:

> First, that, as things are at present, a large proportion of the working class do not receive sufficient nourishment for *efficient* subsistence: and, secondly, that a much larger proportion have absolutely *no margin in their weekly incomes for expenditure upon alcoholic drinks.*

A consideration of the whole range of budgetary requirements reinforced the point (Rowntree and Sherwell, 1899, p. 43):

> If one-fifth of a limited income be spent in drink, economies must be practised somewhere, and since rent, reduced to its lowest limits by unwholesome crowding, remains an inflexible quantity, food must be stinted, and expenditure upon clothing, fuel etc., reduced to limits that are not only relatively, but absolutely, destructive of efficiency.

In this way the efficiency calculation was used to establish the necessity for temperance.

Seebohm Rowntree himself could and did draw equally 'reactionary' conclusions from the efficiency calculation. Four years after *Poverty* had been published, Rowntree used the minimum efficiency calculation to establish the necessity for free trade. In an essay, he argued (Massingham, 1903) that protection would increase the price of working-class consumption staples and thus push below the poverty line those workers who were just above it. The calculation that served temperance first also served free trade; so much for the inherently progressive tendency of the minimum efficiency calculation. In the examples we have considered, the Rowntrees, father and son, used the minimum expenditure calculation to support temperance and free trade, the key totems of an unregenerate nonconformist Liberalism.

Seebohm Rowntree was not simply a temperance free trader, as was obvious from his two other major pre-war studies which followed *Poverty,* namely *Land and Labour* which was first published in 1910 and *Unemployment* which was first published in 1911. In these texts Rowntree did advance radical collectivist solutions but the point is that those were distinctly Edwardian. *Unemployment* contains a long list of policy prescriptions: training for juveniles, employment exchanges, unemployment insurance, decasualisation, labour colonies, decentralisation of population, counter-cyclical public works, and afforestation (Rowntree and Lasker, 1911, pp. 262-89). On this basis, Rowntree appears as the photo-fit, radical Edwardian Liberal. His version of Edwardian radicalism was distinctive in its emphasis on reform in the countryside as a prerequisite for the solution of urban problems. The reasons for this emphasis were explained in the theoretical sections of *Land and Labour* which identified landlords as a parasitic class that captured an unearned increment in the value of land or its rent.

In all Rowntree's pre-1914 texts, there is an insistent reference from urban poverty to the land question and back again. *Poverty*, as we have seen, contained no policy proposals but it is significant that, where this text indicated the dimensions of a 'wider social problem', the list of considerations began with 'questions dealing with land tenure' (Rowntree, 1913, p. 150). In *Unemployment*, the favoured middle-range policy proposal was for decentralisation of population from the towns (Rowntree and Lasker, 1911, pp. 262-89). *Land and Labour* identified land reform as the key to the resolution of almost every urban problem (Rowntree, 1911, pp. 544-5). If the large English landed estates were broken up, the rural districts of Britain could be 'repeopled' with working agriculturalists and a 'decentralised population' who worked in town, but lived on little plots in the country. This would directly ease the burden of excess supply on the urban labour market and excess demand for urban housing, and it would also help check a self-evident process of 'physical deterioration' in the towns. These prescriptions are obviously remote from those of any modern collectivism.

Edwardian Rowntree's connection with the Liberal social reforms was equally tenuous. This connection is in many ways the most plausible of the historians' fairy tales; if the poor suffered from insufficient earnings as the York survey argued, was not the next step to give the poor money and was not this what the Liberal government did in the social reforms that came after 1908 - old-age pensions, health insurance, and sickness insurance? However, this giving of money did not have much connection with the minimum efficiency calculation in *Poverty*. First, the Liberal government was not redressing an insufficiency of wages, but dealing with the interruption of earnings in sickness, unemployment, and old age. Second, the assistance to those whose earnings were interrupted was not designed to maintain a minimally sufficient income level. Subject to various conditions, the Liberal government gave small sums of money: five shillings per week to the old, ten shillings per week to the sick, and seven shillings per week to the unemployed. By way of comparison, a standard unskilled wage in this period was about a pound a week, and, in *Poverty*, this wage was identified as inadequate for a family man.

Generally, it can also be said that the Liberal reforms were not based upon a detailed knowledge. Knowledge of the beneficiaries was not necessary to the operation of the schemes; in both unemployment and sickness insurance, stringent contributory conditions automatically prevented malingering and made it unnecessary to investigate the merits of the beneficiary. Furthermore, a detailed empirical knowledge was not necessary to the formulation of the whole strategy. It is significant here that Rowntree's 1911 text *Unemployment* made a detailed empirical knowledge about the unemployed available for the first time, when the health and insurance schemes were already cut and dried. In the formulation of the strategy, Beveridge's 1909 text *Unemployment* was more important. This text was empirically negligible and theoretically conservative in its economics. Beveridge's *Unemployment* was significant because it articulated a strategy for 'organisation of the labour market' whose reality was to be adjusted, with labour exchanges and decasualisation, to correspond more closely with the economic theory of a free market with perfect information. A detailed knowledge of unemployment or the unemployed was irrelevant at this stage.

In conclusion, therefore, the discovery of primary poverty did not establish a modern poverty problem with its associated solutions. Did Rowntree's later studies of primary poverty make this connection? And, did recalculation resolve problems about the arbitrariness of the poverty line? These questions will be considered in the next section.

Recalculating primary poverty

After *Poverty*, Rowntree's subsequent investigations were more restricted in scope. The first hint of this came in Rowntree's (1903) pamphlet replying to criticism of *Poverty*. Although both total and primary poverty measurements had been criticised by Mrs Bosanquet, Rowntree's pamphlet only defended the primary poverty measurement. The impressionistic measurement of total poverty was then dropped from Rowntree's next major text; *Land and Labour* in 1910 concentrated almost exclusively on the measurement of primary poverty in Belgium. By the inter-war period, Rowntree's texts quite explicitly refused to measure total and secondary poverty, because 'the methods of doing this adopted in 1899 appear to me as too rough to give reliable results' (Rowntree, 1942, p. 461). The second York poverty survey did include a figure of 7 to 10 per cent in secondary poverty, but this figure was clearly labelled as a guestimate.

This restriction placed all the more emphasis on the minimum efficiency calculation which was reworked again and again in Rowntree's later texts. In 1910, *Land and Labour* worked out a primary poverty line for Belgium; in 1918 and 1936, the *Human Needs of Labour* updated the English poverty line. And a second survery, *Poverty and*

Progress, first published in 1941, calculated the extent of primary poverty in York according to the new 'human needs' standard. By emphasising primary poverty, the later texts retreated towards technicist calculation, but their recalculations revealed rather than resolved the problems of arbitrariness in this calculation.

Poverty constantly insisted that only necessities were included, and 'no allowance is made for any expenditure other than that absolutely required for the maintenance of merely physical efficiency' (Rowntree, 1913, p. 167). A subsequently much-quoted paragraph stressed that the 1899 minimum budget did not allow expenditure on trade union subscription or sick club, smoking or drinking, newspapers or letters, presents or pocket money for children and so forth (Rowntree, 1913, p. 167). Rowntree's later texts claimed the *Poverty* standard was 'a standard of bare subsistence' (Rowntree, 1942, p. 102), but this argument was substantially weakened by Rowntree's discoveries about Belgium. Here the poor lived at a cultural level which would have been unacceptable in England and Rowntree therefore drew a poverty line for Belgium which was substantially lower than the English line of 1899.

This is clear with regard to both diet and clothing, which can be considered in turn. To formulate a minimum dietary, *Poverty* took English pauper institutional diets as a bench-mark and modified them in the direction of unattractiveness. Institutional diets were rather different in Belgium. After 1901, English workhouse dietaries included a good deal of variety and two meals of boiled or roast meat per week (Rowntree, 1913, p. 130). At the Merxplas labour settlement in Belgium, apart from breakfast, at every meal the paupers simply got vegetable soup and bread. As the text (Rowntree, 1911, p. 403) observed, this diet 'if adopted among the inmates of an English workhouse would lead to an insurrection'. This difference of institutional diet reflected differences of actual behaviour in the independent working class. The Belgian poor in their own homes were 'living largely on bread and potatoes', drinking little coffee and eating little meat (Rowntree, 1911, p. 391). The English poor ate less austerely and insisted on meat even at the expense of calorie or protein intake. There were similar international differences in clothing where 'national customs' again allowed greater economy in Belgium. In England, actual working-class expenditure per annum on men's clothing was more than twice that of Belgium (Rowntree, 1911, p. 397). The English wore leather boots and not wooden shoes and wore underpants and vests under their shirts.

The English primary poverty line of 1899 was not a subsistence minimum, when in slightly different cultural circumstances in a nearby West European country, the line was lower. It was perhaps in response to this discovery that all Rowntree's texts on England after 1918 drew higher and explicitly cultural poverty lines on the 'human needs standard'. These recalculations only demonstrated the arbitrariness of cultural poverty lines. This can be shown by considering first, how the minimum calculation was reworked, and second, how this reworking altered the percentage in poverty.

In reworking necessary expenditure, the human needs standard made many concessions to cultural behaviour. Nutritional theory did not change dramatically between the 1890s and the 1930s. Only modest changes to the original dietary were necessary to ensure an adequate supply of vitamins. The main changes in diet were made as concessions to behaviour; in the 1918 edition of *Human Needs,* cheap cuts of fresh meat were allowed into the dietary. This text also introduced a new item of expenditure called 'personal sundries' which covered some of the cultural needs explicitly excluded from the 1899 budget. Half the expenditures allowed under personal sundries were necessary expenditures for working men – social insurance contributions, trade union subscriptions, and bus fares to and from work. The other half of 'personal sundries' covered the typical indulgences of the working class in the 1930s – daily newspaper, wireless, beer and tobacco. Rowntree's later texts made some concession to culture on the income side of the equation as well as on the expenditure side. The second York poverty survey relaxed the 1899 assumption that 100 per cent of family income came home to be spent (Rowntree, 1942, p. 102); young wage earners habitually did not turn over their full pay packet, so the second survey assumed only 87.5 per cent of income was available in the home (Rowntree, 1942, p. 125).

Directly or indirectly, all these concessions to culture had the effect of raising the poverty line, but this did not make the line any more rationally defensible. To begin with, most of the modifications were concessions to behaviour of the kind already considered, but some of the human needs standard changes went in the opposite direction. *Poverty* had taken rents actually paid by the poor as the basis for calculating cost of housing. *Human Needs* in 1918 and 1936 calculated housing cost on the basis of the hypothetical rent of an 'efficiency house' which 'will meet the needs of physical efficiency as economically as possible' (Rowntree, 1919, p. 96). By 1936, the efficiency house had acquired three upstairs bedrooms and a separate bathroom. It had better facilities than the average working-class terrace house which dominated the available urban housing stock; the working class could not all have lived in efficiency houses even if they had wanted to.

More seriously, the concessions to culture in the human needs standard were half-hearted and not thought through. Half-heartedness is most obvious in the treatment of expenditure on drink which, as we have seen, was excluded from the original *Poverty* calculation. The second York survey admitted that the average working-class family spent seven shillings per week on drink (Rowntree, 1942, p. 473), but the 1936 human needs standard allowed just under half this sum to cover not only beer but also tobacco, and newspapers, and wireless, and travelling, and an assortment of other items. Furthermore, none of Rowntree's later texts recognised the problems introduced by concessions to actual behaviour. Such concessions threatened to resolve the problem of arbitrariness at the expense of introducing complete circularity into the definition and measurement of poverty. A completely realistic standard would measure poverty on the basis of a calculation about how the poor dispose of their income. But this calculation obviously requires a prior definition of the poor as a social group and this must introduce circularity.

The human needs standard concessions to culture may have been half-hearted and incoherent, but they did dramatically raise the poverty line and increase the number in poverty. For a family of five at 1936 prices, the 1899 subsistence standard required a weekly minimum income of forty-three shillings and six pence, including rent, while the 1936 human needs standard required a minimum income of fifty-three shillings and sixpence, including rent (Rowntree, 1942, pp. 52 and 102). This difference of standard had a major impact on the percentage in poverty, as the second York survey, *Poverty and Progress,* showed. The original survey had worked out all the key percentages in terms of total population, but the second survey worked out these percentages in terms of working-class population. On this base, and by the 1899 subsistence standard, 6.8 per cent of working-class population was in primary poverty in 1936. On the same base and by the 1936 human needs standard, 31.1 per cent of working-class population was in primary poverty in 1936. Some half-hearted concessions to culture increase the percentage in poverty quite spectacularly.

In this way, Rowntree's own calculations undermine the concept of primary poverty more effectively than any subsequent criticism. This must reinforce the earlier conclusion that primary poverty is a fraud in its own pseudo-scientific terms. But it is self-indulgent simply to denounce fraud; it is more important to understand its significance and function.

To begin with, it is necessary to underline the peculiarity of the second survey results. The second survey freely admitted that real wages had risen substantially in the forty years since the first survey; the text estimated that real wages in York had increased by one-third between 1899 and 1936. And yet the apparent size of the social problem group was increased by the use of a higher poverty line and a change in the population base in the second survey. The first survey established that 10 per cent (of total population) was in primary poverty in 1899; the second survey established that 30 per cent (of working-class population) was in primary poverty in 1936. Nor was this the end of the matter when the second survey insisted that the poverty problem was even more serious if it was analysed in dynamic life-cycle terms. The text emphasised that around one half of working-class children were born into primary poverty and were likely to remain in it for five years; this discovery was identified as 'perhaps the most disconcerting fact revealed by this investigation'. It could reasonably be claimed that the second survey substituted a 30–50 per cent problem group for the 10 per cent problem group defined in the first survey nearly forty years earlier.

To understand the rationale and significance of this dramatic increase in the size of the social problem group, it is necessary to make the cross-reference to Rowntree's policy proposals of the inter-war period and to the 'welfare state' of the 1940s, that is, to the changes proposed by the *Beveridge Report* of 1942 and to the measures enacted by the post-war Labour government.

The second York survey maintained an effective silence about policy prescriptions just like the first; 'I have avoided expressing my own views as to the cures which should be applied'. However, Rowntree's other texts show that in the inter-war period, he totally rejected his erstwhile Edwardian collectivism. To begin with, Rowntree had completely changed his position on the strategic role of a policy for re-peopling the countryside; as Briggs (1961, pp. 215-16) shows, by the 1930s Rowntree was increasingly convinced by Eleanor Rathbone's argument production as a progressive tendency. Long before this, he had changed position on what should be done about primary poverty. The two editions of *Human Needs* in 1918 and 1937 established a connection between primary poverty and the social policies of minimum wages and family allowances. These texts mark the point where primary poverty is connected to 'modern' remedies and solutions. In 1918, *Human Needs* proposed that trade boards fix wages which offered adequate subsistence for families with three children, and state child allowances to be paid to larger families. The second edition of *Human Needs* showed how Rowntree was increasingly convinced by Eleanor Ratbone's argument against a high minimum wage and in favour of across the board child allowances paid to all families with children. The second York survey simply produced results which would vindicate the case for family allowances being paid to all employed and unemployed wage earners with children.

Finally, the *Beveridge Report* of 1942 established an important connection between the Rowntree-type of poverty survey and official government strategy. The *Beveridge Report* departed from an analysis of 'the condition of the people as revealed by social surveys between the wars' (Beveridge, 1942, p. 8). From these surveys, the report picked out the conclusion that three-quarters or more of poverty was due to loss or interruption of earning power. This reinforced the *Beveridge*

Report's identification of the social problem as 'a problem of income maintenance' in unemployment, sickness, and old age (Beveridge, 1942, p. 11). Moreover, the definition of a subsistence minimum in the surveys determined a re-definition of the appropriate kind of income maintenance. The aim now was to be 'the abolition of want' (Beveridge, 1942, p. 8), and this was to be achieved by a comprehensive system of insurance benefits 'adequate for subsistence without other means' (Beveridge, 1942, p. 58).

If the Liberal reforms before 1914 had marked the first victory of the strategy of giving people money, the *Beveridge Report* of 1942 marks the emergence of a new strategy of giving people adequate amounts of money. Necessarily, therefore, the *Beveridge Report* accorded a privileged place to the kind of calculation of minimum necessary income pioneered in *Poverty,* subsequently reworked in *Human Needs,* and applied not only in Rowntree's second survey but also in the other poverty surveys of the inter-war period. An expert advisory committee, which included Rowntree, advised on the question of adequate benefits. The Report itself included a minimum necessary income calculation of the classic type; it costed rent, food, clothing, household necessaries and sundries, and then added a margin to allow for inefficiency and waste. It is interesting to compare the *Beveridge Report*'s proposed benefit level with Rowntree's later human needs standard, as applied in the second York survey. The Beveridge benefit was worked out in 1938 prices and the Rowntree standard was worked out in 1936 prices which were nearly the same. At fifty-three shillings per week, Beveridge's proposed cash benefit for a family of five was just six pence below Rowntree's minimum necessary income. Nothing shows more clearly the way in which the *Beveridge Report* was the inter-war social survey transformed into a series of prescriptions for redirecting the existing system of income maintenance.

The *Beveridge Report* proposals were never fully implemented, although the post-war Labour government did enact a comprehensive system of social insurance for sickness, unemployment, and old age. Post-war provision of insurance benefit approached, but did not reach, the *Beveridge Report* level. Under the 1946 National Insurance Act, the insurance benefit for man and wife was set at the level suggested in the *Report.* But inflation eroded the real value of insurance benefits which were adjusted only once every five years. Furthermore, the family allowances paid to all parents were initially set below the *Beveridge Report* level and then not raised until 1956. Nevertheless, the post-war social policy measures had a major impact on poverty, as is demonstated by the results of Rowntree's third York survey of 1950 (Rowntree and Lavers, 1951). This applied substantially the same necessary income standard as the second York survey of 1936 (Rowntree, 1942). By this standard, in 1950, Rowntree found that only 2.77

per cent of the York working-class population were in poverty. The dramatic reduction was partly, but by no means entirely, a consequence of rising real wages and the maintenance of near full employment. Rowntree calculated that when all these improvements were allowed for, if the pre-Beveridge welfare measures of 1936 had been in operation in 1950, then 22 per cent of the working-class population would have been in poverty.

Afterwards, from the mid-1950s, matters became more complicated. The social security system deviated more and more from the Beveridge plan. National Assistance, or non-contributory social security, came to have a large and permanent role, while after 1959, the insurance system increasingly moved away from the flat-rate principle and towards graduated contributions and benefits. This combined insurance and assistance system was increasingly an object for criticisms which were often mutually contradictory. The Fabian left 'rediscovered poverty' in the later 1950s, while the 'hard' right denied that poverty in any meaningful sense still existed. The social administration lobby emphasised the inadequacy of benefit levels while there was widespread political dismay at the escalating cost of the existing system. If nothing else, the criticisms of the later 1950s show that 'the abolition of want' objective could not be so easily defined and achieved, as the technicist calculation in the *Beveridge Report* might suggest. Rowntree's texts, which popularised this kind of technicist calculation, should be discursively situated, not at the beginning of triumphant modernity, but at the origins of the present crisis of the welfare state.

August, 1977

Bibliography

Althusser, L. (1969), *For Marx*, trans. B. Brewster, Allen Lane, London.

Aschrott, P. F. (1888), *The English Poor Law System*, Knight, London.

Ashforth, D. (1976), 'The Urban Poor Law', pp. 128–48, in Fraser, D. (ed.), *The New Poor Law in the Nineteenth Century* (1976), Macmillan, London.

Barthes, R. (1970), *S/Z*, Éditions du Seuil, Paris.

Barthes, R. (1971), *Sade, Fourier, Loyola*, Éditions du Seuil, Paris.

Barthes, R. (1973), *Le Plaisir du Texte*, Éditions du Seuil, Paris.

Baugh, D. A. (1975), 'The Cost of Poor Relief in South East England 1790–1834', *Economic History Review*, vol. 28, February 1975, pp. 50–68.

Beveridge, W. H. (1942), *Social insurance and allied services*, Cmd 6404, HMSO, London.

Blaug, M. (1963), 'The Myth of the Old Poor Law and the Making of the New', *Journal of Economic History*, vol. 23, no. 2, June 1963, pp. 151–84.

Blaug, M. (1964), 'The Poor Law Report Re-examined', *Journal of Economic History*, vol. 24, June 1964, pp. 229–45.

Booth, C. (1886), 'Occupations of the People of the U.K., 1841-81, . . .', *Journal of the Statistical Society*, vol. 49, June 1886, pp. 314–435.

Booth, C. (1887), *Condition and Occupations of the People of the Tower Hamlets 1886-7*, Edward Stanford, London.

Booth, C. (1888), 'Condition and Occupations of the People of East London and Hackney, 1887', *Journal of the Royal Statistical Society*, vol. 51, June 1888.

Booth, C. (1892a), *Pauperism and Endowment of Old Age*, Macmillan, London.

Booth, C. (1892b), 'Dock and Wharf Labour', presidential address, *Journal of Royal Statistical Society*, vol. 55, December 1892, pp. 521–57.

Booth, C. (1894), *The Aged Poor in England and Wales: Condition*, Macmillan, London.

Booth, C. *et al.* (1896), *Family Budgets*, Economic Club, London.

Booth, C. (ed.) (1902–3), *Life and Labour of the People in London*, 17 vols: ser. 1. 'Poverty'. 4 vols; ser. 2. 'Industry'. 5 vols; ser. 3 'Religious Influences'. 7 vols; Final vol. 'Notes on Social Influences and Conclusion', Macmillan, London.

Bosanquet, H. (1903), 'The Poverty Line', *Charity Organisation Review*, January 1903, pp. 1–23.

Boyson, R. (1960), 'The New Poor Law in North East Lancashire 1834–71', *Trans. of the Lancashire and Cheshire Antiquarian Society*, vol. 70, 1960, pp. 35–6.

Briggs, A. (1961), *Social Thought and Social Action. A Study of the Work of Seebohm Rowntree, 1871–1954*, Longman, London.

British Parliamentary Papers (BPP)

Annual Pauperism Returns, 'Statement of the Number of Paupers relieved on 1st Jan. each year', 1852–1939.

Annual Reports of the Poor Law Commission, 1835–48.

Annual Reports of the Poor Law Board, 1849–70.

Annual Reports of the Local Government Board, 1871–1919.

Annual Reports of the Ministry of Health, 1920–1938/9.

BPP, Special Reports and Returns

BPP, 1803–4 (XIII): *Abstract of . . . Returns Relative to the Expense and Maintenance of the Poor* (1802–3).

BPP 1818 (XIX): *Abstract of Returns . . . Relative to the Maintenance of the Poor* (1813–15).

BPP, 1824 (XIX): *Select Committee on Labourers' Wages.*

BPP, 1825 (XIX): *Abstract of Returns Prepared by Order of the Select Committee on Labourers' Wages.*

BPP, 1834 (XXVII): *Report from the Commissioners for Inquiry into the Poor Laws.*

BPP, 1834 (XXX–XXXIV): Royal Commission, *Appendix B, Answers to Rural Queries.*

BPP, 1834 (XXXV–XXXVI): Royal Commission, *Appendix B2, Answers to Town Queries.*

BPP, 1841 (XXI): *Sums Expended in Purchase of and Erection of Buildings and Fitting up of Workhouses* (1838–40).

BPP, 1852–3 (LXXIV): *Number of Persons Relieved as 'Out of Work' or 'In aid of Wages' during the Tenth Week of Christmas Quarter 1852 . . .*

BPP, 1854 (LV): *Regulations of Poor Law Board . . . and Return for each Workhouse.*

BPP, 1854–5 (XLVI): *Return of Amount of Workhouse Accommodation* (in 1854).

BPP, 1857–8 (XLIX): *Cost of Building Workhouses in England and Wales . . . since 1840.*

BPP, 1872 (LI): *Number of Able Bodied Paupers in Receipt of Relief on 1st January, 1872.*

BPP, 1890-1 (LXVIII): *Return . . . of Paupers over Sixty* (Mr Burt's Return).

BPP, 1892 (LXVIII): *Return . . . of Paupers over Sixty Five* (Mr Ritchie's Return).

BPP, 1904 (LXXXII): *Return Showing the Number of Persons (in receipt of relief) . . . over Sixty Years of Age.*

BPP 1909 (XXXVII): *Report of Royal Commission on the Poor Laws and Relief of Distress.*

BPP, 1909 (CIII): *Statistical Memoranda . . . Relating to Public Health and Social Conditions.*

BPP, 1910 (LIII): Royal Commission, Appendix vol. XXV, *Statistical Memoranda and Tables Relating to England and Wales.*

BPP, 1911 (LXIX): *Statement with regard to Persons . . . Ceased to be Chargeable to Guardians during the Four Weeks ended January 1911.*

BPP, 1942-3 (VI): *Social Insurance and Allied Services; Report by Sir William Beveridge.*

Brown, J. (1968), 'Charles Booth and Labour Colonies', *Economic History Review*, 2nd series, vol. 21, no. 2, August 1968.

Brown, J. (1977), 'Social Control and the Modernisation of Social Policy 1890-1929', pp. 126-43, in Thane, P. (ed.), *The Origins of British Social Policy*, Croom Helm, London.

Brundage, A. (1978), *The Making of the New Poor Law*, Hutchinson, London.

Builder, vol. I, 1843-vol. 94, 1908.

Burns, E. M. (1941), *British Unemployment Programs*, Social Science Research Council, Washington.

Chance, W. A. (1895), *The Better Administration of the Poor Law*, Sonnenschein, London.

Checkland, S. G. and E. O. A. (eds) (1974), *The Poor Law Report of 1834*, Penguin, Harmondsworth.

Crowther, M. A. (1978), 'The Later Years of the Workhouse 1890-1929', in Thane, P. (ed.), *The Origins of British Social Policy*, Croom Helm, London.

Cullen, M. J. (1975), *The Statistical Movement in Early Victorian Britain; the Foundations of Empirical Social Research*, Harvester, Hassocks, Sussex.

Deane, P. and Cole, W. A. (1962), *British Economic Growth 1688-1959*, Cambridge University Press, London.

Digby, A. (1975), 'The Labour Market and the Continuity of Social Policy after 1834: the Case of the Eastern Counties', *Economic History Review*, vol. 28, February 1975, pp. 69-83.

Digby, A. (1976), 'The Rural Poor Law', pp. 149-70, in Fraser, D. (ed.), *The New Poor Law in the Nineteenth Century* (1976), Macmillan, London.

Digby, A. (1978), *Pauper Palaces*, Routledge & Kegan Paul, London.

Donajgrodzki, A. P. (ed.) (1977), *Social Control in Nineteenth Century Britain*, Croom Helm, London.

Duke, F. (1976), 'Pauper Education', pp. 67-86, in Fraser, D. (ed.),

The New Poor Law in the Nineteenth Century (1976), Macmillan, London.

Dunkley, P. (1974), ' "The Hungry Forties" and the New Poor Law: a Case Study', *Historical Journal*, vol. 17, no. 2, 1974, pp. 329–46.

Engels, F. (1975), 'The Condition of the Working Class in England', in *Marx-Engels Collected Works*, vol. 4 (1844–5), trans. Jack Cohen *et al.*, Lawrence & Wishart, London.

Feuerbach, L. A. (1854), *The Essence of Christianity*, trans. M. Evans, Chapman, London.

Feuerbach, L. A. (1972), *The Fiery Brook; Selected Writings of Ludwig Feuerbach*, trans. Zawer Hanfi, Anchor Books, New York.

Feyerabend, P. K. (1975), *Against Method*, New Left Books, London.

Flinn, M. W. (1976), 'Medical Services under the New Poor Law', in Fraser, D. (ed.), *The New Poor Law in the Nineteenth Century* (1976), Macmillan, London.

Fogel, R. W. (1964), *Railroads and American Economic Growth*, Johns Hopkins, Baltimore.

Foucault, M. (1967), *Madness and Civilisation*, Tavistock, London.

Foucault, M. (1973), *The Birth of the Clinic*, Tavistock, London.

Foucault, M. (1977), *Discipline and Punish*, Allen Lane, London.

Franklin, B. (1948), *Autobiography*, Dent, London.

Fraser, D. (ed.) (1976), *The New Poor Law in the Nineteenth Century*, Macmillan, London.

Freeman, A. C. (1904), *Hints on the Planning of Poor Law Buildings and Mortuaries*, St Bride's Press, London.

Fripp, C. B. (1839), 'Report of an Inquiry into the Condition of the Working Classes of the City of Bristol', *Journal of the Statistical Society*, vol. 2, October 1839, pp. 368–75.

Glen, W. C. (1898), *The General Orders . . .* (11th edn), Knight, London.

Hammond, J. L. and B. (1911), *The Village Labourer* (1st edn), Longman, London.

Hammond, J. L. and B. (1927), *The Village Labourer*, Longman, London.

Harrison, B. (1967), 'London's Lower Depths', *New Society*, 2 November 1967, pp. 638–9.

Hay, J. R. (1978), 'Employers' Attitudes to Social Policy and the Concept of "social control" 1900–1920', pp. 107–25, in Thane, P. (ed.), *The Origins of British Social Policy*, Croom Helm, London.

Hempel, C. G. (1965), 'The Function of General Laws in History', pp. 231–44, in *Aspects of Scientific Explanation*, Macmillan, London.

Henderson, W. O. (1976), *The Life of Friedrich Engels*, 2 vols, Cass, London.

Henderson, W. O. and Chaloner, W. H. (1958), Editors' Note in Engels, F., *The Condition of the Working Class in England*, Basil Blackwell, Oxford.

Hennock, E. P. (1976), 'Poverty and Social Theory in England', *Social History*, no. 1, January 1976, pp. 67–91.

Heywood, J. (1838), 'Report of an Inquiry in Miles Platting . . . Manchester in 1837', *Journal of the Statistical Society*, vol. 1, May 1838, pp. 34–6.

Himmelfarb, G. (1973), 'The Culture of Poverty', in Dyos, H. J. and
 Wolff, M. (eds), *The Victorian City*, vol. 2, Routledge & Kegan Paul,
 London.
Hobsbawm, E. J. (1968), 'History and the Dark Satanic Mills', in
 Labouring Men, Weidenfeld & Nicolson, London.
Hobsbawm, E. J. (1969), 'Introduction', in Engels, F., *The Conditions
 of the Working Class in England*, Granada (Panther), St Albans.
Holderness, B. A. (1972), ' "Open" and "Closed" Parishes in England in
 the Eighteenth and Nineteenth Centuries', *Agricultural History
 Review*, vol. 20, 1972, pp. 126–39.
Hume, D. (1902), *An Enquiry Concerning the Human Understanding*,
 Oxford University Press, London.
Hume, D. (1911), *A Treatise of Human Nature*, 2 vols, Dent, London.
Humphreys, A. (ed.) (1971), *Voices of the Poor*, Cass, London.
Hunter, W. A. (1894), 'Outdoor Relief', *Contemporary Review*, vol. 45,
 March 1894, pp. 304–25.
Huzel, J. P. (1969), 'Malthus, the Poor Law, and Population in early
 nineteenth-century England', *Economic History Review*, 2nd series,
 vol. 22, December 1969.
Jenner-Fust, H. (1907), *Poor Law Orders* (2nd edn), King, London.
Jenner-Fust, H. (1912), *Poor Law Orders, Relief Regulation Order
 1911 . . .*, King, London.
*Knight's Guide to the Arrangement and Construction of Workhouse
 Buildings* (1889), Knight & Co., London.
Kuhn, T. S. (1962), *The Structure of Scientific Revolutions*, University
 of Chicago Press.
Lakatos, I. (1970), 'Falsification and Methodology of Scientific
 Research Programmes', pp. 91–195, in Lakatos, I and Musgrave, A.
 (eds), *Criticism and the Growth of Knowledge*, Cambridge Uni-
 versity Press, London.
London Statistical Society (1840), 'Report of a Committee . . . on the
 State of the Working Classes in the Parishes of St Margaret and St
 John, Westminster', *Journal of the Statistical Society*, vol. 3, April
 1840, pp. 14–24.
London Statistical Society (1848), 'Report of a Committee . . . to
 investigate . . . Church Lane, St. Giles's', *Journal of the Statistical
 Society*, vol. 11, March 1848, pp. 3–18.
Longley, Inspector H. (1874), 'Outdoor Relief in the Metropolis', pp.
 136–209, in the Local Government Board's *Third Annual Report*,
 1873–4.
McCloskey, D. N. (1974), 'New Perspective on the Old Poor Law',
 Explorations in Economic History, vol. 10, no. 4, 1974, pp. 419–36.
Malthus, T. R. (1826), *An Essay on the Principle of Population . . .* (6th
 edn), Murray, London.
Manchester Statistical Society (1839), 'Report on the Condition of the
 Population in Three Parishes in Rutlandshire in March 1839',
 Journal of the Statistical Society, vol. 2, October 1839, pp. 297–302.
Manchester Statistical Society (1842), 'Report on the Condition of the
 Working Classes in the Town of Kingston-upon-Hull', *Journal of the
 Statistical Society*, vol. 5, July 1842, pp. 212–21.

Marcus, S. (1974), *Engels, Manchester, and the Working Class,* Weidenfeld & Nicolson, London.

Marshall, J. D. (1968), *The Old Poor Law 1795–1834,* Macmillan, London.

Marx, K. (1970), *Economic and Philosophical Manuscripts of 1844,* trans. M. Milligan, Struick, D. J. (ed.), Lawrence & Wishart, London.

Marx, K. and Engels, F. (1968), *Selected Works,* 1 vol., Lawrence & Wishart, London.

Massingham, H. W. (ed.) (1903), *Labour and Protection,* Unwin, London.

Mayhew, H. (1850), 'Report of Speech given at a Public Meeting convened by the Committee of the Tailors of London', printed for the Committee, London.

Mayhew, H. (1851), *Low Wages, Their Causes, Consequences and Remedies,* Office, 16 Upper Wellington Street, Strand, London.

Mayhew, H. (1861–2), *London Labour and the London Poor* (4 vol. edn), Griffin, Bohn & Co., London.

Mayhew, H. and Binny, J. (1862), *The Criminal Prisons of London,* Griffin, Bohn & Co., London.

Mill, J. S. (1843), *A System of Logic,* 2 vols, Parker, London.

Mitchell, B. R. and Deane, P. (1962), *Abstract of British Historical Statistics,* Cambridge University Press.

Moore Lappé, F. (1975), *Diet for a Small Planet,* Ballantine Books, New York.

Mouat, F. J. and Snell, H. Saxon (1883), *Hospital Construction and Management,* Churchill, London.

Neumann, M. (1972), 'Speenhamland in Berkshire', pp. 85–127, in Martin, E. W. (ed.), *Comparative Development in Social Welfare,* Allen & Unwin, London.

Popper, K. R. (1968), *The Logic of Scientific Discovery,* Hutchinson, London.

Popper, K. R. (1969), *Conjectures and Refutations,* Routledge & Kegan Paul, London.

Popper, K. R. (1972), *Objective Knowledge,* Oxford University Press, London.

Popper, K. R. (1974), 'Autobiography' and 'Replies to My Critics', in Schilpp, P. A. (ed.), *The Library of Living Philosophers,* vol. 14, Open Court, Illinois.

Ricardo, D. (1817), *On the Principles of Political Economy, and Taxation,* Murray, London.

Rose, M. E. (1966), 'The Allowance System under the New Poor Law', *Economic History Review,* vol. 19, December 1966, pp. 607–20.

Rose, M. E. (1979), 'The Respectable Poor and the Residuum; the Victorian Crisis of Poor Relief', *Social History Society Newsletter,* vol. 4, Spring 1979, p. 5.

Rowntree, B. S. (1903), *The 'Poverty Line',* Good & Son, London.

Rowntree, B. S. (1905), *Betting and Gambling,* Macmillan, London.

Rowntree, B. S. (1911), *Land and Labour,* Macmillan, London.

Rowntree, B. S. (1913), *Poverty, a Study of Town Life,* Nelson, London.

Rowntree, B. S. (1919), *The Human Needs of Labour*, Nelson, London.

Rowntree, B. S. (1942), *Poverty and Progress. A second Social Survey of York* (2nd edn), Longman, London.

Rowntree, B. S. and Kendall, M. (1913), *How the Labourer Lives,* Nelson, London.

Rowntree, B. S. and Lasker, B. (1911), *Unemployment,* Longman, London.

Rowntree, B. S. and Lavers, G. R. (1951), *Poverty and the Welfare State,* Longman, London.

Rowntree, J. and Sherwell, A. (1899), *The Temperance Problem and Social Reform,* Hodder & Stoughton, London.

Ryan, P. A. (1978), 'Poplarism 1894–1930', in Thane, P. (ed.), *The Origins of British Social Policy,* Croom Helm, London.

Samuel, R. (1973), 'Mayhew and Labour Historians', *Society for the Study of Labour History,* Bulletin 26, Spring 1973, pp. 47–52.

Saussure, F. de (1960), *Course in General Linguistics,* Owen, London.

Searle, G. R. (1971), *The Quest for National Efficiency,* Blackwell, Oxford.

Simey, T. S. and Simey, M. B. (1960), *Charles Booth, Social Scientist,* Oxford University Press, London.

Smith, P. G. (1901), *Hints and Suggestions as to the Planning of Poor Law Buildings,* Knight, London.

Stedman Jones, G. (1971), *Outcast London,* Oxford University Press, London.

Thompson, E. P. and Yeo, E. (1971), *The Unknown Mayhew,* Merlin Press, London.

Tucker, G. S. L. (1975), 'The Old Poor Law Revisited', *Explorations in Economic History,* vol. 12, no. 3.

Vorspan, R. (1977), 'Vagrancy and the New Poor Law in late-Victorian and Edwardian England', *English Historical Review,* vol. 92, no. 362, January 1977, pp. 59–81.

Webb, S. and Webb, B. (1910), *English Poor Law Policy,* Longman, London.

Webb, S. and Webb, B. (1927–9), *English Poor Law History, Part I The Old Poor Law, Part II The Last Hundred Years,* 2 vols, Longman, London.

Weld, C. R. (1843), 'On the Condition of the Working Classes in . . . St George's Parish, Hanover Square', *Journal of the Statistical Society,* vol. 6, February 1843, pp. 17–28.

Willer, D. and Willer, J. (1973), *Systematic Empiricism,* Prentice-Hall, New Jersey.

Williams, K. (1975), 'Popper's Empiricism', *Economy and Society,* vol. 4, August 1975, pp. 309–58.

Williams, K. (1977), ' "Old Corruption" – A Criticism of Althusser', *Lettera,* no. 13, June 1977, pp. 64–109.

Witmer, H. L. (1931), 'Some Effects of the English Unemployment Insurance Acts on the Number of Unemployed Relieved under the Poor Law', *Quarterly Journal of Economics,* vol. 45, February 1931, pp. 262–88.

Wodehouse, E. H. (1871–2), 'Outdoor Relief', pp. 88–215, in *Local Government Board, First Annual Report 1871–2.*

Index